The Sword of Christ

THE SWORD OF CHRIST

Christianity From the Right, or, The Christian Question

GILES COREY

Third edition, second printing 2024,
With new preface by the author.

First edition published by CreateSpace, 2020.
Second edition published by Antelope Hill Publishing, 2023.

Cover art by Swifty.
Edited by Harlan Wallace and Margaret Bauer.
Layout by Margaret Bauer.

Antelope Hill Publishing | antelopehillpublishing.com

Hardcover ISBN-13: 979-8-89252-026-3
Paperback ISBN-13: 979-8-89252-025-6
EPUB ISBN-13: 979-8-89252-027-0

Contents

A Note on Translation

As Steven Anderson has conclusively demonstrated, the 1611 Authorized King James Version is the only Bible translation we can trust.[1] Aside from its incomparable beauty, the King James Version is the *only* English translation that approaches parity with the Greek and Hebrew. When one begins to tinker with the Scripture, Satan easily inserts himself into the text and subverts the Word of God from within. As just one example of many, the execrable New International Version is owned and published by Zondervan, the largest Bible publisher on earth. Zondervan is a subsidiary of the Big Five publisher, HarperCollins, which is itself owned by News Corp, owned by the rampant philo-Semite and fanatical Zionist Rupert Murdoch, whose vast media empire propagates Zionism across the globe. As such, all Scripture in this work is cited from the King James Version. I have deliberately chosen not to specifically cite verses quoted from either Talmudic or other rabbinical sources or the Qur'an. First, these verses are cited in each of the sources that I *have* cited from, each of which is copiously and authoritatively sourced; as such, I encourage the reader to acquire and scrutinize these sources. The second reason is cosmetic; as the reader is in all likelihood unfamiliar with the Talmud, other Jewish texts, or the Qur'an, citations to them would largely be irrelevant, as well as likely to engender confusion. Additionally, these religious texts have several different translations, and the sources I have drawn verses from are not uniform in the translations employed.

---

[1] framingtheworld, "New World Order Bible Versions."

My Mission

The hatred for Christianity on the right truly pains me; this is the reason why I wrote this book. I fully understand the hatred—as I argue in my introductory essay, there is very little to praise about organized Christianity today, if anything. Organized Christianity, including the Catholic Church and the various Protestant denominations, has indeed become yet another instrument of White genocide. Organized Christianity has capitulated and bent the knee to Satan's coalition of the damned, thereby turning its back on our Lord and Savior, Jesus Christ. I despise organized Christianity too, for this same reason. But, usurped though the mantle of the Church may be, that is no reason to simply abandon the faith.

So many of us who observe the collapse of the Church into anti-White leftism have been led to the facile conclusion that Christianity itself is irredeemable. It isn't. Christianity does not even need redemption, for our faith remains what it has always been; the pharisaical teachers of false doctrine whom we witness on parade today simply *are not Christians*, no matter what they may say. Remember Paul's warning:

> For such are false apostles, deceitful workers, transforming themselves into the apostles of Christ. And no marvel; for Satan himself is transformed into an angel of light. Therefore it is no great thing if his ministers also be transformed as the ministers of righteousness; whose end shall be according to their works. (2 Cor. 11:13–15)

They have accomplished Satan's work well, driving good men from the Church in droves to seek a fruitless solace in a pagan history that we are thousands of years removed from. Again, I understand the attraction; there is much to admire in the Indo-European tradition, and, as I discuss in my introductory essay, the inculturation of this tradition into early Christianity ushered the faith into its rightful marriage with Europe as Christendom. This is the very process which the German *Völkisch* movement hoped to recreate in its program of national renaissance. However, to extrapolate a Christophobic paganism from our admiration of that rich tradition is fundamentally wrongheaded, premised upon biblical and historical illiteracy.

This same illiteracy lies behind the more absurd contention that Christianity is some sort of life-denying suicidal Jewish psyop. First, if this is true, why, after nearly two thousand years, did organized Christianity only betray its race and civilization in the twentieth century, *after* the Jewish coup that was accomplished in no small part by the creation and promotion of the heresy of Christian Zionism? Indeed, the Bible is quite anti-Semitic, and, as I explore in my essay on Christian Zionism, historical Christianity was diametrically opposed to Judaism. Christians have always known, until just this past century, that Jews are our greatest enemy. Second, the Jews of the Old Testament are not the Jews of the New Testament, or of today. As I explain, what we now know as Judaism is rabbinical, Talmudic Judaism, a belief system that is wholly disconnected from the faith practiced by the pre-Christian Israelites of the Old Testament. The precursor to the Judaism of today is the Sanhedrin of the New Testament Pharisees, which Christ essentially explicitly tells us are the spawn, whether literal or figurative, of Satan. The key here is that Christianity predates Talmudic Judaism, which arose as a response to Christianity, with the sole organizing principle of annihilating Christianity.

It is my greatest desire that this work will equip *real* Christians with the tools that they need to understand that our faith *is* in total alignment with White racial identity, and with the arguments that they need to refute those egalitarian allegedly Christian leftists who wave the bloody shirt and pervert the Word of God to argue for ethnomasochism and racial suicide. For atheist or pagan Whites, I hope to at least take the sting out of their Christophobia by demonstrating that those who work for our dispossession under the ensign of the cross *are not Christians*.

FOREWORD BY DR. KEVIN MACDONALD

From the First Edition, 2020

Giles Corey has written a book that should be read by all Christians, as well as White advocates of all theoretical perspectives, including especially those who are seeking a spiritual foundation that is deeply embedded in the history and culture of Europeans. This is excellent scholarship combined with a very fluid writing style. He has thought deeply about all the issues confronting the peoples and cultures of the West.

Corey is well aware that contemporary Christianity has been massively corrupted. The Catholic Church and the mainline Protestant Churches have become little more than appendages for the various social justice movements of the left, avidly promoting the colonization of the West by other races and cultures, even as religious fervor and attendance dwindle and Christianity itself becomes ever more irrelevant to the national dialogue. On the other hand, Evangelicals, a group that remains vigorously Christian, have been massively duped by the theology of Christian Zionism, their main focus being to promote Israel.

Until the twentieth century, Christianity served the West well. One need only think of the long history of Christians battling to prevent Muslims from establishing a caliphate throughout the West—Charles Martel at the Battle of Tours, the Spanish Reconquista, the defeat of the Turks at the gates of Vienna. The era of Western expansion was accomplished by Christian explorers and colonists. Until quite recently, the flourishing of science, technology, and art occurred entirely within a Christian context.

Much of my scholarly interest has been to attempt to understand the people and culture of the West, resulting in my book *Individualism and the Western Liberal Tradition: Evolutionary Origins, History, and Prospects for the Future.* As I argue there, individualism lends itself to moral and ethical universalism, which led to the religiously-based eradication of slavery long before the rise of an elite hostile to Christianity itself. And White intellectuals in the nineteenth century attempting to understand their own moral universalism often attributed it to their racial origins.

Such individualism was not disastrously self-destructive. As Corey notes:

> Christian universalism historically posed little to no danger to White survival because it was preached by Whites living in a world ruled by Whites; it was only in the multicultural, egalitarian regime, inaugurated in the aftermath of the Second World War, that Christian sacrifice was transformed into a call for racial suicide. (Page 3)

The individualistic, Christian West was thus highly adaptive—until the rise of a hostile, Jewish-dominated elite bent on corrupting adaptive forms of Christian individualism in favor of a completely deracinated individualism, now accompanied by powerful religious, media, and academic voices preaching White guilt, often from a Christian perspective.

Instead, Corey advocates a revitalization of Medieval Germanic Christianity based on, in the words of Samuel Francis, "social hierarchy, loyalty to tribe and place (blood and soil), world-acceptance rather than world-rejection, and an ethic that values heroism and military sacrifice." (Page 39) This medieval Christianity preserved the aristocratic, fundamentally Indo-European culture of the Germanic tribes. This was an adaptive Christianity, a Christianity that was compatible with Western expansion, to the point that, by the end of the nineteenth century, the West dominated the planet. Christianity per se is certainly not the problem.

The decline of adaptive Christianity coincides with the post-Enlightenment rise of the Jews throughout the West as an anti-Christian elite, and Corey has a great deal of very interesting material on traditional Christian views of Judaism. Traditional Christian theology viewed the Church as having superseded the Old Testament; by rejecting the Church, the Jews had not only rejected God, but were also responsible for murdering Christ. My view, developed in Chapter 3 of *Separation and Its Discontents: Toward an Evolutionary Theory of Anti-Semitism*, is that traditional Christian theology was fundamentally anti-Jewish and was developed as a weapon which was used to lessen Jewish economic and political power in the Roman Empire. Here Corey describes the writings of the fourth-century figure, St. John Chrysostom, who has a chapel dedicated to him inside St. Peter's Basilica in Rome as well as a statue outside the building. His writings on Jews are nothing less than scathing, and reflect long-term tensions between Jews and Greeks in Antioch. Chrysostom was far from alone in his hatred. For example, St. Gregory of Nyssa, also writing in the fourth century:

> [Jews are] murderers of the Lord, assassins of the prophets, rebels against God, God haters, . . . advocates of the devil, race of vipers, slanderers, calumniators, dark-minded people, leaven of the Pharisees, sanhedrin of demons, sinners, wicked men, stoners, and haters of righteousness.

The traditional Church was certainly far from friendly toward Jews.

Although Protestantism was generally far more amenable to Jewish interests even before its current malaise, there certainly are exceptions. Here Corey emphasizes Martin Luther's writings on Jews. Luther emphasizes Jewish hatred toward Christianity and their sense of superiority vis-à-vis Christians, seeing the latter as "not human; in fact, we hardly deserve to be considered poor worms by them." (Page 106) But he is also concerned about Jewish economic exploitation and domination of Germans via usury—certainly the biggest complaint about Jews in traditional Europe. And he is repulsed by Talmudic ethics which promote very different moral codes for Jews and non-Jews.

However, much has changed since the origins of Christianity. In the contemporary United States, Christian Zionism has had a very large influence on evangelical Protestantism, whose theology departs radically from traditional Christianity, particularly with respect to the Jews. Corey has an excellent section on how Jews helped shape this new theology; it should be required reading for Christian Zionists, because it will open their eyes to the sordid history of the movement. The result of such thinking is that Zionism has often become a vehicle of moral idealism in the minds of a great many gentiles, from Lloyd George to the present, who believe that the restoration of Israel is far more important than the fate of their own people.

Jews have not stood by idly on this but have actively supported the Christian Zionism movement. I noted in a 2010 article on the delusional Pastor John Hagee:

> Beginning in 1978, the Likud Party in Israel has taken the lead in organizing this force for Israel, and they have been joined by the neocons. For example, in 2002 the Israeli embassy organized a prayer breakfast with the major Christian Zionists. The main organizations are the Unity Coalition for Israel which is run by Esther Levens and Christians United for Israel, run by David Brog. The Unity Coalition for Israel consists of ~200 Christian and Jewish organizations has strong connections to neocon think tanks such as the Center for Security Policy, headed by Frank Gaffney, pro-Israel activist organizations the Zionist Organization of America, the Likud Party and the Israeli government. This organization claims to provide material for 1,700 religious radio stations, 245 Christian TV stations, and 120 Christian newspapers.[2]

Corey notes that Hagee's organization, A Night to Honor Israel, has donated over $100 million to right-wing causes in Israel over the years. He has been well rewarded financially for his efforts, and is the recipient of numerous awards from Zionist organizations.

---

[2] MacDonald, "Christian Zionism."

Christian Zionism is a fitting reminder of how humans, unlike animals, can be motivated by ideas, including ideas that are completely unrelated to believers' real interests. These ideas may be disseminated by people who are only doing so for selfish reasons, such as the dishonorable Cyrus Scofield, whose annotated Bible has become central to Christian Zionism. Maladaptive ideas may also be disseminated by people who are utterly opposed to the legitimate interests of believers or even hate Christianity and the West in general. Here Corey discusses the role of Felix Untermeyer, a wealthy Jew, in promoting Scofield and his Bible. It was a religious ideology "with a new worship icon—the modern State of Israel," and Corey does an excellent job showing how Christian Zionism is a radical departure from traditional Christian theology. I found the following passage quite stunning:

> The heresy of Christian Zionism, using an arbitrary and self-contradictory literalist and futurist hermeneutic, con-tends that the Jews remain God's chosen people, separate from and superior to the Church; indeed, they believe that earthly Jewish Israel will *replace* the Church, and that as such, "Christians, and indeed whole nations, will be blessed through their association with, and support of, Israel." (Page 92)

Although Christian Zionism is far less influential than the Israel lobby in furthering Jewish interests in the United States, it has certainly had some influence and creates a ready-made cheering section for wars in the Middle East on behalf of Israel. After all, other attitudes typical of Christian Zionists, such as opposition to abortion or pornography, have had much less traction with the current left-oriented establishment despite their powerful commitment to the State of Israel.

Religious thinking is by its nature unbounded—it is infinitely malleable. It is a dangerous sword that can be used to further the legitimate interests of believers, or it can become a lethal weapon whereby believers adopt attitudes that are obviously maladaptive. One need only think of religiously based suicide cults, such as Peoples Temple (Jonestown), Solar Temple, and Heaven's Gate. Mainstream Christianity, from traditional Catholicism to mainline Protestantism, was fundamentally adaptive in terms of creating a healthy family life. It was compatible with a culture characterized by extraordinary scientific and technological creativity and standards of living that have been much envied by the rest of the world.

Corey has great material on Jewish perceptions of Christianity in the Talmud, and on negative Jewish influences on culture in the present West, including pornography and the sexual revolution generally. As is so often the case with Jewish activism, the pornography movement has been motivated not solely by money, but by hatred toward Christian morality and Christian family functioning. The results have been devastating, with huge increases since the 1960s—the breakthrough decade of Jewish power—in all the markers of family dysfunction and poor child outcomes: lower marriage rates, higher births out of wedlock, higher rates of teenage pregnancy, precocious sexuality, high divorce rates, and unstable pair bonds. In other words, the Western family pattern of monogamous nuclear families based on strong husband-wife pair bonds has been under attack from Jewish dominated movements, the most noteworthy of which was psychoanalysis, promising an idyllic future if only people would jettison traditional Christian constraints on sexuality. These negative trends in family functioning have been most pronounced among the lower social classes, and thus have much less effect on high-IQ middle- and upper-income groups, including Jews as a relatively high-IQ group. The disaster in family patterns has fallen far most severely on the White working class.

Corey has an extended treatment of the corrosive effects of pornography, now extended to child pornography and legalized pedophilia as the "final frontier" in the sexual revolution. As in other areas, this starts out by advocating language that makes the activity more or less acceptable depending on the interests of advocates. In the case of pedophilia, the first step is to label them "minor attracted persons," whereas in the area of free speech, we find labels like "hate speech"—even for speech that is reasonable and fact-based. If issues related to free speech are any guide, there will soon be articles in law journals arguing that pedophilia is normal and should not be punished, and eventually courts will begin to adopt this logic in particular cases. Already Supreme Court justices like Elena Kagan have signaled a willingness to curtail speech on diversity issues, and this would be joined by the other liberals, which would mean that curtailing free speech on race is at most one Supreme Court appointment away.[3] And when that happens, it won't be long before it is embraced by conservatives. As Corey notes in the case of pedophilia, "We are presumably one Supreme Court ruling away from the Koch-funded cocktail conservative crowd celebrating pederasty as the next great achievement of individual liberty." (Page 167)

Given the exhaustive summary of the negative effects of pornography—including neurological impairments related to impulsivity and lessened interest in familial relationships of love and nurturance—it is horrifying indeed that Corey discusses a study in which "sixty percent of boys and thirty percent of girls were exposed to pornography in early adolescence, including 'bondage, rape, and child pornography,' and another which concludes that children *under ten years old* now account for over twenty percent of online pornographic consumption." (Page 170) This definitely was not happening when I was growing up in the 1950s, prior to the deluge. I agree with Corey's conclusion:

> We have conclusively established that Jewish leadership and participation was instrumental in, and a necessary condition of, the pornographic war that has struck at the most sacred foundation of the West: the family. (Page 172)

As Freud famously said, "we are bringing them the plague."

Corey has an excellent and exhaustive section on Jewish ritual murder—an absolutely convincing presentation on a topic that, like so much of Jewish history, is a minefield for serious scholars. As he notes:

> There are hundreds of accusations and cases of Jewish ritual murder, each just as sadistically depraved as the last, involving barrels of nails, crucifixion, decapitation, spit-roasting,

[3] MacDonald, "Elena Kagan."

> stoning, and a litany of other barbaric evils; we could fill entire volumes with the accounts of each of these innocent lives so cruelly taken from this world. (Page 206)

This is a topic that I have never written about, although I was somewhat familiar with *Blood Passover*, Ariel Toaff's book on the topic. As to be expected, Toaff's book was condemned by the activist Jewish community, and he was pressured into publishing an apology, promising to prevent distribution of his book, etc. However, we should not be surprised to find that such practices occurred. Ritual murder is an extreme manifestation of normative Jewish hostility toward the surrounding society, which is an important facet of the entire subject. The eighteenth-century English historian Edward Gibbon was struck by the fanatical hatred of Jews in the ancient world:

> From the reign of Nero to that of Antoninus Pius, the Jews discovered a fierce impatience of the dominion of Rome, which repeatedly broke out in the most furious massacres and insurrections. Humanity is shocked at the recital of the horrid cruelties which they committed in the cities of Egypt, of Cyprus, and of Cyrene, where they dwelt in treacherous friendship with the unsuspecting natives; and we are tempted to applaud the severe retaliation which was exercised by the arms of the legions against a race of fanatics, whose dire and credulous superstition seemed to render them the implacable enemies not only of the Roman government, but of human kind.[4]

The nineteenth-century Spanish historian José Amador de los Rios wrote of the Spanish Jews who assisted the Muslim conquest of Spain that:

> Without any love for the soil where they lived, without any of those affections that ennoble a people, and finally without sentiments of generosity, they aspired only to feed their avarice and to accomplish the ruin of the Goths; taking the opportunity to manifest their rancor, and boasting of the hatreds that they had hoarded up so many centuries.[5]

---

[4] Gibbon, *History of the Decline*, Chapter XVI, Part I.
[5] Walsh, *Isabella of Spain*, 196.

As I noted in an article titled "Stalin's Willing Executioners: Jews as a Hostile Elite in the Soviet Union":

> Hatred toward the peoples and cultures of non-Jews and the image of enslaved ancestors as victims of anti-Semitism have been the Jewish norm throughout history—much commented on, from Tacitus ("they regard the rest of mankind with all the hatred of enemies"[6]) to the present.

Toaff brings out the revenge motive:

> In their collective mentality, the Passover *Seder* had long since transformed itself into a celebration in which the wish for the forthcoming redemption of the people of Israel moved from aspiration to revenge, and then to cursing their Christian persecutors, the current heirs to the wicked Pharaoh of Egypt.[7]

Hatred and revenge were clearly on display in the early decades of the Soviet Union, a period in which around twenty million people were murdered. From "Stalin's Willing Executioners," a review of Yuri Slezkine's *The Jewish Century*:

> There can be little doubt that Lenin's contempt for "the thick-skulled, boorish, inert, and bearishly savage Russian or Ukrainian peasant" was shared by the vast majority of shtetl Jews prior to the Revolution and after it. Those Jews who defiled the holy places of traditional Russian culture and published anti-Christian periodicals doubtless reveled in their tasks for entirely Jewish reasons, and, as Gorky worried, their activities not unreasonably stoked the anti-Semitism of the period. Given the anti-Christian attitudes of traditional shtetl Jews, it is very difficult to believe that the Jews engaged in campaigns against Christianity did not have a sense of revenge against the old culture that they held in such contempt. . . .
>
> Slezkine seems comfortable with revenge as a Jewish motive, but he does not consider traditional Jewish culture itself to be a contributor to Jewish attitudes toward traditional Russia, even though he notes that a very traditional part of Jewish culture was to despise the Russians and their culture. (Even

[6] Tacitus, *Histories*, 659.

[7] Toaff, *Blood Passover*, 254.

> the Jewish literati despised all of traditional Russian culture, apart from Pushkin and a few literary icons.) Indeed, one wonders what would motivate the Jewish commissars to revenge apart from motives related to their Jewish identity. . . .
>
> Slezkine's argument that Jews were critically involved in destroying traditional Russian institutions, liquidating Russian nationalists, murdering the tsar and his family, dispossessing and murdering the kulaks, and destroying the Orthodox Church has been made by many other writers over the years. . . .
>
> The situation prompts reflection on what might have happened in the United States had American Communists and their sympathizers assumed power. The "red diaper babies" came from Jewish families which "around the breakfast table, day after day, in Scarsdale, Newton, Great Neck, and Beverly Hills have discussed what an awful, corrupt, immoral, undemocratic, racist society the United States is. . . ."[8] It is easy to imagine which sectors of American society would have been deemed overly backward and religious and therefore worthy of mass murder by the American counterparts of the Jewish elite in the Soviet Union—the ones who journeyed to Ellis Island instead of Moscow. The descendants of these overly backward and religious people now loom large among the "red state" voters who have been so important in recent national elections. Jewish animosity toward the Christian culture that is so deeply ingrained in much of America is legendary. As Joel Kotkin points out, "for generations, [American] Jews have viewed religious conservatives with a combination of fear and disdain." And as Elliott Abrams notes, the American Jewish community "clings to what is at bottom a dark vision of America, as a land permeated with anti-Semitism and always on the verge of anti-Semitic outbursts."

As the quote from neocon Elliott Abrams—and much else—indicates, this fear and loathing continues into the present. Consistent with what we know of the psychology of ethnocentrism, a fundamental motivation of Jewish intellectuals and activists involved in social criticism has simply been hatred of the non-Jewish power structure perceived as anti-Jewish and deeply immoral—Susan Sontag's "the white race *is* the cancer

---

[8] MacDonald, *Culture of Critique*, 46.

of human history," which was published in *Partisan Review*, a prominent literary journal associated with the New York Intellectuals (a Jewish intellectual movement), is emblematic.

As I write this in the summer of 2020, we are experiencing what feels like the end game in the Jewish conquest of White America. Because Jews have become a hostile elite with a powerful position in the media and educational system, Jewish attitudes in the 1950s that the U.S. is an "awful, corrupt, immoral, undemocratic, racist society" are now entirely mainstream, and the cancel culture that we see now is indeed directed most of all toward White red-state voters, particularly in the South. Cancel culture started with toppling Confederate monuments, but of course it didn't stop there, so now statues of the Founding Fathers are being destroyed, and there are demands that statues dedicated to Christian religious figures be removed. Jews in particular have demanded the removal of a statue of King Louis IX of France because of his attempt to curb Jewish moneylending in the interests of his people.

This hatred won't end if and when Whites become a minority. Jews were responsible for the 1965 immigration law that opened up the United States to immigration from all over the world, and they have energetically worked to make alliances with these immigrant groups, who are encouraged to hate White America and often adopt anti-White rhetoric almost as soon as they arrive, because they can see the political advantages of doing so.

This won't end well. As I concluded in my recent book, *Individualism and the Western Liberal Tradition*:

> I agree with Enoch Powell: "as I look ahead, I am filled with foreboding; like the Roman, I seem to see 'the River Tiber foaming with much blood.'" All the utopias dreamed up by the Left inevitably lead to bloodshed—because they conflict with human nature. The classical Marxist Utopian vision of a classless society in the USSR self-destructed, but only after murdering millions of its own people. Now the multicultural utopian version that has become dominant throughout the West is showing signs of producing intense opposition and irreconcilable polarization.

> Given the very large Jewish involvement in these projects consequent to the Jewish rise to elite status throughout the West, the big picture is that the thrust of Jewish power has been to create societies envisioned as being good for Jews, inevitably advertised in idealistic, morally uplifting, humanitarian terms [to appeal to the evolutionary psychology of individualism where social ties are based on belong to moral communities rather than communities based on kinship ties]. Historically, such projects have typically not ended well and have resulted in massive social upheavals. It would thus not be surprising if current social divisions result in a movement characterized by anti-Jewish overtones. . . .
>
> All of the measures of White representation in the forces of social control will continue to decline in the coming years given the continued deterioration of the demographic situation. At this point, even stopping immigration completely and deporting illegals would not be enough to preserve a White America long term.
>
> The left and its big business allies have created a monster. Whites have to realize that if they do nothing, they will be increasingly victimized and vilified in the coming decades as the monster continues to gain power. Better that any blood be shed sooner rather than later.

What happened in the early decades of the Soviet Union is a chilling reminder of what can happen when an alien hostile elite seizes control of a country.

I agree entirely with Corey's conclusions and recommendations for a revival centered around the adaptive aspects of Christianity—the aspects that produced Western expansion, innovation, discovery, individual freedom, economic prosperity, and strong family bonds; a Christianity that is adaptive, in the evolutionary sense of survival and reproduction, and fundamentally cognizant of the mistakes of the past.

> We must not tolerate subversion. Liberalism must go; we cannot afford to repeat the mistakes of the Enlightenment. We cannot afford to countenance any further anti-American, anti-family, anti-White speech, and this should be reflected in a new Constitution. Just as conservatism was not enough, the United States Constitution was not enough, with gaps that left it gaping wide for judicial "interpretation." For another thing,

we must circle the wagons and inculcate the *männerbund*, restraining our individualism at least for the time being. For another, we must return to our Lord and Savior. A nation without faith can have no guiding light, no purpose, no drive, no Mission. Izaak Walton, writing of his friend John Donne's last days, described the body "which was once a temple of the Holy Ghost and is now become a small quantity of Christian dust." His last line: "But I shall see it reanimated." (Page 292)

Resources

Gibbon, Edward. *The History of the Decline and Fall of the Roman Empire*. 1782. Revised 1845.

MacDonald, Kevin. "Christian Zionism." *The Occidental Observer*, March 12, 2010. https://www.theoccidentalobserver.net/2010/03/12/kevin-macdonald-christian-zionism/.

MacDonald, Kevin. "Elena Kagan: Jewish Ethnic Networking Eases the Path of a Liberal/Leftist to the Supreme Court." *The Occidental Observer*, May 20, 2009. https://www.theoccidentalobserver.net/2009/05/20/elena-kagan/.

MacDonald, Kevin. "Research on Pornography and the Sexualization of Culture." *The Occidental Observer*, June 9, 2012. https://www.theoccidentalobserver.net/2012/06/09/research-on-pornography-and-the-sexualization-of-culture/.

MacDonald, Kevin. *The Culture of Critique: An Evolutionary Analysis of Jewish Involvement in Twentieth-Century Intellectual and Political Movements*. Westport, CT: Praeger, 1998.

MacDonald, Kevin. "Stalin's Willing Executioners: Jews as a Hostile Elite in the USSR." *The Occidental Quarterly* 5, no. 3 (2005): 65–100.

Toaff, Ariel. *Blood Passover: The Jews of Europe and Ritual Murder*. Translated by Gian Marco Lucchese and Pietro Gianetti. Lucchese-Gianetti Editori LLC, 2016.

Walsh, William Thomas. *Isabella of Spain: The Last Crusader*. Gastonia, NC: TAN Books, 1987.

Preface by Giles Corey

Written for the Third Edition
June 2024

It has been four years since I wrote *The Sword of Christ.* In that time, Western Christianity's decline has only accelerated. Organized Christianity in America and in Western Europe is today but a dim and fading shadow of its former self. Indeed, the faith now masquerading as Christianity bears no resemblance to the Christianity that animated the men who built our civilization. It would be unrecognizable to any Christian living prior to the late nineteenth century, indeed it would be unrecognizable to the vast majority of Christians alive even just a few decades ago.

Before we embark on our grim journey, I would like to say that I was unduly harsh in my treatment of the Christian churches of the Global South, specifically the African churches. The Christians of Africa are doing commendable, indispensable, and truly brave work in their steadfast refusal to accept or normalize sodomy. I have far more faith in African Christianity at this point than I do in the Western churches.

The Catholic Church as an organization continues to bow to homosexuality more and more every day. Pope Francis has promoted nearly every leftist cause célèbre, but his approval of *Fiducia supplicans* in 2023 will surely be his most lasting legacy. This declaration, subtitled "On the Pastoral Meaning of Blessings," allows Catholic priests to bless same-sex couples, presumably including transgender couples as well.

Fiducia supplicans is quite sinister in its effect. While Francis's apologists argue that the document itself does not actually alter Christian doctrine, given the fact that any individual (including sodomites, transgenders, and other deviants) can receive a blessing from a priest, and that the love of God is available to all who repent of their sins and seek Him, this is a specious argument that fails to address the true significance of the document. While it is true that any individual can be blessed by a priest, and it is true that God will not turn away from any individual who truly repents and seeks His grace, neither of these points is relevant here. In this particular case, we are dealing exclusively with unrepentant, profligate, *proud* deviants, fallen, corroded souls who embrace sodomy and perversion, who fly their rainbow flags as a satanic mockery of God's rainbow covenant with Noah.

While *Fiducia supplicans* does not technically alter Christian doctrine, it is obviously intended to signify to the world that the Church is surrendering its stalwart position. While a devout Christian who has studied the topic might understand that the document does not officially recognize same-sex relationships as sacramental marriages, the casual Christian and the average non-Christian who encounters the document would be led to believe that it *does* officially accept and even celebrate sodomy as compatible with the Christian life. The document clearly paves the way for exactly that. Why else would this document have been approved and published, if not to create the impression that sodomite couples could now enter into a proxy form of sacramental marriage under the auspices of the Catholic Church?

Most of the mainline Protestant churches across Europe and the United States can no longer even be referred to as Christian, having long ago chosen to embrace sodomy, transgenderism, feminism, and various other satanic heresies and ideologies. There are still the evangelicals, those socially conservative Protestants who largely vote for the Republican Party. Although the Republican Party is increasingly indistinguishable from the Democratic Party in any meaningful way, it remains true that a significant (albeit rapidly shrinking) number of Republican voters still remain opposed to homosexuality, and that an overwhelming number of Republican voters remain opposed to transgenderism. This opposition, however, exists only in the abstract, and does not translate to any physical action against the widespread transformation of

American schools into LGBT conversion factories and the weaponization of Child Protective Services and family courts for the enforcement of the new orthodoxy.

In any case, it is American evangelicals, united by the heresy of Christian Zionism, who are doing more than any other Western Christians to lead themselves and their congregations into the jaws of Hell. Nowhere is this more evident than in their reaction to the ongoing genocide of the Palestinian people committed by Jewish Israelis. The reaction of American evangelicals can largely be characterized as one of bloodlust.

The topic of American evangelical devotion to the State of Israel, manifested in gleeful, bloodthirsty revelry at the annihilation of the Palestinian people (both Muslim *and* Christian), can best be illuminated by examining a typical Christian Zionist sermon. The sermon I've chosen is truly remarkable in its ignorance, cruelty, and inhumanity—the pillars of Christian Zionist thought. It was delivered by Bill Monroe, the head pastor at Florence Baptist Temple in Florence, South Carolina, on Palm Sunday, March 24th, 2024.[9] This particular Palm Sunday also happened to fall on the same day as the Jewish revenge holiday of Purim.

Mr. Monroe opens his sermon by asking his congregants to turn to the Book of Esther, noting the date as that of the Feast of Purim, the story of which is related in Esther. He acknowledges that "we don't have very many Jews" in South Carolina, describing Purim as "July Fourth if you're Jewish," and further attempts to make this alien Jewish festival of hatred relatable to his congregation by stating that some Jews celebrate Purim by dressing up in costumes, "like Halloween for us."

Mr. Monroe next gives his flock an abbreviated version of the events narrated in the Book of Esther that gave rise to Purim. In his telling, a royal official called Haman, "enemy of the Jews," hated the Jews because the Jews refused to bow for him. As Mr. Monroe puts it, "Jews didn't bow to anybody," because they only bowed before God. Angered, Haman, "one of the leading anti-Semites in all of recorded history," devised a plot

---

[9] FBT Live, "Sunday Evening at FBT 032424."

to kill all of the Jews. His plot was foiled: "The plot to eliminate the Jews was eliminated."

Purim, in Mr. Monroe's telling, is a celebration of "the freedom of the Jews," as American as apple pie. He says that Jews "go to their synagogues and read the entire Book of Esther, and every time they say the name *Haman*, they hiss and boo, or they don't say it at all," casting the festival of hatred as a jolly, good-natured community picnic. Christians should also celebrate Purim, Mr. Monroe exhorts, because it is the story of how "the good guys win and the bad guys hang on the gallows." Esther, he continues, "is one of the most amazing books of the Bible." Even though the word *God* appears nowhere in the text, "God is working," and the triumph of the Jews over Haman is *prima facie* evidence of "the providence of God . . . orchestrating things to carry out His will."

Mr. Monroe then takes it upon himself to deliver a lecture on the history of Israel. Why? Because "Israel is central to everything that we believe." With a map of the present State of Israel on the projector screen, he begins his story in 1987, with the First Intifada, which he characterizes as unprovoked terrorism against the innocent Jews of Israel. He decries the 1993 Oslo Accords, which, he says, "gave the governing authority of part of Israel to the Palestinians." "Now, keep in mind," Mr. Monroe continues, "Israel had fought to take that land in 1948. They miraculously got a little sliver of land," which was "greatly expanded" in the Six-Day War of 1967. Reiterating, Mr. Monroe declares that "Israel has been under pressure to give up its land since 1987. It fought three wars to gain that land."

In his grotesquely childish and one-sided view of history, Mr. Monroe sees the Palestinians as greedy invaders "demanding that they have a part of Israel." He mocks the Palestinians by chanting, "We want more land, we want more land, we want more land." Hamas, he tells us, wants "to turn Israel into an Islamic republic, to drive the Jews into the sea, to eliminate the Jews."

Concluding his jaundiced history lesson, Mr. Monroe declares:

> I'm going to say something contrary to everything you hear if you watch the news. The Palestinians . . . [t]hat has never been their land. Not one time, not one inch, not in all of history. There is no Palestinian. Never has been. The Palestinians are Arabic people who migrated into Israel since Israel has been a state in 1948. When Israel went there in 1948, that was a wasteland. . . . That land, and more was given to Abraham by Almighty God Himself. The title deed goes back to Genesis chapter 12. That's Israel. That's God's land.

His congregation is delighted, chanting "Amen," and "That's right."

We now pause Bill Monroe's satanic sermon in order to examine the *Nakba*, the true story of the establishment of the State of Israel, as well as to discuss the true origins of the Jews and the Palestinians.

Britain's 1917 Balfour Declaration promised Palestine as the future Jewish homeland; interestingly, there is considerable evidence to suggest that the British issued that document in exchange for influential Zionists orchestrating America's entry into the First World War.[10] In any case, after the Allied victory, Palestine passed from Ottoman to British control. Violence perpetrated by Zionist settlers against the Palestinians continued to escalate, as the Zionists tried to maximize Jewish immigration. British forces, alongside Zionist militias, brutally repressed Palestinian resistance, and by 1939 an estimated 14 to 17 percent of the adult male population of Palestine was killed or imprisoned.[11]

After the Second World War, the Zionists engaged in a campaign of terrorism against the British authorities in order to establish exclusive Jewish control over Palestine. In 1947, the British asked the newborn United Nations to propose a solution, which resulted in a partition plan that would have given 55 percent of Palestine to the Jews. At that time, Jews controlled only 6 percent of Palestine and comprised about a third of the population, the vast majority of whom had arrived only

---

[10] Unz, "Balfour Declaration."

[11] Khalidi, *Hundred Years' War.*

in the previous few years.[12] The Jews, dissatisfied with this massive expansion of territory, resolved to proceed with what they had been planning and preparing for since well before even the Balfour Declaration—the ethnic cleansing of Palestine, a genocide which the Arabs call the *Nakba*.

Supported unconditionally by both the United States and the Soviet Union—and armed with heavy Soviet weaponry—the Zionists declared the State of Israel on May 14th, 1948. The ethnic cleansing of Palestine had begun decades prior, but the *Nakba* proper occurred from late 1947 through the summer of 1949, by which time the Jews had seized 80 percent of Palestine, killing tens of thousands of Palestinians and exiling nearly a million of them from what had been their homeland for almost two millennia. This systematic removal of the Palestinian people was accomplished through the pillaging and destruction of hundreds of villages, marked by ruthless massacres and atrocities.[13]

Jewish forces, then as now, regarded Palestinian villages as enemy military bases, and all Palestinians—including women, children, and infants—were seen as enemy combatants. At Deir Yassin, thirty babies were among the slaughtered; at Safsaf, women and girls were gang-raped in front of the captive villagers, and a pregnant woman was bayoneted; at Dawaymeh, babies were crushed and women were gang-raped and burned alive.[14] Zionist militants threw a young Palestinian boy into an oven and roasted him alive, with his father following close behind.[15] The Jews also engaged in biological warfare, poisoning aqueducts and wells with typhoid and dysentery viruses.[16] Examples like these abound.

One incident is particularly revealing of Jewish bestiality: the elderly father of supermodels Gigi and Bella Hadid recently related the story of how his parents had willingly taken in a family of pitiful Jewish refugees who arrived in their country from Europe. His pregnant mother traveled to a

---

[12] Unz, "American Pravda: The *Nakba* and the Holocaust."

[13] Pappé, *Ethnic Cleansing of Palestine.*

[14] Ibid., 117, 212, 224.

[15] Unz, "Jewish Roots of the Gaza Rampage."

[16] Pappé, *Ethnic Cleansing*, 126–7.

neighboring town for a few days to be with her relatives for the birth of her child. When she returned, she found that the Jewish family they had kindly taken into their home had dispossessed them of it, refusing to allow them entrance to take any of their family photographs or even a blanket for their newborn baby.[17]

Remarkably, large numbers of British troops were still present in Palestine while the *Nakba* occurred. The Palestinians had expected the British to maintain some semblance of order, as they had for the last thirty years, and were thus dismayed as British forces stood by and allowed the Zionists to dispossess them of their land, loot them, and exterminate them with impunity.[18]

In 1967, Israel launched a surprise attack against Egypt and its other Arab neighbors, resulting in another massive expansion of its territory. During the Six-Day War that followed, Israeli forces intentionally attacked an American surveillance ship, the USS *Liberty*, killing or maiming more than two hundred American sailors in what was likely a false flag attempt to draw direct American intervention into the conflict.[19] Today, the Palestinians control less than 2 percent of their homeland.

Since 1967, they have lived under total Israeli occupation, as Zionist settlers armed and supported by the Israeli and American governments have continued to encroach upon what little land they have managed to eke out an existence on. For over fifteen years, more than two million Palestinians have been confined to Gaza, a roughly 140 square mile open-air prison (a space roughly as large as Detroit), at the mercy of the increasingly fanatical Israeli government.[20] In 2018, Israel responded to peaceful protests by butchering and disfiguring many thousands of Palestinians in Gaza.

Christian Zionists like Bill Monroe predicate their entire heretical theology upon the belief that the Jews remain God's Chosen. They believe that the New Testament of our Lord

---

[17] Unz, "American Pravda: The *Nakba* and the Holocaust."
[18] Pappé, *Ethnic Cleansing*, 124.
[19] Unz, "American Pravda: Remembering the *Liberty*."
[20] Unz, "Gaza and the Danger."

Jesus Christ is essentially inoperative, and that the Old Testament remains in effect. This belief is itself premised upon the notion that the Jews of the Old Testament, and even the Jews in Christ's time, are the same as those who call themselves Jews today. Most emphatically, however, they are *not*.

In the first place, rabbinical or Talmudic Judaism is not the religion of the Jews of the Old Testament, and indeed did not arise until long after the Crucifixion and Resurrection of Christ. This Judaism emerged as a reaction *against* Christianity, motivated and fueled entirely by rejection and hatred of Jesus Christ. While it is true that the Jews of Christ's time are responsible for His murder, and thus it is accurate to refer to the Jews as "Christ-killers," it must also be understood that Judaism is not itself the same faith as the one that those Jews practiced.

The vast majority of the Jews whom we see in positions of oligarchic wealth and cultural and political power throughout the West today are Ashkenazim. Their origins remain frustratingly opaque, but it is clear that they are not related to the Jews of the Bible.[21] They are, indeed, "the Synagogue of Satan, which say they are Jews, and are not, but do lie" (Rev. 3:9). Even at the time of the late Roman empire, little if any of the empire's Jewish population had any Judean ancestry; in other words, few if any Jews even at this relatively early period could trace their roots to the Israelites of the Bible.[22]

The Judeans, the Jews of the Bible, in fact remained exactly where they were.

> Over the centuries, many of those Jews eventually converted to Christianity then later to Islam following the Muslim conquest, and they are the ancestors of today's Palestinians, leavened by an admixture from all the various conquering groups of the last two thousand years, including Arabs, Crusaders, and Turks. Thus, the direct descendants of the Judeans lived continuously in their homeland prior to the creation of the State of Israel in 1948. . . . [D]espite a long series of military conquests and foreign overlords, the Israelites of the Old

[21] Unz, "Prof. John Beaty."

[22] Ibid., citing Sand, *Invention of the Jewish People*.

> Testament had remained in place for well over two thousand years, annually plowing their fields until they were brutally uprooted and expelled from their ancient homeland by Zionist militants in 1948.[23]

The tremendous historical irony that the current Palestinians—now suffering horrifying massacres in Gaza—are almost certainly the closest lineal descendants of the biblical Israelites was fully understood by the Zionists, including David Ben-Gurion, Israel's founding father and first prime minister, and Yitzhak Ben-Zvi, Israel's second president. In 1918, Ben-Gurion and Ben-Zvi had written *Eretz Israel in the Past and the Present*, the most important Zionist book of its time, in which "they summarized the strong historical evidence that the local Palestinians were obviously just long-converted Jews, expressing the hope that they would therefore be absorbed into the growing Zionist movement and become an integral part of their planned State of Israel." In 1929, Ben-Zvi published a pamphlet reiterating this argument. It was only after Palestinian resistance emerged to the Zionist project that the Judean ancestry of the Palestinian Arabs became an inconvenient truth to be discarded and obscured.

Where, then, did the Ashkenazim come from? Compelling evidence suggests that they are actually the descendants of the Phoenicians and Carthaginians—Punic peoples widely known as the Canaanites.

The namesake of the Canaanites, Canaan, was a son of Ham, himself a son of Noah. In Genesis 9:20–27, Ham walked in upon his naked father and, rather than cover him up, told his brothers about it. His brothers walked backwards into Noah's tent and covered him. When Noah awoke, he said, "Cursed be Canaan," cursing Ham through his son. Canaan's descendants, as a result of this curse, practiced incest, sodomy, bestiality, and child sacrifice to the demon Moloch. These practices, set forth in Leviticus 18, marked the Canaanites for expulsion from the land of what is now the State of Israel.[24]

---

[23] Ibid.

[24] Erickson, "Religious Implications of the Carthaginian Theory."

Thus the irony is twofold. First, as we have seen, the modern Palestinians are the real descendants of the biblical Israelites; thus, "the entire Zionist project justifies itself off the claim that they are the descendants of the Israelites, but in reality, they are expelling the actual descendants of the Israelites from the Holy Land."[25] If indeed the modern Jews are the descendants of the Canaanites, then "the Zionist settlers are not just a foreign entity attacking the true Israelites, but are actually the descendants of the people that were cursed and explicitly ordered for removal from the land by God."[26]

The Canaanite origins of the Ashkenazim would also at least partially explain the origins of the practice of the Jewish ritual murder of Christian children. Archaeological evidence has incontrovertibly proven that the Carthaginians and other Phoenicians *did* ritually sacrifice children to the demons Baal-Hammon and Tanit, or Astarte, namesake of the demon Astaroth, supporting the biblical accounts of Canaanite child sacrifice. Child sacrifice did not end with the destruction of Carthage, but rather persisted within the religious practice of the Ashkenazim, Carthaginian peoples who converted to rabbinical or Talmudic Judaism.[27]

Another interesting link between Canaanite religion and Ashkenazi practice involves the so-called Star of David, which is both the Israeli flag and the standard of international Jewry. Its origins, like so much about the Ashkenazim, are shrouded in mystery. There is nothing in the Bible that would associate David with the symbol. The Star of David, the hexagram, is almost certainly the "star of your god Remphan" mentioned by St. Stephen in his speech to the Sanhedrin (Acts 7:43), itself a reference to "the tabernacle of your Moloch and Chiun your images, the star of your god" (Amos 5:26).

Remphan is the Egyptian name for Saturn, and Chiun the Hebrew name for Saturn. Furthermore, the Romans associated the Phoenician Baal-Hammon with Saturn, likely reinforced by the fact that Saturn ate his children in Roman

---

[25] Ibid.

[26] Ibid.

[27] Ibid.

mythology. Many Roman and Jewish sources attest to the significance of Saturn in Jewish practice. Tacitus and St. Augustine stated that the Jews had made the Sabbath their day of rest not to honor God, as is commanded in the Old Testament (Exod. 20:8–11), but in order to worship Saturn, an assertion seemingly confirmed by the fact that the Babylonian Talmud refers to Saturn as "Shabbetai," the star of Shabbat, Saturday.[28]

While Jews are today unable or unwilling to discuss the origin of the Star of David, the Jewish Virtual Library states that "the oldest undisputed example is on a seal from the seventh century B.C.E. found in Sidon," which was a prominent Phoenician city, and that Arab and Jewish sources referred to the hexagram as "the seal of Solomon." This connects the symbol with the Testament of Solomon, a noncanonical pseudepigraphic text in which "God gives Solomon a ring engraved with a pentagram that allows him to control demons, and the story ends with Solomon worshipping Moloch and Remphan in exchange for sex." Given, then, that "the oldest example of the Star of David is from around the time of Amos, in a major city of Saturn worshippers, and its first documented appearances also associate it with Saturn in the time of Stephen," it is highly probable that Amos and Stephen were speaking of the hexagram, or Star of David, when they condemned the Star of Remphan or Saturn.[29]

Quite disturbingly, in 1981 the *Voyager* interstellar probe mission revealed a massive hexagonal storm at the north pole of Saturn, something that the Canaanites could not possibly have known. The "black cube" of Saturn, which also happens to be the sixth planet from the Sun, has long been a central concept in occult practices due partially to the association of the numbers 666 with Satan (Rev. 13:18). While this is an esoteric topic, the extreme emphasis on ritualism within rabbinical Judaism makes it a topic that is only to be ignored at our peril, and provides another link between Canaanite Saturn-worship and international Jewry.

---

[28] Ibid.

[29] Ibid.

We return now to the execrable Purim sermon of the Christian Zionist Bill Monroe. Mr. Monroe tells his hopelessly befuddled, semi-lobotomized, and quasi-retarded congregation:

> [On October 7th, 2023] radical terrorists broke out of Gaza. They attacked, they went to kibbutzim, businesses, homes, jerked the doors open, began killing people. At the end of the day, 1,400 Jews had been murdered. Babies, for the first time, became part of the terrorist plan. Little children, babies, were beheaded. Little toddlers were raped. It was the cruelest, wickedest, most evil thing that anybody has seen.

As proof of this narrative, as though his rapt audience would ever ask him for proof, Mr. Monroe cites Tony Perkins, the Southern Baptist pastor and president of the Family Research Council, who, he says, "saw the films."

There are so many lies packed into that paragraph that it is hard to know exactly where to start. In the first place, the Hamas "attack" on the State of Israel was not a surprise attack. In December 2023, law professors Robert Jackson, Jr., and Joshua Mitts, respectively of Columbia University and New York University, published a paper with profound implications that has predictably gone almost entirely unremarked upon, even in alternative media.

They documented a significant spike in short selling in the principal Israeli-company exchange-traded fund in the days immediately prior to the October 7th Hamas raid. The short selling that day far exceeded the short selling that occurred during numerous other periods of crisis, including the recession following the 2008 financial crisis, the 2014 Israel-Gaza war, and the so-called COVID-19 pandemic. They also identified increases in short selling before the raid in dozens of Israeli companies traded in Tel Aviv, as well as a sharp increase, just before the raid, in trading in risky short-dated options (expiring just after October 7th) on Israeli companies on U.S. exchanges. Clearly, then, Israeli traders had foreknowledge of the Hamas raid, and in fact profited from it.[30]

---

[30] Jackson and Mitts, "Trading on Terror?"

Since Israeli traders had foreknowledge of the October 7th Hamas raid, it thus follows that they were informed of it by the Israeli government. Why, then, did Israel allow the raid to happen? There are two reasons, both of which are obvious to anyone who has observed the actions of the State of Israel since: 1) to provide a pretext for the total extermination or removal of every last Palestinian from Palestine; and 2) to escalate the genocide of Palestine into a regional war, with the ultimate goal of drawing the United States, a rapidly declining power, into a direct war against Iran, something that Israel has been trying to accomplish for decades.

For more than thirty years, Benjamin Netanyahu has declared that Iran is on the cusp of producing a nuclear weapon, a claim that continues to animate his Republican errand boys in the United States. While the State of Israel has engaged in an assassination and sabotage campaign within Iran for decades, its most direct attempt to incite a war occurred on April 1st, 2024, with an airstrike on the Iranian embassy in Damascus, Syria. While Israel had successfully directed the Donald Trump administration to assassinate Iranian general Qasem Soleimani in January 2020, this Israeli bombing of traditionally inviolate diplomatic quarters was a blatant act of war obviously designed to provoke the sort of Iranian retaliation that would draw in American intervention.[31]

Israel and its puppets in the American government also claim, again without any evidence, that Iran, acting through Hamas, is the primary culprit of the October 7th raid. Hence Republicans like Nimrata Randhawa (better known as Nikki Haley) wag their fingers on television, declaring that we must finish Iran. Senator Lindsey Graham urges us to "hit Iran. They have oil fields out in the open, they have the Revolutionary Guard headquarters you can see from space. Blow it off the map," while the Biden administration has pledged to do "whatever it takes" to prevent Iran from developing nuclear weapons. There is no evidence to suggest that Iran has a nuclear weapons program, but we can be assured that Israel will be working hard to produce fabricated evidence, just as it did

[31] Unz, "Israeli Assassinations and Public Scrutiny."

with Saddam Hussein's nonexistent weapons of mass destruction in 2003.[32]

Just days after the October 7th Hamas raid, the Biden administration dispatched two aircraft carrier strike groups to the eastern Mediterranean, along with orders to prepare the deployment of two thousand Marines.[33] Lt. Gen. Richard Clark, the Black superintendent of the U.S. Air Force Academy, declared that American soldiers are "prepared to die for the Jewish state."[34]

In the same month, John Hagee of Christians United for Israel (CUFI) delivered a sermon telecast from his Cornerstone Church, a Christian Zionist megachurch in San Antonio, Texas. Flanked by Israeli officials and Republican members of Congress, he cited Christian Zionist "End Times prophecy" to call for war against Iran:

> The righteous rage of America must be focused on Iran. . . . Let me say it to you in plain Texas speech. America should roll up its sleeves and knock the living daylights out of Tehran for what they have done to Israel. Hit them so hard that our enemies will once again fear us.[35]

His congregation cheered and waved Israeli flags—the Star of Remphan.

Hagee's son, Matt, continued: "The Secretary of State is not going to get us out of this one. . . . God tells Ezekiel exactly how he's going to defend Israel. He speaks about raining down fire and hail and brimstone. That's a heavenly air assault." Israel's ambassador to the United Nations, Gilad Erdan, took the stage and again cited the prophet Isaiah to call for increased American aid to Israel: "We need to be partners with God. For those of us in Israel, we are battling on the frontlines, for you my friends, we need you on . . . the political frontlines, making sure your elected officials on the state and national level stand with unwavering support for Israel." House Majority Whip

---

[32] Giraldi, "Israel Goes to Court."
[33] Giraldi, "The Damage Israel Does."
[34] Giraldi, "Marching for Israel?"
[35] Fang, "Televangelists Invoke Holy War."

Tom Emmer declared that "Congress must take deliberate action to give Israel whatever resources they need to end Hamas once and for all and combat Iran's support of terrorism." John Hagee added, "Israel is the apple of God's eye, Israel is unique to God. . . . I encourage you to bless the house of Israel with your financial giving."[36]

The Jewish obsession with inciting a war against Iran is all the more alarming given Israel's massive and illegal arsenal of nuclear weapons, said to number over two hundred. The Israeli nuclear program was only made possible by the theft of enriched uranium and triggers from the United States.[37] (Interestingly, President John F. Kennedy attempted to stop this program in its infancy, and strong evidence supports this being the cause of his assassination.[38])

In any case, the absolutely evil and remarkably reckless government of the State of Israel cannot be trusted with such an arsenal. Netanyahu's heritage minister, Amihai Eliyahu, has suggested using some of its nuclear weapons in Gaza.[39] Perhaps more concerningly, Israel has a nuclear strategy called "the Samson option," whereby it would launch a massive nuclear strike, perhaps including its entire arsenal, if Israel were ever in danger of being overrun.[40] This policy is named for Samson, who broke the pillars of a Philistine temple apart in order to bring down the roof and kill himself and the three thousand Philistines who had gathered to see him humiliated (Judg. 16:25–30).

Former prime minister Ariel Sharon has confirmed this plan:

> We possess several hundred atomic warheads and rockets and can launch them at targets in all directions, perhaps even at Rome. Most European capitals are targets for our air force. Let me quote General Moshe Dayan: "Israel must be like a mad dog,

---

[36] Ibid.

[37] Giraldi, "Gaza Genocide Continues."

[38] See, for instance: Guyénot, "Did Israel Kill the Kennedys?"; Unz, "American Pravda: The JFK Assassination, Part II?"; Guyénot, "Angleton, Mossad, and the Kennedy Assassinations."

[39] Unz, "American Pravda: Gaza and the Antisemitism Hoax."

[40] Hersh, *Samson Option*.

> too dangerous to bother." I consider it all hopeless at this point. . . . We have the capability to take the world down with us. And I can assure you that that will happen before Israel goes under.[41]

The idea that the October 7th Hamas raid was a "surprise attack" has been reinforced by American politicians, who regularly draw comparisons of the event to Pearl Harbor and 9/11. Indeed, Joe Biden described the Hamas raid as the equivalent of "fifteen 9/11s,"[42] and Senator Tom Cotton went further, stating that "this savage atrocity wasn't just the worst slaughter of Jews since World War 2, but one of the worst terror attacks against America since 9/11."[43] Of course, these comparisons are far more accurate than those who make them know, for neither Pearl Harbor nor 9/11 were surprise attacks either. The FDR administration had foreknowledge of and even intentionally provoked the Japanese attack on Pearl Harbor, in order to mobilize popular support for American intervention in the Second World War against the enemies of international Jewry.[44] In the case of 9/11, there is overwhelming evidence of Israeli foreknowledge, complicity, and even the primary carrying-out of the attacks on September 11th, 2001, in a conspiracy involving Jewish and Christian Zionist officials within the Bush administration.[45] This, too, was a false flag intended to draw the United States into a direct war against the enemies and rivals of the State of Israel.

Israel's successful framing of the Hamas raid as a "surprise attack" further allows the Jews to present violent Palestinian resistance as unprovoked, rather than what it is: the natural and just response to almost a century of brutal subjugation, to twenty miserable years of life in the panopticon of Gaza, to generations of slavery where death by bullet, bomb, and

---

[41] Giraldi, "Gaza Genocide Continues."

[42] Ibid.

[43] Fang, "Televangelists Invoke Holy War."

[44] Unz, "American Pravda: Understanding World War II."

[45] Sabrosky, "Demystifying 9/11." See also Bollyn, *Solving* 9-11 and Guyénot, "9/11 Was an Israeli Job."

starvation could arrive at any moment. Indeed, Hamas started nothing on October 7th.

Mr. Monroe cites the number of Jews killed by Hamas on October 7th as fourteen hundred, the number which has been credulously repeated by the media ever since Israel conjured it. Like the magical "six million" which the Jews like to cite regarding the so-called Holocaust, it is an entirely fictitious figure without any evidentiary support.[46] The true number of unarmed Israeli civilians killed by Hamas on October 7th is likely closer to one hundred.[47]

While the total number of Israelis killed on October 7th remains uncertain, there is convincing evidence that the overwhelming majority of these were killed by trigger-happy Israeli forces,[48] perhaps motivated by Israel's long-standing "Hannibal Directive," a policy requiring that any Israelis captured by Palestinians be killed to avoid allowing them to become future bargaining chips.[49] Tellingly, this policy is named for Hannibal, who led the Carthaginians and nearly destroyed Rome in the Second Punic War, and who, later in life, committed suicide rather than be captured by Rome.

Also fictitious is the Israeli atrocity propaganda, parroted by Mr. Monroe and the entirety of the Western media and political establishment, that Hamas had beheaded forty Jewish babies, roasted Jewish babies in an oven, and committed numerous mass rapes and sexual mutilations.[50] These claims, some of which did not emerge until fully two months after October 7th, all came from fanatic Zionist settlers, and each one has been thoroughly disproven.[51] These gruesome tales "echo past Holocaust claims involving Jews rendered into human-skin lampshades and bars of soap, fiendish Nazi atrocities that served as the lurid centerpiece of the Nuremberg Trials and

---

46 Unz, "Gaza and the Danger of Jewish Paranoia."
47 Unz, "American Pravda: Gaza and the Antisemitism Hoax."
48 Unz, "Pro-Israel Propaganda: Lies vs. Reality."
49 Unz, "American Pravda: Israel, Gaza, and Broader Issues."
50 Unz, "Pro-Israel Propaganda: Lies vs. Reality."
51 Unz, "American Pravda: War Crimes and Atrocity-Hoaxes."

other Allied propaganda, but which were eventually admitted to be total fabrications."[52]

The Israeli government has produced a documentary, *Bearing Witness*, allegedly compiled by the Israeli military from raw footage that it claims was captured from body cameras worn by Hamas fighters during the October 7th raid. Israel has organized screenings for influential audiences in America and Europe, who are forbidden from sharing any images from the film. One of these screenings, held at the U.S. Capitol in November 2023, was attended by forty senators, led by Marco Rubio and the Jewish Jacky Rosen. After the screening, many of the senators literally staggered and ran out of the room crying, including Michael Bennet, who claims to be the son of a Holocaust survivor. Ted Cruz described the film thus:

> We saw terrorists celebrating as they murdered children and women, as they desecrated the bodies. We saw them beheading bodies with knives. We heard audio of the terrorists calling their parents celebrating the people that they murdered. There is a level of evil and hate and depravity that defies words.[53]

Elon Musk, one of the wealthiest people on earth, is another individual for whom this propaganda film was screened. Mr. Musk has since visited Auschwitz with the Jewish media figure Ben Shapiro, even donning a yarmulke for the occasion. Describing himself as "aspirationally Jewish," Mr. Musk completed his pilgrimage of submission to Jewish power by visiting Netanyahu in Israel, posing for a photo in which the two men reverently eye an empty crib to symbolize the "forty beheaded babies" hoax.[54]

Atrocity propaganda is central to the entire project of Jewish power; after all, their alleged Holocaust, replete with piles of shoes, is the magic spell with which they have dazzled and hypnotized the Goyim of the West for the last eighty years. With this one word, *Holocaust*, they have masked their

---

[52] Unz, "American Pravda: The *Nakba* and the Holocaust."
[53] Kampeas, "Stark images of murder."
[54] Unz, "Elon Musk Goes to Canossa."

unbridled, monstrous, inhuman, bloodthirsty faces, their total domination of the West, behind the veneer of victimhood. In the case of Hamas, Jews use these outrageous hoaxes to: 1) identify the Palestinian cause, and all who sympathize with it, in the minds of idiot Americans with scenes of raping, roasting, and beheading babies; 2) deflect attention from the ongoing Israeli genocide of the Palestinians; and 3) frame the genocide as a retaliatory war against "terrorists."

The credulous repetition of "Hamas atrocities" allows Jews and their servants to totally elide the very real genocide that the Jews are committing against Christian and Muslim Palestinians. As Southern Baptist Bill Monroe puts it in his Purim sermon, trust not your lying eyes: "Everything you look at on television has been edited over and over. . . . There are always civilian deaths in a war. If I were Jewish, and I saw what happened on October 7th, I would want every single Hamas removed from the walk of life." Stated differently, Mr. Monroe tells his audience that the copiously documented Israeli war crimes against the Palestinians are actually fabricated, that this fabrication is performed by a Western media that is, in his total inversion of reality, *sympathetic* to Palestinians, and that, in any case, the Palestinians deserve anything and everything that his precious Jews decide to do to them.

The heinous crimes against God and against humanity which the Jews have committed since October 7th fill several volumes, and the list increases exponentially with each passing day; here, it is sufficient to give a brief sketch.

Financed by tens of billions of dollars from American taxpayers and supplied with ever-increasing shipments of American heavy weaponry, including many tens of thousands of tons of massive bombs and other equipment, the State of Israel has for eight months now engaged in the heaviest bombing campaign in history, carpet-bombing Gaza's roughly 140 square miles with more tonnage in October 2023 than that corresponding to the nuclear weapons dropped on Hiroshima and Nagasaki. By early December, the devastation was worse than that suffered by the worst-hit German cities after years of Allied bombing in the Second World War.[55]

Just as German civilians melted into liquefied pavement in Dresden in 1945, Palestinians in Gaza are today being burned alive in infernal columns fueled by the hellfire of the Jews and their father Satan (John 8:44). A prominent Israeli politician recently made the comparison himself: "Gaza needs to turn into Dresden! Complete incineration." Israeli U.N. ambassador Gilad Erdan wore a yellow star emblazoned with the words "never again" as he pledged before the Security Council to "eliminate the Nazi Hamas," extending the Jewish narrative of continuity between their enemies in the Second World War and their enemies today.[56]

As I write this, the official Palestinian death toll stands at over thirty-five thousand killed, nearly eighty thousand injured, and essentially the entire population of Gaza, over two million, displaced.[57] By early December 2023, however, the Gazan officials responsible for tabulating the dead had themselves been killed, so the official death toll stagnated and remains implausibly low. The true number of the martyred is orders of magnitude higher, in the hundreds of thousands, with one hundred thousand being a very conservative estimate. Some have speculated that the figure could be greater than two hundred thousand.[58] It bears repeating that these are helpless civilians, the vast majority of them women, children, and infants, being indiscriminately slaughtered before the entire world with impunity.

American officials generously estimate that Israel has killed between 30 and 35 percent of Hamas,[59] but the reality is that Hamas fighters are still in their tunnel network. Over 70 percent of the victims in Gaza, in the early months when they could still be identified, have been women and children, mirroring the general population of Gaza and thus further

---

[55] Unz, "Gazacaust."
[56] Antoniadis et al., "The Unwinnable War."
[57] United Nations Office for the Coordination of Humanitarian Affairs.
[58] Unz, "Israel/Gaza: The Masks Come Off."
[59] Ward, Banco, and Seligman, "Biden admin openly hammering."

indicating that essentially all of the deaths have been of civilians.[60] It cannot be stressed enough that, while Israel and its American protector would have malicious rubes like Bill Monroe believe that the Jews are "fighting Hamas," they are actually deliberately attempting to annihilate every last Palestinian person and render Gaza an uninhabitable, smoldering Hell on earth.

One need only listen to the Jews themselves to understand that their intention is to extinguish the Palestinian flame forevermore. In November 2023, Israel's Rosenbaum Communications produced a video widely circulated by the Israeli government and its constellation of Jewish lobby organizations, entitled "The Friendship Song 2023." In it, a choir of Jewish children sing praise for industrial-scale murder, affirming that "we will show the world how we destroyed our enemy," and that "we will annihilate everyone," meaning all of the Palestinians.[61]

In the same month, Prime Minister Benjamin Netanyahu explicitly identified the Palestinians with the tribe of Amalek, which the Israelites of the Old Testament were ordered by divine mandate to completely exterminate, down to the last newborn baby.[62] Specifically, God commanded the Israelites to "blot out the remembrance of Amalek from under heaven," to "go and smite Amalek, and utterly destroy all that they have, and spare them not; but slay them both man and woman, infant and suckling, ox and sheep, camel and ass" (Deut. 25:19; 1 Sam. 15:3).

In May 2024, Netanyahu again referenced 1 Samuel 15, in which Samuel admonished Saul for having spared the Amalekite king and the best of the Amalekites' animals. The implication, of course, is that he will not make the same mistake as King Saul by not completely eradicating Amalek. He will go all the way. He will "wipe off the seed of Amalek," as Israeli soldiers have been recorded chanting.[63]

---

[60] Unz, "Gaza and the Danger of Jewish Paranoia."
[61] Giraldi, "Toward a Palestine Without Palestinians."
[62] Unz, "American Pravda: War Crimes and Atrocity-Hoaxes."
[63] Ofir, "Netanyahu's response to the ICC."

Netanyahu's call was echoed by both Bezalel Smotrich and Itamar Ben-Gvir, his finance and national security ministers. As Smotrich put it, "There are no half-measures. . . . Total annihilation. . . . There's no place under heaven."[64] Ben-Gvir, whose Jewish Power party is integral to Netanyahu's governing coalition, has publicly endorsed such sentiments and hailed Jewish supremacists like Baruch Goldstein (perpetrator of the 1994 Hebron massacre, in which dozens of Muslims were slaughtered as they prayed) as a martyred hero.[65] Ben-Gvir used to have a portrait of Goldstein in his home.[66] At Goldstein's memorial service in Jerusalem, Rabbi Yaacov Perrin infamously proclaimed that even one million Arabs "are not worth a Jewish fingernail."[67] Ariel Sharon once said, "I vow that if I was just an Israeli civilian and I met a Palestinian, I would burn him and I would make him suffer before killing him."[68] These are merely a few of the innumerable instances of genocidal language regularly employed by Israeli politicians. Each statement is entirely in line with the teachings of Talmudic Judaism regarding Gentiles, who are seen as subhuman Goyim whose only purpose in life is to serve as beasts of burden for Jews.

The Israeli population fully supports the Jewish supremacism of their government and religious authorities, as public opinion surveys have consistently shown that 98 percent of Israeli Jews support the massive destruction inflicted upon Gaza and that over 40 percent think that the Israeli government has been too restrained.[69] Countless videos have appeared on TikTok, Telegram, and other platforms of ordinary Israeli civilians gleefully mocking dead and starving Palestinians.[70] Some of the worst examples have been posted by Israeli soldiers, obviously quite pleased with themselves, such as a video of a starving dog eating the corpse of a Palestinian child,

---

[64] Giraldi, "The Enemy Is Among Us?"
[65] Unz, "Gaza and the Danger of Jewish Paranoia."
[66] Associated Press, "Israel: leader of far-right."
[67] Kraft, "Extremists Pay Tribute."
[68] Weiss, "Sharon's racism was etched."
[69] Unz, "Gazacaust."
[70] Unz, "American Pravda: Gaza, Jewish Power, and the Holocaust."

and an image of a bound Palestinian who had been crushed flat while still alive by an Israeli tank.[71]

The Israeli military offers tours of its detention centers and prisons, where Israeli civilians are invited to observe the detainees, stripped to their underwear, and laugh and jeer as the men are beaten, humiliated, and tortured, with many of the viewers also allowed to film what is happening on their cell phones to share with their friends and families.[72] Israeli medical interns perform surgical experiments on captive Palestinians without anesthesia.[73] On Israeli television, when a journalist joked that Joe Biden's red line was the slaughter of thirty thousand Palestinians, the singer Kobi Peretz asked if that was the number being killed in a single day. The audience erupted in laughter and applause.[74]

Gaza has been rendered an uninhabitable wasteland, with hundreds of thousands of structures completely obliterated, including almost every hospital, school, church, mosque, apartment building, and house.[75] The intention, spelled out explicitly in Israeli government documents, is to murder or expel every Palestinian, and make it impossible for any survivors to ever return.[76]

An additional benefit of the leveling of Gaza is financial. Jared Kushner, Donald Trump's Jewish son-in-law, has noted that Gaza's waterfront property is "very valuable." Indeed, Israeli real estate dealers are already preparing to divide up the land, especially that along the Mediterranean. Stolen Palestinian land and houses are being sold even now at synagogues and Jewish community centers in New York and New Jersey. These sales are advertised by statements such as this: "In a world where uncertainty looms and antisemitism shows its

---

[71] Unz, "Israel/Gaza: The Masks Come Off."
[72] Giraldi, "American Foreign Policy."
[73] Cook, "The Message of Israel's Torture."
[74] Hedges, "Israel's Willing Executioners."
[75] Unz, "Gazacaust." See also Unz, "American Pravda: War Crimes and Atrocity-Hoaxes" and Unz, "American Pravda: Gaza and the Antisemitism Hoax."
[76] Giraldi, "Toward a Palestine Without Palestinians."

ugly face more boldly than ever, the decision to invest in a home in Israel is not just wise—it's exhilarating!"[77]

Israeli soldiers have shared videos of themselves looting their Palestinian victims, one of which shows them grinning from ear to ear in a Palestinian home with the owners tied up and blindfolded in the background.[78] The State of Israel is also motivated by the oil and gas reserves off the coast of Gaza, which are worth billions of dollars, as well as the long-gestating Ben Gurion Canal project, a proposed alternative to the Suez Canal. In any case, the United States will be on hand to pay for the reconstruction of Gaza, having recently announced that it plans to play a "prominent" role in Gaza after the war. From the bones and ashes of the Palestinians, luxurious seafront properties can be developed for Israeli and international Jewish buyers, which would produce a windfall both for the Israeli government and for Jewish investors like Kushner.[79]

A central component of Israeli strategy is the inculcation of famine. Even before the October 7th Hamas raid, Israel tightly restricted the importation of food, water, and medicine into Gaza, resulting in some of the highest rates of malnutrition on earth. This situation has rapidly degenerated into actual famine, with the Palestinians of Gaza constituting roughly 80 percent of all of the people on the planet facing catastrophic hunger and thirst.[80] Of the half of Gaza's population now at risk of imminent famine, at least fifteen thousand are pregnant women.[81]

Israeli soldiers and Zionist settlers regularly block food deliveries, even to the point of destroying and burning the food. Even the sea is patrolled, so that any Gazans who attempt to fish for food are killed. This program of starvation extends also to the West Bank, under Israeli occupation since 1967, where Zionist settlers armed by the Israeli government destroy olive

---

77 Giraldi, "Where Does Israel-Gaza Go from Here?"

78 Hedges, "Israel's Willing Executioners."

79 Giraldi, "Where Does Israel-Gaza Go from Here?" See also Ward, "US preparing for 'prominent' role."

80 Unz, "Gazacaust."

81 Barrett, "UN: 15,000 Pregnant Women."

trees and close the roads so that Palestinians cannot harvest the major cash crop, olive oil.[82] Israel's bombing campaign has also created large accumulations of hazardous waste, further poisoning the air and water.[83]

When desperate, starving Palestinians flock to the few food deliveries that are allowed through, the Israeli military massacres them by the hundreds.[84] Israeli troops have even started placing bombs disguised as food tins in the rubble of Gaza, with the intention of killing or maiming starving Palestinians when they open them.[85]

Along with doctors, the aid workers who attempt to bring food, water, and medicine to the Palestinians are themselves deliberately targeted for death by Israeli forces.[86] Several hundred aid workers, including over one hundred United Nations employees, have been butchered with impunity, including consecutive drone strikes on a clearly marked convoy belonging to the World Central Kitchen charity.[87]

Israel has also claimed that twelve employees (out of thirty thousand total) of the United Nations Gaza Relief and Works Agency (UNRWA), participated in the October 7th Hamas raid,[88] a claim to which the United States responded by immediately cutting all funding to the organization.[89] The alleged confessions of these alleged Hamas operatives were extracted under torture, as the men were being beaten, waterboarded, and mauled by attack dogs.[90] The goal is to terrify any humanitarian relief organizations from even attempting to help the Palestinian people as they are incinerated. Indeed, as of May 2024, the United Nations has given up its efforts to distribute food.[91]

---

[82] Giraldi, "Old Genocide Joe Has Got to Go!"
[83] "'Slow poisoning': How Israeli Bombing."
[84] Unz, "Israel/Gaza: The Masks Come Off."
[85] Hedges, "Israel's Willing Executioners."
[86] Giraldi, "Israel Goes to Court."
[87] Giraldi, "More Deaths in Gaza."
[88] Giraldi, "Israel Keeps Killing Civilians."
[89] Unz, "Gazacaust."
[90] Cook, "Torture, Executions, Babies."
[91] Associated Press, "UN suspends Rafah aid."

Just as Israel designates food distribution zones in order to draw crowds of Palestinians and slaughter them *en masse*,[92] Israeli forces routinely designate "safe zones" and refugee camps in order to corral large numbers of Palestinians and massacre them.[93] Videos from the aftermath of these "safe zone" attacks show desperate parents trying to dig the charred corpses of their children out from under the rubble, and vice versa; one man can be seen cradling the headless, smoking remains of a toddler, presumably his son.[94] This latter video, from Rafah in southern Gaza, was widely shared by government-affiliated Israeli Telegram channels for Jews to laugh at, with captions calling Rafah "the central bonfire of the year." In what is surely not coincidental, that atrocity took place on Lag BaOmer, a Jewish holiday celebrated with bonfires.[95]

Israeli quadcopters broadcast the sounds of screaming women and crying babies in order to lure Palestinians out to be killed.[96] Jewish snipers murdered a pair of Catholic women, mother and daughter, taking refuge in a church.[97] Unarmed people waving white flags of surrender and begging for mercy are regularly cut down,[98] including some of the Israeli "Hamas hostages" that the Western media never ceases to remind us to worry about.[99] Israeli soldiers came across a group of Palestinian women, children, and infants taking shelter in a school and summarily executed them all.[100] Palestinians, including those seeking refuge at hospitals, were shackled and buried alive by Israeli bulldozers, just after the deputy mayor of Jerusalem, Fleur Hassan-Nahoum, publicly suggested that exact method of murder.[101]

Mass graves have been discovered at the sites of many destroyed hospitals, each filled with hundreds of corpses of

---

[92] Unz, "American Pravda: War Crimes and Atrocity-Hoaxes."
[93] Giraldi, "Biden's America Surrenders."
[94] Whitney, "Israeli Missile Attack."
[95] Menahan, "Israeli Airstrike on Gaza."
[96] Hedges, "Israel's Willing Executioners."
[97] Giraldi, "The Antisemitic Moment."
[98] Ibid.
[99] Unz, "Gaza and the Danger of Jewish Paranoia."
[100] Ibid.
[101] Ibid.

doctors and patients of all ages, stripped naked and bound with their hands behind their backs.[102] Many of the bodies showed signs of hasty surgery, indicating that their lucrative organs had been harvested by the Jews, a regular practice performed on Palestinians by Israeli forces for decades.[103] Israel has preyed upon the organs of its defenseless Palestinian population to such a degree that it is one of the world's primary organ trafficking hubs.[104] Inside the hospitals, newborn babies in incubators were abandoned to die,[105] their parents and the doctors caring for them having already been killed.[106]

Patients who manage to survive these assaults on hospitals, including those with gangrenous wounds, cancer, and neurodegenerative diseases, have their hands bound above their heads and are left to decompose.[107] When they are not immediately executed outright, Palestinian women of all ages, including those who are pregnant, are often detained and raped by Israeli soldiers,[108] some of whom have posted sadomasochistic, pornographic photos and videos of their conquests.[109] There are also reports of female infants being taken from their mothers, never to be seen again.[110]

Along with doctors and aid workers, journalists are favored targets for Israeli assassination, and hundreds of them have now have paid the ultimate price for attempting to document these monstrous Jewish atrocities.[111] A particularly horrific example is that of Wael Dahdouh, the Palestinian bureau chief for *Al Jazeera*. On October 25th, 2023, just days after the Israeli government complained about *Al Jazeera*'s coverage of its operations in Gaza, an Israeli missile strike took the lives of almost his entire family, including his wife, his fifteen-year-old

---

[102] Unz, "Israel/Gaza: The Masks Come Off."
[103] Giraldi, "Students are Taking the Lead." See also Giraldi, "The Enemy Is Among Us?"
[104] Euronews, "Israel 'stealing organs' from bodies."
[105] Giraldi, "Biden's America Surrenders."
[106] Giraldi, "American Foreign Policy."
[107] Cook, "Torture, Executions, Babies."
[108] Reed, "State Dept downplays reports."
[109] Cook, "Torture, Executions, Babies."
[110] Ibid.
[111] Unz, "Israel/Gaza: The Masks Come Off."

son, his seven-year-old daughter, and his one-year-old grandson. They were, as is so often the case, well within a "safe zone" to which Israel had told the Palestinians to flee.[112] *Al Jazeera* has since been expelled from Israel.[113]

In May 2022, the celebrated Palestinian-American journalist Shireen Abu Akleh was murdered by an Israeli army sniper while reporting from the occupied West Bank, with the single precisely-aimed round striking her in the back of the head just above her flak-jacket, which was clearly emblazoned "Press."[114] She was neither the first nor the last American citizen murdered by Israel in cold blood. Just as Israel does not prosecute or punish Jews who kill Arabs,[115] the United States imposes no penalties upon Jews who kill American citizens.[116] American taxes and munitions will never cease to flow into Israel, no matter how many Americans are slain.

Among those Americans killed are Rachel Corrie of Washington, run over and crushed to death in 2003 by an Israeli armored bulldozer while protesting the demolition of Palestinian houses in Gaza; Furkan Dogan, a Turkish-American teenager, shot and killed in 2010 by the Israeli navy along with eight others while attempting to deliver humanitarian aid to Gaza; Omar Abdalmajeed As'ad of Milwaukee, an eighty-year-old Palestinian-American beaten to death by Israeli soldiers; and, most recently, the Palestinian-American teenager Tawfic Abdel Jabbar of Louisiana, killed by Zionist settlers in the West Bank in January 2024, apparently for the crime of being Palestinian.[117]

We return again to Bill Monroe and his Purim sermon, as he perfectly exemplifies Christian Zionist theology in an act of verbal fellation of his Jewish masters that would be comical, were it not so grotesque. He tells his congregants that "God's eye is upon the land of Israel. He has never taken His eye off of Israel. . . . What God is going to do in the future is going to

---

[112] Al Jazeera Staff, "To kill a family."
[113] Al Jazeera Staff, "Israel bans Al Jazeera."
[114] Unz, "American Pravda: War Crimes and Atrocity-Hoaxes."
[115] Giraldi, "The Enemy Is Among Us?"
[116] Giraldi, "Israel Keeps Killing Civilians."
[117] Ibid.

involve the State of Israel. Israel is the key to biblical prophecy, the key to understanding the future." Emphasizing yet again that the Israel of the Bible is literally the present-day political entity of the State of Israel, he says, to a chorus of amens from his congregation, that "God is displeased with anybody who tries to make Israel give up their land. . . . If you get on the bandwagon of getting Israel to give up its land, you're gon' make God mad."

Legions of Christian Zionists take charlatans like Mr. Monroe at his word. They fall over themselves to donate their hard-earned money, tears streaming down their faces as they see the ubiquitous International Fellowship of Christians and Jews (IFCJ) television advertisements featuring Yael Eckstein, former Arkansas Governor Mike Huckabee, and former Representative Michele Bachmann exhorting us to "feed the hungry Jews." There are many such organizations of hucksters.

The Hayovel organization, for example, raises millions of dollars from Christian Zionists in the United States to finance the illegal occupation of the West Bank, sending violent, fanatical Zionist settlers such supplies as bulletproof vests, drones, and night-vision binoculars. After the October 7th Hamas raid, Hayovel sent a crew of fifteen young Christian Zionist "cowboys" from rural America to the West Bank to help the settlers install security roads, build warehouses, and "stand guard." One of Hayovel's cowboys in the West Bank, Yosef Strain of Montana, 22, wears a large Star of David belt buckle. His family trains rodeo horses. He said, "We want to live for Israel; that is our goal." Charles Hutsler, 19, of Huntsville, Arkansas, added that he wasn't scared of Hamas because "God has my back." Johnny Plocher, 24, explained that "God put a special calling on my life" to serve the State of Israel.[118]

Morgan Waller, Hayovel's director of operations, explained the rationale:

> Everyone is talking about a proportionate response. A proportionate Christian response would be to bring the supplies needed to stop another Jewish massacre from happening. . . .

---

118 Jaffe-Hoffman, "Meet the Christian Cowboys."

> No one wants to say it, but these Palestinians, many of them are also involved with Hamas or another terrorist organization, and if they believe they are strong enough and Israel is weak enough, they will strike. . . . Americans support Israel. . . . The Biden Administration believes in a two-state solution and would like to see 500,000 Jews pushed out of here, their biblical heartland. These cowboys represent the America behind Israel and the Bible. We are here to say no way to have to cut the State of Israel in half and the ability to create an Arab state in the middle of Israel's heartland. These cowboys are not going to see it.[119]

Mr. Monroe next turns his ire on "replacement theology," which is to say the entire New Testament as understood by every Christian for two thousand years. "There are those that believe in the replacement theology," he continues, "that Israel has been replaced in God's plans, that God's plans now involve only the Church, and that Israel lost their privileges when they crucified Christ." This, essentially a call to trivialize and disregard the New Testament and Christ Himself, is one of the two or three mentions of Jesus Christ in this entire ostensibly Christian pastor's Palm Sunday Purim sermon.

Next, Mr. Monroe reads long, sickening excerpts from "a wonderful book here that I got when I was in the Holy Land," containing Gentile tributes to Jews. From Leo Tolstoy's 1891 essay "What is a Jew?" he reads: "A Jew is a sacred being. . . . A Jew is eternal; he is an embodiment of eternity." From Mark Twain's 1899 essay "Concerning the Jews," he reads: "The Jews constitute but one percent of the human race. It suggests a nebulous dim puff of stardust lost in the blaze of the Milky Way. Properly the Jew ought hardly to be heard of; but he is heard of. . . . His commercial importance is extravagantly out of proportion to . . . the weakness of his numbers. . . . He could be vain of himself, and be excused for it." He notes the passing of empires such as Rome, and continues, "The Jew saw them all, beat them all, and is now what he always was. . . . *All things are mortal but the Jew; all other forces pass, but he remains.* What is the secret of his immortality?"

---

[119] Ibid.

Mr. Monroe reveals his complete and utter detachment from reality by claiming that every president of the United States, with "the one exception" of Ronald Reagan, has "pressured Israel to give up its land." He attacks the Biden administration, the European Union, and the United Nations for "pressuring Israel to give up land to have a two-state solution." He reserves particular scorn for Senator Chuck Schumer's recent call for Netanyahu's resignation—remarks that Schumer almost certainly made in an attempt to at least nominally pacify the millions of Democratic voters opposed to the Israeli genocide of Gaza. Remarkably, Mr. Monroe compares the cartoonishly Jewish Chuck Schumer to Haman from the Book of Esther for the unthinkable sin of criticizing Bibi.

Before we proceed any deeper into the warped, corroded mind of Bill Monroe, let us take a look at American government support for Israel. Aside from the unending deluge of American dollars and munitions, it is abundantly clear that the American government is a Jewish xenocracy in which a hostile, alien elite rules with an iron fist.

The Chuck Schumer-led United States Senate has voted 97–0 pledging its full and unconditional support for the State of Israel and whatever it chooses to do, with the House following by 412–10.[120] In May, 2024, shortly before the International Criminal Court (ICC) issued an arrest warrant for Netanyahu for war crimes and crimes against humanity, Speaker of the House Mike Johnson called on the White House to prevent such an "abomination" from transpiring, and twelve senators, all Republicans, sent a letter to Karim Khan, the ICC's chief prosecutor, ending in a threat:

> The United States will not tolerate politicized attacks by the ICC on our allies. Target Israel and we will target you. If you move forward with the measures indicated in this report, we will move to end all American support for the ICC, sanction your employees and your associates, and bar you and your family from the United States. You have been warned.

---

[120] Giraldi, "Gaza Genocide Continues."

The senators include Mitch McConnell, Tom Cotton, Marsha Blackburn, Katie Britt, Ted Budd, Kevin Cramer, Ted Cruz, Bill Hagerty, Pete Ricketts, Marco Rubio, Rick Scott, and Tim Scott.[121]

Upon his arrival on the first of his many visits to Israel after the October 7th Hamas raid, Jewish Secretary of State Antony Blinken declared:

> I come before you . . . as a Jew. My grandfather . . . fled pogroms in Russia. My stepfather . . . survived concentration camps—Auschwitz, Dachau, Majdanek. So . . . I understand on a personal level the harrowing echoes that Hamas's massacres carry for Israeli Jews—indeed, for Jews everywhere.[122]

Blinken is just one of the many Jews who occupy top-level positions within the Biden administration, a figure that comes to around 70 percent and includes Attorney General Merrick Garland, Director of National Intelligence Avril Haines, Secretary of Homeland Security Alejandro Mayorkas, White House Chief of Staff Jeff Zients, and Secretary of the Treasury Janet Yellen.[123] Kamala Harris is married to a Jew, and all three of Joe Biden's children married Jews.[124]

Jewish bloodlust for the Palestinians is almost matched by Christian Zionists in America and the Republican politicians they support. Nikki Haley and Mike Pence, for example, have both been photographed near the Israel–Lebanon border signing and writing messages on American-made artillery shells that were about to be fired into Lebanon, ostensibly against Hezbollah.[125] Haley wrote "Finish them!" and "America ♥ Israel always" on her artillery shells.[126] Mike Pompeo was filmed laughing and dancing with Israeli soldiers, celebrating after a long day of slaughtering Palestinian children.[127] Senator Lindsey Graham has said that there should be "no limit" to the

---

[121] Giraldi, "Protecting Israel."
[122] Blinken, "Secretary Antony J. Blinken."
[123] Unz, "Israel/Gaza: The Masks Come Off."
[124] Connelly, "Everything you need to know."
[125] Giraldi, "Israel Goes to Court."
[126] Astor, "Nikki Haley Writes 'Finish Them.'"
[127] Giraldi, "American Foreign Policy."

number of Palestinians murdered.[128] Representative Tim Walberg, a former evangelical pastor, has echoed Israeli politicians by suggesting that nuclear weapons be used not just to annihilate Palestinians, but Russians as well. Representative Andy Ogles has called on Israel to "kill them all."[129]

Representative Brian Mast, a Christian Zionist who volunteered with the Israeli military, has stated that there are no innocent Palestinians, and has even worn his Israeli uniform on the floor of the United States House of Representatives. There are more than twenty-three thousand American citizens serving in the IDF as of February 2024. Some Israeli army reservists living in the United States have also been summoned back to Israel to fight. Prior to the October 7th Hamas raid, there were an estimated six hundred thousand American citizens living in areas under Israeli occupation, mostly consisting of dual-national settlers who are fanatically Zionist, support Jewish atrocities against the Palestinians, and commit vigilante murders themselves.[130]

Representatives Guy Reschenthaler and the Jewish Max Miller have sponsored legislation that would provide direct support for Americans in the Israeli military by extending to them the legal, financial, and employment protections that have previously only been available to American servicemembers.[131] Miller, who gleefully stated that Palestine was "about to get eviscerated," believes that there should be "no rules of engagement" in Gaza, which should be turned "into a parking lot."[132]

Former Representative Tulsi Gabbard, who made a name for herself by opposing military adventurism in the Middle East and Ukraine, spoke in support of the Jewish genocide of Palestine at a rally organized by the Conference of Presidents of Major American Jewish Organizations and the Jewish Federations of North America. Other speakers included Chuck Schumer, Mike Johnson, House Minority Leader Hakeem

---

[128] Giraldi, "Gaza Genocide Continues."
[129] Giraldi, "More Deaths in Gaza."
[130] Giraldi, "Washington Digs in Deeper."
[131] Ibid.
[132] "US congressman: 'Palestine will be turned into a parking lot.'"

Jeffries, Senator Joni Ernst, John Hagee, and Israeli President Isaac Herzog.[133] Robert F. Kennedy, Jr., another self-styled "anti-war" politician, whose father and uncle were almost certainly assassinated by the State of Israel, is perhaps the most vicious of all of Israel's legion of Shabbos Goyim.

Kennedy has falsely claimed that the Palestinian Authority has offered to pay a bounty to any Palestinians who "kill a Jew anywhere in the world" while also claiming that Palestinian children are all "being raised as serial killers." He has praised Israel's "unique moral approach" to war, echoing Jared Kushner's delusional statement that "Israel's gone way more out of their way than a lot of other countries would, to try to protect civilians from casualties."[134] Kennedy has pledged his "unequivocal support for the Jewish state's right to self-defense," and has derisively referred to what he calls "Palestinian settlements within Israel" when describing Palestinians living in what is left of their former land, as though the Palestinians are the ones colonizing the Israelis![135]

More egregious still is his statement that the Palestinians are "the most pampered people in the world," even as hundreds of thousands of them have been burned alive and crushed to death on an industrial scale, their women and children brutalized by some of the most unimaginable cruelty in history.[136] Kennedy is advised by Zionists like the rabbi and sex-toy entrepreneur Shmuley Boteach.[137]

Bill Monroe continues his Purim sermon by lamenting the "explosion of anti-Semitism on our college campuses." Starting at Columbia University, students at over thirty universities in at least forty-five states nationwide have formed pro-Palestinian encampments to protest the genocide of Gaza, in what is surely the most significant student protest movement since the end of the Vietnam War. Their demands are simple, including a call for an Israeli ceasefire, a halt to institutional investment in Israel and the corporations that do business

---

133 Giraldi, "Marching for Israel?"

134 Giraldi, "Where Does Israel-Gaza Go from Here?"

135 Giraldi, "Who is the Antiwar Candidate?"

136 Ibid.

137 Unz, "Elon Musk Goes to Canossa."

with it, and the termination of academic ties with Israeli institutions. The response—from the State of Israel, the Jewish lobby, and the American politicians they control—has been swift. We are witnessing nothing less than the death of the First Amendment.

The students participating in these protests have been roundly demonized by the Jews and their puppets. The entirely Jewish-run *Breitbart* regularly refers to these students as "Hamas Youth," smearing these college students as terrorists. The Trump campaign echoes this, calling them "terrorist sympathizers."[138] The prominent Jewish attorney Alan Dershowitz has called them "Hitler Youth."[139] The University of Southern California labeled its own students "homegrown violent extremists."[140]

Anti-Defamation League leader Jonathan Greenblatt calls them "Jew-haters,"[141] and stated without any evidence that the protests are funded by foreign governments like Iran and China.[142] In November 2023, Greenblatt called for the IRS to investigate student organizations like Students for Justice in Palestine (SJP) for "providing material support to Hamas, which is a foreign terrorist organization." The very next day, the House Ways and Means Committee approved a bill to do exactly that.[143] The bill passed the House in April 2024, by a vote of 382–11.

Donald Trump promised to a group of Jewish donors in New York that he would crush the protests and deport the students engaging in them.[144] A bill to that effect, calling for the deportation of "anti-Semites" and introduced by Representative Beth Van Duyne, is currently before Congress.[145] Florida Attorney General Ashley Moody has directed prosecutors to "exercise zero tolerance" in dealing with the

---

[138] King, "Donald Trump vowed to toss."
[139] Campanile, "Alan Dershowitz compares."
[140] Giraldi, "Enemy Is Among Us?"
[141] Ibid.
[142] Perkins, "Anti-Defamation League ramps."
[143] Ibid.
[144] Dawsey, DeYoung, and LeVine, "Trump told donors."
[145] Bickerton, "Republican Bill Calls for Antisemites."

protesters, whose criticisms of Israel she refers to as "anti-Jewish hate crimes." Ron DeSantis, who says that Palestinians are "all anti-Semites" and "Jew-haters," has banned SJP from state universities and threatened its members with prosecution for "hate crimes."[146] DeSantis, who infamously refused to meet with survivors of the Israeli attack on the USS *Liberty*,[147] has also vowed to expel any pro-Palestinian students from college, a sentiment also expressed by Governor Greg Abbott of Texas.[148]

Abbott, after dispatching police to violently disperse and arrest student protesters at the University of Texas, declared: "These protesters belong in jail. Antisemitism will not be tolerated in Texas. Period."[149] Senator Tom Cotton has repeatedly advocated that the student protesters, whom he describes as "pro-Hamas criminals," be confronted by angry citizens who ought to "take matters into [their] own hands" and directly punish the offenders.[150] Cotton also introduced legislation to deny student loan relief to the protesters. More bizarrely, House Republicans led by Andy Ogles introduced the Antisemitism Community Service Act, which would deport student protesters to do six months of "community service" in Gaza. As Representative Randy Weber explained, "I am going to bet that these pro-Hamas supporters wouldn't last a day, but let's give them the opportunity."[151]

At Harvard, a coalition of more than thirty student groups published an open letter accurately characterizing Israel as "entirely responsible" for the violence in Gaza. Though this letter did not include the names of individual students, the names and personal information of the students connected to the signatory groups were published online by Jewish activists within days. One of these Jewish activists circled Harvard Square in a truck with a digital billboard flashing these students' photos and names, accompanied by the headline

---

[146] Giraldi, "Damage Israel Does."
[147] Giraldi, "Who is the Antiwar Candidate?"
[148] Giraldi, "Enemy Is Among Us?"
[149] Fang, "Wave of Legislation Seeks."
[150] Giraldi, "Students are Taking the Lead."
[151] Giraldi, "Protecting Israel."

"Harvard's Leading Antisemites." The same Jew then purchased online domain names using the students' names to create websites identifying them as "anti-Semites."[152]

This treatment has been extended to pro-Palestinian student protesters at every American university. Their families back home have been threatened;[153] they have lost jobs, internships, fellowships, and academic appointments;[154] some have been evicted from student housing, suspended, expelled, and prevented from graduating or receiving their diplomas;[155] and their names have been circulated on a national blacklist, endorsed by a group of federal judges, to prevent their ever being gainfully employed in the future.[156]

For the crime of allowing the protests to start in the first place, the presidents of the University of Pennsylvania, Harvard, and MIT were hauled before Congress and subjected to a struggle session led primarily by Representative Elise Stefanik, a mentee of the Jewish billionaire Paul Singer. Stefanik and other members framed student protesters, rightfully enraged at the American-funded Jewish genocide of Palestine, as calling for the genocide of Jews. During their testimonies, the three presidents were deemed insufficiently critical of "anti-Semitism," and the Jewish lobby thus decided to make examples of them.[157]

Within days, Liz Magill of Penn was forced to resign, along with the chairman of the board of trustees, who was immediately replaced by the head of the Jewish Federations of North America.[158] Claudine Gay of Harvard was subjected to a months-long harassment campaign, including by members of Congress, and was eventually also forced to resign. The Department of Justice, headed by the Jew Merrick Garland, is

---

152 Giraldi, "Damage Israel Does."
153 Tiberius, "Jews Declare War on America."
154 Giraldi, "Old Genocide Joe Has Got to Go!"
155 Giraldi, "Students are Taking the Lead."
156 Unz, "Israel/Gaza: The Masks Come Off."
157 Giraldi, "A Week Like No Other."
158 Giraldi, "Antisemitic Moment."

investigating a number of other universities for failing to "protect the civil rights of Jewish students."[159]

House Speaker Mike Johnson visited Columbia to address "Jewish students" and attack the university administration for failing to "guarantee the safety of Jewish students," whom he described as "running for their lives." He pointedly dismissed the fact that the protests are legally protected expressions of free speech.[160] The president of Columbia University, Minouche Shafik, was hauled before Congress and given a browbeating about permitting the protests and causing Jewish students to "feel unsafe." Remembering the fates of Magill and Gay, she vowed to take action.[161] During this same grilling, Representative Rick Allen asked Shafik if she was concerned that God might "curse" the university, repeating the Christian Zionist belief that God will curse those who curse the State of Israel and adding that Jerusalem is "the center of the universe."[162]

Just days after Netanyahu called for a ruthless crackdown on these American student protesters, calling them "antisemitic mobs" reminiscent of Nazi rallies, American authorities launched a wave of police and paramilitary violence against them.[163] Hundreds of New York City riot police stormed the Columbia campus, arresting students for "trespassing" on their own campus.[164] In Georgia, a number of police agencies stormed the campus of Emory University, where a tenured professor was brutally thrown to the ground, hogtied, and arrested.[165] At the University of California Los Angeles, police officers stood aside as over two hundred Jewish thugs with no connection to the university attacked the student protesters with bars, clubs, and fireworks, causing serious injuries. The violent mob was organized and financed by Jewish billionaire Bill Ackman. Police officers are also preventing food from

---

159 Giraldi, "Are We Losing Free Speech in America?"

160 Giraldi, "Students are Taking the Lead."

161 Unz, "Israel/Gaza: The Masks Come Off."

162 Giraldi, "Enemy Is Among Us?"

163 Giraldi, "Students are Taking the Lead."

164 Unz, "Israel/Gaza: The Masks Come Off."

165 Associated Press, "Police break up pro-Palestinian camp."

being delivered to the UCLA students, taking a page from the Israeli military playbook of starvation.[166]

To date, well over three thousand college students nationwide have been beaten, gassed, and arrested for the crime of having sympathy for the Palestinian people. The police officers tasked with breaking up these student protests are heavily-armed, helmeted, burly thugs equipped with rifles, shotguns, grenade launchers, armored vehicles, helicopters, and drones. The Jewish billionaires that fund American universities have threatened to withhold their donations unless the "anti-Semitic" protests are crushed, including Bill Ackman, Ross Stevens, Robert Kraft, Leon Cooperman, Len Blavatnik, Idan Ofer, Leslie Wexner, Marc Rowan, and many more, all of whom have ties with the Israeli government.[167]

The invasion of the Columbia campus is instructive. A private WhatsApp group of over a dozen Jewish billionaires and multimillionaires working directly in concert with the Israeli government successfully pressured New York City mayor Eric Adams to order the invasion, partly by offering and making bribes in the form of political donations. The group included Ackman, Blavatnik, Barry Sternlicht, Daniel Lubetzky, Daniel Loeb, Joseph Sitt, Howard Schultz, Michael Dell, and Joshua Kushner, brother to Jared. Members of the group attended private briefings with Israeli officials including former Prime Minister Naftali Bennett, war cabinet minister Benny Gantz, and Michael Herzog, Israel's U.S. ambassador. Members of the group also organized screenings of the "Bearing Witness" propaganda film.[168]

Not only did Jewish billionaires working with the Israeli government conspire to suppress American protests by bribing American politicians; the militarized invasion of the Columbia campus was directed by the Jewish Rebecca Weiner, an adjunct Columbia professor who also serves as the civilian executive in charge of the NYPD Intelligence and Counterterrorism Bureau, which maintains an office in Tel Aviv. Weiner,

---

[166] Reilly, "Cops thwart robot delivery."

[167] MacLeod, "Follow the Money."

[168] Natanson and Felton, "Business titans privately urged."

the granddaughter of a Jew who worked on the Manhattan Project, stated at a post-raid press conference that the student protesters had not been "expressing ideas," but rather normalizing and "mainstreaming rhetoric associated with terrorism." Mayor Adams declared it "despicable that schools will allow another country's flag to fly in our country." However, as an enthusiastic participant in New York City's annual Celebrate Israel parade, Adams is no stranger to waving another country's flag.[169]

Aside from attacking the student protesters and the administrations of their universities, the Jewish lobby has attacked the social media platforms on which the students continue to be exposed to the horrific footage of Israeli atrocities which first spurred the protests. As Jonathan Greenblatt of the Anti-Defamation League (ADL) said in a leaked November 2023 phone call, "We have a major TikTok problem." Pro-Palestinian content exponentially outpaced pro-Israeli content, by a factor of at least forty. In March 2024, Representative Mike Gallagher and fifty-four co-sponsors introduced a bill to ban or force the sale of TikTok. This original bill, passed 352–65, is virtually identical to the one that was included in the recent $95 billion aid package to Israel, Ukraine, and Taiwan, which passed the House 360–58, passed the Senate 79–18, and was signed into law by Joe Biden. It empowers the president to unilaterally ban any app or website that he deems to be owned or controlled by a "foreign adversary," defined as China, Russia, Iran, and North Korea .[170]

Every single co-sponsor of the original bill has received donations from the American Israel Public Affairs Committee (AIPAC), which heavily lobbied for the TikTok ban alongside the ADL.[171] For his efforts, Representative Michael McCaul saw his contributions from AIPAC increase by over 1,400 percent.[172] The comically stupid Nikki Haley responded to the bill by stating, "We really do need to ban TikTok once and for all and let me tell you why. For every 30 minutes that someone

---

[169] Reed and Blumenthal, "Columbia crackdown led by university."
[170] Martin, "TikTok and the Gen Z problem."
[171] Ibid.
[172] DeMartino, "Sponsor of TikTok Ban."

watches TikTok every day they become 17% more antisemitic, more pro-Hamas based on doing that."[173] Because the Chinese parent company ByteDance owns TikTok, Congress and its Jewish handlers framed the bill as a national security measure necessary to counter Chinese influence. ByteDance has stated that it does not intend to submit to the sale of TikTok, so the platform will certainly be banned. However, if ByteDance does decide to submit to the sale, a group of investors led by Donald Trump's former Treasury Secretary, the Jew Steven Mnuchin, has announced their intention to buy it.[174] Functionally, then, the United States is ordering the ownership of one of the world's most popular media platforms to be transferred to Jews.

Watching scenes of pro-Palestinian protesters being mercilessly beaten by militarized police officers, both on and off college campuses, it is clear that "anti-Semitism," which is to say any criticism of or difference of opinion with individual Jews or the State of Israel, has already been de facto criminalized. Those who dare to speak against the Jews are ruined financially, beaten, arrested—and, if many Republican politicians have their way, deported. The same police officers who are even now gleefully cracking the skulls of "anti-Semites" sat by and watched—and even knelt down in solidarity—as Black Lives Matter and Antifa rioters burned down American cities in the summer of 2020.[175] As Andrew Anglin notes:

> The only possible conclusion that can be drawn here, is that it is illegal in America to criticize the Israeli government. If you criticize Jews, militarized police will come and beat the shit out of you. They don't have to explain or justify anything. They just do it.[176]

Most Americans seem to have already internalized the idea that "hate speech" is illegal; witness Bill Monroe's Purim sermon, in which he refers to the case of Jamin Fite: "We have

---

[173] Giraldi, "Israel Uber Alles?"
[174] Hadero and Chapman, "Former Treasury Secretary Steve."
[175] Dunderhoff, "Watch: Cops in Riot Gear."
[176] Anglin, "Watch: Psycho NYC Cops Attack."

problems right in our own city. A man was arrested in Florence this week for disseminating antisemitic literature and other vile propaganda here in our own city . . . stirring up hatred for the nation of Israel." So, at least as far as Mr. Monroe and his congregation of the damned are concerned, "anti-Semitic literature" and "hatred for the nation of Israel" are already crimes.

Mr. Fite is accused of dropping "anti-Semitic" flyers in driveways in Florence, South Carolina, in March 2024.[177] The Florence County Sheriff's Office initially stated—correctly—that the flyers were protected political speech, and that there were thus no grounds for a criminal response.[178] Less than a week later, the same office arrested Mr. Fite and charged him with seven counts of "communicating obscene messages" and "littering." The "communicating obscene messages" charge carries a possible sentence of three years in prison—per count. The "littering" charges carry a sentence of thousands of dollars and over two hundred days in jail. The police also seized all of Mr. Fite's "antisemitic literature."[179] In 2023, he had been arrested and convicted in Myrtle Beach for dropping similar flyers, and was fined several hundred dollars. Just two weeks after Mr. Fite is supposed to have dropped the flyers in Florence, the Florence City Council passed a "hate intimidation" ordinance, punishable by up to thirty days in jail.[180]

Ironically, it is Republicans—who for the past decade have touted themselves as the champions of "free speech"—who are leading the charge to criminalize anti-Semitism.

Ron DeSantis and the Florida state legislature are first among these. In April 2023, a bill innocuously titled "Public nuisances" was introduced by state representatives Randy Fine (Jewish) and Mike Caruso to make "antisemitic littering" (i.e., leafleting) a felony punishable by five years in prison. Promoting the bill, Fine said:

---

[177] Taylor, Henson, and Fedor, "Antisemitic flyers tossed."
[178] Fedor, "Man arrested for spreading."
[179] Taylor, "2 weeks after antisemitic incident."
[180] Fedor, "Man accused of spreading."

> Nazis, take note. You're done in Florida. . . . There is no First Amendment right to conduct. If you graffiti a building, it is a crime now, but if your motivation is hate, it will be a third-degree felony and you will spend five years in prison. If you want to litter, it's a crime right now, but if you litter and your motivation is a hate crime, it will be a third-degree felony and you will spend five years in jail.

Caruso, who admits that the bill "makes antisemitism a hate crime," stated that "if we do nothing we are going to have 1930s Nazi Germany all over again."[181]

The bill was unanimously approved by both houses of the Florida legislature, and signed into law by Ron DeSantis on foreign soil, in Jerusalem. This cannot be overstated: the governor of an American state transported his entire cabinet to a foreign capital to sign and enact legislation that will be used to imprison his own constituents for criticizing that same foreign government. DeSantis had done the same thing before, transporting his cabinet to Jerusalem in May 2019 for the purpose of signing into law a bill to punish Floridians for boycotting the State of Israel.[182] Florida is merely one of the thirty-eight states to date that have adopted laws, executive orders, or resolutions to punish their citizens for boycotting Israel.[183]

As of May 2024, Governors Brian Kemp of Georgia, Kristi Noem of South Dakota, and Henry McMaster of South Carolina have all signed legislation criminalizing "anti-Semitic" speech. These laws, like Florida's, directly expand the scope of behavior subject to criminal prosecution and enhance sentences for existing violations when related to Jews or the State of Israel. Kemp stood beside Elan Carr of the Israeli-American Council (IAC), another major Jewish lobby organization, as he signed Georgia's bill into law. IAC lobbyists also guided the South Dakota legislation.[184]

The most alarming legislation in its implications for freedom of speech in America is the Antisemitism Awareness Act.

---

[181] Menahan, "Florida Passes Harshest Hate."

[182] Ibid.

[183] Jewish Virtual Library, "Anti-BDS Legislation."

[184] Fang, "Wave of Legislation Seeks."

This bill, along with all of the aforementioned state laws, requires the government to adopt and codify the definition of anti-Semitism promulgated by the International Holocaust Remembrance Association (IHRA).[185] The IHRA defines the following as examples of anti-Semitism:

- Making mendacious, dehumanizing, demonizing, or stereotypical allegations about Jews as such or the power of Jews as collective—such as, especially but not exclusively, the myth about a world Jewish conspiracy or of Jews controlling the media, economy, government or other societal institutions.
- Accusing Jews as a people of being responsible for real or imagined wrongdoing committed by a single Jewish person or group, or even for acts committed by non-Jews.
- Denying the fact, scope, mechanisms (e.g., gas chambers) or intentionality of the genocide of the Jewish people at the hands of National Socialist Germany and its supporters and accomplices during World War II (the Holocaust).
- Accusing the Jews as a people, or Israel as a state, of inventing or exaggerating the Holocaust.
- Accusing Jewish citizens of being more loyal to Israel, or to the alleged priorities of Jews worldwide, than to the interests of their own nations.
- Denying the Jewish people their right to self-determination, e.g., by claiming that the existence of a State of Israel is a racist endeavor.
- Applying double standards by requiring of it a behavior not expected or demanded of any other democratic nation.
- Using the symbols and images associated with classic antisemitism (e.g., claims of Jews killing Jesus or blood libel) to characterize Israel or Israelis.
- Drawing comparisons of contemporary Israeli policy to that of the Nazis.
- Holding Jews collectively responsible for actions of the state of Israel.

This definition, aside from banning any criticism of the State of Israel, further prohibits us from, among other things: 1)

---

[185] International Holocaust Remembrance Association, "Working definition of antisemitism."

simply pointing out the total domination of our government, economy, and media by Jews; 2) documenting any Israeli atrocities in its war of extermination against Palestinians; 3) investigating the shoddy narrative of the so-called Holocaust; and 4) questioning the motivations of the Jewish neoconservatives and neoliberals who dominate the foreign policies of Republican and Democratic administrations and lead the United States into wars and other entanglements that are devoid of any national interest or directly harmful to our national interests.

Most chillingly of all, though, this definition clearly includes the Bible, in which the Jews *did* incite the crucifixion of our Lord and Savior. Not only would this definition silence all criticism of Jews, whether individually or collectively, and the Israeli government, it would also outlaw the Bible and Christianity.[186] So, whether out of ignorance or malice, the heavily Christian Zionist Republican politicians with "their Scofield Bibles firmly embedded between their ears where their brains are supposed be," who have wholeheartedly endorsed this legislation, have in fact wholeheartedly endorsed banning the Bible.[187]

The Antisemitism Awareness Act ostensibly deals primarily with educational institutions, for the purpose of suppressing the pro-Palestinian student protest movement. Specifically, the bill requires the Department of Education Office for Civil Rights to use the IHRA definition of anti-Semitism when investigating discrimination complaints in programs or activities that receive federal funding. In other words, universities that are determined to have permitted the speech or writing by faculty or students of any of the forms of expression deemed anti-Semitic by the IHRA will lose their federal funding and be subjected to investigation and prosecution for civil rights violations. Given the fact that virtually every college and university in America receives federal funding, including in the form of federal student loans, this legislation would

---

[186] Giraldi, "Old Genocide Joe Has Got to Go!"
[187] Unz, "Israel/Gaza: The Masks Come Off."

effectively proscribe any criticism of Jews and the Israeli government on every college campus in the country.[188]

The bill would certainly lead to the creation of a legion of "anti-Semitism" commissars within every American institution of higher learning, but its ramifications are far greater in scope. In the first place, this legislation would also be enforced at every public school in America, as well as most charter schools and many private schools, as many of those receive public money. Moreover, the bill would probably be adopted by a variety of private organizations, surely to include businesses, hospitals, insurance companies, and the denial of their services to customers deemed to be "anti-Semites." Once criticism of Jews and Israel has been banned from all respectable venues, "much of the public, perhaps even including some confused law enforcement officers, may vaguely begin to assume that they have actually become illegal."[189]

More importantly, though, the Antisemitism Awareness Act would establish a precedent for criminalizing speech deemed to be "anti-Semitic." Such a direct attack on the First Amendment by the federal government as this clearly signifies that we are well on our way to the actual criminalization of anti-Semitism. It is but a short logical step between designating any and all criticism of Jews to be a civil rights violation punishable by federal defunding and designating such speech as crimes punishable by prosecution. Florida, as we have seen, already uses "anti-Semitism" as a sentence enhancement to turn simple littering into a major felony, just as hate crime sentence enhancements are on the books throughout the country and at the federal level. The Antisemitism Awareness Act thus represents the end of academic freedom, freedom of speech, and even freedom of thought in the United States.

The Zionist logic goes something like this, according to Giraldi:

> If you criticize the Jewish state and/or Zionism you are therefore by definition an antisemite. Antisemitism is a "hate crime."

---

[188] Hoffman, "Secret History of the Anti-Semitism Awareness Act."
[189] Unz, "Israel/Gaza: The Masks Come Off."

> If you advocate or argue for any Palestinian group like Hamas, which the US government has labeled "terrorist," you are providing "material assistance to terrorism" which is a crime for which you can be fined or imprisoned. Even if you merely criticize Jewish groups supporting Israel you are likewise an antisemite and have committed a "hate crime." Neat, isn't it? And the end result is that Israel, which is immune from the consequences of its actions internationally, also increasingly cannot be criticized at all without serious consequences for the critic. In other words, freedom of speech in the United States only exists, insofar as it does, if you are not disparaging Israel or even its friends due to their demonstrable behavior.[190]

In the era of CIA black sites and drone assassinations of American citizens accused of terrorism, this is a terrifying portent.

The Antisemitism Awareness Act, sponsored by Representative Mike Lawler (reportedly a Catholic) and sixty-one co-sponsors, sailed through the House in May 2024 by a vote of 320–91. It is currently before the Senate, where Tim Scott and Katie Britt are sponsoring a companion bill, and Joe Biden has already stated his intent to sign it into law.[191] Jewish Lobby organizations such as the ADL and the Israeli-American Coalition for Action, a sister of IAC, have invested heavily in its passage, dating back at least to 2018.[192] In part to accomplish this feat, the ADL is on track to spend nearly $1.6 million on lobbying this year, a sixteen-fold increase on what it spent in 2020. The ADL also successfully lobbied for a massive funding increase for investigations under Title VI of the 1964 Civil Rights Act, which already employs the IHRA definition of anti-Semitism under a 2019 executive order by President Trump.[193]

Conveniently, the Antisemitism Awareness Act joins the recently reauthorized Foreign Intelligence Surveillance Act (FISA), which allows for the warrantless surveillance of American citizens. The ADL also lobbied for the FISA renewal to "protect Jews" by making it easier to spy on suspected anti-

---

[190] Giraldi, "Week Like No Other."

[191] Lee Fang, "Wave of Legislation Seeks."

[192] Perkins, "Anti-Defamation League ramps."

[193] Ibid.

Semites.[194] The ADL claims that all of this is vital to prevent another Holocaust, citing a 388 percent increase in "anti-Semitic incidents" in the United States since the October 7th Hamas raid; these "anti-Semitic incidents," however, when they are not fictitious in their entirety, consist of Jews passing by a pro-Palestinian message and claiming to feel offended.[195]

Assisting the ADL in these claims of surging anti-Semitism is a litany of lunatic Republicans, such as Elise Stefanik, who lied that students marched through a Brooklyn high school chanting "Kill the Jews"; Aaron Bean, who claimed that anti-Semitism is such a "dominant force" that second-grade children across America are "spewing Nazi propaganda"; and Burgess Owens, who said that the student protesters, many of whom wear the iconic keffiyeh, are "antisemitic bigots" who "have swapped out the KKK hoods for terrorist scarfs [sic]."[196]

A constellation of Jewish lobby organizations and Jewish billionaires possesses practically unlimited money and wields far more political power than the corporations which we are often told control the government. These groups, which boast about the hundreds of millions of dollars they spend to defeat politicians critical of Israel and install and reinstall politicians who will do their bidding, are blatant foreign agents of the State of Israel.

And yet somehow they have avoided registering as such with the Department of Justice under the Foreign Agents Registration Act of 1938, which would require American oversight of their finances and political activities. One reason for this might be related to the fact that the last president who tried to register what became the Jewish lobby—and also, as aforementioned, sought to stop Israel's illegal nuclear weapons program—was John F. Kennedy.[197]

A senior AIPAC official once boasted that he could write anything on a napkin and, within twenty-four hours, have the signatures of seventy senators to endorse it.[198] In 2001, Ariel

---

[194] Giraldi, "Enemy Is Among Us?"
[195] Giraldi, "Marching for Israel?"
[196] Wallace, "Republicans Pledge Allegiance to Israel."
[197] Giraldi, "Antisemitic Moment."
[198] Unz, "Israel/Gaza: The Masks Come Off."

Sharon stated explicitly during a cabinet meeting that "We, the Jewish people, control America, and the Americans know it. . . . I own the Congress!" In the same year, shortly after 9/11, Netanyahu was recorded saying that "America is a thing you can move very easily."[199] Indeed, only absolute Jewish control of the United States could explain a remark like then-Speaker of the House Nancy Pelosi's comment at the 2018 IAC conference: "I have said to people when they ask me if this Capitol crumbled to the ground, the one thing that would remain is our commitment to our aid . . . and I don't even call it aid . . . our cooperation with Israel. That's fundamental to who we are."[200]

The American government is complicit in and accessory to the Jewish genocide of Palestine, enabling the carnage by funding and arming the State of Israel as it rapes, tortures, pulverizes, and incinerates the Palestinian people, racking up a death toll that is already well into the hundreds of thousands, and with no end in sight. The American government has lost what thin veneer of legitimacy it had yet retained and has "demonstrated to the entire world that our country has now become nothing more than a political colony of Israel, run by a puppet government under the complete control of the pro-Israel Lobby and its financial donors."[201]

Clearly, then, the government of the United States of America is a Jewish xenocracy, a Zionist Occupation Government, one eerily reminiscent of the Bolshevik Jewish government of Russia. At the dawn of the twentieth century, Jews only comprised about 4 percent of the population of the Russian Empire. Thus, when the overwhelmingly Jewish Bolsheviks seized the Russian state, one of their first actions was to outlaw anti-Semitism, punishable by summary execution.[202] The Bolsheviks, before, during, and after their ascent to power, butchered tens of millions of Christian Russians. Here, for example, is what the White armies found in Kiev in late August 1919, after they had temporarily driven the Bolsheviks from the area:

[199] Giraldi, "Israel Exception to Free Speech."
[200] Giraldi, "Biden's America Surrenders."
[201] Unz, "Jewish Roots of the Gaza Rampage."
[202] Unz, "Israel/Gaza: The Masks Come Off."

> The place had formerly been a garage, and then the provincial Che-Ka's main slaughter-house. And the whole of it was coated with blood—blood ankle deep, coagulated with the heat of the atmosphere, and horribly mixed with human brains, chips of skullbone, wisps of hair, and the like. Even the walls were bespattered with blood and similar fragments of brain and scalp, as well as riddled with thousands of bullet holes. In the center was a drain about a quarter of a meter deep and wide, and about ten meters long. This led to the sanitary system of the neighboring house, but was choked to the brim with blood. The horrible den contained 127 corpses, but the victims of the previous massacre had been hurriedly buried in the adjacent garden. What struck us most about the corpses was the shattering of their skulls, or the complete flattening out of those skulls, as though the victims had been brained with some such instrument as a heavy block.... And in every case the corpses were naked.... [A grave in the courtyard] contained eighty bodies which in every instance bore almost unimaginably horrible wounds and mutilations. In this grave we found corpses with, variously, entrails ripped out, no limbs remaining (as though the bodies had literally been chopped up), eyes gouged out, and heads and necks and faces and trunks all studded with stab wounds. Again, we found a body which had had a pointed stake driven through its chest, whilst in several cases the tongue was missing.[203]

When they possess power, this is the inevitable outcome of Jewish rule. To the Jews, we are all Palestinians. Worse, actually, for the Talmudic authorities are explicit in their hatred of Jesus Christ and His people, more so than of any other Goyim. We are lower than animals in the Jewish mind, fit for nothing but short, squalid lives of slavery, and they would kill us all exactly as they are doing to the Christians and Muslims of Palestine if they could. The Synagogue of Satan is a threat to all life on earth.

We return one last time to Bill Monroe and his Purim sermon in Florence, South Carolina. He concludes his toxic stream of bile with a prayer:

---

[203] Melgounov, *Red Terror in Russia*, 176.

> We pray again for Israel. . . . I pray, Lord, that you will give us people in America who will stand by them, that in the election cycle there will be a group of leaders elected who will not threaten them to remove their support. . . . Pray for the peace of Jerusalem.

Mr. Monroe, like so many self-proclaimed Christians in America, leads his congregation in prayer not to God, but to Satan. He leads his congregation into eternal damnation, without even the slightest care or concern for the Christians of Palestine.

The ancient Christian community of Palestine—divided between Gaza, the West Bank, Israel proper, and East Jerusalem, with each community unable to visit another, even before the October 7th Hamas raid—is at risk of extinction. The majority of Palestinian Christians live in Gaza, and are the descendants of refugees originally displaced during the *Nakba*. Their homes are now craters in the dirt. With nowhere else to go, they seek refuge in their churches, where they starve to death, die of curable illnesses without any medicine or medical care, get picked off by Jewish snipers, or get crushed to death by falling rock as ancient churches are obliterated by Israeli airstrikes. They thought that their churches would be protected, a notion which they were quickly and ruthlessly disabused of. When the St. Porphyrius Church (built in the fifth century) was destroyed, at least eighteen Christians sheltering inside were killed, including nine children. And yet, as one Palestinian Christian put it to their pastor, "If I'm going to die, I'd rather die in the church."[204]

Christian evangelism is illegal in the State of Israel, and thus Christians are forbidden from sharing their faith. Christian churches are regularly attacked, even with arson. Jewish mobs spit on Christians and their clergymen. Zionist settlers cry, "Death to Arabs! Death to Christians!"[205] Christian graves are desecrated. Statues of Christ are destroyed. In the Armenian Quarter of Jerusalem's Old City, the Armenian Christian community, which has lived there since the fourth century,

---

204 Carlson, "Uncensored: Munther Isaac."

205 Al Jazeera Staff, "'Death to Christians'."

faces expulsion by violent Jewish settlers.[206] In December 2021, the Patriarchs and Heads of Local Churches in Jerusalem warned that these "countless incidents" of Jewish attacks on Christians amounts to "a systematic attempt to drive the Christian community out of Jerusalem and other parts of the Holy Land."[207]

So-called Christians, self-styled Christian leaders, and Christian media outlets in America—the "religious right," in other words—are wholly silent about the evil manner in which Christians are treated and targeted by Jews and the State of Israel. They are totally unsympathetic, blinded by their Christian Zionist theology. Lunatic, ignorant End Times "prophecy watchers" have created a situation in which the Jews are deified as literally sacred. Israel uses American tax dollars and church offerings to finance the construction of Zionist settlements on land stolen from Palestinian Christians. Israel uses American weaponry to slaughter Palestinian Christians wholesale. In other words, pious American Christians fall over themselves to enable a satanic government to brutalize Christians.[208]

Because of the Christian Zionist conflation of the biblical Israel with the modern State of Israel, we witness solemn pronouncements such as this, from Mike Johnson at a meeting of John Hagee's CUFI:

> The United States must show unwavering strength and support for Israel. . . . We have to make certain that the entire world understands that Israel is not alone and God is going to bless the nation that blesses Israel. We understand that that's our role. It's also our biblical admonition. This is something that's an article of faith for us. It also happens to be great foreign policy.[209]

---

[206] Loffredo, "VIDEO: Armenian Christians under siege by Israel."
[207] Shoaib, "Church leaders warn." See also Carlson, "Uncensored: Munther Isaac."
[208] Ibid.
[209] Elkind, "Speaker Johnson says."

Johnson's very first act as Speaker of the House was to call up and pass a resolution pledging for the umpteenth time America's unconditional support for Israel.[210]

The Reverend Dr. Munther Isaac, pastor of the Evangelical Lutheran Christmas Church in Bethlehem, emphasizes that "every time an evangelical says something that implies unconditional support to Israel, people ask, is this what you stand for?" The "credibility of the Christian witness . . . is at stake." Indeed, just as American support for Israel's ongoing genocide of Palestine has irredeemably ruined what little standing the United States still retained on the world stage, so too does American Christian support for the genocide ruin the global reputation of Christianity. Referring to Lindsey Graham and Tim Walberg's suggestion that Gaza be nuked, Dr. Isaac asks, "Is that really the way of Christ? Is this how we walk in Jesus's footsteps as Jesus followers?"[211]

The eradication of Christians and Christianity is obviously a foreign policy priority of the United States. During the American occupation of Iraq, the ancient Christian community there was almost totally destroyed. Saddam Hussein had been their protector, just as Bashar al-Assad has protected the Syrian Christians for the entirety of his rule. ISIS and other terrorist organizations, all funded, armed, and trained by the United States, massacred and continue to massacre Christians in the ongoing Western attempt to depose Assad's government. The entirely Jewish government of the artificial state known as Ukraine has ruthlessly suppressed Russian Orthodoxy. We could go on, but it will suffice to say that the American government spends hundreds of billions of dollars every year to extinguish Christianity. As Dr. Isaac puts it, the government of the United States has ensured that "there is no future for us."[212]

This black record of tragedy and doom, the rivers of blood contained in the pages you have thus far read, *this* is what Christian Zionism has accomplished. American Christians

---

[210] Zengerle, "Pro-Israel resolution."
[211] Carlson, "Uncensored: Munther Isaac."
[212] Ibid.

have made our entire nation complicit in the worst genocide since antiquity. I will leave you with these words, from Andrew Anglin:

> Every time I think about the evangelicals who support these Jewish Satan worshippers, I get a flash of anger. Then I remind myself to pray for them. The people who use Jesus's name to support this kind of evil are going to go to the deepest and darkest part of Hell, and they're going to be there forever.[213]

---

[213] Anglin, "Israel Torturing Palestinian Prisoners."

Resources

"Slow Poisoning: How Israeli Bombing Poisoned Gaza's Water." *Palestine Online*, December 15, 2021. https://palestineonline.org/slow-poisoning-how-israeli-bombing-poisoned-gazas-water/.

"US congressman: Palestine will be turned into a parking lot." *Middle East Monitor*, October 26, 2023. https://www.middleeastmonitor.com/20231026-us-congressman-palestine-will-be-turned-into-a-parking-lot/.

Al Jazeera Staff. "Israel bans Al Jazeera: What does it mean and what happens next?" *Al Jazeera*, May 6, 2024. https://www.aljazeera.com/news/2024/5/6/israel-bans-al-jazeera-what-does-it-mean-and-what-happens-next.

Al Jazeera Staff. "To Kill a Family: The loss of Wael Dahdouh's family to Israeli bombs." *Al Jazeera*, November 1, 2023. https://www.aljazeera.com/news/2023/11/1/to-kill-a-family-the-loss-of-wael-dahdouhs-family-to-israeli-bombs.

Al Jazeera Staff. "Under Netanyahu, violence against Christians is being normalised." *Al Jazeera*, April 9, 2023. https://www.aljazeera.com/features/2023/4/9/under-netanyahu-violence-against-christians-is-being-normalised.

Anglin, Andrew. "Watch: Psycho NYC Cops Attack Protesters on the Street for Criticizing Israel, Arrest at Least a Dozen." *Daily Stormer*, May 19, 2024. https://dailystormer.in/watch-psycho-nyc-cops-attack-protesters-on-the-street-for-criticizing-israel-arrest-at-least-a-dozen/.

Antoniadis, Nikolai, Monika Bolliger, Oliver Imhof, et al. "The Unwinnable War: Israel faces international headwinds as the ground offensive commences." *Der Spiegel*, November 3, 2023. https://www.spiegel.de/international/world/the-unwinnable-war-israel-faces-international-headwinds-as-the-ground-offensive-commences-a-86d184af-a86f-4476-a8d5-e4d59b8af9ce.

Associated Press. "Israel: Leader of far-right Jewish Power party pays tribute to late racist rabbi." *The Guardian*, November 10, 2022. https://www.theguardian.com/world/2022/nov/10/israel-leader-of-far-right-jewish-power-party-pays-tribute-to-late-racist-rabbi.

Associated Press. "Police break up pro-Palestinian camp at the University of Michigan." *The Guardian*, May 21, 2024. https://www.theguardian.com/us-news/article/2024/may/21/pro-palestinian-camp-university-michigan.

Associated Press. "TikTok, Mnuchin eyed for subpoenas by House, Senate panels." *AP News*, May 21, 2021. https://apnews.com/article/tiktok-mnuchin-house-senate-ffdf37776e63a09bb6966d741df7093b.

Associated Press. "UN suspends Rafah aid distribution and warns US pier may fail." *The Guardian*, May 21, 2024.

https://www.theguardian.com/world/article/2024/may/21/un-suspends-food-aid-in-rafah-over-lack-of-supplies-and-insecurity.

Astor, Maggie. "Nikki Haley: 'Finish Them' Israel." *The New York Times*, May 29, 2024. https://www.nytimes.com/2024/05/29/us/politics/nikki-haley-finish-them-israel.html.

Barrett, Kevin. "UN: 15,000 Pregnant Women Facing Famine in Gaza." *The Unz Review*, May 29, 2024. https://www.unz.com/kbarrett/un-15000-pregnant-women-facing-famine-in-gaza/.

Bickerton, James. "Republican Bill Calls for Antisemites to be Deported." *Newsweek*, May 8, 2024. https://www.newsweek.com/republican-bill-calls-antisemites-deported-1898244.

Blinken, Antony. "Secretary Antony J. Blinken and Israeli Prime Minister Benjamin Netanyahu after their meeting." October 12, 2023. https://www.state.gov/secretary-antony-j-blinken-and-israeli-prime-minister-benjamin-netanyahu-after-their-meeting-2/.

Bollyn, Christopher. *Solving 9-11: The Deception That Changed the World*. LaVergne, TN: Lightning Source, 2012.

Campanile, Carl. "Alan Dershowitz likens campus protests to Nazi Germany." *New York Post*, May 26, 2024. https://nypost.com/2024/05/26/us-news/alan-dershowitz-likens-campus-protests-to-nazi-germany/.

Carlson, Tucker. "Uncensored: Munther." *TuckerCarlson.com*, April 11, 2024. https://tuckercarlson.com/uncensored-munther/.

Connelly, Irene Katz. "Joe Biden's Jewish Relatives: Everything to Know." *Forward*, November 7, 2020. https://forward.com/news/453023/joe-bidens-jewish-relatives-everything-to-know/.

Cook, Jonathan. "The Message of Israel's Torture Chambers Is Directed at Us All, Not Just Palestinians." *The Unz Review*, May 24, 2024. https://www.unz.com/jcook/the-message-of-israels-torture-chambers-is-directed-at-us-all-not-just-palestinians/.

Cook, Jonathan. "Torture, Executions, Babies Left to Die, Sexual Abuse: These Are Israel's Crimes." *The Unz Review*, March 16, 2024. https://www.unz.com/jcook/torture-executions-babies-left-to-die-sexual-abuse-these-are-israels-crimes/.

Dawsey, Josh, Karen DeYoung, and Marianne LeVine. "Trump told donors he will crush pro-Palestinian protests, deport demonstrators." *The Washington Post*, May 27, 2024. https://www.washingtonpost.com/politics/2024/05/27/trump-israel-gaza-policy-donors/.

DeMartino, Ian. "Sponsor of TikTok Ban, Iran-Palestine Sanctions Gets 1400% Bump in AIPAC Donations." *Sputnik Globe*, April 22, 2024. https://sputnikglobe.com/20240422/sponsor-of-tiktok-ban--iran-palestine-sanctions-gets-1400-bump-in-aipac-donations-1118047522.html.

Dunderhoff, Elvis. "Israel Torturing Palestinian Prisoners." *Daily Stormer*, May 19, 2024. https://dailystormer.in/israel-torturing-palestinian-prisoners.

Dunderhoff, Elvis. "Watch: Cops in Riot Gear Assault Students at University of Michigan Gaza Camp." *Daily Stormer*, May 22, 2024.

https://dailystormer.in/watch-cops-in-riot-gear-assault-students-at-university-of-michigan-gaza-camp/.

Elkind, Elizabeth. "Speaker Johnson says US biblical admonition to help Israel." *Fox News*, April 15, 2024. https://www.foxnews.com/politics/speaker-johnson-says-us-biblical-admonition-help-israel.

Erickson, Lawrence. "Religious Implications of the Carthaginian Theory." *The Unz Review*, May 10, 2024. https://www.unz.com/article/religious-implications-of-the-carthaginian-theory/.

Euronews. "Israel 'stealing organs from bodies in Gaza', alleges human rights group." *Euronews*, November 27, 2023. https://www.euronews.com/2023/11/27/israel-stealing-organs-from-bodies-in-gaza-alleges-human-right-group.

Fang, Lee. "Televangelists Invoke Holy War to Push for Weapons for Israel, Strikes on Iran." October 27, 2023. https://www.leefang.com/p/televangelists-invoke-holy-war-to.

Fang, Lee. "Wave of Legislation Seeks to Penalize Criticism of Israel as Antisemitism ." May 2, 2024. https://www.leefang.com/p/wave-of-legislation-seeks-to-penalize.

FBT Live. "Sunday Evening at FBT 032424." YouTube video, March 24, 2024. https://www.youtube.com/watch?v=bVMZ5Gu3uIg.

Fedor, Tyler. "Anti-Semitic fliers: Innocent plea for Jamin Fite of Florence on littering." *The Post and Courier*, April 17, 2024. https://www.postandcourier.com/pee-dee/news/anti-semiticflyers-innocent-plea-jamin-fite-florence-littering/article_0f4b6070-fcc4-11ee-8d65-dba2bfd1fd20.html.

Fedor, Tyler. "Anti-Semitic flyers lead to charges for Jamin Fite in Myrtle Beach, Florence, South Carolina." *The Post and Courier*, March 12, 2024. https://www.postandcourier.com/pee-dee/news/antisemitic-flyers-jamin-fite-myrtle-beach-florence-south-carolina/article_4f31e252-e079-11ee-aac8-470f999b9402.html.

Giraldi, Philip. "A Week Like No Other." *The Unz Review*, December 14, 2023. https://www.unz.com/pgiraldi/a-week-like-no-other-2/.

Giraldi, Philip. "American Foreign Policy Seems to Have Nowhere to Go." *The Unz Review*, February 15, 2024. https://www.unz.com/pgiraldi/american-foreign-policy-seems-to-have-nowhere-to-go/.

Giraldi, Philip. "Are We Losing Free Speech in America?" *The Unz Review*, January 4, 2024. https://www.unz.com/pgiraldi/are-we-losing-free-speech-in-america/.

Giraldi, Philip. "Biden's America Surrenders to War Criminal Netanyahu." *The Unz Review*, December 28, 2023. https://www.unz.com/pgiraldi/bidens-america-surrenders-to-war-criminal-netanyahu/.

Giraldi, Philip. "Israel Goes to Court for the Crime of Genocide." *The Unz Review*, January 12, 2024. https://www.unz.com/pgiraldi/israel-goes-to-court-for-the-crime-of-genocide/.

Giraldi, Philip. "Israel Keeps Killing Civilians and Rejects Any Sovereignty for Palestinians." *The Unz Review*, February 1, 2024.

https://www.unz.com/pgiraldi/israel-keeps-killing-civilians-and-rejects-any-sovereignty-for-palestinians/.
Giraldi, Philip. "Israel Uber Alles." *The Unz Review*, March 15, 2024. https://www.unz.com/pgiraldi/israel-uber-alles-2/.
Giraldi, Philip. "Marching for Israel." *The Unz Review*, November 24, 2023. https://www.unz.com/pgiraldi/marching-for-israel/.
Giraldi, Philip. "More Deaths in Gaza." *The Unz Review*, April 4, 2024. https://www.unz.com/pgiraldi/more-deaths-in-gaza/.
Giraldi, Philip. "Old Genocide Joe Has Got to Go." *The Unz Review*, May 17, 2024. https://www.unz.com/pgiraldi/old-genocide-joe-has-got-to-go/.
Giraldi, Philip. "Protecting Israel Is Washington's Number One Job." *The Unz Review*, May 8, 2024. https://www.unz.com/pgiraldi/protecting-israel-is-washingtons-number-one-job/.
Giraldi, Philip. "Students Are Taking the Lead in Denouncing Gaza Atrocities." *The Unz Review*, April 25, 2024. https://www.unz.com/pgiraldi/students-are-taking-the-lead-in-denouncing-gaza-atrocities/.
Giraldi, Philip. "The Antisemitic Moment." *The Unz Review*, December 21, 2023. https://www.unz.com/pgiraldi/the-antisemitic-moment/.
Giraldi, Philip. "The Damage Israel Does." *The Unz Review*, October 23, 2023. https://www.unz.com/pgiraldi/the-damage-israel-does/.
Giraldi, Philip. "The Enemy Is Among Us." *The Unz Review*, May 2, 2024. https://www.unz.com/pgiraldi/the-enemy-is-among-us/.
Giraldi, Philip. "The Gaza Genocide Continues." *The Unz Review*, November 4, 2023. https://www.unz.com/pgiraldi/the-gaza-genocide-continues/.
Giraldi, Philip. "The Israel Exception to Free Speech." *The Unz Review*, November 10, 2023. https://www.unz.com/pgiraldi/the-israel-exception-to-free-speech/.
Giraldi, Philip. "Towards a Palestine Without Palestinians." *The Unz Review*, December 7, 2023. https://www.unz.com/pgiraldi/towards-a-palestine-without-palestinians/.
Giraldi, Philip. "Washington Digs in Deeper on Its Support for Israel." *The Unz Review*, May 23, 2024. https://www.unz.com/pgiraldi/washington-digs-in-deeper-on-its-support-for-israel/.
Giraldi, Philip. "Where Does Israel-Gaza Go From Here?" *The Unz Review*, March 22, 2024. https://www.unz.com/pgiraldi/where-does-israel-gaza-go-from-here/.
Giraldi, Philip. "Who Is the Antiwar Candidate?" *The Unz Review*, January 25, 2024. https://www.unz.com/pgiraldi/who-is-the-antiwar-candidate/.
Guyénot, Laurent. "9/11 Was an Israeli Job." *The Unz Review*, September 10, 2018. https://www.unz.com/article/911-was-an-israeli-job/.
Guyénot, Laurent. "Angleton, Mossad, and the Kennedy Assassinations." *The Unz Review*, June 5, 2022. https://www.unz.com/article/angleton-mossad-and-the-kennedy-assassinations/.
Guyénot, Laurent. "Did Israel Kill the Kennedys?" *The Unz Review*, June 3, 2018. https://www.unz.com/article/did-israel-kill-the-kennedies/.
Hadero, Haleluya, and Michelle Chapman. "Former Treasury Secretary Steve Mnuchin Says He's Putting Together Investor Group to Buy TikTok." *The Business Journal*, March 14, 2024.

https://thebusinessjournal.com/former-treasury-secretary-steve-mnuchin-says-hes-putting-together-investor-group-to-buy-tiktok/.

Hedges, Chris. "Israel's Willing Executioners." *The Unz Review*, May 13, 2024. https://www.unz.com/article/israels-willing-executioners/.

Hersh, Seymour. *The Samson Option: Israel's Nuclear Arsenal and American Foreign Policy*. New York: Random House, 1991.

Hoffman, Michael. "Secret History of the Anti-Semitism Awareness Act." *The Unz Review*, May 16, 2024. https://www.unz.com/article/secret-history-of-the-anti-semitism-awareness-act/.

International Holocaust Remembrance Alliance. "Working Definition of Antisemitism." https://holocaustremembrance.com/resources/working-definition-antisemitism.

Jackson, Jr., Robert J., and Joshua Mitts. "Trading on Terror?" SSRN, December 6, 2023. SSRN:4652027. https://ssrn.com/abstract=4652027.

Jaffe-Hoffman, Maayan. "Meet the Christian Cowboys defending Israel's heartland." *The Jerusalem Post*, November 9, 2023. https://www.jpost.com/israel-news/article-772559.

Jewish Virtual Library. "Anti-BDS Legislation." https://www.jewishvirtuallibrary.org/anti-bds-legislation.

Kampeas, Ron. "Stark images of murder and torture in Israel leave US senators in tears and silence." *JTA*, November 28, 2023. https://www.jta.org/2023/11/28/politics/stark-images-of-murder-and-torture-in-israel-leave-us-senators-in-tears-and-silence.

Khalidi, Rashid. *The Hundred Years' War on Palestine*. New York: Metropolitan Books, 2020.

King, Ryan. "Donald Trump assured donors he'd deport anti-Israel student protesters: report." *New York Post*, May 27, 2024. https://nypost.com/2024/05/27/us-news/donald-trump-assured-donors-hed-deport-anti-israel-student-protesters-report/.

Kraft, Scott. "Extremists Pay Tribute to Killer of 48 at Funeral." *Los Angeles Times*, February 28, 1994. https://www.latimes.com/archives/la-xpm-1994-02-28-mn-28250-story.html.

Loffredo, Jeremy. "Armenian Christians siege Israel." *The Grayzone*, April 11, 2024. https://thegrayzone.com/2024/04/11/armenian-christians-siege-israel/.

Macleod, Alan. "Follow the Money." *The Unz Review*, May 22, 2024. https://www.unz.com/article/follow-the-money-how-israel-linked-billionaires-silenced-us-campus-protests/.

Martin, Jenna. "TikTok and the Gen Z Problem: Government Races to Ban App Most Favored by Young Adults." *Alabama Reflector*, May 29, 2024. https://alabamareflector.com/2024/05/29/tiktok-and-the-gen-z-problem-government-races-to-ban-app-most-favored-by-young-adults/.

Melgounov, Sergey. *The Red Terror in Russia*. Westport, CT: Hyperion Press, 1976.

Menahan, Chris. "Florida Passes Harshest Hate Crime Bill in America to 'Combat Anti-Semitism'; Gov DeSantis Signs Bill in Israel." *Information*

Liberation, April 26, 2023. https://www.informationliberation.com/?id=63730.
Menahan, Chris. "Israeli Airstrike on Gaza Refugee Camp in Rafah Decapitates Small Child, Kills Dozens." *Information Liberation*, May 26, 2024. https://www.informationliberation.com/?id=64465.
Natanson, Hanah and Emmanuel Felton. "Business titans privately urged NYC mayor to use police on Columbia protesters, chats show." *The Washington Post*, May 16, 2024. https://www.washingtonpost.com/nation/2024/05/16/business-leaders-chat-group-eric-adams-columbia-protesters/.
Office for the Coordination of Humanitarian Affairs (OCHA). https://www.ochaopt.org.
Ofir, Jonathan. "Netanyahu invoked another genocidal Biblical reference in his response to the ICC." *Mondoweiss*, May 6, 2024. https://mondoweiss.net/2024/05/netanyahu-invoked-another-genocidal-biblical-reference-in-his-response-to-the-icc/.
Pappé, Ilan. *The Ethnic Cleansing of Palestine*. Oxford: Oneworld Publications, 2006.
Perkins, Tom. "Anti-Defamation League ramps up lobbying to promote controversial definition of antisemitism." The Guardian, May 15, 2024. https://www.theguardian.com/us-news/article/2024/may/15/adl-lobby-antisemitism-definition.
Reed, Wyatt, and Max Blumenthal. "Columbia crackdown: University, NYPD." *The Grayzone*, May 2, 2024. https://thegrayzone.com/2024/05/02/columbia-crackdown-university-nypd/.
Reed, Wyatt. "State Dept.: Israeli soldiers 'sexually abusing, slaughtering' Palestinian women." *The Grayzone*, February 23, 2024. https://thegrayzone.com/2024/02/23/state-dept-israeli-soldiers-sexually-abusing-slaughtering-palestinian-women/.
Reilly, Patrick. "Police stop robot from delivering food to UCLA anti-Israel encampment." *New York Post*, May 23, 2024. https://nypost.com/2024/05/23/us-news/police-stop-robot-from-delivering-food-to-ucla-anti-israel-encampment/.
Sabrosky, Alan. "Demystifying 9/11: Israel and the Tactics of Mistake." *The Unz Review*, June 27, 2011. https://www.unz.com/article/demystifying-9-11-israel-and-the-tactics-of-mistake/.
Sand, Shlomo. *The Invention of the Jewish People*. London: Verso, 2020.
Shoaib, Alia. "Israel's systematic attempt to drive Christians out of Jerusalem." *Business Insider*, December 2021. https://www.businessinsider.com/israel-systematic-attempt-to-drive-christians-out-of-jerusalem-2021-12.
Taylor, Seth, G. E. Hinson, and Tyler Fedor. "Antisemitic fliers found in Florence, South Carolina driveways." *The Post and Courier*, March 5, 2024. https://www.postandcourier.com/pee-dee/news/antisemitic-fliers-florence-south-carolina-driveways/article_9cc2ce98-dafa-11ee-af95-837002d37771.html.
Taylor, Seth. "Florence hate crime law: Antisemitic incident." *The Post and Courier*, March 18, 2024. https://www.postandcourier.com/pee-

dee/news/florence-hate-crime-law-antisemitic-incident/article_e95b351e-dfd3-11ee-b5e9-6b74009fe1a7.html.

Tiberius, Josephus. "Jews Declare War on America." *The Unz Review*, November 5, 2023. https://www.unz.com/article/jews-declare-war-on-america/.

Unz, Ron. "American Pravda: Gaza and the Anti-Semitism Hoax." *The Unz Review*, November 27, 2023. https://www.unz.com/runz/american-pravda-gaza-and-the-anti-semitism-hoax/.

Unz, Ron. "American Pravda: Gaza, Jewish Power, and the Holocaust." *The Unz Review*, February 19, 2024. https://www.unz.com/runz/american-pravda-gaza-jewish-power-and-the-holocaust/.

Unz, Ron. "American Pravda: Israel, Gaza, and Broader Issues." *The Unz Review*, October 23, 2024. https://www.unz.com/runz/american-pravda-israel-gaza-and-broader-issues/.

Unz, Ron. "American Pravda: Remembering the Liberty." *The Unz Review*, October 18, 2021. https://unz.com/runz/american-pravda-remembering-the-liberty/.

Unz, Ron. "American Pravda: The JFK Assassination, Part II – Who Did It?" *The Unz Review*, June 25, 2018. https://www.unz.com/runz/american-pravda-the-jfk-assassination-part-ii-who-did-it/.

Unz, Ron. "American Pravda: The Nakba and the Holocaust." *The Unz Review*, December 11, 2023. https://unz.com/runz/american-pravda-the-nakba-and-the-holocaust/.

Unz, Ron. "American Pravda: Understanding World War II." *The Unz Review*, September 23, 2019. https://www.unz.com/runz/american-pravda-understanding-world-war-ii/.

Unz, Ron. "Elon Musk Goes to Canossa." *The Unz Review*, February 12, 2024. https://www.unz.com/runz/elon-musk-goes-to-canossa/.

Unz, Ron. "Gaza and the Dangers of Jewish Paranoia." *The Unz Review*, December 18, 2023. https://www.unz.com/runz/gaza-and-the-dangers-of-jewish-paranoia/.

Unz, Ron. "Gazacaust: Placing the Blame Where It Belongs." *The Unz Review*, February 5, 2024. https://www.unz.com/runz/gazacaust-placing-the-blame-where-it-belongs/.

Unz, Ron. "Israel/Gaza: The Masks Come Off in American Society." *The Unz Review*, May 6, 2024. https://www.unz.com/runz/israel-gaza-the-masks-come-off-in-american-society/.

Unz, Ron. "Israeli Assassinations and Public Scrutiny." *The Unz Review*, April 15, 2024. https://www.unz.com/runz/israeli-assassinations-and-public-scrutiny/.

Unz, Ron. "Prof. John Beaty and the True Origin of the Jews." *The Unz Review*, January 29, 2024. https://www.unz.com/runz/prof-john-beaty-and-the-true-origin-of-the-jews/.

Unz, Ron. "Pro-Israel Propaganda: Lies vs. Reality." *The Unz Review*, October 30, 2023. https://www.unz.com/runz/pro-israel-propaganda-lies-vs-reality/.

Unz, Ron. "The Balfour Declaration and 116,000 American Lives." *The Unz Review*, November 20, 2023. https://unz.com/runz/the-balfour-declaration-and-116000-american-lives/.

Unz, Ron. "The Jewish Roots of the Gaza Rampage." *The Unz Review*, March 11, 2024. https://unz.com/runz/the-jewish-roots-of-the-gaza-rampage/.

Unz, Ron. "War Crimes and Atrocity Hoaxes in the Israel-Gaza Conflict." *The Unz Review*, November 6, 2023. https://www.unz.com/runz/war-crimes-and-atrocity-hoaxes-in-the-israel-gaza-conflict/.

Wallace, Hunter. "Republicans Pledge Allegiance to Israel." *Occidental Dissent*, May 9, 2024. https://occidentaldissent.com/2024/05/09/republicans-pledge-allegiance-to-israel/.

Ward, Alexander, Erin Banco, and Lara Seligman. "Biden admin openly hammering Israel's military strategy in Gaza." *Politico*, May 21, 2024. https://www.politico.com/news/2024/05/21/biden-admin-hammering-israel-military-strategy-gaza-00159262.

Ward, Alexander. "US preparing for 'prominent' role in postwar Gaza." *Politico*, May 23, 2024. https://www.politico.com/news/2024/05/23/us-postwar-gaza-00159723.

Weiss, Philip. "Sharon's 'most brutal Israeli officer' dies." *Mondoweiss*, January 12, 2014. https://www.mondoweiss.net/2014/01/sharons-israeli-officer/.

Whitney, Mike. "Israeli Missile Attack Turns Refugee Camp into Rafah Hellscape." *The Unz Review*, May 27, 2024. https://www.unz.com/mwhitney/israeli-missile-attack-turns-refugee-camp-into-rafah-hellscape/.

Zengerle, Patricia. "Pro-Israel resolution is first act of new U.S. House leader." *Reuters*, October 25, 2023. https://www.reuters.com/world/us/pro-israel-resolution-is-first-act-new-us-house-leader-2023-10-25/.

PART I

The Christian Question: Engulfed Among the Fallen

The prevailing attitude toward Christianity in our movement is one of disdain, occasionally tempered with a begrudging tolerance. Is this justified? Yes and no. This work is an attempt to resolve, to whatever extent resolution is possible, the Christian Question. As the late Samuel Francis posed it, the Christian Question is an inquiry into whether the Christian faith is a force that *supports* or *opposes* "the efforts of the Right to defend the European-American way of life."[214] While we argue here that Christianity is inextricable from Western civilization, and that any rightist attempt to save our homelands and our peoples is futile in the absence of Christianity, there are greater numbers in our ranks (all of whom are just as committed to White nationalism) who agree with Oswald Spengler that "Christian theology is the grandmother of Bolshevism," who see that Christian universalism undermines the familial, national, and racial foundations of society, weakening us and leaving us susceptible to the cultural evisceration of the egalitarian regime.[215] As such, they attempt to either bypass thousands of years of history to return to the pagan roots of Germanic Europe, or to dispense with faith altogether and rely on secular philosophical, political, and scientific theories. Central to our examination of the Christian Question is the glaringly

---

[214] Francis, "Christian Question."

[215] Spengler, *Hour of Decision*, 123.

stark distinction between traditional Christianity and contemporary Christianity.

We begin our inquiry by agreeing with Francis that, indeed:

> What is indisputably happening today is the deliberate extirpation from Christianity of the European heritage by its enemies within the churches. The institutional Christianity that flourishes today is no longer the same religion as that practiced by Charlemagne and his successors, and it can no longer support the civilization they formed. Indeed, organized Christianity today is the enemy of the West and the race that created it.[216]

We examine the treacherous depths of ethnomasochistic self-flagellation to which organized Christianity has fallen, but we proceed to conclude that Christianity is redeemable. Indeed, as Revilo Oliver acknowledged, Christianity is "irreplaceable."[217] Christianity has sunken, yet it lives and remains fully salvageable. While we understand, and wholeheartedly participate in, the criticism of and hostility toward organized Christianity, we must understand that what cloaks itself in the garb of Christianity today *is not Christian*, nor even close to it; modern Christianity is a disgusting aberration from the faith. The egalitarian "Christians" of the left and of the cocktail conservative class *are not Christians*. It is therefore incumbent upon the right to reclaim Christianity from the heretics who have seized it; we can under no circumstances allow our enemies to co-opt that which built the West. Christianity is the foundation of our Occidental heritage, and of everything else that has been stolen from us.

---

[216] Francis, "Christian Question."

[217] Oliver, *Christianity and the Survival*.

1

Christianity Today

Michael Masters writes that Christianity "must now share the blame for the dissolution of the West," that it "has abandoned the defense of our people and has become an accomplice" of those who would exterminate us.[218] When we needed the Church the most, it not only abandoned us, but joined in the vanguard of dispossessory efforts against us. How did the faith that once served as our anchor, that so nobly prevented us from spinning away into the ether of oblivion, become our enemy? Masters summarizes the most common criticisms leveled at Christianity, that it "has subverted inbred traits of altruism that help family and tribe survive, and has transmuted those traits into agents of passivity and surrender," that it "has universalized altruism, thus stripping us of our defense against multiracialism," and that its "preoccupation with eternal reward in the world to come blinds some Christians to the consequences of their actions today." Interestingly, Masters ascribes the bastardization of Christian soteriology to contemporary narcissistic humanism, whereby Heaven is emphasized as "an entirely *personal* reward, which can be pursued at the expense of family, tribe or race." Yet, "if, in their fervor to enter Heaven, Christians fail to have children or to build a nation in which their children can maintain their way of life, the race will not continue." All of this is true. Christian universalism historically posed little to no danger to White

[218] Masters, "How Christianity Harms the Race."

survival because it was preached by Whites living in a world ruled by Whites; it was only in the multicultural, egalitarian regime, inaugurated in the aftermath of the Second World War, that Christian sacrifice was transformed into a call for racial suicide.

The National Council of Churches lobbies to achieve the goals of its "Social Creed," including "restorative justice" and the racial "rehabilitation" of the legal system, the abolition of the death penalty, and "just immigration policies." One of the most notable examples where Christianity is used to accelerate White dispossession is the invasion of the West by Black and Brown immigrants and "refugees." As Michelle Malkin documents in *Open Borders, Inc.*, the Catholic Church is one of the largest financiers and facilitators of illegal Central and South American immigration into the United States. Once these aliens have made it across the border, the Church finances the legal and political activism that keeps them here, working with such organizations as the Southern Poverty Law Center. Malkin notes that six of the nine voluntary agencies resettling "refugees" in America are nominally "religious," including the Catholic Charities and the United States Conference of Catholic Bishops, the Lutheran Immigration and Refugee Services, and the Episcopal Migration Ministries. In most cases, these "Christian charities" actually profit financially from their international human trafficking operations. Evangelical pastors across Central and South America are known to actually match "migrants" with *coyotes*, human traffickers, taking a percentage of the profits.

Cardinal Timothy Dolan, Archbishop of New York, refers to anti-immigration demonstrators as "un-American," "un-biblical," and "inhumane."[219] The United Methodist Church, in the midst of a schism over homosexuality, holds prayer vigils to "make room for refugees." Russell Moore, President of the Ethics and Religious Liberty Commission of the Southern Baptist Convention, led a delegation of Southern Baptist leaders to visit "refugee" detention centers in Texas. Moore said that "the anger directed toward vulnerable children is deplorable

---

[219] Breitman, "Coulter hits 'moral show-off' Dolan."

and disgusting." In 2014, a coalition of evangelical and mainline Protestant denominations, including the Disciples of Christ, the Episcopal Church, the Evangelical Lutheran Church, the Presbyterian Church USA, the Unitarian Universalist Association, and the United Church of Christ, along with the Catholic Church, lobbied against the deportation of "refugees." In *L'invasione silenziosa*, their exposé of radicalized Catholic clergy, Alberto Carosa and Guido Vignelli document the Italian Catholic hierarchy's support for Muslim immigration, as well as the Catholic Church's endorsement of state support for Islamic cultural activities. In 2018, Pope Francis said that Catholics should treat "compassion for migrants" as the equivalent of opposing infanticide. In 2019, the Evangelical Lutheran Church (which in 1995 passed a resolution attacking its theological progenitor, Martin Luther, for his anti-Semitism) declared itself a "sanctuary church," committed to supporting and sheltering illegal aliens, at a Milwaukee event in which clergy participated in a march against Immigration and Customs Enforcement.[220]

That same year, Arturo Sosa, the Superior General of the Jesuits, sometimes known as the Black Pope, absurdly declared that immigrants "come to make a contribution, which is greater than what they receive from the host country," and that Europeans and Americans must "thank them for it."[221] Sosa continued, saying that "those who live in a given territory have no right to turn away migrants, because they have no absolute right to that territory. They do not own it; the goods of the land are for everyone." In 2020, at the height of the coronavirus pandemic, the Christian Council of Sweden, which includes the Church of Sweden, called for prioritizing the provision of financial aid to Muslim "refugees." The Church of Sweden has also installed altarpieces featuring homosexual couples and uses gender-neutral language to refer to Jesus Christ. In the United States, evangelical leaders—including the ubiquitous Russell Moore, Walter Kim (President of the National Association of Evangelicals), and Samuel Rodriguez

---

[220] Miller, "ELCA declares self a 'sanctuary church body.'"
[221] Williams, "Jesuit Chief."

(President of the National Hispanic Christian Leadership Council, who delivered a prayer at the inauguration of President Donald Trump)—urged the Trump Administration to release immigration detainees, using the pandemic as an excuse and citing "our Christian belief that each human life is made in the image of God and thus precious." For the "World Day of Migrants and Refugees," Pope Francis compared "migrants" to our Lord and Savior, proclaiming:

> The child Jesus experienced with His parents the tragic fate of the displaced and refugees. . . . In each of these people, forced to flee to safety, Jesus is present as He was at the time of Herod. In the faces of the hungry, the thirsty, the naked, the sick, strangers and prisoners, we are called to see the face of Christ who pleads with us to help. If we can recognize Him in those faces, we will be the ones to thank Him for having been able to meet, love and serve Him in them.[222]

Let us continue to take the pulse of contemporary Christianity. If we focus inordinate attention on the Southern Baptist Convention, it is because the Southern Baptists are the best bellwether for gauging just how far the Church has gone astray. The Catholic Church has long been corrupt, honeycombed with homosexual pedophiles in spite of the efforts by traditional Catholics to enforce the Church's teaching against sodomy. Popes John Paul II, Benedict XVI, and Francis have apologized for the Crusades, colonialism, slavery, the Inquisition, and the mistreatment of gypsies. The mainline Protestant denominations have openly supported homosexuality and "racial reconciliation" for decades longer than the Southern Baptists. Indeed, as Samuel Francis emphasized in the column that set into motion his excommunication from movement conservatism, what has happened and is happening to the Southern Baptists is all the more important "because they were fortunate enough to flourish in a region where the false sun of the Enlightenment never shone."[223] We may trace the beginning of the Southern Baptists' decline to the period of

---

[222] Francis, "Message for the 106th World Day."
[223] Francis, "All Those Things to Apologize For."

Massive Resistance, the decade or so of White resistance between *Brown v. Board of Education* and the Civil Rights Act. While the Southern people needed leadership, the Convention was nowhere to be found; in fact, it actually endorsed *Brown* almost immediately, contrary to the will of essentially its entire congregation.

In 1845, the Southern Baptists split with the virulently anti-Southern Northern Baptists over several doctrinal issues, including that of slavery, which we will examine in our Christian Racialism essay. One hundred and fifty years later, at its annual meeting in June 1995, the Southern Baptist Convention repudiated its own foundation. The Convention passed a resolution, "On Racial Reconciliation on the 150th Anniversary of the Southern Baptist Convention," officially apologizing for the "sins" of "racism" and slavery, which, as we will show, are *not* sins. This resolution disavowed the Southern Baptist's ancestors who participated in or supported the "particularly inhumane" institution of antebellum slavery, which, as we shall see, was not particularly inhumane in any respect. The resolution decried the generations of Southern Baptists who failed to support civil rights vociferously enough, continuing to claim that "racism has divided the body of Christ . . . and separated us from our African-American brothers and sisters," and that "racism profoundly distorts our understanding of Christian morality, leading some Southern Baptists to believe that racial prejudice and discrimination are compatible with the Gospel." The resolution ultimately declared that "we . . . unwaveringly denounce racism, in all its forms, as deplorable sin," and that "we lament and repudiate historic acts of evil such as slavery from which we continue to reap a bitter harvest, and we recognize that the racism which yet plagues our culture today is inextricably tied to the past."

The resolution went on to say, "We apologize to all African-Americans for condoning and/or perpetuating individual and systemic racism in our lifetime; and we genuinely repent of racism of which we have been guilty, whether consciously or unconsciously." It got worse:

> We ask forgiveness from our African-American brothers and sisters, acknowledging that our own healing is at stake. . . . We hereby commit ourselves to eradicate racism. . . . We commit ourselves to be doers of the Word by pursuing racial reconciliation in all our relationships.

After this expiation of their "White privilege," Francis remarked, "the assembled repentants humbly kissed the toe of the only black minister in their leadership, who was pleased to accept their apology and enjoined them to sin no more."[224] In his aforementioned column, Francis saw this resolution for exactly what it was: More than "a politically fashionable gesture intended to massage race relations," this represented:

> A radical split from their own church traditions as well as from their determination to let the modern world go to Hell by itself. Now that they've decided to join the parade toward that destination, we can expect them to adopt some even more modern resolutions that will pave the road for them.

A point that we will continue to make is that the Bible must be accepted in an all-or-nothing manner; the 1995 resolution, Francis understood, placed the Southern Baptists:

> On the path to a modernist, secularized, and socially radicalized vision of Christianity that breaks with their own traditions and history as well as with the historic meaning of the New Testament. . . . Now, having turned the corner on slavery and racism, we can look forward to the Baptists marching forward with the army of Progress. For fundamentalists in particular, that may be serious. You can dismiss the New Testament passages about slaves obeying their masters as irrelevant today, but they happen to occur in the same places that enjoin other social responsibilities—such as children obeying their parents, wives respecting their husbands, and citizens obeying the law. If some passages are irrelevant, why should anyone pay attention to the others, and if you shouldn't, why not sign up with the feminists, the children's rights crusaders and—

[224] Francis, "All Those Things to Apologize For."

> dare I suggest it—the Bolsheviks? So much for "Christian family values."[225]

The oft-maligned "slippery slope" argument is rarely inaccurate, and such slopes are especially slippery when it comes to matters of theology. Just as Francis foresaw, the not just *un*-biblical, but indeed *anti*-biblical reinterpretation of "racism" and "slavery" as sins broke the Southern levy that protected the last bastion of Christian, and thus Western, traditionalism.

In 2015, Russell Moore's Ethics and Religious Liberty Commission held a conference on "the Gospel and racial reconciliation." Before an audience of hundreds of Southern Baptist leaders, Moore heaped scorn and vitriol upon Dixie, proclaiming:

> We are not the State Church of the Confederate States of America. The cross and the Confederate battle-flag cannot co-exist without one setting the other on fire. White Christians, let's listen to our African-American brothers and sisters. Let's care not just about our own history, but also about our shared history with them.[226]

What disgusting hubris. The enlightened Moore would have us believe that his pious Southern ancestors were simply wrong, satanic even, that *he* knows better than the men who built the Church, the same men who built the West. The conference chose its topic in response to the death of Eric Garner in New York, one of the patron saints of Black Lives Matter. Also included in the conference were panels on "White privilege," "immigration" advocacy, "the perils of gentrification," and "racial disparities" in the legal system. One speaker, a Muslim convert, attacked Americans for celebrating the death of Osama bin Laden. Moore prattled on about his hobbyhorse, the forced "diversification" of Southern Baptist churches, and suggested that Black Lives Matter embodies the "biblical definition of justice." The conference closed with a call-to-arms for "confession and accountability" regarding "racism" by a

---

[225] Francis, "All Those Things to Apologize For."
[226] Moore, "The Cross and the Confederate Flag."

Black pastor, following which Moore offered a prayer, ending with "Give us the power to fight."

Later in the year, Moore wrote an editorial in *The New York Times* attacking then-candidate Donald Trump as a "cartoonish . . . authoritarian":

> [Trump] incites division, with slurs against Hispanic immigrants and with protectionist jargon that preys on turning economic insecurity into ugly 'us versus them' identity politics. When evangelicals should be leading the way on racial reconciliation, as the Bible tells us to, are we really ready to trade unity with our black and brown brothers and sisters for this angry politician?[227]

If Christians vote for Trump, Moore wrote, they have "lost their values." Moore followed this up with even more egalitarian gobbledygook in a 2016 editorial, titled "A White Church No More," also in *The New York Times*. He wrote that the election:

> Has cast light on the darkness of pent-up nativism and bigotry all over the country. There are not-so-coded messages denouncing African-Americans and immigrants; concern about racial justice and national unity is ridiculed as "political correctness." Religious minorities are scapegoated for the sins of others, with basic religious freedoms for them called into question. Many of those who have criticized Mr. Trump's vision for America have faced threats and intimidation from the "alt-right" of white supremacists and nativists who hide behind avatars on social media.[228]

All of this is so self-evidently and pervasively mendacious that we need not undertake a full refutation. Moore reveled in declaring that evangelical Christianity is no longer old and White, celebrating the idea that "the next Billy Graham probably will speak only Spanish or Arabic or Persian or Mandarin." Moore went on to say, even more outrageously and spitefully:

---

[227] Moore, "Have Evangelicals Who Support?"

[228] Moore, "A White Church No More."

> The Bible calls on Christians to bear one another's burdens. White American Christians who respond to cultural tumult with nostalgia fail to do this. They are blinding themselves to the injustices faced by their black and brown brothers and sisters in the supposedly idyllic Mayberry of white Christian America. That world was murder, sometimes literally, for minority evangelicals. . . . A vast majority of Christians, on earth and in heaven, are not white and have never spoken English. A white American Christian who disregards nativist language is in for a shock. The man on the throne in heaven is a dark-skinned, Aramaic-speaking 'foreigner' who is probably not all that impressed by chants of "Make America Great Again."

At their 2017 meeting, the Southern Baptists adopted another noxious resolution, "On the Anti-Gospel of Alt-Right White Supremacy," which again decried the "racist history" of the Convention and congratulated itself on the aforementioned 1995 resolution. The 2017 resolution commended itself for having "nominated and elected individuals from a variety of ethnicities, including electing our first African-American president in 2012," and for recent resolutions: in 2014, the Convention called on "all Christian men and women to pray and labor for the day when our Lord will set all things right and racial prejudice and injustice will be no more"; in 2015, the Convention expressed continued grief "over the presence of racism and the recent escalation of racial tension in our nation"; and in 2016, the Convention urged fellow Christians to discontinue using the Confederate battle-flag, acknowledging that it is "used by some and perceived by many as a symbol of hatred, bigotry, and racism, offending millions of people." The new resolution encouraged the acceleration of the blackening and browning of the Church, and penitently highlighted its "continuing need to root out vestiges of racism from our own hearts as Southern Baptists," as "racism and white supremacy are, sadly, not extinct but present all over the world in various white supremacist movements, sometimes known as 'white nationalism' or 'alt-right.'" Again, the Convention resolved itself to "decry every form of racism, including alt-right white supremacy, as antithetical to the Gospel of Jesus Christ," and to "denounce and repudiate white supremacy and every form of racial and ethnic hatred as a scheme of the Devil intended to bring suffering and division to our society."[229] Catch that? White survival is a scheme of Satan. In November of the same year, the Alabama Baptist Convention followed suit, condemning "racism" and "white nationalism."

In August 2017, the doomed Unite the Right rally was held in Charlottesville, Virginia. The ensuing events were a prime example of media malfeasance. James Alex Fields, Jr., was sentenced to two life sentences in a "hate crime" prosecution for the death of a (White) female protester struck by his car. Video clearly shows a panicked Fields plowing into the crowd, braking, and then backing up. Before he drove into the crowd, eyewitnesses report his car being trapped and set upon by a leftist mob. The same mob continued to attack Fields' car after he braked, smashing in his windows with baseball bats; rightfully fearing for his life, he backed up again to escape. Had he not done so, he almost certainly would have received the Danny Gilmore, Reginald Denny, and Steve Utash treatment. In any case, the Charlottesville city government and police force engineered the circumstances by purposely and maliciously encouraging the day's violence. Of course, the truth never matters to our enemies.[230]

Russell Moore was one of the first Christian leaders to enter the feeding frenzy, writing an editorial in *The Washington Post* a mere two days later. Moore snarled:

> As we watched the televised images of the noxious, violent White Nationalist protests in Charlottesville this week, many of us felt our blood pressures rise. Many of us were, and are, angry. Many of us have been for some time about the resurgence of white supremacy and anti-Semitism we see all over the world. . . . If you are feeling distressed and heated, you have reason to be. White supremacy makes Jesus angry. [Blood and soil nationalism is] idolatry of the flesh, the human being seeking to deify his own flesh and blood as God. The Scripture defines this attempt at human self-exaltation with a number:

---

[229] Strode, "SBC denounces 'alt-right white supremacy.'" For all.

[230] For further reading on the alternative narrative of the James Fields incident at Charlottesville, VDARE's archives on Fields contain a wealth of sources, and it is from these archives that I drew.

> 666. White supremacy does not merely attack our society and the ideals of our nation; white supremacy attacks the image of Jesus Christ himself. White supremacy exalts the creature over the Creator, and the wrath of God is revealed from heaven against it. . . . The Church should call white supremacy what it is: terrorism, but more than terrorism. White supremacy is Satanism. Even worse, white supremacy is a Devil-worship that often pretends that it is speaking for God.[231]

With false sobriety, Moore closed his editorial by stating, "White supremacy angers Jesus of Nazareth. The question is: Does it anger his church?"

Moore, of course, was not alone. Evangelical leaders wrote on Twitter such hogwash as: "Every evangelical I know condemns antisemitism, white nationalism, and supremacism. The Christian church is proudly and increasingly the most ethnically diverse movement in the world" (@JohnnieM, August 12, 2017). Christian Zionist Robert Jeffress of the First Baptist Church of Dallas wrote, "Let there be no misunderstanding. Racism is sin. Period." (@robertjeffress, August 12, 2017) Another pastor wrote that white nationalism is:

> [E]vil personified, and we denounce it. This is what hatred and sin looks like. Their hate will not win. Racism is still alive and well, the only answer is God's love and the church of Jesus Christ standing hand in hand with our brothers and sisters of every race (@Jentezen, August 12, 2017) .

The Catholic Church joined in on the action as well, with the President of the US Conference of Catholic Bishops condemning "the evil of racism, white supremacy and neo-Nazism."[232] The President of the USCCB also celebrated the violent, godless mobs of leftists who initiated the hostilities and hijacked the rally as a peaceful group "who offered a counter-example to the hate marching in the streets." The Archbishop of Philadelphia said:

> The wave of public anger about white nationalist events in Charlottesville this weekend is well warranted. Racism is a

[231] Moore, "Perspective."

[232] USCCB, "Call for prayer and unity."

> poison of the soul. It's the ugly, original sin of our country, an illness that has never fully healed. Blending it with the Nazi salute, the relic of a regime that murdered millions, compounds the obscenity.[233]

Ralph Reed, former executive director of Pat Robertson's Christian Coalition, wrote after the events at Charlottesville that "those who twist the cross of Christ into a swastika exchange his message of love and redemption for one of hatred and evil." (@ralphreed, August 12, 2017) Reed is the same Christian who agreed with Abraham Foxman (of the Anti-Defamation League) that "American Christians were not sufficiently sorry about the history of Christian anti-Semitism," and lamented "the failure of American Christians to come to terms with either the Spanish Inquisition or the Holocaust."[234] Reed also spoke at the first Congress of Racial Justice and Reconciliation in 1997, where he argued that racial injustice was "widespread in bank loans, housing, inner-city funding, and in prison sentences."[235] He also fed the totally discredited conspiracy theory that racist Whites are involved in a vast scheme to burn Black churches, and committed the Christian Coalition to financing the construction of Black churches. As H. A. Scott Trask has pointed out, Reed and the Christian Coalition "are largely responsible for stopping Pat Buchanan's insurgent drive for the Republican presidential nomination in 1996." Moreover, Trask notes, the same "Christian" organization:

> [H]elped defeat proposed legislation in Congress that would have cut legal immigration by a modest one-third on the grounds that it would have prevented immigrants from bringing in relatives, thereby thwarting 'family reunification.' Such an objection is sentimental nonsense, for it is immigrants who first chose to separate from their families and people. Americans are not obligated to end such freely chosen separations by throwing open their borders.[236]

---

[233] Chaput, "Statement."
[234] Gottfried, *Multiculturalism and the Politics*, 49.
[235] Ibid., 51.
[236] Trask, "Christian Doctrine of Races."

Almost two weeks later, dozens of Christian leaders promulgated and signed the "Charlottesville Declaration," which stated:

> The violence of white supremacy visited our nation once again; its demonic presence has not been exorcised from us. From the founding of this nation until the present hour, the idolatry of whiteness has been a pro-death spirit within our republic.[237]

The declaration exhorted Christians to "cry loud and spare not" against "America's national sin," the "invidious doctrine" of "white supremacy." After the obligatory deification of Martin Luther King, Jr., the document called specifically for white Christians to:

> [C]ondemn in the strongest terms the White supremacist ideology that has long existed in the Church and our society. Nothing less than a full-throated condemnation can lead to true reconciliation in the Lord's body. Additionally, this condemnation must not be in word only, but also in deeds that "bring forth fruits worthy of repentance."

Former Southern Baptist Convention President Ronnie Floyd encapsulated the regnant egalitarian leftism well, stating:

> White nationalism and white supremacism are anathema to the teachings of Christ, who called us to love and to serve our neighbor—regardless of skin color, gender or religion—to give up our life for our friends and to even love our enemies.[238]

Russell Moore, lamenting the death of a violent criminal in Minnesota, declared that "racism is not swept away by the upward march of history. Racism is a religion, and that religion is Satanism, the idolatry of the flesh and the will-to-power."[239] This teacher of false doctrine refers to "the images by video done secretly of these killings," as if these videos were surreptitious; evidently, he has never heard of body cameras, nor has

---

[237] Tisby, "Black ministers release Charlottesville Declaration."
[238] Shellnut, "Evangelical Advisers."
[239] Moore, "Weight of Glory."

he seen the video in question, wherein the tarred and feathered police officer is calmly looking into the camera for almost its entirety. The Southern Baptist Convention issued a statement which references a supposed "long history of unequal justice in our country, going back to the grievous Jim Crow and slavery eras," and declares that "there is much more work to be done to ensure that there is not even a hint of racial inequity in the distribution of justice in our country."[240] This fully comports with the Convention's hastily-adopted 2019 resolution affirming anti-White and anti-Christian "critical race theory" and "intersectionality." In lieu of its canceled annual meeting, Convention President J. D. Greear delivered a speech in which he declared:

> We realize that, especially in a moment like this one, we need our brothers and sisters of color. . . . Southern Baptists, we need to say it clearly: As a gospel issue, Black lives matter. Of course, Black lives matter. Our Black brothers and sisters are made in the image of God.[241]

Perhaps the most illustrative microcosm of Christianity today is the tragedy of Chick-Fil-A. The fast-food corporation has billed itself a Christian company since its inception, its signature feature being that its locations are closed on Sundays. The restaurant chain has long been the target of the homosexual-transgender lobby, generally because the company dared to openly refer to its Christian values, but specifically for the 2012 remarks of Dan Cathy, the founder's son, then the company's chief operating officer and now its chief executive, against sodomite "marriage." For this, Chick-Fil-A thrived, with Christians across our nation going out of their way to spend their hard-earned money there, to support what, along with Hobby Lobby, appeared to be the only courageous Christian corporation in America. Former Arkansas Governor Mike Huckabee launched Chick-Fil-A Appreciation Day, and preachers urged their congregants to support this "godly" business. After founder S. Truett Cathy passed away, his son

[240] BP Staff, "Southern Baptist Leaders Issue."
[241] Banks, "Southern Baptist President."

evidently had a change of heart; by 2015, Chick-Fil-A was sponsoring a sodomite film festival.[242] In 2019, it was revealed that for at least the last two *years*, Chick-Fil-A had been donating thousands of dollars to the anti-White and Christophobic Southern Poverty Law Center, among a laundry list of other groups representing the infanticide and homosexual-transgender lobby.[243]

The "Christian" company also announced that it would no longer contribute to the (Christian) Salvation Army, the Fellowship of Christian Athletes, or the (Christian) Paul Anderson Youth Home, donating those millions of dollars instead to organizations such as Covenant House International, a homosexual-transgender activist group that targets children through such nefarious activities as "Drag Queen Story Hour." In response to the American Kristallnacht of summer 2020, Dan Cathy truly jumped the shark, declaring at a "roundtable discussion" that Whites should not condemn rioting, looting, or arson, but rather have empathy for Black "frustration." Cathy genuflected:

> My plea would be for the White people, rather than point fingers at that kind of criminal effort, would be to see the level of frustration and exasperation and almost the sense of hopelessness that exists . . . within the African-American community.[244]

After calling for Whites to "repent for racism," the pathetic ethnomasochist got down on the floor and shined a Black rapper's shoes, much to the delight of the Negro. The sickening display continued, culminating in Cathy stating that "we as Caucasians, until we're willing to just pick up the baton and fight for our Black, African-American brothers and sisters, which they are as one human race, we're shameful." Shameful, indeed. Disgusting. Chick-Fil-A still closes on Sunday, undoubtedly to keep up the ruse and trick Christians into

---

[242] Filloon, "Chick-fil-A is sponsoring an LGBT film festival."
[243] Duffy, "Chick-Fil-A once inspired me."
[244] Leggate, "Chick-fil-A CEO Dan Cathy on racism in America."

continuing to patronize them and indirectly fund whatever satanic cause catches Cathy's fancy.

What are the consequences of the conversion of Christianity into a suicidal cult? Paul Gottfried sees the vast egalitarian regime of multiculturalism as a "secular theocracy," which would not have been possible to create in the absence of a mangled, bastard Christianity. Indeed, Gottfried argues:

> Neither social engineering as a political project nor the victim-therapy practiced and exported by the American political class would be enjoying its present success without a deformed Protestant culture. The stress on individual salvation, unmediated by ecclesiastical authorities, prepared the way for a late modern society, without strong communal ties or respect for a collective past.[245]

Lest we travel too far back, Gottfried cautions that the roots of this present condition are not found in "the dense Calvinist tradition that suffused early American morals and manners," but rather in the conscious and concurrent annihilation and dilution of that Calvinist tradition, that Christianity:

> [H]ad to be dismembered before a consumerist and egocentric society could triumph. A religion that stresses human depravity and the need for divine grace for even a minimally good human act should not be seen . . . as leading into sentimental or moral self-indulgence.[246]

Nevertheless, the anticommunitarian and antihierarchical traits exhibited by the mutilated Christianity of today "may have been *embryonically* present all along."

Gottfried observes:

> Individual sensitivity, social guilt, and the personal overcoming of one's depraved ancestral society are the common attributes of modern managerial subjects; all of these traits have a particularly strong resonance in a progressively deformed but also recognizable Protestant culture. . . . A less self-reliant type, this latter-day Protestant is the self-absorbed but

---

[245] Gottfried, *Multiculturalism and the Politics*, 15.

[246] Ibid.

> spiritually uneasy materialist. He looks to the State and media for moral direction while professing belief in therapeutic sentiments and plastic 'human rights.'[247]

As Jared Taylor restates, American Christianity "prepared Whites . . . for neutering," laying the foundation for what Taylor calls "the White man's disease."[248] Guilt is the order of the day; this guilt is unilateral, a fact that is exceedingly bizarre. As Gottfried notes:

> It is one thing for a member of an ethnic or racial minority . . . to work to neutralize the traditional majority culture by which he feels threatened. It is quite another to have members of the majority group constantly dwelling on their collective sins and proposing public expiation. [249]

As we prostrate ourselves at the feet of our colored conquerors, they actually despise us *more*. This "expiating majority" perpetuates:

> [A] spiraling process of confessing to and compensating for historical burdens. It is allowed to feel righteous individually while being part of a historically wicked society . . . as a country redeemed from its own racist, sexist, homophobic past, the repentant Protestant is allowed to go forth and bring enlightenment to others. Thus, the humbled, self-debasing sinner achieves ultimate purpose as a crusader on a never-ending global mission.[250]

He continues, saying:

> [Ritual acts of condemnation] by a nonvictim group directed against their civilization, gender, race, or ancestors indicates sanctified living in a world or society held to be reprobate. The society that offends this visibly redeemed consciousness must be swept aside to make room for . . . the "Messianic State," a

---

[247] Ibid., 16.

[248] Taylor, "White Man's Disease."

[249] Gottfried, *Multiculturalism and the Politics*, 16.

[250] Ibid.

> world in which Christ, as a synecdoche for all designated victims, will no longer be crucified.[251]

We proclaim our guilt for "crimes" that we have not committed because "public contrition serves to showcase the self-consciously virtuous, while at the same time satisfying those embattled minorities that are demanding public recognition as victims."[252] Every day, we witness excommunicative ostracism marked by "Two Minutes' Hate" for anti-egalitarian heretics, in a striking phenomenon whereby "the recycling of religious themes [serves] to advance therapeutic-managerial rule partly by discrediting moral opposition. Insofar as Americans are still idealistic, they have come to believe in the special claims of those held to be the 'suffering just.'"[253] Taylor remarks that "the mind of the Salem witch-burners is not unlike that of today's 'anti-racists' and other liberal crusaders."[254] Having been the subject of a stereotypical outrage mob myself, I can assure the reader that it is indeed something akin to an excommunication; the pitchfork-carrying mass feeds on its own self-righteousness, in a ritual vampirism whereby the "fascist victimizer" is drained of his zero-sum moral tenor, the surplus of which is then divided among the "crusaders."

Gottfried explains:

> The Protestant framework of sin and redemption . . . now responds to two cultural particularities, general indifference to or ignorance of biblical texts . . . and an equally strong indifference to theology as a subject or existential concern. Cultural and historical illiteracy shapes the theology of guilt by turning the past into a *tabula rasa*. For example, a majority of Americans polled consider the Holocaust to have been the worst 'tragedy in history' and something about which Americans should be constantly reminded but also something about which the respondents 'know little or nothing.' Given this popular devotion to somber responsibility for the factually

---

[251] Ibid., 58.
[252] Ibid., 64.
[253] Ibid., 135.
[254] Taylor, "White Man's Disease."

> unknown, it is easy to understand . . . a reformulated Protestantism that incorporates politically correct martyrologies.[255]

Transpositions have taken place, substituting the deification of designated victims and even classes of victims for "the older adoration of religious martyrs or that of successive utopian visions for the biblical final age."

Taylor expands upon this, stating:

> The Church is now the handmaiden of the State in promoting the new religion of tolerance, giving clerics a moral influence [that] they lost at the end of the Middle Ages. In just one generation, the very nature of its teachings [has] shifted, and it agrees that its own past is just one more chapter in the depraved history of the White, male Gentile oppressor. Christians now apologize for the Crusades, for having permitted slavery, sexism, and colonialism.[256]

Gottfried also remarks upon the startling fact that "the politics of atonement has spilled over to the American 'Christian Right,'" noting:

> The insistence by Christian conservative Republican hopeful Gary Bauer that as President he would exclude from consideration for a Supreme Court nomination 'first of all anyone who is a bigot.' The bigotry that Bauer deplores is exclusively the white Christian kind, seeing that the prejudice of minorities is now widely viewed as reactive.[257]

Biblical illiteracy and misconstruction are perpetuated in the seminaries; documented by Paul Wilkes, Gottfried discusses:

> [T]he replacement of traditional theological and classical training in Protestant divinity schools by rote invectives about 'race, sex, and class oppression.' Seminarians can get by without acquiring what had once been requisite learning for their vocation; meanwhile, Yale, Harvard, and Princeton Divinity

---

[255] Gottfried, *Multiculturalism and the Politics*, 56.
[256] Taylor, "White Man's Disease."
[257] Gottfried, *Multiculturalism and the Politics*, 49.

> Schools have centered their training on combating sexism, homophobia, and misogyny.[258]

One Yale Divinity School professor observed that his students "'don't know the names of half of the books of the Bible, whether Calvin lived before or after Augustine, what it means to say that Christ descended to the dead or acted 'in accordance with the Scriptures.'"[259] This theological erosion and ignorance, particularly with respect to the concept of forgiveness, is perhaps most darkly manifested in the most obscene form of pathological altruism, the sacrifice of White martyrs in the name of "diversity," as the propitiation of sin for "White privilege."

We can fill innumerable volumes full of instances of racial idealists and egalitarians being gruesomely murdered by the snakes that they chose to trust, an undertaking which we will not here attempt. Something even more sinister than this, though, is occurring, and we must state that the only explanation for this phenomenon is religious in nature. In 1992, the father of a twelve-year-old White girl brutally raped on her way to school by a Black man made an appeal for racial harmony and "healing" at the rapist's sentencing hearing, calling the death penalty, and even life imprisonment, "harsh and divisive," stating that "an *incident* [emphasis mine] such as this fuels racial hatred among those who do not think."[260] After Reginald Denny was famously dragged from his truck during the 1992 Los Angeles riots and beaten to within an inch of his life by vicious Blacks:

> [He] embraced the mother of one of his assailants and excused their behavior because of the hard times they had faced. He decided that racism was to blame for his beating—but racism on the part of the police, not his attackers. He and three other Whites who were attacked filed . . . [a] suit against the city of Los Angeles, claiming that police did not put down the riots because they didn't care what was going on in the non-White

---

[258] Ibid., 40.

[259] Ibid., 41.

[260] AR News, "O Tempora, O Mores!"

> parts of town. Police 'racism' therefore left them at the mercy of understandably angry Blacks.[261]

In 1993, White Negrophile activist Amy Biehl was beaten and stabbed to death by Blacks in South Africa who sang "Kill the Boer" while they murdered her; the Black-ruled government freed the killers with no punishment. Biehl's parents forgave her killers, honoring those who "lost their lives in the struggle" against Apartheid, and hired two of them at the charity they established in her name.

In 2000, a Sudanese "migrant" resettled in Arlington, Massachusetts, by the White congregation of the local Evangelical Lutheran Church raped a young woman who passed by him in the street. The Lutherans stood by him, and posted bail of fifty thousand dollars, as, according to the pastor, "He's part of the family."[262] One congregant chalked the rape up to a "cultural misunderstanding." In 2001, a British man was robbed and beaten by a Somali gang on a bus in South London; in the attack, his assailants tore one of his eyes out of its socket and damaged the other, leaving him legally blind. His response? "It might sound strange but I feel sorry for the people who did this to me. They have totally messed up their lives."[263] On Christmas Eve, 2006, a drunk illegal alien crashed into a White family of six in Salt Lake City, Utah. The mother and two children were killed; yet what was the widowed father's response to losing the love of his life and two of his children? *Sympathy.*

> He has to endure all the pain that I have to endure, plus knowing that he was the cause of it. I have hundreds of people coming to visit and thousands of people praying for me. But who's praying for him?[264]

In 2015, two Blacks broke into the home of Indianapolis pastor Davey Blackburn and raped his pregnant wife before murdering her, along with her thirteen-week-old unborn child. Blackburn "forgave" the killers, stating that "I choose the

---

[261] Roberts, "When One Crime Becomes Two."

[262] Taylor, "Church, Community Stand."

[263] Roberts, "When One Crime Becomes Two."

[264] Ibid.

route of forgiveness, grace, and hope . . . love, not hate," and expressed his desire "to share the Gospel with these guys."[265] He added, "Jesus takes what the world says is a tragedy and makes it beautiful." After the 2018 murder of Mollie Tibbetts by an illegal alien, her father delivered a eulogy at her funeral, expressing his undying love for immigrants. He declared that "the Hispanic community are Iowans. They have the same values as Iowans. As far as I'm concerned, they're Iowans with better food."[266] Death, we see, is the price for your greasy enchilada. Enjoy it.

In 2016, an Afghan "migrant" raped and murdered a teenage German girl. Her family asked mourners to donate to a "refugee charity" in her memory, for which her parents won the "Citizen of the Year" prize from the Federal Association of German Newspaper Publishers. This sorry list goes on and on *ad infinitum*. What else is this but a perverted form of Christianity, Gottfried's secular theocracy? The "moral vision" of this secular theocracy is the egalitarian ideal, a fantasy to which even the lives of our own children are subordinated. The egalitarian God demands the blood of Isaac. The capitulation of organized Christianity has also destroyed the Church itself, driving Christian marginalization and an ever-burgeoning atheism. The self-destructive paroxysms of penitence for imagined generational "sins" accomplish nothing but the accelerated collapse of Western faith. Because organized Christianity has no response to the orgiastic fire consuming our nation, our *civilization* itself, aside from enthusiastically heaping fuel into the conflagration, our people have rightly left the Church in droves. This bastard "Christianity" has abandoned the people, and so have the people abandoned it; this is why Christianity in the West has entered into its death throes. For the Church, it is, of course, simply *easier* to forgo the arduous and thankless task of fighting *real* sin, of fighting Satan, of combating the rampant nihilistic decadence that afflicts our nation. It is easy for preening "Christian" leaders to denounce "racism" and pat themselves on the back for a job well done

---

[265] Kimble, "Pastor Speaks Out."
[266] Rosenberg, "Mollie Tibbetts' father decries vitriol."

than to condemn our usurious and ruthlessly extractive ruling class, or the breakdown of sexual traditionalism, or Christian persecution, or anything else that might make them seem "mean" or less "respectable." These egalitarian "Christian" heretics crave the praise of the world that hates them, of Satan himself. The cost of Christian silence is all around us.

Trask observes:

> While liberal Protestants prate about the endless benefits of "diversity," conservative Protestants boast they will convert the newcomers. So lost have they become in the mists of political correctness, so effeminate has become their Christianity, they do not realize the erection of mosques . . . in the formerly Christian lands of the West is not a sign of progress in world evangelism but is terrible regress and defeat.[267]

Billy Graham once told White Christians that they had a religious and moral *duty* to commit racial suicide and foster total racial integration "in our homes, in our worship services, even in our marriages." Trask continues:

> Most Christians never mention, much less oppose, policies that directly harm Whites: racial quotas, affirmative action, anti-discrimination laws, forced busing, extortion-motivated "civil rights" lawsuits, black-on-white hate crimes, interracial marriage, and Third-World immigration. They believe Martin Luther King, Jr., was an American Christian hero who truly deserves to be the only American with a national holiday in his honor. They believe "racism" is a sin, but a sin only when it is White racial consciousness or loyalty, never non-White racial consciousness or identity. They believe whites have a moral and Christian obligation to "bridge the racial divide," integrate their churches, reach out to people of color, etc. It therefore seems a bad joke to speak of Christian conservatives or the Christian Right, for there is nothing conservative about acquiescing in a demographic revolution to turn whites into a minority.

---

[267] Trask, "Christian Doctrine of Nations."

The Church has allowed itself to be subverted and devoured by the world that it is sworn never to be *of*, merely *in*; the Church gave in to the darkness, its ramparts fallen, and slit its own wrists.

2

Christianity Yesterday and Tomorrow

The corruption of Christianity is both cause and symptom of White genocide; Revilo Oliver saw clearly that "the loss of Christian faith as the West's bond of union was a disaster; the spiritual vacuum thus created was a catastrophe."[268] Yet Christianity also offers the last hope for White survival. Only a Christian revival can reverse the White fertility crisis and instill in our women once again that lost sexual morality, with marriage restored as the foundation of our civilization. Only Christianity saved me from the addiction that has claimed the lives of some of my friends, along with hundreds of thousands of other Whites. Only Christianity can reanimate the values which once served as the animating spirit of the West. We cannot state it better than the late American soldier killed defending Rhodesia, John Alan Coey:

> The basis of race, culture, and nation is vital for the survival of Western Civilization. Blood and soil, conservation and nationalism are what make a country and civilization sound, strong, and healthy. But faith is needed, faith in our way of life, our civilization, and faith in a Higher Destiny and the Divine Sanction of God.[269]

Europe was Christendom; as Oliver noted, so complete was the Christian monoculture that, "after the fall of the Roman Empire and the evanescence of hopes for its restoration, we

---

[268] Oliver, *Christianity and the Survival*, 39.
[269] Coey, *Martyr Speaks*, 49.

of the West regarded our religion as the bond that united us and distinguished us from the rest of the human species." Our forefathers did not call themselves *Europeans*, but *Christians*:

> [Our White ancestors] were all members of the great race that we now call Indo-European or Aryan, but they had in their languages no word to designate their blood relationship and biological unity. Thus, when they referred to the unity of which they were always conscious as something transcending the constantly shifting territorial and political divisions of Europe, they called themselves Christendom. And for many centuries that word was adequate and misled no one.[270]

Christianity is not only *a* religion of the West, but *the* religion of the West; importantly, Oliver argued, Christianity is *only* of the West. As we will examine in our Christian Racialism essay, while Christianity might not *necessarily* be White, it *is* in practice White, and only White. Indeed, Oliver continued, Christianity is most certainly *not* "a universal religion, for experience has proved that it cannot be successfully exported to populations that are not Indo-European." Christianity, the faith of the West:

> [H]as *never* been comprehensible to the rudimentary minds of Congoids, Capoids, and Australoids, races so primitive that they were congenitally incapable of inventing a wheel and even of using one without supervision—races that could not develop for themselves even the first and simplest preliminaries of a civilization.[271]

He continues:

> Christianity embodied all the moral instincts of our race, such as our concepts of personal honor, of personal self-respect and integrity, of fair play, of pity for the unfortunate, of loyalty—all of which seem preposterous to other races, at least in

---

[270] Oliver, *Christianity and the Survival*, 2

[271] Ibid., 5.

> the form and application that we give to them. They simply lack our instincts.[272]

It seems obvious that, were we and our European brethren still Christian nations:

> [W]e should not find ourselves in our present plight. We should have other difficulties, of course; we should, no doubt, continue to quarrel among ourselves, and we should have to face, as now, the open hostility or covert hatred of the rest of the world. But if we Occidentals were still Christian nations, we should have no need to worry about International Bankers, Illuminati, Bolsheviks, Jews, "Liberals," or any other *internal* menace that you may choose to name or imagine.[273]

We must unequivocally stress the vast fissure between historical Christianity and the deracinated and godless "Christianity" promulgated today. As Michael Masters notes, the systematized racial suicide of the present is an extraordinarily recent aberration. For centuries, racial consciousness never posed a moral dilemma, real or imagined, for Christians; Christianity was good enough for Charles Martel, Pope Urban II, Christopher Columbus, the American Founders, and such pious stalwarts as Stonewall Jackson. It was "good enough for European colonial masters who ruled millions of non-Whites, untroubled by egalitarian scruples."[274] Victor Craig argues that, over the centuries:

> Not only did Christianity preside over vigorous expressions of racial nationalism, it created the very culture that men of the West claim to defend. Far from causing the decline, Christianity has itself been debased along with so many other principles that once guided us. Christianity must therefore be rescued and revived, not reviled.[275]

He goes on to say:

---

[272] Ibid., 10.
[273] Ibid., 20.
[274] Masters, "How Christianity Harms the Race."
[275] Craig, "Defense of the Faith."

> The Church has been one of the final citadels of resistance against assaults on tradition and the social and moral decay that follow. The same revolutionary forces that undermined Europe's civilizational and racial identity have only recently succeeded in undermining its religious identity. Therefore, to condemn the Church for what amounts to an eleventh-hour conversion to a movement it has adamantly opposed for generations is short-sighted and unfair. No student of history can argue that Christianity is somehow "inherently" defective in ways that weaken the race.

If this were the case, if Christianity were inherently egalitarian all along, why would it only have shown its "true colors" in the mid-twentieth century? This break might be traced to the Enlightenment, and there were strains of egalitarian "Christian" leftism present in America as early as the late eighteenth century, but in our view, Christianity did not truly fall until the post-Second World War campaign for the erasure of White identity. Stated differently, Craig argues:

> Those who talk of the "inherent" flaws of Christianity seem to forget that it has taken a very long time for those alleged flaws to reveal themselves. . . . For 14 *centuries*, European man has lived and conquered with this Bible in his hand. It is implausible to argue that it suddenly revealed its true, race-destroying character only in the last few years.

Craig notes that the last bastions of Western traditionalism were the devoutly Christian societies of the American South and Afrikaner South Africa, neither of which found anything in their faith to stunt White racial consciousness. Though Craig concedes, as indeed we must, that there is an *element* of universalism inherent in Christian evangelism, "universalism does not require equality. . . . A concern for another man's soul does not imply that I think him my equal. He may be superior or inferior to me in any number of ways." Christianity was *Christendom*, encouraging ethnonational loyalty; as we will see in our Christian Racialism essay, ethnonationalism is not only compatible with Christianity, but is a Christian *doctrine* found throughout the Bible. Craig explains that "it is true that for the man devoted to the Lord, race will not be his only loyalty or even his first," but it yet remains a loyalty. Craig asks:

> How can whites claim to be defenders of a people and of a race and yet scoff at the deepest convictions of their ancestors? How can they speak of "preservation" when they oppose the faith that has for so long defined and guided our race? Today's whites are the final link in a chain of faith that reaches more than a thousand years into the past. If they can throw off their ancient religion so easily what else might they cast aside? Their language, their culture, *their race*? Should we not be suspicious of men who invoke the wisdom of their ancestors' views on blacks or immigrants but who reject the spiritual foundation on which their ancestors built their lives—who reject what their ancestors would have said was the *source and strength* of all wisdom?

If we truly love and respect our race, if we wish to honor our ancestors and the legacy that they bequeathed us, if we wish for it not merely to survive, but to *thrive*, we must not ridicule or condemn the Church; though, as Craig acknowledges, "it is not given to all men—not even to all good men—to believe," we must still respect and honor the Church, and even join it. Craig continues:

> As a duty to your ancestors, in solidarity with the ancient traditions of your people, as an act of participation in the faith that suffuses our culture, stand with the believers even if, in your hearts, you do not believe.

Our people cannot be saved in the absence of faith. As Craig asks, "Can it be a coincidence that racial consciousness in the West collapsed at precisely the moment liberalism invaded the Church?"

There has, to our knowledge, *never* been a healthy secular nation; only the faithful survive. Whites cannot build our ethnostate on "conservative," "constitutional," materialist, or scientific grounds alone. As Craig writes, "Those who think of Christianity as an obstacle and a stumbling block should ask themselves whether it may be that Christianity must be cured of liberalism before the West can be cured." Those of us who may attempt to salvage Europe without also resurrecting and reforming the Christianity that served as its beating heart, will, as Craig says:

> [F]ind that Europe cannot be Europe without the faith. Even if some biologically authentic remnant of the race succeeds in securing a material corner of the earth, it will have established a nation without an identity and a body without a soul.

For our race to survive, we *must* restore the faith. This brings us to the guiding purpose behind our study of the Christian Question. In order for our movement to succeed, we *absolutely* must win over White Christians to our cause.

Obviously, conservatives are the population most receptive to our ideology; to clarify, we do not refer here to the self-appointed leaders of movement conservatism, but rather to the good, decent, rank-and-file conservatives that cast their votes into the Republican ether each and every election cycle. These are the patriotic, *Christian* Americans who understand that a deep, insidious putrefaction has infected our society. The Deep State, Hollywood, the academy, Wall Street, the immigration lobby, the infanticide lobby, the New World Order, and the neoconservative monsters whom the average American conservative has come to despise all share one thing in common: they constitute the anti-White egalitarian regime. We share the same enemies; we simply know more about them, such that we are able to "call a spade a spade," and name the Jewish Enemy. While these conservatives might not be *explicitly* pro-White, they are explicitly anti-anti-White, and thus *implicitly* pro-White. American nationalism *is* White nationalism. America was established as a White, Christian ethnostate. It will not take much to teach all of this to Republican voters, the overwhelming majority of whom already deeply distrust the regime. The only real obstacle in our path is the Republican Party, which must be destroyed at all costs. As Oliver observed, any pro-American, anti-leftist, and implicitly pro-White organization in American history is constituted by Christians, even where their mission is not explicitly Christian; it is thus *this* population that we must focus our energies on. It is my hope that the present effort will contribute to this mission.

3

Christian Reformation

It is clear that we must reform Christianity, and retrieve it from the clutches of the demons that captured and exenterated it. We need only *return* Christianity to what it once was; in other words, we must "Make Christianity Great Again." Encouragingly, this has been done before, though under much different circumstances. James Russell has traced the process whereby early medieval Christianity was "Germanized," that is, transformed into that form of Christianity that animated the historical Occident, "from the entrance of the Visigoths into the Eastern Roman Empire in 376 until the death of Saint Boniface in 754."[276] As Samuel Francis explained the argument:

> Early Christianity flourished in the decadent, deracinated, and alienated world of late antiquity precisely because it was able to appeal to various oppressed or dissatisfied sectors of the population—slaves, urbanized proletarians, women, intellectuals, frustrated aristocrats, and the odd idealist repelled by the pathological materialism, brutality, and banality of the age.[277]

Early Christianity, like the bastard Christianity of the Third World, tended to take root in rootless, "heterogeneous societies in which there exist high levels of anomie, or social

---

[276] Russell, *Germanization of Early Medieval Christianity*, 3.
[277] Francis, "Christian Question."

destabilization."[278] Christianity provided an intimate, cohesive community of solidarity that stood in stark contrast with pervasive social alienation; these "early Christian communities were not perceived as a means for social advancement, but rather as a social refuge and a center for egalitarian resocialization for those who experienced status inconsistency or cognitive dissonance."[279] Russell continues:

> Featuring greater organizational stability and solidarity than other religious or philosophical groups, Christianity offered the alienated individual, without regard to sex, ethnicity, or socioeconomic status, membership in a caring community, together with the hope of bodily resurrection.[280]

When Christian missionaries attempted to Christianize the Germanic peoples of Europe, they ran into a brick wall, for the cohesive community offered by Christianity was simply unnecessary—Germanic society did not suffer from the anomie that suffused other pre-Christian societies. So, Francis wrote, "when Christian missionaries tried to appeal to the Germanic invaders by invoking the universalism, pacifism, and egalitarianism that had attracted the alienated inhabitants of the empire, they failed." Russell explains:

> The worldview of the Indo-European Greek, Roman, and Germanic religions was essentially folk-centered and "world-accepting," whereas the worldview of . . . early Christianity was essentially soteriological and eschatological, hence "world-rejecting."[281]

In other words, Francis noted, "the Germans practiced a folk religion that reflected ethnic homogeneity, social hierarchy, military glory and heroism." Therefore, Russell writes:

> For Christianity to be accepted by the Germanic peoples, it was necessary that it be perceived as responsive to the heroic,

---

[278] Russell, *Germanization of Early Medieval Christianity*, 212.
[279] Ibid., 88.
[280] Ibid., 91.
[281] Ibid., 4.

> religiopolitical, and magicoreligious orientation of the Germanic worldview. A religion which did not appear to be concerned with fundamental military, agricultural, and personal matters could not hope to gain acceptance among the Germanic peoples.[282]

The process by which Christianity was Germanized in its attempt to Christianize the Germanic peoples:

> [W]as not the result of organized Germanic resistance to Christianity, or of an attempt by the Germanic peoples to transform Christianity into an acceptable form. Rather, it was primarily a consequence of the deliberate inculturation of Germanic religiocultural attitudes within Christianity by Christian missionaries. This process of accommodation resulted in the essential transformation of Christianity from a universal salvation religion to a Germanic, and eventually European, folk religion.[283]

During the period of Germanization, Francis summarized:

> The saints and Christ Himself were depicted as Germanic warrior heroes; both festivals and locations sacred in ancient Germanic cults were quietly taken over by the Christians as their own; and words and concepts with religious meanings and connotations were subtly redefined in terms of the new religion. Yet the final result was not that the Germans were converted to the Christianity they had originally encountered, but rather that that form of Christianity was "Germanized," coming to adopt many of the same Indo-European folk values that the old pagan religion had celebrated.

Russell notes that it was during this time that the Christmas festival cycle emerged as a rival to that of Easter. In addition to the portrayal of Christ as a "victorious Germanic warlord," the Church sought to harness the Germanic war ethos. Russell explains:

---

[282] Ibid., 4.

[283] Ibid., 39.

> The Church subsumed and did not reject the warlike moral qualities of its converts. . . . The apotheosis of the Christian assimilation of the Germanic warrior code may be found in St. Bernard of Clairvaux's "recruitment tract" for the military order of the Knights Templar, *De laude novae militiae*, in which the killing of non-Christians in battle is justified, if not encouraged.[284]

What is the significance of all of this? First, Russell emphasizes that, "were it not for its Germanization, Christianity might never have spread throughout Northern and Central Europe."[285] More importantly, though, Russell observes that this process of Germanization is being *undone* today. As we have discussed, what we witness today is:

> [T]he de-emphasis, if not the repudiation, of the early medieval Germanic influence on Christianity. The recently accelerated, and hence more perceptible dissociation of the . . . Christian churches from their European heritage may have contributed toward a reciprocal dissociation of many Christians of European descent from these churches, and possibly from Christianity altogether. Alienation appears most likely to occur among those Euro-Christians for whom religiosity and cultural identity are closely related.[286]

Continuing on this point, Francis wrote:

> It is precisely this rejection of the European heritage that may have driven many Christians of European background out of Christianity altogether and into alternative forms of paganism that positively affirm their racial and cultural roots.

So, our task might better be stated as a mission to re-Germanize Christianity, to retrieve it from the abyss to which it has been cast. Following Russell, Francis concluded:

> The early Christianity that the Germans encountered contained . . . many universalist tendencies, adapted and

[284] Ibid., 41.
[285] Ibid., 40.
[286] Ibid., 211.

reinforced by the disintegrating social fabric and deracinated peoples of the late empire. But thanks to Germanization, those elements were soon suppressed or muted and what we know as the historical Christianity of the medieval era offered a religion, ethic, and world-view that supported what we today know as "conservative values"—social hierarchy, loyalty to tribe and place (blood and soil), world-acceptance rather than world-rejection, and an ethic that values heroism and military sacrifice. In being "Germanized," Christianity was essentially reinvented as the dynamic faith that animated European civilization for a thousand years and more.

PART II

The Heresy of Christian Zionism

Christian Zionism is the greatest heresy that has ever afflicted our faith. Its malignantly twisted doctrine has brought the Church to its knees and rendered us servants to our most ancient enemy; institutional Christianity now worships those whom we formerly treated as the monsters that we knew them to be. We now idolize those who tormented and murdered our Lord and Savior Jesus Christ. Our forefathers would never have allowed this to happen. It is crucial that we understand how Judaism co-opted Christianity from within, for this is how our greatest enemy was able to complete its coup and take control of our nation, bringing it to its present state of sordid deterioration. It is through Christian Zionism that the West allowed itself to be murdered, that Christian America allowed itself to be subverted and consumed. We will briefly trace the history of this heresy's development and proceed to expose its rotten and decayed theological foundations. Following our refutation of Christian Zionism, we will go on to shatter the myth of Judeo-Christianity and investigate the strange religion known as Judaism. As to the issue of Judaism, we will focus our efforts particularly on the disquieting interaction of Judaism with Christianity, an interaction that can only be characterized as visceral hatred. This hatred does much to explain how our ruthlessly extractive ruling class has presided over the controlled decline, as well as the cultural and economic impoverishment, of America, including the evisceration of the American kulaks, our middle class.

4

The History of Christian Zionism

Zionism is the nationalist movement for the Jewish ethnostate of Israel; specifically, Zionism began as the movement for the return of global Jewry to, and resumption of sovereignty over, the physical land of Israel. The term was first coined in 1892 by Nathan Birnbaum, who published a pamphlet that Theodor Herzl later expounded upon in his 1896 *Der Judenstaat*. We need not examine the various strains of Zionism, for they are beyond our purview. A form of proto-Christian Zionism actually predates Jewish Zionism, while fully-formed Christian Zionism as we encounter it today emerged shortly after the 1967 Six-Day War. The simplest definition of Christian Zionism, a term first coined by Herzl, is Christian support for Zionism, or political philo-Semitism. Restated, Christian Zionism is Jewish Zionism cloaked in the garb of Christian theology.

The roots of Christian Zionism can be found in the Protestant Reformation. John Calvin espoused a belief that the covenants of the Old and New Testaments were concurrent. Calvin and Luther understood "Israel" in Romans 11:25–27, the promise that "all Israel shall be saved," to mean Jewish and Gentile believers, while their successors, Theodore Beza and Martin Bucer, preferred to apply the word to unbelieving Jews and Judaism. The 1557 and 1560 editions of the Geneva Bible defined "Israel" as "the nation of the Jews," a definition that was later expanded to suggest the future conversion of Jews to Christianity: "He sheweth that the time shall come that the whole nation of the Jews, though not everyone particularly, shall be joined to the church of Christ." Through this translation, which was the preferred translation of the Puritans, and the most popular among all English-speaking Protestants until the 1611 publication of the Authorized Version, "the idea of the conversion of the Jewish people spread in Britain and the American Colonies."[287] It was thus under Protestantism that:

> A proto-Zionist movement emerged, convinced the Bible promised that the Jewish people, once "converted" to Christianity, would then return to Palestine and enjoy a national existence alongside other Christian nations prior to the Second Advent.[288]

This is important, for Christian Zionism in its nascency was predicated upon the *conversion* of Jews to Christianity.

The postmillennial Puritan eschatology advanced by Thomas Brightman was elaborated on by men such as Henry Finch, John Owen, Samuel Rutherford, and Richard Sibbes. Postmillennialism is an optimistic eschatological interpretation of Revelation 20, whereby the Second Coming, or Second Advent, will occur *after* a thousand-year golden age of Christianity. Postmillennialists hold that this utopia of Christian ethics will result in the salvation of a majority of humanity. As such, most Protestants during this period were convinced of a "restoration" of the Jews, that eventually the Jewish people would come to faith in Jesus Christ and *join* the Church. This belief was written into the *Westminster Larger Confession* and the 1658 Congregationalist Savoy Declaration. Throughout the seventeenth and eighteenth centuries, especially during the First Great Awakening, postmillennialism was dominant. Jonathan Edwards and George Whitefield preached that the millennium had arrived, that the gospel was ascendant, and that God's blessing would soon follow the conversion of entire nations; Edwards believed that "Jewish infidelity will be

---

[287] Sizer, *Christian Zionism*, 28.
[288] Ibid., 30.

overthrown. Jews will cast away their old infidelity. . . . They shall then be gathered into one fold together with the Gentiles."[289]

In the late eighteenth and early nineteenth centuries, a movement away from the optimism of postmillennialism commenced. In quick succession, the American War of Independence, the French Revolution, and the Napoleonic Wars formed the basis for a growing popular interest in apocalyptic prophecy and premillennialism, concurrent with the Second Great Awakening, Charles Finney's innovative revivalism, and the creation of Joseph Miller's Adventism and Charles Russell's Jehovah's Witnesses. Premillennialist eschatology holds that Christ will return to earth *before* the Christian millennium, establishing a thousand-year kingdom on earth. Premillennialists generally believe in the rapture of the faithful either before or after the carnage of a Tribulation period.

A litany of other factors converged to create "a growing interest among evangelical Christians in a futurist interpretation of Old Testament prophecy, in the rediscovery of the land of Palestine and in the conversion and restoration of the Jewish people,"[290] including the burgeoning literary romanticism of the Orient and the Jews by the likes of Robert Browning, Byron, Walter Scott, Wordsworth, and George Eliot, whose novel *Daniel Deronda* decoupled Jewish emancipation from Christian conversion, instead linking Jewish restoration to Israel to ethnic Hebraic heritage. Travelogues of the Near East were also popularized by writers such as Gertrude Bell, Robert Graves, Alexander Kinglake, Rudyard Kipling, T. E. Lawrence, Arthur Stanley, Freya Stark, and William Thackeray. In 1865, clergymen and academics founded the Palestine Exploration Fund, and four years later, Thomas Cook began to offer tours to Jerusalem.

Stephen Sizer illustrates that, in Britain, "as the postmillennialism of the Reformation and Puritanism gave way to a more pessimistic premillennialism of the nineteenth century, two differing views regarding the relationship of the church

---

[289] Quoted in Sizer, *Christian Zionism*, 30.

[290] Sizer, *Christian Zionism*, 34.

to the Jewish people."[291] This shift from postmillennialism to premillennialism appears to quite clearly presage the disengagement and retreat of Christianity from public life. The two strains of premillennial Christian Zionism that simultaneously arose were historic or covenantal premillennialism and dispensational premillennialism. We will focus on dispensationalism, but a brief glance at covenantal premillennialism is in order.

Covenantal premillennialists generally believe in the eventual incorporation of the Jews into the Church, seeing Palestine, the physical land of Israel, as one converted nation among many other Christian nations. The Jews are merely a part of the universal Church, though they still retain a position of some prominence given their status as the people of the Old Testament covenant. This eschatological branch provided the foundations for British Christian Zionism and the associated movement to "restore" the Jewish people to the land of Israel. The keynote to remember is that covenantal premillennialism still believes that Jews will be converted to Christianity. The most influential figures in this strain were George Faber, Charles Simeon, Charles Spurgeon, Lewis Way, and Joseph Wolff. In 1809, the London Society for Promoting Christianity amongst the Jews, or London Jews' Society (LJS), became the first of many philo-Semitic missionary societies. LJS is now known as the Church's Ministry Among Jewish People (CMJ), and holds to the covenantal premillennialist belief that "if the Bible is true, literally, then Israel would be restored, first physically, then spiritually," and that "God continues to have an ongoing covenant relationship with the Jews who remain God's 'chosen people.'"[292]

The aforementioned figures embraced the twin objectives of Christian evangelism and Jewish restoration, giving Christian Zionism "its first distinct identity as an embryonic movement."[293] Spurgeon affirmed covenantal premillennialism and rejected dispensationalism:

---

[291] Ibid.

[292] Ibid., 98.

[293] Ibid., 35.

> Spurgeon saw the church and Israel one day united spiritually; . . . the church and Israel facing the tribulation together; and the millennial kingdom on earth the culmination of God's purposes for both Jewish and Gentile believers in one church of which Jesus is the head.[294]

Israel was thus not excluded from the millennium, nor was the millennium its exclusive domain. Sizer summarizes these figures as sharing:

> [A] common passion to see Jewish people come to faith in Jesus Christ. Their literal reading of the Bible and premillennial eschatology gave them confidence that the Jewish people as a nation would soon turn to Christ and be restored to the land of Palestine, after which Jesus would return to set up his millennial kingdom. Support for restorationism was a personal matter and secondary to the priority of gospel ministry among the Jews.[295]

Though covenantal premillennialism is best seen as a minor heresy, neutralized by its insistence upon Jewish conversion to Christianity, dispensational premillennialism, otherwise known as dispensationalism, is a far more pernicious doctrine. Dispensationalists assert that there are seven periods of time, during which humanity has been or will be tested accorded to prophetic revelation, which only they are capable of discerning. Dispensationalism reverses the priorities of covenantal premillennialism, "giving greater emphasis to political restoration than evangelism as it became increasingly preoccupied with interpreting Biblical prophecy from a futurist perspective and publicizing what it saw as its contemporary fulfilment."[296] Indeed, dispensationalists interpret the New Testament in the light of Old Testament prophecy, rather than interpreting those prophecies with the New Testament as their interpretive lodestar.

Dispensationalists today generally hold that the Jews will return to Palestine *before* their conversion (although, as we

---

[294] Ibid., 40.

[295] Ibid., 41.

[296] Ibid.

shall see, conversion has essentially been dropped altogether), and that the Jewish people remain distinct and separate from the Church. We will delve much deeper into the theological heresies undergirding this strain of thought, but for now it is enough simply to understand that dispensationalists believe that the Old Covenant exists parallel to the New Covenant established with the death and resurrection of Jesus Christ. In other words, dispensationalists believe that there are two paths to salvation. Dispensationalism is the foundation of American Christian Zionism.

Figures such as Edward Irving (influenced by the layman James Frere and the Spanish Jesuit Manuel Lacunza), Henry Drummond, and Hugh McNeile led the vanguard of dispensationalism; they predicted the "apostasy of Christendom, the subsequent restoration of the Jews and imminent return of Christ," as well as "the imminent repentance and then restoration of the Jews, and finally their pre-eminence on earth, a blessing to the whole world."[297] A group of early dispensationalists formed a group known as the Albury Circle, which Sizer describes as:

> [A] product of its own age and thus a theology shaped by romanticism's love for grand all-inclusive systems, the enlightenment's rational methodology and their own subjective polemic. These coalesced to form a system that was tacitly understood to be God's final revelation. . . . Its self-fulfilling character affirmed its validity that in turn locked the Circle into a system and perspective beyond which they could see nothing else.[298]

It was John Darby, however, who would do the most lasting damage among these early theorists. Darby was a founder of the Plymouth Brethren sect, and used his American contacts to inseminate Christian Zionism in the fertile ground of the United States. Lady Powerscourt was an avid financier of prophecy conferences, at which Darby spoke and gathered followers. Darby and his associates interpreted current events

---

[297] Ibid., 44.

[298] Ibid., 49.

in the pessimistic light of revelatory apocalyptic prophecy, and promulgated a millennial (and beyond the millennium) distinction between Jews and the Church. One Darby associate, Benjamin Newton, recognized "Darby's elevation of Israel above the church as heresy, and repudiated the idea that the Jews could be blessed apart from faith in Jesus Christ," adding that it was "to say there are two kinds of Christianity, two Gospels, two ways, and two ends of salvation."[299] F.W. Newman wrote of Darby's pessimistic dispensational preoccupation with the Second Advent that "it totally forbids all working for earthly objects distant in time," and told the story of a young mathematics enthusiast who sought Darby's advice on whether he should continue his studies.[300] Darby had told the young man:

> Such a purpose was very proper, if entertained by a worldly man. Let the dead bury their dead; and let the world study the things of the world . . . such studies cannot be eagerly followed by the Christian, except when he yields to unbelief.[301]

As we shall see, Darby's missionary activities and American visits exercised vast influence in America over Cyrus Scofield, helping to shape emerging evangelical Bible schools and prophecy conferences, which dominated American evangelicalism at the turn of the century.

Darby's distinctive dispensationalism, asserting that God's purposes for Jews and for Gentiles are separate:

> Received increasingly enthusiastic endorsement from contemporaries. . . . Their influence over these two branches . . . had an impact not only on American fundamentalism but, more significantly, on British foreign policy in the late 19th and early 20th and indeed, to inspire the birth of the Jewish Zionist movement itself.[302]

---

[299] Ibid., 53.
[300] Ibid.
[301] Ibid.
[302] Ibid., 55.

Indeed, Zionism would most probably have remained a theological position "were it not for the intervention of a handful of influential aristocratic politicians who came to share the theological convictions of Way, Irving, and Darby and translated them into political reality." One such politician, the philanthropist Lord Shaftesbury, was convinced that "the restoration of the Jews to Palestine was not only predicted in the Bible, but also coincided with the strategic interests of British foreign policy," a view shared by Prime Minister Lord Palmerston, as well as future Prime Ministers Lord Balfour and David Lloyd George.[303]

Shaftesbury lobbied Palmerston to secure the appointment of a restorationist consul and Anglican bishop in Jerusalem, and was instrumental in the founding of the aforementioned Palestine Exploration Fund. Expecting the land to be empty, his mission was to "survey the land, and . . . prepare it for the return of its ancient possessors, for I believe that the time cannot be far off before that great event will come to pass."[304] Shaftesbury coined the slogan "A country without a nation for a nation without a country," later adapted by Herzl as "a land of no people for a people with no land." William Hechler, Anglican Chaplain to the British Embassy in Vienna and the son of an LJS missionary, was Herzl's chief Christian ally, one of only three Christians invited to the World Congress of Zionists.

> Hechler's advocacy and diplomacy highlighted a progressive and radical shift in Christian Zionist thinking away from the views of Way and Simeon, who saw evangelism as a priority and restoration to the land as a consequence of Jewish people coming to faith in Jesus Christ. Now, Hechler was insisting instead that it was the destiny of Christians simply to help restore the Jews to Palestine.[305]

---

[303] Ibid.
[304] Ibid., 59.
[305] Ibid., 61.

This prefigured American dispensational Christian Zionists' belief that the establishment of a Jewish state fulfilled their Christian mandate to bless Israel.

Lloyd George was a self-professed Zionist and proselyte of Chaim Weizmann, who later served as the first President of Israel. Lloyd George was philo-Semitic to his core, once declaring:

> I was taught far more about the history of the Jews than about the history of my own land. I could tell you all the kings of Israel. But I doubt whether I could have named half a dozen of the kings of England.[306]

Balfour, however, was to make the greatest stride yet in political Zionism. Balfour was a dispensationalist who regarded history as "an instrument for carrying out a Divine purpose," and was easily convinced by Weizmann that Palestine was the Jewish homeland. Balfour is famous for his 1917 letter to Lord Rothschild, Zionist leader and scion of the Rothschild family, officially declaring British commitment to "the establishment in Palestine of a National Home for the Jewish people."[307] British troops occupied Jerusalem the very next month. This letter became known as the Balfour Declaration, which was a factor in the entry of the United States into the First World War.[308] The first draft of this momentous document was produced by the Zionist Organization, and its final draft was also written by a Jew, Leopold Amery, who served as Assistant Secretary to the War Cabinet. Amery had changed his middle name from Moritz to Maurice in order to conceal his Jewish identity; he later went on to found the Jewish Legion, forerunner to the Israel Defense Forces. Sizer notes:

> It is ironic that the Jewish Zionist movement led by Herzl was essentially secular, and yet it relied heavily on Christian Zionists . . . who had a deep reverence for the Hebrew Scriptures and a passionate certainty that Eretz Israel [Greater Israel, the

---

[306] Ibid., 62.
[307] Ibid., 63.
[308] Weir, *Against Our Better Judgment*, 31.

> lands God had promised to Abraham and his descendants, about which more later] was the Jewish destiny.[309]

It was in the United States that dispensational Christian Zionism bore its bloodiest fruit. Through the end of the War for Southern Independence, during which the Confederate Army experienced a Third Great Awakening, American Protestantism was postmillennial. Fortified by the Wesleyan Holiness movement, emphasis was placed on evangelism, personal morality, and civic responsibility. There were, however, cracks in the foundation. As we have already mentioned, the American Revolution had been a stimulus for apocalyptic speculation; this, combined with the French Revolution, caused historic premillennialism to gradually gather converts, concomitant with an explosion of millennial sects such as the Millerites, Mormons, and Shakers.

It was in this atmosphere that, in the devastation wrought by the War for Southern Independence:

> Darby's premillennial dispensational views about a failing church and revived Israel came to have a profound and increasing influence upon American evangelicalism. It resulted not only in the birth of American dispensationalism but also influenced the millenarianism associated with the prophecy-conference movement and, later, fundamentalism.[310]

The most important promulgators of American dispensationalism were Darby's associate James Brookes, Dwight Moody, William Blackstone, and Cyrus Scofield. The nuances of their theological differences are relatively unimportant, but they all shared a restorationist conviction that Jews had a divinely ordained right to Palestine, along with the belief that the Abrahamic covenant was immutable, that the Jewish people were always and forever God's chosen people, apart from the Church. With Darby's influence, the most consequential innovation of this nascent American Christian Zionism was that "no longer were Christian Zionists expecting Jewish national

---

[309] Sizer, *Christian Zionism*, 63.

[310] Ibid., 66.

repentance to precede restoration; it could wait until after Jesus returned."[311] The logical consequence of believing that God has separate purposes for Israel and the Church is that evangelism and restoration come to be seen as equally *valid*, instead of mutually *exclusive*.

Moody founded what became the Moody Bible Institute in 1886, the prototype for scores of Bible schools, training tens of thousands of preachers and missionaries in dispensationalism each year. Organizations like Bible Study Fellowship, Precept Ministries, and other national Bible study organizations continue this work today. Blackstone, like his contemporaries, saw the secular Zionist movement as a sign of the imminent Second Coming, a worldly means for divine ends. Blackstone was a fervent devotee of, as Spurgeon called it, "exegesis by current events." He lobbied President Benjamin Harrison and Secretary of State James Blaine, as well as future president Woodrow Wilson, gathering over four hundred prominent Christian and Jewish signatories, including John and William Rockefeller, for the Blackstone Memorial, a petition to organize an "international conference on the restoration." Blackstone was a close friend of Supreme Court Justice Louis Brandeis, who led the Jewish Zionist movement in America after 1914. Brandeis praised him as "the Father of Zionism." At one Zionist meeting, Blackstone said that "true Zionism is founded on the plan, purpose, and fiat of the everlasting and omnipotent God, as prophetically recorded in His Holy Word, the Bible," adding that Jews had three options: convert to Christianity, become a Zionist, or renounce Judaism and assimilate into secularism.[312]

Dispensationalism was finally systematized and canonized in American Christianity by Cyrus Scofield, the man who made the single greatest impact in enshrining Christian Zionism in American life. There exists a curious dearth of biographical information on Scofield, unlike his fellow dispensationalist contemporaries; only two biographies of the man were produced, one a eulogy by a devotee and the other exposing him

[311] Ibid., 71.
[312] Ibid., 73.

"as a charlatan, accused of perjury, fraud, and embezzlement."[313] There are numerous gaps in his life, but of what we do know, he appears as a man devoid of any scruples whatsoever. Born in Michigan, Scofield's mother died three months after his birth and his father remarried twice thereafter. Scofield was poor and by all accounts largely illiterate about Christian matters.

As a teenager, living with unnamed relatives in Lebanon, Tennessee, Scofield enlisted in the Seventh Tennessee Infantry of the Confederate Army; he successfully petitioned for a discharge, but was soon conscripted back into service. En route to his new assignment, Scofield deserted, fleeing behind Union lines in Bowling Green, Kentucky. After pledging allegiance to the Federals, Scofield settled in St. Louis, Missouri. He was elected to the Kansas House of Representatives in 1871, and a few years later was appointed to be the U.S. District Attorney for Kansas. In less than one year, Scofield was forced to resign for a litany of financial crimes, including accepting railroad bribes, embezzling political contributions, and forging signatures on promissory banknotes. He appears to have served time in jail on at least some of these charges, but no official records attest to this. A known alcoholic, Scofield abandoned his wife and two daughters around this time, declined to pay for their maintenance, and married another woman only three months after his first wife divorced him on grounds of desertion.

Somehow, Scofield was introduced to James Brookes, the aforementioned Darby associate and dispensationalist leader. Brookes seems to have trained the unlearned Scofield, and, consequentially, introduced him to Darby. Scofield became a dispensationalist preacher, and began to style himself as the Reverend C.I. Scofield, D.D., despite never actually earning or even being honorarily granted the Doctor of Divinity degree. Sometime between 1887 and 1888, the idea that was to forever alter our faith and nation came to him—the *Scofield Reference Bible*. In 1901, Scofield was, seemingly inexplicably, admitted as a member of the prestigious and highly exclusive Lotos

---

[313] Ibid., 74.

Club in New York. Founded by a group of esteemed creatives, the men's club took its name from Lord Tennyson's "The Lotos-Eaters," and lifelong member Mark Twain referred to the place as "the Ace of Clubs."

The stated mission of the Lotos Club was:

> [T]o promote and develop literature, art, sculpture, music, architecture, journalism, drama, science, education and the learned professions, and to that end to encourage authors, artists, sculptors, architects, journalists, educators, scientists and members of the musical, dramatic, and learned professions in their work, and for these purposes to provide a place of assembly for them and other persons interested in and sympathetic to them, and their objectives, effort and work.

The names associated with this establishment over the years have included Astor, Carnegie, Chrysler, Clemens, Eisenhower, Guggenheim, Hearst, Lansbury, Marsalis, Mead, Meredith, Paley, Schwab, Sondheim, Sulzberger, Welles, Wodehouse, and Wolfe. It was at the Lotos Club that George Harvey, editor of *Harper's Weekly*, launched Woodrow Wilson's presidential campaign. The Club has held dinners for such luminaries as Amelia Earhart, Robert Frost, Supreme Court Justice Oliver Wendell Holmes, and Presidents Grant, Wilson, Truman, and Eisenhower, alongside dozens of creative celebrities.

How, then, did a nobody like Scofield gain admission to the hallowed halls of such an institution? As Joseph Canfield suggests, "the admission of Scofield to the Lotos Club, which could not have been sought by Scofield, strengthens the suspicion that has cropped up before, that someone was directing the career of C. I. Scofield."[314] Just who was this "someone"? Canfield, along with David Lutz, believes that it was none other than the Zionist, Wall Street lawyer, and Democrat fundraiser Samuel Untermyer.[315] Untermyer is alleged to have been the man who directed President Wilson to appoint Louis Brandeis to be the first Jewish member of the Supreme

---

[314] Canfield, *Incredible Scofield and His Book*, 220.

[315] Lutz, "Unjust War Theory."

Court.[316] Scofield's brand of dispensationalism was instrumental in gaining American Christian support for Untermyer's Zionism, and it appears that Untermyer and his circle of powerful Zionist friends financed and promoted Scofield, organizing trips for the untrained "theologian" to visit Europe. Maidhc Ó Cathail reports that "on one of these European trips, Oxford University Press publisher Henry Frowde expressed immediate interest in Scofield's project."[317] Frowde was associated with the Exclusive Brethren, a breakaway group of Darby devotees spun out of the Plymouth Brethren.

Sizer demonstrates how, upon its publication by Oxford University Press in 1909, the *Scofield Reference Bible* quickly became "the most influential book among evangelicals during the first half of the twentieth century" and "the most important single document of all fundamentalism . . . the Bible of fundamentalism," with at least "half of all conservative evangelical student groups in the 1950s" using the *Scofield Reference Bible*.[318] Indeed, "the theology of the notes approached confessional status in many Bible schools, institutes, and seminaries." Scofield's Bible was the foundational text of American dispensational Christian Zionism, and made the enigmatic man fabulously wealthy. C. E. Carlson emphasizes:

> Scofield's Bible was not to be just another translation, subverting minor passages a little at a time. No, Scofield produced a revolutionary book that radically changed the context of the King James Version. It was designed to create a subculture around a new worship icon, the modern State of Israel, a state that did not yet exist, but which was already on the drawing boards of the committed, well-funded authors of World Zionism.[319]

The Bible's popularity was the result of several factors, including "an attractive format, illustrative notes and cross references"; these reference notes were largely plagiarized from

---

[316] Freedman, *Hidden Tyranny*.
[317] Ó Cathail, *Scofield Bible*.
[318] Sizer, *Christian Zionism*, 75.
[319] Carlson, "Source of the Problem."

Darby. The footnotes of the *Scofield Reference Bible* are also extraordinarily selective, "appearing on less than half the pages of the Bible."

Scofield's commentary was printed *alongside* the Scripture, in the margins, between verses and chapters, and in footnotes, instead of separately—the first Bible to do so since the 1560 Geneva Bible. Moreover, Scofield also imposed "comprehensive headings embedded within the Biblical text" which included:

> [N]ot only . . . chapter and paragraph titles but also, in many cases, verse by verse headings in chapters deemed significant to dispensationalists that would otherwise prove obscure were it not for such 'helps.' . . . Had Scofield's notes been published as a separate commentary, in all probability his views would have eventually been forgotten or superseded.[320]

Carlson notes:

> [Scofield] wisely chose not to change the text of the King James Edition. Instead, he added hundreds of easy-to-read footnotes at the bottom of about half of the pages, and as the Old English [sic] grammar of the King James becomes increasingly difficult for progressive generations of readers, students become increasingly dependent on the modern language footnotes.[321]

Within only a few years, Scofield was able to get his notes accepted *as* Scripture. Aside from the millions of dollars spent by unknown parties to promote the book, it is also important to understand that Scofield's Bible was published shortly before World War One; the carnage of that "war to end all wars" shattered the regnant postmillennial optimism that had until then prevailed in American Christianity, and thus, as Mark Brahmin writes:

> [World War I] was popularly seen as vindicating the dispensationalist scheme in the Scofield Bible. After World War I, the

---

[320] Sizer, *Christian Zionism*, 118.
[321] Carlson, "Source of the Problem."

> *Scofield Reference Bible* flew off the rack, exceeding two million copies by the end of World War II. Hence the pointless carnage of the World Wars literally sold the Scofield Bible and its apocalyptic pro-Israel message.[322]

The 1948 creation of the State of Israel also made Scofield's premillennialism seem prophetic.

Since its initial 1909 publication, the *Scofield Reference Bible* has undergone numerous revisions, the first of which came in 1917; seven consulting editors had been added, most of whom were Moody associates. Their names, Sizer suggests, "appear to have been added, together with their academic qualifications, to give greater credibility to the work." Sizer continues by stating:

> Scofield's footnotes and his systematized schemes of hermeneutics have been memorized by many as religiously as have verses of the Bible. It is not at all uncommon to hear devout men recite these footnotes prefaced by the words: 'The Bible says.' . . . Many a pastor has lost all influence with members of his congregation and has been branded a liberal for no other reason than failure to concur with all the footnotes. . . . Many ministers use the teachings of Scofield as tests of orthodoxy.[323]

Carlson argues that the capture of the Southern Baptist Convention was "World Zionism's crowning achievement." The editor of the *Sunday School Times* described the *Scofield Reference Bible* as a "God-planned, God-guided, God-energized work." In other words, the format of Scofield's Bible essentially led his fraudulent Zionist commentary to *become* a part of the Scripture. The ultimate reason behind Americans' undying devotion to Israel above itself is that Christian Zionists have been duped into believing that Scofield's words are actually God's.

An interesting aside is a brief glance at Arno Gaebelein, a Brookes disciple and a source of Scofield's prophetic notes;

---

[322] Brahmin, "'1917': A Fateful Reference."

[323] Sizer, *Christian Zionism*, 73.

Gaebelein believed *The Protocols of the Elders of Zion* to be the work of a Jew and said:

> They certainly laid out a path for the revolutionary Jews that has been strictly and literally followed. That the Jew has been a prominent factor in the revolutionary movements of the day, wherever they may have occurred, cannot truthfully be denied, any more than . . . that a very large majority of the present Bolshevist government in Moscow, are Jews: while along other lines, in the assembly of the League of Nations, the Jew's voice is heard, and it is by no means a plaintive, timid, or uninfluential one.[324]

Gaebelein drew a distinction between secular apostate Jews and "the God-fearing, law-abiding, peace-loving kind," and, just like his other dispensational confederates, "distinguished between God's purposes for the Jews in this church dispensation from those of the millennium to follow, keeping them in separate watertight compartments chronologically as well as eternally."[325]

In the 1890s, Scofield served as the head of the Southwestern School of the Bible, forerunner to the Dallas Theological Seminary that his disciple, Lewis Chafer, founded in 1924. Chafer wrote the first systematic theology of dispensational Christian Zionism, and his Dallas Theological Seminary has been the most influential academic exponent of dispensationalism, training whole generations of evangelical pastors, promulgated further through the writings of such figures as Charles Dyer, Charles Ryrie, John Walvoord, and Hal Lindsey. As fundamentalism declined through the Great Depression and Second World War, Jewish Zionists "discovered more influential friends among liberal church leaders who had greater leverage with the presidency and were more interested in Jewish rights than in converting Jews or fulfilling Biblical prophecy."[326] Conservative evangelicals were preoccupied with countering the theory of evolution and the liberal

[324] Quoted in Ibid., 78.
[325] Quoted in Ibid., 79.
[326] Ibid., 80.

theology of the social gospel, rather than with prophetic eschatological speculation; gradually, though, they "welcomed the support of dispensationalists against a common liberal enemy," thereby legitimizing and spreading dispensational eschatology.[327] The principal Zionist allies, however, were mainline Protestants like William Albright, Reinhold Niebuhr, and Paul Tillich.

The Six-Day War was the single event that did the most work to solidify the current iteration of neoconservative Christian Zionism; as Sizer describes:

> With the annexation of the West Bank, liberal Protestants and organizations such as the World Council of Churches increasingly distanced themselves from Zionism, whereas the same events fueled a resurgence of enthusiasm for Eretz Israel among fundamentalists and evangelicals.[328]

Through the mid-twentieth century, dispensationalists like M.R. DeHaan, Harry Ironside, and Reuben Torrey "maintained a vocal commitment to a 'Biblical' basis for the imminent realization of a Jewish restoration to Palestine."[329] The 1948 establishment of the State of Israel, as aforementioned, "came to be seen . . . as the most significant fulfilment of Biblical prophecy," a conviction that deepened with Israel's blitzkrieg victory over Egypt in 1967, in which the ethnostate doubled its territory.[330] Sizer writes that "at a time when America was bogged down in the Vietnam War, Israel's lightning victory over the Palestinian forces in just six days had a profound effect," projecting an image of military invincibility and moral righteousness that stood in stark contrast to the impression of Vietnam on the American psyche.[331]

After the Six-Day War, Nelson Bell, editor of *Christianity Today* and father-in-law of Billy Graham, wrote that, "for the first time in more than two thousand years, Jerusalem is now

---

[327] Ibid., 81.
[328] Ibid., 84.
[329] Ibid., 84.
[330] Ibid., 90.
[331] Ibid., 90.

completely in the hands of the Jews," and that this "gives a student of the Bible a thrill and a renewed faith in the accuracy and validity of the Bible."[332] In 1968, President Lyndon Johnson, who had covered up Israel's unprovoked and deliberate attack on the USS *Liberty* the year before, made comments similar to what Lloyd George had said decades ago. Johnson declared that "the Bible stories that are woven into my childhood memories as the gallant struggle of modern Jews to be free of persecution are also woven into our souls."[333] In 1976, Jimmy Carter was elected with a wave of "born-again" evangelical support, and the following year Menachem Begin and his Likud Party came to power in Israel. This period concretized the "tripartite coalition . . . between the political Right, evangelicals and the U.S. Israeli lobby."[334] Despite Carter's 1978 description of Israel as "a return at last, to the Biblical land from which the Jews were driven so many hundreds of years ago. . . . The establishment of the nation of Israel is the fulfilment of Biblical prophecy and the very essence of its fulfilment," he supported the idea of a homeland for Palestinians, leading to the overwhelming evangelical-Zionist coalition that delivered Ronald Reagan to the Oval Office in 1980.[335]

The Reagan administration signified the complete dominance of Christian Zionism over American Christianity, to the point that the two were virtually indistinguishable from one another. Reagan was "raised on premillennial dispensational theology, influenced not only by his mother Nelle, but also by leaders such as Billy Graham, Pat Boone and George Otis"; the president was an avid reader of Hal Lindsey's Armageddon prophecies, often discussing them with aides. Reagan interpreted every geopolitical development through this apocalyptic premillennial lens, fitting events into his conviction that "God was bringing the Jews back to Israel." Reagan memorized the 1948 date that Israel was "reconstituted as a nation," and believed that "we could be the generation that sees

[332] Quoted in Ibid., 85.
[333] Quoted in Ibid., 86.
[334] Mearsheimer & Walt, *Israel Lobby*.
[335] Quoted in Sizer, *Christian Zionism*, 86.

Armageddon."[336] In a 1976 interview with Otis, when asked what America should do if Israel were ever attacked, Reagan replied, "We have a pledge to Israel to the preservation of that nation. . . . We have an obligation, a responsibility, and a destiny."[337] Reagan believed that Libya was "one of the prophesied enemies of Israel and therefore an enemy of God's."[338] Christian Zionists in the Reagan administration, including Attorney General Edwin Meese, Secretary of Defense Casper Weinberger, and Secretary of the Interior James Watt, invited Jerry Falwell to brief the National Security Council on the possibility of nuclear war with Russia, while Lindsey was invited to the Pentagon. Presidents George H. W. Bush, Clinton, and George W. Bush continued full steam ahead with Zionism, most particularly the latter Bush, despite none of the three appearing to share Reagan's fervent dispensational premillennialism; this is simply because these three politicians were not as religious as Reagan had been.

Sizer shows that "three Christian leaders, each first given a White House platform by Reagan, have probably done more than any others in ensuring American foreign policy remains resolutely pro-Zionist."[339] These three are Hal Lindsey, Jerry Falwell, and Pat Robertson, to which we will add a fourth, John Hagee. Lindsey's *The Late Great Planet Earth* has sold tens of millions of copies, and Lindsey is one of a select few authors to have had three simultaneous *New York Times* bestsellers. Through over a dozen books, as well as his radio and television programs, Lindsey popularized apocalyptic prophecy in mainstream American Christianity. He insists that "contemporary geopolitical events are the fulfilment of Biblical prophecy" and asserts that "the end of the world is imminent." Sizer notes:

> Lindsey's apocalyptic scenarios are highly speculative yet continue to enjoy popular support, especially among dispensationalists in the US. . . . His particular reading of history, colored by a literal exegesis of highly selective

---

[336] Quoted in Ibid., 87.
[337] Quoted in Ibid., 88.
[338] Quoted in Ibid., 87.
[339] Ibid., 88.

> Scriptures . . . justifies the demonization of Russia [and] encourages the continued military and economic funding of Israel.[340]

Indeed, Lindsey's so-called "plain meaning" literalism is nothing but a license for "uninhibited exegetical exploitation." For example, Lindsey said that in the Book of Revelation, John "actually saw . . . supersonic jet aircraft with missiles . . . intercontinental ballistic missiles with Multiple Independently Targeted Re-entry Vehicles tipped with thermonuclear warheads, . . . aircraft carriers, missile cruisers, nuclear submarines, laser weapons, space stations and satellites"; Lindsey and his ilk even go so far as to add words to the Scripture that were not there, supposedly to "let the reader understand."[341] In his effort at assimilating all of his predictive prophetic interpretations, Lindsey employs constantly shifting goalposts to accommodate every geopolitical development within prior predictions. Holding to Scofield's theology, Lindsey has also said that "Christians are not obligated to keep the Ten Commandments because they were given only to the nation of Israel in a previous dispensation."[342]

Falwell was the founder of Liberty University, and operated a popular television ministry. In 1979, Falwell founded the Moral Majority, a major organization in the American "religious right." Israel provided Falwell with a personal Learjet, and in 1980 he became the first Gentile to be awarded the Vladimir Ze'ev Jabotinsky Medal for Zionist excellence by Prime Minister Begin. When Israel bombed Iraq in 1981, Begin called Falwell before Reagan to "explain to the Christian public the reasons for the bombing."[343] Falwell regularly defended and minimized Israeli atrocities, and in 1985 pledged to the Rabbinical Assembly in Miami to "mobilize seventy million conservative Christians for Israel and against anti-Semitism."[344] Continuing the pattern, in 1998, then-Prime Minister

---

[340] Ibid., 95.
[341] Quoted in Ibid., 124.
[342] Quoted in Ibid., 133.
[343] Ibid., 90.
[344] Ibid., 91.

Benjamin Netanyahu met with Falwell before President Clinton, and in 2000 Falwell revived the Moral Majority as People of Faith 2000, a pro-Israel "movement to reclaim America as one nation under God." Sizer writes that Falwell "succeeded, probably better than any other American Christian leader, in ensuring his followers recognize that their Christian duty to God involves providing unconditional support for the State of Israel."[345]

Robertson is the founder of Regent University. In 1960, he founded Christian Broadcasting Network, the most influential Christian satellite television network; his flagship program, *The 700 Club*, reaches a weekly audience of over seven million people. His Christian Coalition, founded in 1989, bills itself as a "pro-family citizen action organization" that works to elect "Christian candidates," but practically functions as part of the Israel lobby. The influence of these figures is such that:

> By the end of the 1970s, Christian Zionism had become synonymous with American evangelicalism. Since then, the relationship between Christians and Zionism has been sustained with increasing effectiveness to the point that it is rare to find a single elected politician . . . willing to express public criticism of the Israeli government.[346]

These leaders, however, are merely the figureheads of a vast alliance of hundreds of Christian leaders, such as Jim Bakker, Kenneth Copeland, Paul Crouch, James Dobson, Mike Evans, Tim LaHaye (author of the bestselling *Left Behind* series), Edward McAteer, Chuck Missler, Oral Roberts, Jimmy Swaggart, Peter Wagner, and David Wilkerson, who regularly meet with Israeli officials.

John Hagee is the most influential Christian Zionist at work today. Hagee founded and leads the Cornerstone Church in San Antonio, which boasts over twenty-two thousand members and reaches a combined radio and television audience of ninety-nine million homes. Cornerstone's website features a

[345] Ibid., 91.
[346] Ibid., 93.

Star of David under a section touting its "commitment to Israel" and continuing:

> We believe in the promise of Genesis 12:3 regarding the Jewish people and the nation of Israel. We believe Christians should bless and comfort Israel and the Jewish people. Believers have a Bible mandate to combat anti-Semitism and to speak out in defense of Israel and the chosen people.

Hagee and Republican celebrity Mark Levin host an annual "Night to Honor Israel" at Cornerstone, the last of which took place on the first anniversary of the Pittsburgh synagogue shooting. This event raised nearly one-and-a-half million dollars; Hagee celebrated, saying:

> Think about it, never in the history of Christianity have millions of Christians united for the sole purpose of defending the nation of Israel and to protect the Jewish people from every vestige of anti-Semitism. Anti-Semitism is a daily event in America and . . . should concern us all.[347]

He continued that his church is "ready to fulfill the words of the Prophet Isaiah, 'For Zion's sake we will not keep silent, and for Jerusalem's sake, we will never be quiet." Levin added that "America and Israel are forever bound. The people who love America love Israel. . . . The one place that Christians flourish in the Middle East is the State of Israel." This claim will be critically examined later on, but this night was merely one of innumerable fundraisers that Hagee Ministries has organized; to date, Hagee and his misled Christian Zionists have collected and donated over one-hundred million dollars to Jewish organizations.

Sizer sees the contemporary internal division within Christian Zionism not as covenantal-dispensational, but rather evangelical-political; the political has trounced the evangelical, as prominent evangelicals "have disavowed evangelism in order to gain recognition from the Israeli government, set up headquarters in Jerusalem and collaborate with Jewish Zionist

---

[347] Quoted in Parke, "Mark Levin, John Hagee fight anti-Semitism."

organizations."[348] Christian Zionism is "dominated by the activities of a small number of para-church, non-denominational organizations which have successfully harnessed grass-roots evangelical political support for Israel," including Bridges for Peace (BFP) and International Christian Embassy Jerusalem (ICEJ).[349]

As we shall see in the next section, these organizations promulgate a "Biblical responsibility before God to be faithful to Israel and the Jewish community" which "does not include Jewish evangelism since they claim the promises made to Israel were both prior to and independent of the church."[350] They believe that "God's covenant promises between the land and His people Israel were everlasting and unconditional," and have therefore "reinterpreted the Christian message and made the teachings of Jesus subservient to a political Zionist ideology."[351] Christian Zionists see their artificial heresy as biblical, claiming, "We simply believe the Bible. And that Bible, which we understand has not been revoked, makes it quite clear that God has given this land as an eternal inheritance to the Jewish people."[352] Sizer writes:

> These Christian leaders and their organizations have regular access to over one-hundred million American Christians and more than one-hundred thousand church leaders. With a combined budget of well in excess of three-hundred million dollars per annum, they are shaping the Christian Zionist agenda today.[353]

---

348 Sizer, *Christian Zionism*, 97.
349 Ibid., 97.
350 Ibid., 100.
351 Ibid., 102.
352 Ibid., 122.
353 Ibid.

5

THE THEOLOGY OF CHRISTIAN ZIONISM

Christian Zionism is predicated upon the supposition that, in Sizer's words:

> God has a continuing special relationship with, and covenantal purpose for, the Jewish people, apart from the Church, and that the Jewish people have a divine right to possess the land of Palestine . . . based on a literal and futurist interpretation of the Bible and the conviction that Old Testament prophecies concerning the Jewish people are being fulfilled in the contemporary State of Israel.[354]

As such, Christian Zionists believe that their foremost duty is to unconditionally support any and all actions taken by the State of Israel, for they are "orchestrated by God, and should be condoned, supported, and even praised." Because dispensationalism is premillennial, Christian Zionists have come to believe that the restoration of the Jewish people to the physical land of Palestine is *the* necessary precondition for the Second Coming; furthermore:

> [Christian Zionists] increasingly came to recognize that restoration was indeed being achieved, but in 'unbelief,' and, therefore, Biblical predictions were found to confirm it. . . . There was no imperative or necessity to share the gospel with Jews, since their national repentance would occur only after their

[354] Ibid., 20.

> restoration and Jesus' return. Offering practical and financial support to bring about their restoration became the principal means of its fulfilment.[355]

This heresy has gained control over mainstream evangelical, charismatic, and independent denominations, including the Assemblies of God, Pentecostalists, and Southern Baptists, as well as most of the independent mega-churches.

All that we need understand with respect to covenantal premillennialism is that it holds that a restored Israel, and thus the Second Coming, is based upon faith in Jesus Christ; covenantal Christian Zionists, of which there are few today, believe that Jews and Gentiles will share God's blessing *together* during the millennium. Dispensationalists contend that God has *separate* and *different* purposes for Israel and the Church, in distinct dispensations; Jews are seen as God's "earthly bride," while the Church is his "spiritual bride." Sizer delineates three strains of post-1970s dispensational Christian Zionism: Apocalyptic, "preoccupied with the 'signs of the times'"; Messianic, "evangelizing Jews for Jesus," of which Jews for Jesus (JFJ), founded in 1973 in the hippie enclave of Haight-Ashbury in San Francisco, is the largest organization; and Political, "defending and 'blessing' Israel." Political Christian Zionism, as briefly outlined previously, reigns ascendant today. There are three other minor divisions, each regarding the Rapture: Pre-tribulationists hold that Christians will be raptured prior to the Tribulation, mid-tribulationists hold that Christians will be raptured during the Tribulation, and post-tribulationists hold that Christians will be raptured after the Tribulation.

For Christian Zionists, God's promise to Abraham is unconditional and eternal; they point to God promising to:

> [M]ake of thee a great nation, and I will bless thee, and make thy name great; and thou shalt be a blessing: And I will bless them that bless thee, and curse him that curseth thee: and in thee shall all families of the earth be blessed . . . unto thy seed have I given this land. (Gen. 12:1–3, 15:18, and 17:8)

---

[355] Ibid., 80.

Scofield argued, and generations of Christians credulously accepted, that Abraham's descendants need do no more than "abide in their own land to inherit every blessing."[356] He believed that "the mission of Jesus was, primarily, to the Jews. . . . The Sermon on the Mount is Law, not Grace . . . the doctrines of Grace are to be sought in the Epistles, not in the Gospels."[357] In these shockingly heterodox positions, Scofield imposed nonexistent divisions and ignored the only division that truly exists between the Old and New Testaments. Mark *begins* by emphatically pronouncing that it is "the beginning of the gospel of Jesus Christ, the Son of God." (Mark 1:1)

In his misguided and perhaps even malevolent literalism, Scofield took Paul's urging of clergymen to "study to shew thyself approved unto God, a workman that needeth not to be ashamed, rightly dividing the word of truth" (2 Tim. 2:15) as a command to literally impose divisions within the Bible. The correct meaning of "rightly dividing," the only occurrence of this Greek verb in the New Testament, properly refers to expounding something rightly, or teaching something correctly. Here, what needs to be handled correctly is the word of truth. Another way to translate "study" is "be zealous," again meaning that we must be cautious in handling the Scripture correctly. The futurist, literalist hermeneutic of dispensationalism created "a frozen Biblical text in which every word was supported by the same weight of Divine authority,"[358] an error which directly initiated the argument that Old Testament references to Israel apply to contemporary Jews and the State of Israel rather than the Church, and that Christ's earthly kingdom was to be a restoration of physical Israel, rather than the consummation of the Church. This distinction between the Church and Israel was entirely new, without any historical or doctrinal precedent. As Bass shows:

> It is not that exegetes prior to [Darby's] time did not see a covenant between God and Israel, or a future relation of Israel to the millennial reign, but they always viewed the church as a

---

[356] Ibid., 115.
[357] Ibid., 116.
[358] Ibid., 134.

> continuation of God's single program of redemption begun in Israel. It is dispensationalism's rigid insistence on a distinct cleavage between Israel and the church, and its belief in a later unconditional fulfilment of the Abrahamic covenant, that sets it off from the historic faith of the church.[359]

Paul illuminated the "basic hermeneutical error" of Christian Zionism when he wrote:

> Let no man therefore judge you in meat, or in drink, or in respect of an holyday, or of the new moon, or of the sabbath days: Which are a shadow of things to come; but the body is of Christ. (Col. 2:16–17)

Paul was explaining that, because God has reconciled Christians to himself through His Son, Christians are freed from the customs that God's *past* covenant people were required to perform, and cannot therewith be judged; in other words, Christ is the fulfillment of the Law, "the end of the law." (Rom. 8:1 and 10:4) Christ, the *new* covenant, supersedes and replaces the old; Paul's use of the words "shadow" and "body" to juxtapose the ephemeral, incomplete nature of the former obligations with the fulness of Christ. God established the dietary and holy day customs to foreshadow the Messiah, "for the law having a shadow of good things to come, and not the very image of the things, can never with those sacrifices which they offered year by year continually make the corners thereunto perfect." (Heb. 10:1) Thus, as Sizer puts it, "the question is not whether the promises of the covenant are to be understood literally or spiritually; it is instead a question of whether they should be understood in terms of old covenant shadow or new covenant reality."[360]

As we have already shown, Scofield's dispensational scheme was basically plagiarized from Darby; though Scofield claimed his dispensational eras were natural and self-evident, this is belied by the fact that their names and the Bible verses they are ostensibly based upon have varied from revision to

---

[359] Bass, *Backgrounds to Dispensationalism*, 27.
[360] Sizer, *Christian Zionism*, 75.

revision. Interestingly, Oxford University Press retained ownership, paying Scofield generous royalties; this may explain why the *Scofield Reference Bible* has grown *more* dispensational with new revisions, and "in many cases, references to contemporary Israel are appended to verses on which Scofield originally made no comment at all." For example, Carlson argues that the 1967 *New Scofield Reference Bible* deifies the State of Israel. One newly inserted footnote to Genesis 12:3 reads: "For a nation to commit the sin of anti-Semitism brings inevitable judgment." These words, which might as well have been written by Theodor Herzl or Ariel Sharon, are found in a Bible "that is followed by millions of American churchgoers and students and is used by their leaders as a source for their preaching and teaching." Carlson explains that Oxford has hereby made "antipathy toward the 'State of Israel' a 'sin.' Israel is made a god to be worshiped, not merely a 'state.' David Ben-Gurion could not have written it better." Another footnote to the same verse reads: "It has invariably fared ill with the people who have persecuted the Jew, [and] well with those who have protected him. The future will still more remarkably prove this principle." Carlson accurately describes these as "Zionist propaganda that has been tacked onto the text of a Christian Bible. Most of them make no sense, except to support the Zionist State of Israel." [361]

It is unimportant to delve into these dispensations, as we are better served to explain and refute the essential doctrines of dispensational Christian Zionism. Sizer summarizes these doctrines:

> Injunctions and promises concerning the ancient Jews are applied to the contemporary State of Israel rather than to the Church [and promulgate the] conviction that the Jews remain God's 'chosen people,' distinct from the Church . . . into eternity, as affirmed by most dispensationalists. God's end-time purpose for the Jews is expressed in restorationism [to] reclaim the inheritance promised to Abraham and his descendants forever. The role of the Church is to assist in this 'end-time' event. . . . Jerusalem is recognized to be their exclusive,

[361] Carlson, "Source of the Problem."

> undivided and eternal capital. . . . At the heart of Jerusalem will be the rebuilt Jewish temple to which all the nations will come to worship God. Just prior to the return of Jesus, there will be seven years of calamities and war, known as the Tribulation, which will culminate in a great battle called Armageddon, during which the godless forces opposed to *both* [emphasis mine] God and Israel will be defeated. Jesus will then return as the Jewish Messiah and king to reign in Jerusalem for a thousand years and the Jewish people will enjoy a privileged status and role in the world.[362]

Chosen Peoples: Israel and the Church

Christian Zionists believe that the Old Testament covenant with the Jews was never superseded, that the Jews remain God's eternally chosen people, "enjoying a unique relationship, status and eternal purpose within their own land, separate from any promises made to the Church."[363] This doctrine of two different covenants has cascaded into a belief that "the status of Israel is superior to the Church; that the role of Israel supersedes that of the Church; and that, as a consequence, the primary purpose of the Church is to 'bless Israel.'"[364] Scofield argued that Christ, when he told Peter that "upon this rock I will build my church; and the gates of hell shall not prevail against it," was referring to the physical land of Israel. (Matt. 16:18) Scofield asserted that "Israel was the true 'church' but not in any sense the New Testament church—the only point of similarity being that both were 'called out' and by the same God. All else is contrast."[365] The proper meaning of this verse, contrary to Scofield's obtuse interpretation, is that Christ is responsible for the growth of his Church; while in the Old Testament, *ekklesia* referred to sacred Jewish assemblies, Christ's use of the word signifies something wholly new, an

[362] Sizer, *Christian Zionism*, 107.
[363] Ibid., 135.
[364] Ibid., 136.
[365] Ibid., 137.

implication that his followers, Christians, constitute the *new* Israel, the *true* chosen of God.

Following Scofield's doctrine, Christian Zionists like Chafer and Ryrie assert:

> Israel is an eternal nation, heir to an eternal land, with an eternal kingdom, on which David rules from an eternal throne . . . never the twain, Israel and church, shall meet. . . . When the Church was introduced, God did not abrogate His promises to Israel nor enmesh them into the Church.[366]

Hagee wildly extrapolates from God's blessing Abraham that he "will multiply thy seed as the stars of heaven, and as the sand which is on the sea shore; and thy seed shall possess the gate of his enemies," contending that the verse illustrates:

> God has two Israels, one physical and one spiritual . . . since God mentions two separate and distinct elements, the stars in the sky and the sand of the seashore, He is referring in dispensational terms to the heavenly church and the earthly Israel. . . . Just so, the nation of Israel and spiritual Israel, the church, exist at the same time and do not replace each other.[367]

This interpretation requires such tortured mental gymnastics that we need not refute its manifest falsity.

Because Christian Zionists believe in two covenants, they necessarily imply that there are two paths to salvation. Christ clearly dispels this absurdity by declaring firmly that "I am the way, the truth, and the life: no man cometh unto the Father, but by me." (John 14:6) Jesus is the door through which men are saved, the *singular* way to salvation, for it is he *alone* who purged our sins. (John 10:9, Heb. 1:3) Christ declares that "verily, verily, I say unto you, He that entereth not by the door into the sheepfold, but climbeth up some other way, the same is a thief and a robber" and that "except a man be born again, he cannot see the kingdom of God." (John 3:3, 10:1) Christians alone have everlasting life, while "he that believeth not the

---

[366] Quoted in Ibid., 138.

[367] Quoted in Ibid., 139.

Son shall not see life; but the wrath of God abideth on him." (John 3:36)

Christian Zionists also misinterpret God's words to Isaiah, "Speak ye comfortably to Jerusalem, and cry unto her, that her warfare is accomplished, that her iniquity is pardoned: for she hath received of the Lord's hand double for all her sins." (Isa. 40:1–2). They believe that these verses mandate "political and practical support for Jews, encouraging them to . . . settle the land God promised to Abraham";[368] in fact, here Isaiah is being commanded to bring words of comfort, rather than judgment, to the Jews, in anticipation of their exile to Babylon. This "comfort" refers to the atonement, incarnation, and resurrection, and in any case is a historically specific directive from God to the prophet Isaiah. Christian Zionists further misconstrue Christ's exhortation that "inasmuch as ye have done it unto the least of these my brethren, ye have done it unto me," contending that this verse is a "mandate for providing material support rather than evangelistic witness to the State of Israel." (Matt. 25:40)

As one Christian Zionist organization stated:

> In the same sense that the first apostles were commissioned by the Lord to be his witnesses from Jerusalem to the uttermost parts of the earth, we also feel compelled to proclaim the word of Israel's restoration, and the Christian's response to it, to every country and in every place where there are believers.[369]

As such, Christian Zionists believe that they have a biblical obligation "to do everything scripture requires of us to help the Jewish people regain the fulness of their God-appointed inheritance." Sizer ably points out:

> This equation of the 'restoration' ministry . . . with that of the apostolic commission to preach the Gospel to the whole world is simply without precedent [and] invests Biblical terms such

[368] Ibid., 141.
[369] Ibid., 142.

> as 'message' and 'proclaim' with new meaning, redefining the Christian purpose to that of 'blessing Israel.'[370]

Hagee digs his grave even deeper by preaching:

> I believe that every Jewish person who lives in the light of the Torah, which is the word of God, has a relationship with God and will come to redemption . . . trying to convert Jews is a waste of time. The Jewish person who has his roots in Judaism is not going to convert to Christianity. . . . Everyone else . . . needs to believe in Jesus. But not Jews. Jews already have a covenant with God that has never been replaced by Christianity.[371]

Hagee continues that "many Christian theologians are anti-Semitic, because they say the covenant with the Jews is gone, that Jews have been replaced by Christianity and that Israel does not deserve American military and financial support."[372] Hagee also preaches that Jesus was not the Messiah, and that he was not murdered, even indirectly, by the Jews.

The conviction of two covenants has led Christian Zionists to conclude, quite shockingly, that Jews do not need to believe in Jesus as the Son of God, either before or after the Second Coming. Sizer notes that "conveniently, it also ensures they receive favored status as 'Christian' representatives within the State of Israel."[373] By traveling down this inexorable path, "by regarding the Church as a digression from God's continuing purposes for Israel," Christian Zionists elevate Israel to a position superior to the Church. Christian Zionist organizations regard "the last two-thousand-year history of the Church as merely 'a parenthesis' to God's future plans for the Jews" and believe that "the promises originally made to Abraham are unconditional, eternal and exclusively reserved for the physical descendants of Isaac, Jacob and Joseph. Therefore, Israel today is truly blessed."[374] They even go so far as to

---

[370] Ibid.
[371] Ibid., 143.
[372] Ibid.
[373] Ibid.
[374] Ibid., 144.

suggest that "Jewish people who have rejected Jesus are still in a more advantageous position than Gentiles," arguing that, "since the unconditional covenant with the Jews was made prior to the cross, it was not annulled by it either."[375] This is blatantly at odds with Christ's own teaching, which very clearly emphasized the distinction between ignorance and rejection, saying "if ye were blind, ye should have no sin: but now ye say, We see; therefore your sin remaineth." (John 9:41)

Christian Zionists also misinterpret Paul's assurance that "all Israel shall be saved" to literally mean the Jewish people and their physical homeland, today represented by the State of Israel. (Rom. 11:26) This is clarified when Paul writes, "For they are not all Israel, which are of Israel." (Rom. 9:6) Christian Zionists take a further step by using Ephesians 3:6 to argue that "if physical Israel is disinherited, then there is no inheritance for the Gentiles to share in," that the Jews "remain elect of God, and without the Jewish nation His redemptive purposes for the world will not be completed." On its face, that verse, "That the Gentiles should be fellowheirs, and of the same body, and partakers of his promise in Christ by the gospel," might be seen as supporting a dispensational reading. Context helps us dispel such an erroneous reading. It occurs shortly after Paul describes how Gentiles, once separated from God, were reconciled unto him through Christ, who "hath made both one, and hath broken down the wall of partition" between Jew and Gentile; Christ fulfilled and abolished the law, reconciling "both unto God in one body by the cross, having slain the enmity thereby," establishing that "now therefore ye are no more strangers and foreigners, but fellow citizens with the saints, and of the household of God." (Eph. 2:11–19) Thus, Christians *became* the new Israel, together with Jews who accept Jesus as the Messiah, i.e., Christians who are no longer Jews at all.

These political dispensationalists believe that by "blessing Israel," they are hastening the Second Coming; they assert:

---

[375] Ibid.

> With the founding of the State of Israel in 1948 and the reunification of Jerusalem in 1967 under exclusive Israeli control, the 'church age' or 'dispensation of grace' came to an end or is at least nearly over. They believe Christians will soon be . . . raptured to heaven and the Jewish people will become the center of divine government in the world during the millennium. Before then the purpose of the Church . . . is to serve and 'bless Israel.'[376]

By "blessing" the State of Israel, Christian Zionists believe that, as Scofield said, "Gentiles today are thereby blessed in association with Israel." They frequently misapply God's promise to Abraham that "I will bless them that bless thee, and curse him that curseth thee: and in thee shall all families of the earth be blessed." In context, this promise is clearly God's *solely* to Abraham, *not* to the future nation of Israel. Following their misapprehension, Christian Zionists believe that their primary purpose is to "comfort Zion."

At the Third International Zionist Congress in 1966, a resolution was passed which stated, "The Lord in His zealous love for Israel and the Jewish People blesses and curses peoples and judges nations based upon their treatment of the Chosen People of Israel." Hagee often declares that "the man or nation that lifts a voice or hand against Israel invites the wrath of God." Basilea Schlink, founder of the Evangelical Sisterhood of Mary, said that "anyone who disputes Israel's right to the land of Canaan is actually opposing God and his holy covenant with the Patriarchs. He is striving against sacred, inviolable words and promises of God, which he has sworn to keep."[377] As we have shown, there is absolutely no evidence that God's promise to Abraham was intended to extend beyond Abraham himself. Even if we were to apply the aforementioned blessing to them, God's promise to Abraham that "unto thy seed will I give this land" would speak of *God* blessing them, "not of entire nations 'blessing' the Hebrew nation, still less the contemporary and secular State of Israel."[378]

---

[376] Ibid.
[377] Ibid., 148.
[378] Ibid.

Furthermore, the "seed" of Abraham is Jesus Christ, and by extension, Christians. Paul writes that "the blessing of Abraham [comes] on the Gentiles through Jesus Christ," that "to Abraham and his seed were the promises made. He saith not, And to seeds, as of many; but as of one, And to thy seed, which is Christ." (Gal. 3:14–16). Paul continues, saying, "if ye be Christ's, then are ye Abraham's seed, and heirs according to the promise." (Gal. 3:29) Matthew's Gospel opens by naming itself, "The book of the generation of Jesus Christ, the son of David, the son of Abraham." The promise of God's blessing, therefore, "is offered to Gentiles not on the basis of how well they treat the Jews but on whether they have responded to Jesus Christ." Sizer emphasizes that "the idea that the Jewish people continue to enjoy a special status by virtue of the covenants made with the Patriarchs is in conflict with the clear and unambiguous statements of the New Testament."[379]

For example, Jesus urges his Jewish audience:

> Bring forth therefore fruits worthy of repentance, and begin not to say within yourselves, We have Abraham to our father: for I say unto you, That God is able of these stones to raise up children unto Abraham. And now also the axe is laid unto the root of the trees: every tree therefore which bringeth not forth good fruit is hewn down, and cast into the fire. (Luke 3:8–9)

The fruits of our repentance, being our lives transformed by our faith in Christ, render claims of Jewish lineage utterly meaningless. Indeed, physical descent is further problematized by Paul's command that we "neither give heed to fables and endless genealogies" and "avoid foolish questions, and genealogies, and contentions, and strivings about the law; for they are unprofitable and vain." (1 Tim. 1:4, Titus 3:9)

Perhaps Christ's greatest clarification of the issue comes when he says to the Jews, "If ye continue in my word, then are ye my disciples indeed; And ye shall know the truth, and the truth shall make you free." When the Jews reply that they are Abraham's seed, and thus "never in bondage," Christ responds:

---

[379] Ibid.

> Whosoever committeth sin is the servant of sin. And the servant abideth not in the house for ever: but the Son abideth ever. If the Son therefore shall make you free, ye shall be free indeed. I know that ye are Abraham's seed; but ye seek to kill me, because my word hath no place in you. I speak that which I have seen with my Father; and ye do that which ye have seen with your father. (John 8:34–38)

When the Jews, who Christ acknowledges are the *physical* seed of Abraham, but not the *true* seed of Abraham, reply that "Abraham is our father," Christ admonishes them:

> If ye were Abraham's children, ye would do the works of Abraham. But now ye seek to kill me, a man that hath told you the truth, which I have heard of God: this did not Abraham. Ye do the deeds of your father. . . . If God were your Father, ye would love me: for I proceeded forth and came from God; neither came I of myself, but he sent me. Why do ye not understand my speech? even because ye cannot hear my word. Ye are of your father the devil, and the lusts of your father ye will do. He was a murderer from the beginning, and abode not in the truth, because there is no truth in him. When he speaketh a lie, he speaketh of his own: for he is a liar, and the father of it. And because I tell you the truth, ye believe me not. Which of you convinceth me of sin? And if I say the truth, why do ye not believe me? He that is of God heareth God's words: ye therefore hear them not, because ye are not of God. (John 8:39–47)

Abraham's barren wife, Sarah, gave her slave, Hagar, to her husband as a means of fulfilling God's promise to make him the "father of many nations"; Hagar bore him Ishmael, whom many have postulated to be the progenitor of the Arabic people, but once Sarah bore Abraham his legitimate son, Isaac, Sarah cast Hagar and Ishmael out. In so doing, Sarah tells Abraham to "cast out this bondwoman and her son: for the son of this bondwoman shall not be heir with my son, even with Isaac"; God confirmed that it was in Isaac that "thy seed be called." (Gen. 21:10–12) Paul appropriates these very words, applying them to the Judaizers who were corrupting the faith of the Galatian church; he writes:

> Abraham had two sons, the one by a bondmaid, the other by a freewoman. But he who was of the bondwoman was born after the flesh; but he of the freewoman was by promise. Which things are an allegory: for these are the two covenants. (Gal. 4:22–24).

Paul drew a distinction between the earthly Jerusalem, "in bondage with her children," and the "Jerusalem which is above . . . free, which is the mother of us all." (Gal. 4:25–26) Abraham conceived with Hagar out of impatience and, by implication, mistrust in God's promise, while Isaac was conceived of the barren womb of Sarah. Paul writes:

> Rejoice, thou barren that bearest not; break forth and cry, thou that travailest not: for the desolate hath many more children than she which hath an husband. Now we, brethren, as Isaac was, are the children of promise. But as he that was born after the flesh persecuted him that was born after the Spirit, even so it is now. Nevertheless, what saith the scripture? Cast out the bondwoman and her son: for the son of the bondwoman shall not be heir with the son of the freewoman. So then, brethren, we are not children of the bondwoman, but of the free. (Gal. 4:27–31).

We, the new Israel, the "children of promise," are Abraham's seed through our faith in Christ. Though God's children in the Old Testament were the Israelites, this is conclusively no longer the case in the *new* and *singular* covenant established by Christ; as we have seen, only those born of *God* are his children. As John writes, Jesus came unto his own, the Jews, and they rejected him:

> But as many received him, to them gave he power to become the sons of God, even to them that believe on his name: Which were born, not of blood, nor of the will of the flesh, nor of the will of man, but of God. (John 1:11–13)

Sizer explains:

> The promises made to Abraham, Isaac, Jacob and Joseph are therefore now to be understood as fulfilled through those who

> demonstrate the faith of Abraham and follow Jesus Christ, for they alone are designated the true children of Abraham and Sarah. Jews who reject Jesus Christ are outside the covenant of grace and are . . . now to be regarded as children of Hagar.[380]

The Jews rejected Christ by persecuting and murdering him. Peter warned that the consequence for rejection was severance; he promised that "every soul, which will not hear that prophet, shall be destroyed from among the people." (Acts 3:23) Just as God rejects those who reject him and forgets those who forget him, Christ vows:

> Whosoever therefore shall be ashamed of me and of my words in this adulterous and sinful generation; of him also shall the Son of man be ashamed, when he cometh in the glory of his Father with the holy angels. (Mark 8:38)

The New Testament thus repeatedly "repudiates the notion that the Jewish people continue to enjoy a special status or relationship with God, apart from faith in Jesus Christ." "Chosenness" is the gift of God's grace to *all* Christian believers; Christians "are a chosen generation, a royal priesthood, an holy nation, a peculiar people . . . which in time past were not a people, but are now the people of God: which had not obtained mercy, but now have obtained mercy." (1 Pet. 2:9–10) In the New Testament, "chosen" is used only to refer to the Church, the body of Christ.

Restorationism: The Jewish Return to Zion

Scofield taught that "it was God's intention to restore the Jewish people to Palestine," that "the gift of the land is modified by prophecies of three dispossessions and restorations," and that, because two dispossessions and restorations had already occurred, Israel was now in its third dispersion, "from

[380] Ibid., 149.

which she will be restored at the return of the Lord as King under the Davidic Covenant." Scofield's speculation was based on two presuppositions, the first being that Israel had never taken all of the land that had been promised to Abraham. However, as the Book of Joshua attests, "Joshua took the whole land, according to all that the Lord said unto Moses; and Joshua gave it for an inheritance unto Israel. . . . And the land rested from war." (Josh. 11:23) The Lord "gave unto Israel all the land which he sware to give unto their fathers; and they possessed it, and dwelt therein." (Josh. 21:43) This is further reinforced with the penitential prayer in which it is stated concretely that "thou gavest them kingdoms and nations. . . . Their children also multipliedst thou as the stars of heaven, and broughtest them into the land, concerning which thou hadst promised to their fathers, that they should go in to possess it." (Neh. 9:23) All that God has promised his people had been fulfilled by him. Scofield's second presupposition was that not all of the messianic promises had been fulfilled during the First Advent, thus holding that Christ's work had been incomplete, a notion at odds with the orthodox teaching that Christ's ministry, death, and resurrection is the final and fixed point around which history turns.

Sizer notes that Scofield placed great import in James' citation of the prophets Amos and Isaiah to say:

> Simeon hath declared how God at the first did visit the Gentiles, to take out of them a people for his name. And to this agree the words of the prophets; as it is written, After this I will return, and will build again the tabernacle of David, which is fallen down; and I will build again the ruins thereof, and I will set it up: That the residue of men might seek after the Lord, and all the Gentiles, upon whom my name is called, saith the Lord, who doeth all these things. Known unto God are all his works from the beginning of the world. (Acts 15:14–18)

This passage illustrates how God ordained that the Gentiles would be called by his name; James is affirming that the rebuilt tabernacle Christ is referencing is what we now know as the Church, fixed not in one physical location but rather emblematic of the body of Christ. Sizer explains that Scofield, however, interpreted "after this" "not simply as meaning 'after James' or even 'after Pentecost,' but after a further 1,900 years," ignoring the fact that James is appealing to Amos in order to vindicate the universality of the gospel.[381] Extrapolating from this passage a prediction of the State of Israel and scriptural support thereof seems to be at odds with James' own clear meaning.

Christ urges us always to be prepared for His return; in His description of the Second Coming, He says:

> Now learn a parable of the fig tree; When his branch is yet tender, and putteth forth leaves, ye know that summer is nigh: So likewise ye, when ye shall see all these things, know that it is near, even at the doors. . . . This generation shall not pass, till all these things be fulfilled. (Matt. 24:32–34)

"All these things" refers to the Tribulation that will precede his return, not the return itself, for which "of that day and hour knoweth no man, no, not the angels of heaven, but my Father only. . . . Therefore be ye also ready: for in such an hour as ye think not the Son of man cometh." (Matt. 24:36–44) This is an exhortation to live each day as if it were the day that Christ will return, or, in other words, to live Christian lives. A preoccupation with observing geopolitical events is thus fruitless and presumptuous, for we are called to be perpetually ready for a future that even the angels cannot foresee.

Sizer describes how Lindsey has distorted the analogy of the "fig tree" in the Olivet discourse; crucially, we must be cognizant of who Jesus was speaking to.

> Whereas first-century Christians understood Jesus to be warning them to observe the signs and flee Jerusalem when the city came under Roman siege, Lindsey reverses its meaning. He claims Jesus was predicting the restoration of the Jews to Palestine in the twentieth century rather than their departure in the first century. . . . Nothing in Matthew 24, however, indicates that Jesus intended his hearers to understand that he was promising that Israel would become a nation state once

[381] Ibid., 157.

> more.... Nevertheless, Lindsey has popularized the notion that the return of Jewish people to Palestine since 1948 is the fulfilment of Biblical prophecy.[382]

Indeed, Christ categorically denied "any notion that Israel would enjoy a divinely mandated national identity as a kingdom in the future." Christ told the Pharisees that "the kingdom of God shall be taken from you, and given to a nation bringing forth the fruits thereof." (Matt. 21:43) Ryrie reverses Christ's meaning by asserting that "you" refers to the leaders of Israel, i.e. the Pharisees, and that "nation" refers to physical Israel.

Christ tells the centurion that

> I have not found so great faith, no, not in Israel. And I say unto you, That many shall come from the east and west, and shall sit down with Abraham, and Isaac, and Jacob, in the kingdom of heaven. But the children of the kingdom shall be cast out into outer darkness: there shall be weeping and gnashing of teeth. (Matt. 8:10–12)

The kingdom of heaven has been removed from the Jews, who rejected God and who would murder his Son; Christians inherit the kingdom of God, not the "children" in the verse, those Jews to whom the kingdom was originally promised. Another of Christ's parables, that of a great supper, signals, as Sizer puts it, "The end of the nation of Israel as the chosen people of God. They have been tried and found wanting. God's patience has been exhausted."[383]

In his parable, Christ tells:

> A certain man made a great supper, and bade many: And sent his servant at supper time to say to them that were bidden, Come; for all things are now ready. And they all with one consent began to make excuse. The first said unto him, I have bought a piece of ground, and I must needs go and see it: I pray thee have me excused. And another said, I have bought five yoke of oxen, and I go to prove them: I pray thee have me

---

[382] Ibid., 158.
[383] Ibid., 159.

> excused. And another said, I have married a wife, and therefore I cannot come. So that servant came, and shewed his lord these things. Then the master of the house being angry said to his servant, Go out quickly into the streets and lanes of the city, and bring in hither the poor, and the maimed, and the halt, and the blind. And the servant said, Lord, it is done as thou hast commanded, and yet there is room. And the lord said unto the servant, Go out into the highways and hedges, and compel them to come in, that my house may be filled. For I say unto you, That none of those men which were bidden shall taste of my supper." (Luke 14:16–24)

This "great supper" symbolizes a banquet in the future kingdom of God; all of those that were initially invited, the Jews and their leaders, make excuse after excuse as to why they cannot partake. Christ thus invites the Gentiles to *replace* those ingrates who had refused His kindness, the *only* door through which God's grace may be experienced.

Eretz Israel: The Promised Land

As we have seen, Christian Zionists insist that the Abrahamic covenant remains fixed upon the Jewish people, and that as a consequence, they have a divine and unconditional right to the promised land. This is a demonstrable fallacy, for throughout the Old Testament it is clear that the promised land was and is God's, not the Jews', whose residence was always conditional; as Sizer describes:

> The land is never at the disposal of Israel for its national purposes. Instead, it is Israel who are at the disposal of God's purposes. The Jews remain tenants in God's land. The ethical requirements for continued occupancy are clearly outlined in the Law.[384]

---

[384] Ibid., 163.

Additionally, tenancy in God's land was less a function of inherent "chosenness" than of God's contingent grace, as is evidenced by God's words when told His chosen people:

> Not for thy righteousness, or for the uprightness of thine heart, dost thou go to possess their land: but for the wickedness of these nations the Lord thy God doth drive them out from before thee, and that he may perform the word which the Lord sware unto thy fathers, Abraham, Isaac, and Jacob. (Deut. 9:5)

This is even further reified in Ezekiel's warning from God:

> Son of man, they that inhabit those wastes of the land of Israel speak, saying, Abraham was one, and he inherited the land: but we are many; the land is given us for inheritance. Wherefore say unto them, Thus saith the Lord God; Ye eat with the blood, and lift up your eyes toward your idols, and shed blood: and shall ye possess the land? Ye stand upon your sword, ye work abomination, and ye defile every one his neighbour's wife: and shall ye possess the land? Say thou thus unto them, Thus saith the Lord God; As I live, surely they that are in the wastes shall fall by the sword, and him that is in the open field will I give to the beasts to be devoured, and they that be in the forts and in the caves shall die of the pestilence. For I will lay the land most desolate, and the pomp of her strength shall cease; and the mountains of Israel shall be desolate, that none shall pass through. Then shall they know that I am the Lord, when I have laid the land most desolate because of all their abominations which they have committed." (Ezek. 33:24–29)

The Christian Zionist understanding of Eretz Israel is utterly wrongheaded, as, in Sizer's words, it is by *faith* in Christ that Christians, the true "seed" descended from Abraham:

> [A]re now promised not just Canaan but the entire world, including the cosmos itself. . . . It is no longer merely a portion of the earth that is the consummation of God's work of redeeming a fallen world, but one in which the entire cosmos participates. So paradise restored is not just a return to the land but a reconstructed cosmos, a new heaven and a new

> earth which becomes the home of the resurrected faithful remnant.[385]

Paul affirms this when he writes:

> For the promise, that he should be the heir of the world, was not to Abraham, or his seed, through the law, but through the righteousness of faith. For if they which are of the law be heirs, faith is made void, and the promise made of none effect: Because the law worketh wrath: for where no law is, there is no transgression. Therefore it is of faith, that it might be by grace; to the end the promise might be sure to all the seed; not to that only which is of the law, but to that also which is of the faith of Abraham; who is the father of us all. (Rom. 4:13–16)

To reiterate, those that are of the law, the Jews, are *not* heirs to the new covenant, which has *replaced* and *superseded* the old; God's promise still exists, but its recipient has changed from Jew to Christian. The Jews may only receive God's grace through faith in Jesus Christ, the only means by which man may enter the kingdom of God.

Jerusalem: Heaven and Earth

Christian Zionists are fixated upon the physical city of Jerusalem as the eternal and indivisible capital of the physical Israel that they believe is the Jewish destiny; in their approbation, Jerusalem is to be the eternal focal point and final fulfillment of God's covenant with the Jews, his "earthly bride." Just as restoring the Jews to Palestine has come to be seen as a prerequisite for the Second Coming, so too has the ideal of Jewish political control over the worldly Jerusalem. Jerusalem, though, is rendered irrelevant in the New Testament. For example, Christ tells the Samaritan woman at Jacob's Well, "Woman, believe me, the hour cometh, when ye shall neither

---

[385] Ibid., 164.

in this mountain, nor yet at Jerusalem, worship the Father." (John 4:21) "This mountain" refers to Gerizim, the site where Moses commanded an altar to be built, and where blessings were pronounced for keeping the covenant; in tandem with Jerusalem, Christ is declaring that physical sites will not have any connection to his heavenly kingdom.

Indeed, Christ emphasizes that "my kingdom is not of this world: if my kingdom were of this world, then would my servants fight, that I should not be delivered to the Jews: but now is my kingdom not from hence." (John 18:36) Paul, quoting Isaiah, speaks of the "Jerusalem which is above," the only Jerusalem of any significance—the heavenly Jerusalem. (Gal. 4:26) *This* Jerusalem is, as Sizer describes, "the home of all who believe in Jesus Christ" and "nullifies any future exclusive Jewish claim to be the authentic children of Abraham, with all its covenantal privileges, apart from through faith in Jesus Christ." Sizer argues:

> There is . . . no evidence that the apostles believed that the Jewish people still had a divine right to the land, or that the Jewish possession of the land would be important, let alone that Jerusalem would remain a central aspect of God's purposes for the world. On the contrary . . . Jerusalem as much as the land, has now been superseded. They have been made irrelevant in God's redemptive purposes.[386]

Sizer explains that "the turning point for the disciples comes with the resurrection encounters and Pentecost. . . . They had looked forward to God's intervention which would at last restore political sovereignty to the Jews in Israel."[387] Two of Christ's disciples, when they encountered him at Emmaus after his resurrection, remarked that they "trusted that it had been he which should have redeemed Israel." (Luke 24:21) These disciples thereby admitted that the murder of Christ had sunk their hope that he was the Messiah; between his resurrection and ascension, Christ appeared before other of his disciples, and they asked him, "Lord, wilt thou at this time

---

[386] Ibid., 168.
[387] Ibid., 169.

restore again the kingdom to Israel?" (Acts 1:6) To this misguided query, John Calvin once remarked that "there are as many mistakes in this question as there are words."[388] Christ answers his disciples by telling them:

> It is not for you to know the times or the seasons, which the Father hath put in his own power. But ye shall receive power, after that the Holy Ghost is come upon you: and ye shall be witnesses unto me both in Jerusalem, and in all Judaea, and in Samaria, and unto the uttermost part of the earth. (Acts 1:7–8)

The restoration of physical Israel was a dream shared by all first-century Jews (and by Jews ever since), who believed that the Messiah would accomplish this; Christ deflected his disciples' question and reaffirmed their missionary commission. Sizer notes that Christ's reply:

> [R]edefines the boundaries of the kingdom of God and thereby the meaning of chosenness. The expansion of the kingdom of God throughout the world requires the exile of the apostles from the land. They must turn their backs on Jerusalem and on their hopes of a materialistic kingdom. They are sent out into the world but never told to return.[389]

By failing to recognize this truth, Christian Zionists make the same mistake that the apostles made before Pentecost, interpreting Christ's death as the postponement of the messianic promise, rather than the fulfillment thereof.

---

[388] Bouwsma, *John Calvin*, 94.
[389] Sizer, *Zion's Christian Soldiers?* 93.

The Temple: Rebuilding for Desecration

Sizer describes the Zionist doctrine of the third temple:

> On the basis of a few allegedly unfulfilled Old and New Testament prophecies, many Christian Zionists are convinced that a third temple will be built in place of, or near, the Dome of the Rock in Jerusalem and believe that a Jewish priesthood will once again offer sacrifices . . . [and that the] temple will then be desecrated by the Antichrist and replaced during the millennium by a much larger temple.[390]

Christian Zionists ignore the fact that the Temple was desecrated on numerous occasions, as well as the fact that Christ never actually promised that it would be rebuilt; Sizer shows that "there is not a single verse in the New Testament which promises that the Jewish temple would be rebuilt or that a two-thousand year 'parenthesis' should be placed between references to its desecration and destruction."[391] Sizer continues:

> This viewpoint is incompatible with the way the New Testament describes the Temple as an illustration, a copy and a shadow for the atoning work of Jesus Christ . . . the movement in the progressive revelation of Scripture is always from the lesser to the greater. It is never reversed. The New Testament repeatedly sees such Old Testament concepts as the Temple, high priest and sacrifice as 'types' pointing to and fulfilled in Jesus Christ. Typology in Scripture never typifies itself, nor is it ever greater than that which it typifies. . . . Christians who advocate the rebuilding of the Temple are regressing to a pre-Christian sacrificial system, superseded and annulled by the finished work of Jesus Christ. The New Testament portrays the Temple as a temporary edifice, a shadow and type anticipating the day when God will dwell with people of all nations because

---

[390] Sizer, *Christian Zionism*, 182.
[391] Sizer, *Zion's Christian Soldiers?* 129.

> of the atoning work of the true temple, Jesus Christ. The purpose of the Temple . . . finds its ultimate significance and fulfilment not in another man-made sanctuary but in Jesus Christ and His Church.[392]

Indeed, in the Epistle to the Hebrews, we see:

> If that first covenant had been faultless, then should no place have been sought for the second. For finding fault with them, he saith, Behold, the days come, saith the Lord, when I will make a new covenant. . . . Not according to the covenant that I made with their fathers . . . because they continued not in my covenant, and I regarded them not, saith the Lord. For this is the covenant that I will make. . . . I will put my laws into their mind, and write them in their hearts: and I will be to them a God, and they shall be to me a people. . . . In that he saith, A new covenant, he hath made the first old. Now that which decayeth and waxeth old is ready to vanish away. (Heb. 8:7–13)

The Future: Teleology and Eschatology

Christian Zionists like the exegetical madman Lindsey have moved outside the quaint boundaries of eschatology, concerned with interpretations of the Second Coming, and into the realm of teleology, concerned with interpretations of history. As Sizer notes, "Lindsey has to perform 'acrobatic stunts,' twisting Biblical texts to fit his future scenario . . . a modern form of Gnosticism."[393] As briefly touched upon already, dispensationalists have essentially crossed the line into believing in a crude form of salvation by works, for they hold that "God will judge the world on the basis of how people have treated the Jews." DeHaan declares:

> The solution of this world's ills lies in this one formula: bring God's covenant people into God's Holy Land . . . there can be

---

[392] Sizer, *Christian Zionism*, 183.
[393] Ibid., 188.

> no peace in this world until the nation and the land, according to God's purposes are again wholly united. . . . When Jerusalem is at peace the world will be at peace. . . . God is on the side of those who recognize His program.[394]

This statement belies the unbridgeable chasm between traditional Christianity, with its position that our judgment will be based solely upon how we have responded to the gospel, and the bastard theology of Christian Zionism, which is centered upon Israel.

This doctrine would have us believe that the eternal destiny of entire peoples and nations is dependent upon whether or not they have provided the State of Israel with material support. This is the natural consequence of the Christian Zionist doctrine holding that the Jews possess a superior covenant to the one established by Christ's death and resurrection. This artificial superimposition, this "teaching for doctrines the commandments of men," cannot help but pave the way for:

> [A] reductionist eschatology in which Jesus is devalued, salvation and judgment redefined, and Israel sacralized. . . . If Israel is actually the measure for, and mediator of, ultimate justice and peace, then 'blessing' Israel has become synonymous with believing in Jesus.[395]

Christians have been indoctrinated to believe that their support (and by extension America's support) for the State of Israel is the basis of the Second Coming and of their salvation.

The heresy of Christian Zionism, using an arbitrary and self-contradictory literalist and futurist hermeneutic, contends that the Jews remain God's chosen people, separate from and superior to the Church; indeed, they believe that earthly Jewish Israel will *replace* the Church, and that as such, "Christians, and indeed whole nations, will be blessed through their association with, and support of, Israel."[396] Christian Zionists, following this logic, believe in a final restoration of the

[394] Quoted in Ibid., 201.
[395] Ibid.
[396] Ibid., 203.

Jews to Eretz Israel, the eternally and unconditionally promised land, of which the present city of Jerusalem will serve as capital; they have been led to believe that the Temple "must be rebuilt and sacrifices re-instituted in order that it can be desecrated by the Antichrist before Jesus returns," hubristically attempting to hasten the Second Coming, which they take as a matter of faith to be imminent.[397] As we have demonstrated, though, every single one of these claims is in total opposition to the New Testament and the new covenant of Jesus Christ.

The Christian Zionist commitment to literalism presents a great irony; in their presumed quest for "plain meaning," they construct sandcastles in the sky. They ignore the Scriptural exposition of Christ and his apostles, and in so doing have made the Old Testament a strange dogma. Their assumption that the two covenants run parallel to, and concurrent with, each other is inconsistent with the New Testament's own insistence that Christ has fulfilled all of the promises given in the Old Testament.

Most troublingly, Zionism and the State of Israel have been sacralized, ultimately subordinating the cross to the Star of David. We must recognize this as the apostasy that it is. The *Scofield Reference Bible* allowed our most ancient enemy to advance its agenda by way of Christian hands, mouths, and money, indoctrinating whole generations of American Christians that they must do *whatever it takes* to support the State of Israel because "the Bible tells them so."

It would be difficult to overstate the impact that this particular doctrine has had on our nation. A December 2017 poll of American evangelical Christians found the following:

- 67 percent have a positive perception of Israel.
- 80 percent believe that the 1948 establishment of the State of Israel was the fulfillment of biblical prophecy that shows that the Second Coming is nearing.
- 80 percent agree that God's promise to Abraham and his [literal] descendants is eternal.

---

[397] Ibid.

- 41 percent disagree that the Christian Church has fulfilled or replaced the nation of Israel in God's plan.
- 69 percent agree that the Jewish people have a historic right to the land of Palestine.
- 51 percent disagree that the Jewish people lost the promised land by rejecting Christ.
- 63 percent disagree that biblical passages about the Jewish right to the promised land do not apply today.
- 76 percent agree that Christians should support the Jewish right to live in the State of Israel.
- 24 percent support the State of Israel *no matter what.*
- 24 percent believe that the United States does not do enough for the State of Israel, while 31 percent believe that America provides Israel the correct amount of support now.
- 45 percent say that the Bible has most influenced their opinions on Israel
- 51 percent of those who have never traveled to Israel are very interested in doing so.[398]

A vast array of Christian Zionist organizations have convinced American Christians that they must "bless Israel with [their] donations," that they must lobby their government on behalf of the State of Israel, that they must write articles and letters whenever and wherever the State of Israel is criticized, that they must promote Israeli goods, that they must host pro-Israel events, and that anti-Zionism is anti-Semitism. The state of Florida recently passed a law (HB 741, 2019) prohibiting "anti-Semitic discrimination" or speech at state educational institutions; in the bill, "anti-Semitism" is defined as:

> Making mendacious, dehumanizing, demonizing, or stereotypical allegations about Jews . . . or the power of Jews as a collective, especially . . . the myth about a world Jewish conspiracy or of Jews controlling the media, economy, government or other societal institutions . . . accusing Jews . . . or the State of Israel of inventing or exaggerating the Holocaust . . . using the symbols and images associated with classic anti-Semitism, e.g., claims of Jews killing Jesus or blood libel . . . accusing Jewish citizens of being more loyal to Israel.

[398] Smietana, "Millennial Evangelicals on Israel."

The bill defines “anti-Semitism related to Israel” as

> [B]laming Israel for all inter-religious or political tensions . . . applying a double standard to Israel by requiring behavior of Israel that is not expected or demanded of any other democratic nation . . . delegitimizing Israel by denying the Jewish people their right . . . and denying Israel the right to exist.

Florida Governor DeSantis signed the bill into law at a ceremony in Jerusalem. At the time of writing, twenty-six other states have followed suit in some form or other; there will certainly be more.

In December 2019, President Trump followed suit, signing an executive order which deems Jews as a protected group under Title VI of the 1964 Civil Rights Act; in the executive order, the aforementioned definition of “anti-Semitism” was employed—the same definition, we must add, adopted by the Department of State. This is the definition promulgated by the International Holocaust Remembrance Alliance. In recent years, hundreds of representatives and senators have co-sponsored bills that would deem boycotts of Israel a federal felony. In one case, a children’s speech pathologist was fired from the public-school system of Austin, Texas, because she refused to sign an oath swearing that she “does not” and “will not” boycott the State of Israel. Keith Preston notes that

> The full force of the state is being weaponized for such purposes, including the withholding of funding for routine government services . . . professional sanctions and threats of termination of employment, and even criminal law . . . a phenomenon . . . where compulsory fealty to a foreign state is being mandated.[399]

So-called “solidarity tours” transport hundreds of thousands of American Christians to “the Holy Land” each year. On these tours, the Holocaust Museum is a key destination, serving to “remind those who come that Christians are guilty of

---

[399] Preston, “Zionism and the Power Elite.”

perpetrating the Holocaust, and to represent Israel as a victim."[400] These tours are planned by the Israeli government and:

> [F]ocus on the religious and political significance of contemporary Israel with speakers from the Israeli government and visits to the settlements to reinforce Israel's claim to the land and place in prophecy.[401]

Sizer notes that nearly all of these tours:

> [F]ail to make any contact with the indigenous Christian community. . . . The principal motivation among Christian Zionists for visiting the Holy Land is primarily to bring a blessing to the Jewish people, especially the settlers . . . to show solidarity with the State of Israel and witness the literal fulfilment of Biblical prophecy. . . . With greater contact occurring between Western Christians and the State of Israel, Christian Zionists return home galvanized in their support for agencies encouraging Jewish people to make *aliyah* [the return of global Jewry to Israel] and claim their inheritance.[402]

Christian Zionists have twisted the Scripture to read that it is the utmost duty of Christians to financially and militarily support the State of Israel, no matter the cost. Hundreds of organizations are singularly devoted to lobbying for the Israeli government; one, the Christian Israel Public Affairs Committee (CIPAC), modeled on the infamous American Israel Public Affairs Committee (AIPAC), was founded by Ed McAteer, founder of the Religious Roundtable. In December 2017, President Trump, whose son-in-law Jared Kushner, along with much of the Trump's inner circle, is Jewish, recognized Jerusalem as the capital of Israel. Trump moved the American embassy from Tel Aviv to Jerusalem, and at its May 2018 dedication invited the Christian Zionist Robert Jeffress to give the opening prayer. Jeffress, pastor of the fourteen-thousand-member First Baptist Church in Dallas, firmly believes that the

---

[400] Sizer, *Christian Zionism*, 207.
[401] Ibid., 208.
[402] Ibid.

city is "the touchstone of prophecy," and that "most importantly, God gave Jerusalem—and the rest of the Holy Land—to the Jewish people."

A large part of Christian Zionist fundraising, and especially that of televangelists, is aimed at the facilitation of *aliyah*; Sizer notes:

> [Christian Zionists have] facilitated one of the largest mass migrations of people since 1948. Raising tens of millions of dollars, they have assisted many of the seven hundred thousand Jewish émigrés from the former Soviet Union and Eastern Europe to make *Aliyah* [and settle in the Occupied Territories].[403]

A substantial amount of fundraising is also directed to these settlements by means of "adopt-a-settlement" programs, through which financial and material support is delivered, including such equipment as bulletproof vests, armored vehicles, and medical and school supplies. Christian Zionist donations are also used to prop up otherwise unsustainable ventures like farms. Hundreds of millions of dollars have also been injected into quixotic schemes that entail the design and construction of the Temple, the training of its priests, and the breeding of sacrificial animals like the red heifer; one of these "temple funds" was founded by a member of the terrorist Stern Gang. All of this money is raised through television, radio, and churches, raping the Scripture to siphon off the lifeblood of American Christians to those who hate us.

It is important that we recall that a form of nascent Christian Zionism predated Jewish Zionism by at least sixty years. Without the work of British Christian statesmen and evangelists in the nineteenth century, the Jewish Zionist dream would not have materialized. Similarly, Christian Zionists, and the American security state apparatus, have proved indispensable in propping up the Israeli government and furthering its otherwise untenable occupation of the West Bank, largely funded through the voluntary donations of evangelicals and the involuntary taxation of American citizens. The United

---

[403] Ibid., 224.

States has taken the mantle of Zionist berserker from Britain. Falwell told us that "God has been kind to America because America has been kind to the Jew."[404] We are told that "Israel is the key to America's survival. . . . If Israel falls, the United States can no longer remain a democracy."[405]

Christians have been brainwashed into believing that America and the State of Israel have inextricably linked twin destinies, that the State of Israel is the lynchpin of our salvation. Christian Zionists argue:

> Peril awaits those who presume to say that God is finished with His chosen people. . . . Just as God judged the nation of Egypt for her ill treatment of His people, so will He judge nations today.[406]

Financial criminal Jim Staley stated that "opposition to Israel is opposition to God." Senator Ted Cruz declared that "those who hate Israel hate America. Those who hate Jews hate Christians." Robertson warned us that if our nation does not support the State of Israel unconditionally, "we are going to see the wrath of God fall on this nation that will make tornadoes look like a Sunday school picnic."[407] To this, our only response must be that thus far, our deification and worship of Israel has not *blessed* our nation, but has rather irredeemably *destroyed* it.

---

[404] Ibid., 120.
[405] Ibid.
[406] Ibid., 250.
[407] Ibid., 251.

6

The Myth of Judeo-Christianity

We are bombarded from cradle to grave with gobbledygook about America's great "Judeo-Christian" heritage and our magnificent "Judeo-Christian" Founding. To these claims, we must state definitively that they are fantasies. There was no "Judeo-Christian" Founding, nor do we share a heritage with the Jews. There was only a Christian Founding of a Christian America, steeped in a European Christian heritage. "Judeo-Christianity" thus serves as nothing but a vehicle for the Jew to insert himself into our history, to vitiate any notion of a Christian America, to have us believe that we owe just as much to him as we do our European forebears, to further perpetuate the myth that we share a destiny; this is the myth by which he latches on to our minds as a fungal cordyceps, exploiting our labor for his benefit until finally he is risen and we are expended, dead in a ditch.

When Mark Levin asserts that the American Founding was rooted in "Judeo-Christian beliefs and values," when John Hagee says that "America was founded when our Pilgrims landed, and they made a covenant with God," thereby implying a kinship between American Christians and the Jews of the Old Testament, they are simply lying. While the American colonists certainly did make metaphorical parallels with Old Testament Israelites, seeing the Arcadian idyll and their nascent nation as a "new Israel," this does not mean that Judaism played any role in the Founding. Neither does it mean that the early Americans felt any affinity for Judaism; furthermore, even if they did feel an intimacy with the Jews of the Old Testament, those Israelites of yore were not the rabbinical Jews of the eighteenth century, let alone today. When Ben Shapiro referred to Notre-Dame as "a central monument to Western civilization, which was built on the Judeo-Christian heritage," he was engaging in cultural plunder.

Vernon Thorpe dispelled that particular act of appropriation by noting that, as the Israeli *Haaretz* reported, during the period that Notre-Dame was built, the Jews were expelled from France twice.[408] On the gorgeous West Façade of Notre-Dame, below the Gallery of Kings, on both sides of the portico are adorned the figures of Ecclesia and Synagoga. The statues represent the biblical truth that *all* of our forefathers knew, the doctrine of supersession. Ecclesia, representing the Church, stands tall and proud with crown and scepter. Synagoga, the Synagogue, hangs her head, a menacing, fangs-bared snake wrapped around her eyes, blinding her. In her hand are the tablets of the Law, falling from her grasp, and a crown crushed at her feet. Judaism was crushed, blinded, and defeated. The new superseded and replaced the old, as Christianity reigned triumphant over prostrate Judaism. One prominent Zionist, the rabbi Shlomo Aviner, celebrated the destruction of Notre-Dame as divine retribution for the thirteenth-century Disputation of Paris, in which thousands of copies of the Talmud were burned; the rabbi wrote that the destruction of the cathedral demonstrated that "there is justice and there is a Judge."

The origin of the term "Judeo-Christian" is unknown, but its early uses did not signify the meaning that it has come to today. Arthur Cohen traces the concept back to a "Christo-Jewish" tradition targeted by Enlightenment rationalism, wherein Christianity was assailed; Cohen argues that "it could not be helped that in the attack on Christianity Judaism should suffer, for Christianity depended upon Judaism for the internal logic of its history."[409] However, we must state that the implied claim that Judaism is the faith of the Old

---

[408] Thorpe, "Ben Shapiro and the Myth of the Judeo-Christian West."

[409] Cohen, "Myth of the Judeo-Christian Tradition."

Testament has no basis. Cohen also describes a nineteenth-century Christian disentanglement from Judaism as a purgative Christian attempt:

> [T]o demonstrate that what had been correctly denigrated by the Enlightenment was, in fact, the teaching of the ancient Jews whose additions to and alterations of the pure Hebrew vision corrupted the source of Christianity. . . . The Judaism which survives the onslaught of Protestant higher criticism is buried under a mountain of historicist formulations, while a pure, virtuous Kantian Christianity—freed from Jewish accretion—is defined.

Though Cohen's somewhat hollow claims here are unimportant for our purposes, what is to be taken away is that these early concepts of a "Judeo-Christian" tradition are attempts to emphasize or negate supposed theological continuity, and not to serve any political purpose. Ferdinand Christian Baur, in the tradition of higher criticism, employed the term for just that purpose—to examine theological continuity in light of his belief in supersessionism. In an 1821 letter, Alexander McCaul, an early London Jews' Society member, used the term to refer to Jewish converts to Christianity, and in 1829 Joseph Wolff used the term to describe a sort of amalgamated Christianity, retaining Jewish traditions for the purposes of Christian conversion.

Cohen does strike a note of truth, however, when he asserts:

> The renewal of the doctrine of the Judeo-Christian tradition . . . is a postwar phenomenon. Christianity has had a bad conscience and Jews seem justifiably content to pique it. Unfortunately, the penance which some Christians seem willing to perform and which some Jews seem anxious to exact, whatever its personal value, does not legitimate the creation of a "Judeo-Christian tradition."

Cohen thus correctly acknowledges "Judeo-Christianity" to be an American political invention, the product of an American Christian addiction "to proclaiming a tradition in which distinctions are fudged, diversities reconciled, differences overwhelmed by sloppy and sentimental approaches to falling in love after centuries of misunderstanding and estrangement." Thus, Cohen argues, as described by Raymond Apple of *The Jerusalem Post* that "the Judeo-Christian ethic is a myth produced by 'Christian guilt and Jewish neurasthenia,' to obscure the fact that Christians and Jews are 'theological enemies . . . living in the same street as neighbors.'"[410] In other words, there is a Christian tradition and a Jewish tradition, and never the twain shall meet.

As Cohen alluded to, the concept of "Judeo-Christian ethics" as a system of values is a modern invention; George Orwell may well have been one of the first to employ it, when in 1939 he wrote of "the Judaeo-Christian scheme of morals." Appropriating this language to describe the very character of the United States seems to have arisen during the 1940s as a political program in the context of the Second World War; Thorpe cites that the term

> [F]irst came into the public lexicon as a symbolic vehicle of liberal Jewish and Christian leaders . . . looking to signal their contempt for, and provide an alternative to, pro-Fascist sympathizers and anti-Semites in the United States who had mobilized around the term Christian. Specifically, the term Judeo-Christian was intended to include Jews as one of the three "fighting faiths" of democracy. During the war years, this new creed expressed a distinctive and essentially pluralist American religious faith that underpinned American democracy.

Thorpe speculates that, quite probably, the term served the Jewish interest to obscure the association of Judaism and Bolshevism, as it was more commonly known then that communism was a Jewish movement. Precursors of the National Conference of Christians and Jews organized three-man teams consisting of a Catholic priest, a rabbi, and a Protestant minister, to travel the country and promote "interfaith pluralism."

---

[410] Apple, "There is no 'Judeo-Christian' Tradition."

Thorpe points to noontime on December 22nd, 1952, as the "the precise day, nay, the precise hour, the term 'Judeo-Christian tradition' achieved its vaunted victory over the term, 'Christian tradition.'" President-elect Dwight Eisenhower declared that the American republic "is founded in a deeply-felt religious faith, and I don't care what it is. With us, of course, it is the Judeo-Christian concept, but it must be a religion that [teaches] all men are created equal." In one fell swoop, Eisenhower reconfigured the American Founding to be *Judeo*-Christian, an unprecedented and ahistorical superimposition. Our latter-day saint, Martin Luther King, Jr., who shares with Jesus Christ the honor of a federal holiday for his birthday, utilized "Judeo-Christian" as a way of grafting historical logic onto the Black Power movement. By the 1980s, the appellation of a Judeo-Christian heritage, having begun its life as a slogan of Jewish revolutionaries, had achieved mainstream status, such that it became a signature expression particularly among the religious right.

Thus, it is during this pivotal period of America's controlled demolition that "Judeo-Christian" became the standardized descriptor for the invidious liberalism which holds that Western values rest upon an "Abrahamic" consensus. Christ and the Bible, upon whose shoulders rested our nation, were shoved aside to make way for an intruder in their midst: the Jew. The Jew took a seat, and with it the credit due Christ alone. One pseudonymous author makes the fantastic observation that "Judeo-Christianity" is proceeding under the same revisionist banner as that mendacious canard "a nation of immigrants," manufactured to legitimize the Jewish coup consummated in the 1965 Hart-Celler Act, the final death knell of our nation and the pollination of our long fade to brown.[411] "Judeo-Christianity" was retroactively grafted over our history to abolish and rewrite our *Christian* Founding.

[411] VD, "'Judeo-Christian' is Anti-Christian."

7

Historical Christianity on Judaism

We must remember that Christianity has *always* been anti-Semitic. Christians have *always* known that God rejected the Jews for their rejection of him. Such luminaries as John Calvin, John Chrysostom, Martin Luther, Peter the Venerable, and Saint Augustine preached the truth about Judaism. For example, Chrysostom delivered eight homilies known as *Adversus Judaeos*, or *Against the Jews*, writing that Christians must "flee the gatherings and holy places of the Jews. Let no man venerate the synagogue because of the holy books; let him hate and avoid it because the Jews outrage and maltreat the holy ones," that "the Jews disdained the beauty of virginity," that "today the Jews, who are more dangerous than any wolves, are bent on surrounding my sheep; so, I must spar with them and fight with them so that no sheep of mine may fall victim to those wolves."[412] Chrysostom continues, saying:

> The difference between the Jews and us is not a small one, is it? Is the dispute between us over ordinary, everyday matters, so that you think the two religions are really one and the same? Why are you mixing what cannot be mixed? They crucified the Christ whom you adore as God. Do you see how great the difference is? How is it, then, that you keep running to those who slew Christ when you say that you worship him whom they crucified . . . ? The synagogue is worse than a brothel . . . it is the den of scoundrels and the repair of wild beasts . . . the

[412] Chrysostom, *Against the Jews*, 45.

> Temple of demons devoted to idolatrous cults . . . the refuge of brigands and debauchees, and the cavern of devils. It is a criminal assembly of Jews . . . a place of meeting for the assassins of Christ . . . a house worse than a drinking shop . . . a den of thieves, a house of ill fame, a dwelling of iniquity, the refuge of devils, a gulf and an abyss of perdition. . . . I would say the same things about their souls. . . . As for me, I hate the synagogue. . . . I hate the Jews for the same reason.[413]

Saint Augustine wrote that "the Jews can never understand the Scriptures and forever will bear the guilt for the death of Jesus," and Martin Luther chose to devote his very last sermon to the Jewish menace, preaching:

> They are our public enemies and incessantly blaspheme our Lord Jesus Christ, they call our Blessed Virgin Mary a harlot and her Holy Son a bastard and to us they give the epithet of changelings and abortions . . . their synagogues should be set on fire, and whatever does not burn up should be covered or spread over with dirt . . . their homes should likewise be broken down and destroyed. They should be deprived of their prayer-books and Talmuds in which such idolatry, lies, cursing, and blasphemy are taught.[414]

In 1543, Luther published *On the Jews and Their Lies*, exposing "the synagogue of Satan" and employing a strong biblical argument that Judaism is satanic. (2 Chron. 19:2, Rom. 2:28–29, 2 John 1:9–11, Rev. 2:9 and 3:9) One disturbing fact that has more recently come to light is the largely unknown origin of the Star of David, on which there is a strange scarcity of research and an unusual rabbinical reticence. (Acts 7:43, Amos 5:26–27)

In *On the Jews and Their Lies*, Luther breathed righteous fire. Luther knew that the Jews "boast of being the noblest, yes, the only noble people on earth. In comparison with them and in their eyes we Gentiles are not human; in fact, we hardly deserve to be considered poor worms by them." He saw that:

---

413 Ibid., 53.

414 Luther, *On the Jews*.

> The Jews will not give up their pride and boasting about their nobility and lineage . . . their hearts are hardened. Our people, however, must be on their guard against them, lest they be misled by this impenitent, accursed people who give God the lie and haughtily despise all the world. For the Jews would like to entice us Christians to their faith, and they do this wherever they can. . . . They are real liars and bloodhounds who have not only continually perverted and falsified all of Scripture with their mendacious glosses from the beginning until the present day. Their heart's most ardent sighing and yearning and hoping is set on the day on which they can deal with us Gentiles as they did with the Gentiles in Persia at the time of Esther. Oh, how fond they are of the book of Esther, which is so beautifully attuned to their bloodthirsty, vengeful, murderous yearning and hope. The sun has never shone on a more bloodthirsty and vengeful people than they are who imagine that they are God's people who have been commissioned and commanded to murder and to slay the Gentiles. In fact, the most important thing that they expect of their Messiah is that he will murder and kill the entire world with their sword. They treated us Christians in this manner at the very beginning throughout all the world. They would still like to do this if they had the power, and often enough have made the attempt, for which they have got their snouts boxed lustily.[415]

Luther wrote that "it became apparent that they were a defiled bride, yes, an incorrigible whore and an evil slut with whom God ever had to wrangle, scuffle, and fight."[416] He warned Christians, our European ancestors:

> Be on your guard against the Jews, knowing that wherever they have their synagogues, nothing is found but a den of devils in which sheer self-glory, conceit, lies, blasphemy, and defaming of God and men are practiced most maliciously and vehming his eyes on them . . . where you see or hear a Jew teaching, remember that you are hearing nothing but a venomous basilisk who poisons and kills people merrily by fasten-And with all this, they claim to be doing right. . . . A person who is unacquainted with the devil might wonder why they are so particularly hostile toward Christians. They have no reason to

---

[415] Ibid., 12.

[416] Ibid.

> act this way, since we show them every kindness. They live among us, enjoy our shield and protection, they use our country and our highways, our markets and streets. Meanwhile our princes and rulers sit there and snore with mouths hanging open and permit the Jews to take, steal, and rob from their open money bags and treasures whatever they want. That is, they let the Jews, by means of their usury, skin and fleece them and their subjects and make them beggars with their own money. For the Jews, who are exiles, should really have nothing, and whatever they have must surely be our property. They do not work, and they do not earn anything from us, nor do we give or present it to them, and yet they are in possession of our money and goods and are our masters in our own country and in their exile. A thief is condemned to hang for the theft of ten florins, and if he robs anyone on the highway, he forfeits his head. But when a Jew steals and robs ten tons of gold through his usury, he is more highly esteemed than God himself.[417]

Luther was wise to Judaism, noting that the Talmud regards murder, theft, and usury as sins only when the victim is a fellow Jew—Gentiles are fair game. He did limit his inquiry, however, noting that a refutation of every article of Jewish teaching would oblige him "to write against them as much and for as long a time as they have used for inventing their lies—that is, longer than two thousand years."[418] He answered potential detractors by stating:

> Someone may think that I am saying too much. I am not saying too much, but too little—for I see their writings. They curse us *Goyim*. In their synagogues and in their prayers, they wish us every misfortune. They rob us of our money and goods through their usury, and they play on us every wicked trick they can. And the worst of it is that they still claim to have done right and well, that is, to have done God a service. And they teach the doing of such things. No pagan ever acted thus.[419]

---

[417] Ibid., 36.
[418] Ibid.
[419] Ibid., 61.

On Jewish deconstruction and critique, practiced widely in Western academia today, Luther remarked that "this is the way the Jews tear apart the text wherever they can, solely for the purpose of spoiling the words of Scripture for us Christians."[420] We must remember that Christianity is the only faith which permitted rational inquiry into itself; see the consequences we have thus reaped.

Luther asked:

> How does it happen that we poor Christians nourish and enrich such an idle and lazy people, such a useless, evil, pernicious people, such blasphemous enemies of God, receiving nothing in return but their curses and defamation and every misfortune they may inflict on us or wish us? Indeed, we are as blind and unfeeling clods in this respect as are the Jews in their unbelief, to suffer such great tyranny from these vicious weaklings, and not perceive and sense that they are our lords, yes, our mad tyrants, and that we are their captives and subjects. Meanwhile they wail that they are our captives, and at the same time mock us—as though we had to take this from them . . . ! If they are caught in the act or charged with something, they are bold enough to deny it impudently, even to the point of death, since they do not regard us worthy of being told the truth. In fact, these holy children of God consider any harm they can wish or inflict on us as a great service to God. Indeed, if they had the power to do to us what we are able to do to them, not one of us would live for an hour. But since they lack the power to do this publicly, they remain our daily murderers and bloodthirsty foes in their hearts. Their prayers and curses furnish evidence of that, as do the many stories which relate their torturing of children and all sorts of crimes for which they have often been burned at the stake or banished. Therefore, I firmly believe that they say and practice far worse things secretly than the histories and others record about them, meanwhile relying on their denials and on their money.[421]

[420] Ibid.

[421] Ibid., 148.

As we no doubt understand by now, Luther, if he "had power over the Jews . . . would deal severely with their lying mouths."[422]

[422] Ibid.

8

Jewish Hatred for Christianity, and for Gentiles Generally

We must note at the outset, categorically, that Judaism is *not* the religion practiced by the Jews of the Old Testament. What goes by the name Judaism today is rabbinical, or Talmudic, Judaism. Quite importantly, this means that Christianity predates Judaism. Our exploration of the Jewish religion is limited solely to its teachings on Christianity and on all non-Jews. In this respect, it is important to note that while Judaism reserves a very special hatred for Christianity, its texts are suffused with an extraordinarily visceral animosity toward *all* Gentiles. We must also remember that the West is traditionally Christian; to reiterate, then, do not believe that merely because Whites are losing (or rather have already lost) their Christian faith, Jewish hatred toward them has slackened. It most assuredly is not.

Christian, and by extension Western, ignorance of Judaism is the greatest strength that international Jewry may claim. This is a major reason, along with Christian Zionism, for "the substitution of Auschwitz for Calvary,"[423] as Michael Hoffman has so wonderfully described it. Hoffman also notes that

> One encounters in almost any "conservative Christian" bookstore in America shelves groaning under the weight of tomes purporting to boldly unmask the religion of Islam, but not one slim volume will be found delving into the depravities of Orthodox Judaism, the religion which is the self-confessed

---

[423] Hoffman, *Judaism's Strange Gods*, 106.

> ideological and spiritual heir of the Pharisees who persecuted Jesus Christ.[424]

Israel Shahak has quite tellingly observed:

> The crude accusation of "anti-Semitism" against anybody who . . . points out any fact about the Jewish religion or the Jewish past which conflicts with the "approved version" comes with greater hostility and force from non-Jewish "friends of the Jews" than from Jews.[425]

Contrary to popular understanding in the United States, Judaism is *not* based on the Old Testament. In fact, the "Torah" that Jews claim is *not* merely the Torah that we understand as the Old Testament, but rather includes previously oral traditions of the Pharisees. The Old Testament, when read at all, is understood *through* the Talmud, which is supreme over it; thus, the Old Testament that we know is something entirely different from the Old Testament known by Jews. For example, the Talmud teaches that Adam had bestial intercourse with "all of the animals in Eden," and that Eve copulated with the snake, identified as Satan. To the Jew, the Old Testament is a negligible relic that is useful only insofar as it can be twisted and distorted. The Talmud, and its concomitant Jewish texts, are a vast accumulation of rabbinical commentaries compiled hundreds of years *after* the resurrection of Christ. It is the central literary work of Judaism, developed in parallel, with the Palestinian version edited in the fifth century and the much more significant Babylonian version edited in the early seventh century. As Rabbi Jacob Neusner put it, "The Talmud is the prism, receiving, refracting all light . . . into that writing all prior canonical writings emerged; to it, all appeal is directed; upon it, all conclusions ultimately rest."[426]

Alexander McCaul wrote, nearly two hundred years ago, that "modern Judaism is the religion of the oral law. The dogmas, rites, ceremonies, and prayers, all rest upon its authority

---

[424] Hoffman, *Judaism's Strange Gods*, "Preface."
[425] Shahak, *Jewish History*, 30.
[426] Quoted in Hoffman, *Judaism's Strange Gods*, 80.

. . . the Jews have been more than eighteen centuries the disciples of error."[427] Though the Talmud is totally comprehensive and rigidly dogmatic, it lends itself to infinite development without any alteration to its core, for it is a case study in multiplicity—to each verse is attached endless loopholes for all occasions. Jewish morality is thus almost always relative. Things are never what they appear to be in the Talmud or other Jewish texts; behind each seemingly objective statement is a multiverse of, as Hoffman writes, "internal modifications, loopholes and escape clauses. These are made possible because Judaism is two-tiered: the face it presents to the Gentile world and the face it presents to fellow [Jews]."[428] The universal loophole is that any and every command and injunction may be broken whenever necessary to assist the Jewish people. As McCaul put it, "Judaism has for its authors wicked men, unworthy of credit."[429] We must remember that Christ called the Pharisees a "generation of vipers," later continuing, "Woe unto you, scribes and Pharisees, hypocrites! for ye are like unto whited sepulchres, which indeed appear beautiful outward, but are within full of dead men's bones, and of all uncleanness." (Matt. 12:34 and 23:27)

Let us begin with the Talmudic teachings regarding Christ. According to the Talmudic account, there was no virgin birth; Jesus was a bastard, conceived during menstruation, the "son of a whore," "the prostitute's son," as Mary, referred to as "excrement," "played the harlot with carpenters." Christ's father is portrayed as a common Roman centurion, the story of the virgin birth merely her cover to conceal her promiscuity from Joseph. Jews thus most emphatically do *not* believe that Jesus Christ was the Messiah, let alone the Son of God. One version of the Talmudic account was recapitulated by the Neoplatonic pagan philosopher, Celsus:

> Jesus came from a Jewish village and from a poor country woman who earned her living by spinning. . . . She was driven out by her husband, who was a carpenter by trade, as she was

[427] McCaul, *Talmud Tested*, 81.
[428] Hoffman, *Judaism's Strange Gods*.
[429] McCaul, *Talmud Tested*, 210.

> convicted of adultery. . . . After she had been driven out by her husband and while she was wandering about in a disgraceful way she secretly gave birth to Jesus. . . . Because Jesus was poor he hired himself out as a workman in Egypt, and there tried his hand at certain magical powers on which the Egyptians pride themselves; he returned full of conceit, because of these powers, and on account of them gave himself the title of God.[430]

Jesus is also portrayed as a "frivolous disciple," who was rebuked by his rabbi for his sexually scurrilous thoughts; in retaliation, Christ became apostate and established the cult that became known as Christianity. This "cult" was characterized by, according to the Talmudic account, cannibalistic and infanticidal sexual orgies. The Talmud further suggests that Christ was married to Mary Magdalene and that he was an adulterous sexual deviant. Orthodox Jews today refer to "that sick bastard, Jesus."

The biblical account of the crucifixion and resurrection are wholly subverted and mocked by the Talmudic account. In the Bible, after Christ's arrest, he is presented before the Roman Governor, Pontius Pilate. It is heavily implied that Pilate and his wife know exactly who Christ is, that they know that Jesus is the Messiah, the Son of God. It was common custom to release a prisoner for Passover, based on popular will, and so Pilate presented the Jewish mob with the choice of releasing Jesus Christ or releasing Barabbas, whom some early Church figures refer to as Jesus Bar Abbas; if indeed the latter was Barabbas' full name, this indicates that he was the son of an influential rabbi. Barabbas was described as both a thief and a murderous insurgent. Leading rabbis persuaded the Jewish crowd, who, it must be noted, appear to have needed little persuasion, to choose Barabbas over Christ. The bloodthirsty horde cried, "Crucify him." Pilate, who wanted to release Jesus, asked the mob to exculpate him from responsibility for his crucifixion, to which they gladly agreed, declaring that "His blood be on us, and our children." Pilate then "delivered Jesus to their will." (John 18:38–19:16) Interestingly, the pariah

---

[430] Origen, *Contra Celsum*, 105.

of Jewish Hollywood is Mel Gibson, whose 2004 film, *The Passion of the Christ*, unabashedly shows the foregoing biblical narrative.

According to the Talmud, Jesus was a blasphemous and idolatrous sorcerer, having learned black magic in Egypt, who was rightfully tried and executed; in other words, Jews believe that Jesus *got exactly what he deserved.* As Alexander McCaul elucidates, "They think that if Jesus . . . had been the true Messiah, that the Sanhedrin, the great Jewish council of the time, would have acknowledged him, and conclude that, as they rejected him, he cannot be the true Messiah."[431] Jesus "was not crucified but, according to Jewish law, stoned to death and then, as the ultimate postmortem punishment reserved for the worst criminals, hanged on a tree."[432] This took place on the eve of Passover, which was the eve of the Sabbath.

By the Jewish version of events, a herald announced his death sentence forty days prior to his execution, in order to allow witnesses to come forward and testify in his defense. Nobody came forward. What is the significance of this formulation? Peter Schäfer explains:

> In emphasizing that the herald announced Jesus' execution, and not just immediately before it took place but precisely 40 days in advance, [the account] directly contradicts Jesus' own prediction. Why all this fuss about him playing the prophet by dramatically prophesying His trial, sentence, and death. . . . We all know, the Talmud counters, that He was going to be executed: because [the Jewish] court had made this decision in public proceedings . . . and moreover had sent out a herald to proclaim this sentence publicly 40 days before the execution (an unusually long period, not required), so that everybody could know it and, if necessary, had ample time to come up with exonerating evidence to prevent a wrong judgment. Hence, in providing the 40-day period [the Talmud] intends to expose Jesus once more as a swindler and false prophet who makes a fool of himself in claiming to predict what everybody already knew.[433]

---

[431] McCaul, *Talmud Tested*, 8.

[432] Ibid., 9.

[433] Schäfer, *Jesus in the Talmud*, 70.

Furthermore, the rabbis chose to transform the crucifixion into a stoning because crucifixion was a *Roman* punishment, while stoning furthers the narrative that Jesus was executed as just another Jewish heretic, rightfully punished by Jewish law. The Talmudic account gleefully exculpates Rome, noting that "although the Romans probably could not care less, we insisted. . . . We even convinced the Roman governor (or more precisely: forced him to accept) that this heretic and impostor needed to be executed—and we are proud of it." The Talmud gloats that Jesus was murdered so young, for "bloody and deceitful men shall not live out half their days." Christ, "the fool," is also portrayed as having been close to the Romans, something that could not be further from the truth.

The Talmudic account also contends that there was no resurrection, but that instead, Christ was buried in a "dirt heap . . . where they throw the dead bodies of dogs and asses," from which Christians exhumed and stole Christ's corpse. The message? That nothing remains of Jesus Christ or his teachings. Jesus is depicted as being punished in Gehinnom, the Jewish Hell, forever, along with his followers, all Christians. Schäfer notes that this sends a "strong message to his followers, telling them that they better give up any hope for an afterlife for themselves: as with their hero, there is no afterlife reserved for them; they will be punished in Gehinnom forever."[434] Jesus is described as sharing his position in Hell with the other archenemies of Judaism, Titus and Balaam. Titus is punished for his destruction of the Temple by being cremated, reassembled, and cremated *ad infinitum*, while Balaam is punished by perpetual immersion in scalding semen. As for Christ, the Talmud states that he is sitting forever in boiling excrement. If this is not purely malicious, as it most likely is, Schäfer offers two possible explanations for why *this* punishment was chosen.

First, it might be understood as an especially spiteful attack on Christ's statement "out of the heart proceed evil thoughts, murders, adulteries, fornications, thefts, false witness, blasphemies: These are the things which defile a man: but to eat

[434] Ibid., 90.

with unwashen hands defileth not a man." (Matt. 15:17–20) This had been his response to the question of why Christians did not follow the Pharisaic rules of food purification and ritual handwashing. Christ was essentially declaring that the rabbinical purity rules were meaningless, that what is important is not the purity of the hands or of the food, but the purity of the heart. This runs wholly counter to the essence of Judaism, for, as Shahak tells us, "Faith and beliefs play an extremely small part in classical Judaism. What is of prime importance is the ritual act, rather than the significance which that act is supposed to have or the belief attached to it."[435] It matters not if, while praying in the direction of the Temple, a Jew mentally directs his prayers to Satan. It is the act itself that is important, not the underlying meaning, if there even is one.

If the bizarre concept of being punished with boiling excrement is understood in this light, Schäfer argues that "the rabbinic counternarrative about Jesus' punishment would then ironically invert his attack on the Pharisaic purity." Schäfer speculates as to another possible interpretation of the Talmudic account, understood in light of the Eucharist. In this light, Schäfer explains that the Talmud posits:

> Jesus is dead and remains dead, and eating his flesh won't lead to life. Not only that those who follow his advice and eat his flesh will not live forever, as he has promised; rather, he is punished in the Netherworld forever and not granted the milder punishment of those who will be released after 12 months into merciful nonexistence. And the peak of irony: the initiator of this . . . heresy is appropriately punished by sitting in what his followers excrete, after allegedly having eaten him: excrement.[436]

Much of the Talmudic verses regarding Christ, Christians, and Gentiles more generally are written in a sort of roundabout code. This is by design; before the thirteenth century, Christian attacks on Judaism were not grounded in the Talmud, but rather in biblical argumentation. During the thirteenth

---

[435] Shahak, *Jewish History*, 35.
[436] Schäfer, *Jesus in the Talmud*, 93.

century, however, increased Jewish conversion to Christianity led to greater awareness within the Church of what the Talmud actually contained. The penalty for Jews who "inform" on Judaism to Christians, or any Gentiles, was brutal torture and eventual execution. Thus, direct attacks on the Talmud began after this period. Jews responded in a myriad of ways, one of which was simply to bribe corrupt churchmen.

Shahak described another response:

> [One of] surreptitious defiance, combined with outward compliance. . . . Talmudic passages directed against Christianity or against Gentiles had to go or to be modified. . . . A few of the most offensive passages were bodily removed from all editions printed in Europe after the mid-16th century. In all other passages, the expressions "Gentile," "non-Jew," "stranger" . . . were replaced by terms such as "idolater," "heathen," or even "Canaanite" or "Samaritan," terms which could be explained away but which a Jewish reader could recognize as euphemisms. . . . At the same time, lists of *Talmudic Omissions* were circulated in manuscript form, which explained all the new terms and pointed out all the omissions. . . . Following the establishment of the State of Israel, once the rabbis felt secure, all the offensive passages and expressions were restored without hesitation in all new editions.[437]

The Talmud holds that Jewish infidels, in which category are Jesus Christ and his followers, must be "exterminated with one's own hands." Rabbi Ovadia Yosef, a former Chief Rabbi of Israel, acknowledged that "in messianic times Jews would be more powerful than non-Jews and would then be obligated to conquer the land of Israel, to expel all non-Jews, and to destroy the idolatrous Christian churches."[438] He cautioned, however, that the messianic period had not yet arrived, and that as such, "Israel is not sufficiently strong to destroy Christian churches on its territory." When the time comes in which Christian churches can be obliterated without serious repercussions for Jews, Yosef considered it an obligation. How deep does this Christophobia go? Israeli educational authorities

---

[437] Shahak, *Jewish History*, 20.

[438] Shahak, *Jewish Fundamentalism in Israel*, 20.

actually removed the international plus (+) sign from its elementary schools' arithmetic textbooks, believing that this "cross" symbol might "religiously corrupt Jewish children." In place of the standard plus symbol was substituted a capital "T." Shahak noted, quite perceptively, that "if this substitution had been made by the Taliban in Afghanistan, by the Iranian regime, or by China during the Cultural Revolution, it would probably have been discussed at length."[439] Orthodox Jewish papers refuse to even print terms like "Red Cross."

Rabbi Shlomo Min-Hahar taught that "all Christians without exception hate the Jews and look forward to their deaths."[440] In a now-unavailable 1996 *Haaretz Magazine* article by Rami Rosen, discussed by Shahak, a plethora of evidence was detailed, exposing Jewish massacres of Christians which took place in the late ancient period into the early Middle Ages, as well as in sixteenth-century Poland. During the celebration of Purim, mock repetitions of the crucifixion are common. The Talmud teaches that, when passing by a Gentile cemetery, Jews *must* curse the mothers of the dead and otherwise disrespect the cemetery by spitting or by urination, practices that are still common today.

Shahak explains:

> In one of the first sections of the daily morning prayer, every devout Jew blesses [the Jewish] God for not making him a Gentile. The concluding section of the daily prayer opens with the statement: "We must praise the Lord of all . . . for not making us like [Gentiles] . . . for they bow down to vanity and nothingness and pray to a god that does not help. . . ." In the most important section of the weekday prayer . . . there is a special curse, originally directed against Christians. . . . "And may the apostates have no hope, and all the Christians perish instantly. . . ." Some time before the fourteenth century it was softened. . . . After the establishment of Israel, the process was reversed, and many newly printed prayer books reverted. . . . After 1967, several congregations . . . have restored the first version and now pray daily that the Christians "may perish instantly." This process of reversion happened in the period

[439] Ibid., 23.

[440] Ibid., 76.

> when the Catholic Church removed from its Good Friday service a prayer which asked the Lord to have mercy on Jews. . . . This prayer was thought by most Jewish leaders to be offensive and even anti-Semitic.[441]

Christianity is considered to be a blot on the earth to be totally exterminated, the apotheosis of idolatry, a condemnation not even bestowed upon Islam. Indeed, the Talmud has nicer things to say about Muhammad and the Qur'an than Christ and the New Testament. The very *name* of Jesus is the Jewish symbol for "all that is abominable," abbreviated as "may his name and memory be blotted out," and the Gospels are categorically banned from Israeli schools. The New Testament is abhorred, as evidenced by the Talmudic command that Jews *must* burn any New Testaments that they come across, publicly if possible. Burning and burying Bibles is indeed common practice to this day. In March 1980, for example, hundreds of New Testaments were ritually burnt in Jerusalem by an organization subsidized by the Israeli Ministry of Religions. A more recent example occurred in 2008, when the mayor of Or Yehuda ordered all New Testaments in the city to be gathered and burned. Churches in Israel are often vandalized in a phenomenon known as "price-tagging," with phrases such as "Jesus is garbage," "Jesus is dead," "Jesus was a monkey," "Death to Christians," and "Mary is a prostitute." In one church arson, the tag triumphantly declared that "the false gods will be eliminated." Christian clergymen are commonly spat upon. Crucifixes are routinely desecrated and urinated on. The Talmud compares Christian conversion to prostitution. Christians are said to be "allied with [the Jewish] Hell, and Christianity is worse than incest." Those who read the Gospels are "deniers of the Law," doomed to Gehinnom, to share the fate of Jesus Christ. Christian saints are called "fairies" and "whores."

When the Jewish Messiah arrives, the Talmud declares that he will destroy the Christians. The preeminent Talmudic rabbi and philosopher Maimonides taught that Christians should be killed, whenever possible. In the 1948 paroxysm of violence

---

[441] Shahak, *Jewish History*, 106.

that accompanied the establishment of the State of Israel, a Catholic priest reported that "Jewish soldiers broke down the doors of my church and robbed many precious and sacred objects. Then they threw the statues of Christ down into a nearby garden."[442] Christian sites were attacked on numerous occasions, with clergymen, nuns, and children being massacred. Christian missionaries are often attacked in Israel today, where proselytizing Christianity is forbidden. Israel's many atrocities committed against the Palestinians often claim Christian victims, whom the American media simply characterize as Muslims and disregard. Need we even mention the fact that Jewish Bolshevism totally annihilated Christianity from Eastern Europe, tearing churches asunder and raping and slaughtering clergymen and nuns, while synagogues remained untouched? Joseph Sobran quite incisively asked, "Might the Talmudic imprecations against Christ and Christians have helped form the Bolshevik Jews' anti-Christian animus? Did the Talmud help form the 'cultural framework' for the persecution of Christians, and for the eradication of Christian culture in America today?"

When Jews do admit to a moderated level of atavistic disdain for Christianity, they point to "Christian persecution." First, this is not an adequate explanation, for, as Shahak explains,

> Oriental Jewish rabbis, and to a lesser extent their followers who came from Muslim countries, wherein they were generally not persecuted by Christians, have expressed *more* hate of Christianity and its symbols than the fundamentalist European rabbis and their followers who were persecuted by Christians.[443]

The deep hatred for Christianity that pervades the Jewish religion may have been aggravated by past conflict, but it exists largely independent of this; it goes back to the earliest days of the Christian religion, when Christians were far outnumbered

---

[442] Weir, *Against Our Better Judgment*, 44.
[443] Shahak, *Jewish Fundamentalism*, 154.

by the Jews who persecuted them, and it is shared even by Jews who were never subject to Christian rulers.

Second, we must examine the nature of this "Christian persecution." As we shall soon see, Jews absolutely *loathe* non-Jews; this is clearly evidenced in Jewish religious texts. This total lack of sympathy for, or empathy with, non-Jews made them ideal tax collectors and enforcers for the ruling classes of whatever country they inhabited; Jews could be trusted to ruthlessly extract every last drop from the peasantry without any of the mercy and human sympathy that a Christian might show. This continues today, as the sociopathic financial elite demonstrated in the aftermath of the global financial crisis. Indeed, the Talmud strictly forbids a Jew to take any interest whatsoever on a loan made to another Jew, but ruthlessly usurious behavior was *commanded* when dealing with Gentiles. In other words, while usury is strictly forbidden in Christianity, for Jews "it is a religious duty to take as much interest as possible on a loan made to a Gentile."

Jews were the immediate faces of exploitation for the peasantry; as Shahak elaborates:

> The full weight of the Jewish religious laws against Gentiles fell upon the peasants. . . . These laws are suspended or mitigated in cases where it is feared that they might arouse dangerous hostility towards Jews; but the hostility of the peasants could be disregarded as ineffectual so long as the Jewish bailiff could shelter under the "peace" of a great lord.[444]

Thus, each of the periodic anti-Semitic peasant revolts was initiated from the grassroots, as an organic reaction; the ruling class was *always* aligned with Jewry, and thus state actors were virtually *never* organizers of these upswells. As Shahak remarks, "An enslaved peasant is transformed into a racist monster, if Jews profited from his state of slavery and exploitation."[445] We must recall the illuminating Polish proverb: "The Jew cries out in pain as he strikes you."

---

[444] Shahak, *Jewish History*, 63.
[445] Ibid., 73.

Though European Jews are often cast today as destitute serfs, this simply was never the case. Jewish society, composed of craftsmen, peddlers, and clerks, was decidedly urban, and any merchant or tradesmen was automatically better off than the Christian serfs who worked the soil. Judaism held agricultural labor in contempt—clearly, the charge of being "rootless cosmopolitans" was well earned. Indeed, one Talmudic verse states that "agriculture is the lowest form of labor." Hayim Bialik, Israel's national poet, has a very popular poem, *My Father*, still taught in Israeli schools; in this poem, Bialik describes his "saintly father" selling vodka to the besotted peasants, depicted as ignorant beasts of burden, in full accord with the Jewish religion. Aleksandr Solzhenitsyn documented "the extremely exploitative relationship between Jews and Slavic peasants in pre-revolutionary times, based on liquor-dealing and money-lending."

The "Christian persecutions" that are woven into the fabric of that bloody shirt which the Jew so loves to wave thus appear to have been anything *but* irrational. Indeed, it is remarkable that, across time and in all places, Jews are always stereotyped as exhibiting the same vices. This recurrence of the same evil attributes lends credibility to the notion that "several prominent themes of anti-Semitic writings have had a firm basis in the reality of Judaism as a group evolutionary strategy."[446] Jews have controlled every cultural, economic, and governmental institution, every lever of the American state, for at least a century.

The American middle class has been eviscerated and crushed underfoot, our productive industries decimated, our once-proud population reduced to debt-slavery and addiction. Recall the Sackler family of Purdue Pharma sneering at the OxyContin launch party that "the prescription blizzard will be so deep, dense, and white."[447] The United States have been brought to ruin, as a silent genocide erased the men and women who built our nation. Ron Unz has made the obvious connection, that "our population has been reduced to a

---

[446] MacDonald, *Separation and Its Discontents*, 33.

[447] Walters, "OxyContin maker expected a 'blizzard of prescriptions.'"

twenty-first century version of the drunken, ignorant, exploited, indebted, impoverished, and immiserated Slavic peasantry of the Jewish-dominated Pale of Settlement," noting the striking fact that the controlled demolition of America has coincided with the ascendance of the new Jewish ruling class.[448] Almost sixty percent of Americans possess less than a thousand dollars in savings.

We now proceed to examine the cornucopia of Talmudic teachings on Gentiles, which can be summarized as: *The Goyim Must Perish!* Non-Jews are essentially subhuman beasts of burden for their Jewish masters, with no intrinsic value to speak of. Before we go any further, however, we must answer the doubts that many readers may by now have entertained—surely, every Jew is not well-versed in the Talmud, right? Of course, this is correct, but it matters not, for the Talmud is the foundation of Jewish social and intellectual life, the undergirding for the culture that Jews are steeped in. Talmudic teachings regarding Gentiles explain much, if not all, of the florid hatred which the Jew feels for Whites.

As Ron Unz notes,

> it is important to keep in mind that until just a few generations ago, almost all European Jews were deeply Orthodox, and even today . . . the overwhelming majority of Jewish adults had Orthodox grand-parents. Highly distinctive cultural patterns and social attitudes can easily seep into a considerably wider population, especially one that remains ignorant of the origin of those sentiments, a condition enhancing their unrecognized influence. A religion based upon the principal of . . . "Hate Thy Neighbor" may be expected to have long-term cultural ripple effects that extend far beyond the direct community of the deeply pious. If nearly all Jews for a thousand or two thousand years were taught to feel a seething hatred toward all non-Jews and also developed an enormous infrastructure of cultural dishonesty to mask that attitude, it is difficult to believe that such an unfortunate history has had absolutely no consequences for our present-day world, or that of the relatively recent past.

---

[448] Unz, "American Pravda."

The skeptical reader might ask, "What about the rabbis you quote—surely these are decontextualized and cherry-picked fragments from fringe figures, right?" Wrong. These rabbis are some of the most important and influential leaders of Judaism, all of whom are explicitly or implicitly supported by the State of Israel, with honors and political protection, along with significant popular support from Israeli and American Jews. "When you reference *the* Talmud, aren't you generalizing?" When we reference *the* Talmud, we are referring to the vast corpus of rabbinical literature which constitutes both the Talmud *per se* and its associated Jewish religious texts. We simply call it *the* Talmud for the sake of convenience and comprehension.

Rabbi Menachem Schneerson gives us the best starting point, declaring that Gentiles are an entirely separate species. Schneerson was asked about the Talmudic injunction that, while Gentiles should be punished for infanticide of a Gentile, Jews should not be punished even for infanticide of a Jew. He responded:

> Why should a non-Jew be punished if he kills even a non-Jewish embryo while a Jew should not be punished even if he kills a Jewish embryo? The answer can be understood by [considering] the general difference between Jews and non-Jews: A Jew was not created as a means for some [other] purpose; he himself is the purpose, since the substance of all [divine] emanations was created only to serve the Jews. . . . [Everything] was created for the sake of the Jews, who are called the "beginning." This means everything, all developments, all discoveries, the creation, including the "heavens and the earth"—are vanity compared to the Jews. The important things are the Jews, because they do not exist for any [other] aim; they themselves are [the divine] aim . . . the embryo is not a self-contained reality, but rather is subsidiary; either it is subsidiary to its mother or to the reality created after birth when the [divine] purpose of its creation is then fulfilled. In its present state the purpose is still absent. A non-Jew's entire reality is only vanity. . . . The entire creation [of a Gentile] exists only for the sake of the Jews.[449]

---

[449] Quoted in Weir, *Against Our Better Judgment*.

This alarming statement is not even controversial to Jews. Indeed, Schneerson's birthday is commemorated every year in the United States as "Education and Sharing Day." At the behest of Congress, Jimmy Carter designated the holiday in 1978. In 1994, Schneerson was posthumously awarded the Congressional Gold Medal.

This raises two points. First, there is no Jewish restriction on infanticide; indeed, to murder Gentile children is encouraged. The fetus is "mere water" and is "not a person." Gentile children are viewed as nascent threats, and rabbis thus authorize that they be "chopped up in the womb." Maimonides wrote that "the fetus is . . . pursuing her to kill her. . . . It is permitted to dismember the fetus within her, either by drugs or surgery." Isser Unterman, a former Chief Rabbi of Israel, said that "the fetus before birth need not be protected and his status renders abortion not murder." Another Chief Rabbi of Israel, Ben-Zion Uziel, stated that "it is clear that abortion is not permitted without reason. . . . But for a reason, even if it is a slim reason . . . then we have precedent and authority to permit it." Rabbi Yitzhak Shapira, who urged Israel Defense Forces soldiers to use Palestinians as human shields, claiming that it was against "true Jewish values" for a soldier to endanger his life for the sake of enemy soldiers or civilians, wrote that "there is justification for killing babies if it is clear that they will grow up to harm us, and in such a situation they may be harmed deliberately, and not only during combat with adults."

The second point is that Gentiles are considered to be subhuman animals whose very existence is to serve their Jewish masters. Servitude, indeed slavery, is considered to be the natural state of Gentiles. Jews historically played a major role in the international slave trade. White lives simply do not matter; if they do have any modicum of value, it is only that value which Jews can extract and exploit. As one rabbi proclaimed, "A thousand non-Jewish lives are not worth a Jew's fingernail."

As American-born Rabbi Yitzchak Ginsburgh says:

> If you saw two people drowning, a Jew and a non-Jew, the Torah says you save the Jewish life first. If every single cell in a

> Jewish body entails divinity, and is thus part of [the Jewish] God, then every strand of DNA is a part of [the Jewish] God. Therefore, something is special about Jewish DNA.[450]

Ginsburgh has written that "a Jew's killing non-Jews does not constitute murder according to the Jewish religion and that killing innocent [Gentiles] for reasons of revenge is a Jewish virtue."[451] Gentiles are considered to be satanic, literally "limbs of Satan," their defective souls "called evil, not good, and are created without [divine] knowledge." According to the Kabbalah, Jewish converts are in fact:

> Jewish souls consigned firstly to non-Jewish bodies as punishments and later redeemed by conversion to Judaism either because the punishment ended or because a holy man interceded. . . . A satanic soul cannot be transformed into a divine soul by mere persuasion.

None of this stands in conflict with "the Torah," for the Talmud relativizes the Old Testament such that it only addresses the Jews. Thus, for example, the Eighth Commandment, "Thou shalt not steal," is taken to be:

> A prohibition against . . . kidnapping a *Jewish person*. . . . According to the Talmud all acts forbidden by the Decalogue are capital offenses. Stealing property is not a capital offense, while the kidnapping of Gentiles by Jews is allowed by Talmudic law.[452]

The command, "Thou shalt not follow a multitude to do evil; neither shalt thou speak in a cause to decline after many to wrest judgment," is twisted into its exact opposite meaning, ripped out of context and interpreted as "an injunction to follow the majority." General biblical terms such as "thy fellow," "stranger," and "man," are recast in terms of Jewish exclusionism and separatism. For example, the command that "thou shalt love thy neighbour as thyself" is understood as a

---

450 Shahak, *Jewish Fundamentalism*, 63.
451 Alexis, *Christianity and Rabbinic Judaism*, 296.
452 Shahak, *Jewish History*, 36.

command to "love one's fellow *Jew*, not any fellow human." (Lev. 19:18) The injunction that "neither shalt thou stand against the blood of thy neighbour" is understood to mean that "one must not stand idly by when the life of a fellow *Jew* is in danger, [but] a Jew is in general forbidden to save the life of a Gentile, because 'he is not thy fellow.'" (Lev. 19:16)

The generous injunction against gleaning for oneself, that "thou shalt not glean thy vineyard, neither shalt thou gather every grape of thy vineyard; thou shalt leave them for the poor and stranger," is reinterpreted to refer exclusively to the *Jewish* poor and the *Jewish* stranger. (Lev. 19:10) The Sixth Commandment, "Thou shalt not kill," does not apply to the murder of a Gentile, for Gentiles are not human. The taboos related to corpses are dealt with in the same manner; as Shahak elaborates, "the word 'man' is taken to mean 'Jew,' so that only a Jewish corpse is taboo. . . . Pious Jews have a tremendous magic reverence towards Jewish corpses and Jewish cemeteries, but have no respect towards non-Jewish corpses and cemeteries."[453] This lack of reverence toward dead Gentiles can be seen in the repeated destruction of Muslim cemeteries, which are often razed so that condos and Hilton hotels can be constructed to house the Jewish occupiers.

Even the chillingly minimal prohibition on directly murdering a Gentile applies only to "Gentiles with whom [the Jews] are not at war," leading to the logical conclusion that in wartime, or rather any period of hostility, all Gentiles—men, women, and children—not only *can* be killed, but *must* be. IDF medics are ordered "to withhold medical help from 'Gentile wounded.'" The chaplain of the IDF Central Area Command, which includes the West Bank, wrote in a standard-issue booklet:

> When our forces come across civilians during a war or in hot pursuit or in a raid, so long as there is no certainty that those civilians are incapable of harming our forces, then . . . they may and even should be killed. . . . In war, when our forces

---

[453] Ibid., 36.

> storm the enemy, they are allowed and even enjoined . . . to kill even . . . civilians who are ostensibly good.[454]

Minnesota-based rabbi Manis Friedman agreed, saying:

> I don't believe in Western morality, i.e. don't kill civilians or children, don't destroy holy sites. . . . The only way to fight a moral war is the Jewish way: Destroy their holy sites. Kill men, women, and children. And cattle.[455]

Even when not engaged in a period of hostilities, rabbinical commentaries declare, "The best of Gentiles—kill him; the best of snakes—dash out its brains." The Talmud teaches that "Gentiles who fall into a well should not be helped out, but neither should they be pushed into the well to be killed, which means that they should neither be saved from death nor killed directly."[456] Gentiles are "neither to be lifted out of the well nor hauled down into it." Maimonides wrote that Jews should "show no mercy to a non-Jew. If we see a non-Jew being swept away or drowning in the river, we should not help him. If we see that his life is in danger, we should not save him." As we have seen, there is a "wartime" exception, as well as the universal loophole, the exception to everything, that *anything goes if a Jew might stand to benefit*. Indeed, Shahak explains that "the duty to save the life of a fellow Jew is paramount. It supersedes all other religious obligations and interdictions. . . . As for Gentiles, the basic Talmudic principle is that their lives *must not* be saved."[457] Rabbi Eleazar ben Shammua wrote that "it is lawful to split open the nostrils" of a Gentile, and other Talmudic verses confirm that "it is lawful to rend [a Gentile] like a fish."

Jews are forbidden to do anything that might even tangentially benefit a Gentile, including giving them good advice, though, of course, there is an exception; Jews may assist Gentiles if their refusal would engender hostility toward Judaism.

---

[454] Ibid., 76.

[455] Vezner, "St. Paul rabbi's comments spark outrage."

[456] Shahak, *Jewish History*, 78.

[457] Ibid., 80.

Maimonides, who also served as the personal physician for Saladin, wrote that "it is forbidden to heal a Gentile even for payment, but if you fear him or his hostility, cure him for payment, though you are forbidden to do so without payment," though it is allowed "even *gratis*, if it is unavoidable." Incidentally, Maimonides wrote that "it is permissible to try out a drug on a heathen, if it serves a purpose." There is an exception to this exception, however—the Sabbath. Shahak notes:

> The provision that a Gentile may be saved or cared for in order to avert the danger of hostility is curtailed on the Sabbath. A Jew called upon to help a Gentile on a weekday may have to comply because to admit that he is not allowed, in principle, to save the life of a non-Jew would be to invite hostility. But . . . the Jew can use Sabbath observance as a plausible excuse. A paradigmatic case . . . in the Talmud is that of a Jewish midwife invited to help a Gentile woman in childbirth . . . the midwife is allowed to help on a weekday "for fear of hostility," but on the Sabbath she must not do so.[458]

Indeed, the Talmud forbids any Jew to help "multiply the seed" of Gentiles; in other words, Gentile reproduction, and thus Gentile children, must be eliminated. If the Sabbath excuse does not work, Jews are urged to employ whatever other excuses might be necessary; the point is to let the Gentile suffer. If aid is unavoidable, Jews may help Gentiles *only* if the Jew does so with the sole intent of protecting himself and the Jewish people from retaliation. For example, in light of the historical Jewish dependence on ruling classes, Shahak noted that "Jewish doctors, who are in general forbidden to save the lives of ordinary Gentiles . . . are commanded to do their utmost in healing magnates and rulers."[459]

This does not violate any Talmudic command of honesty, for there isn't one. Indeed, the Yom Kippur rite of *Kol Nidrei* dissolves all vows that a Jew will make for the *coming* year; Jews may lie at any time about anything, provided that some thin veneer of justification exists in the Jewish interest. This

---

[458] Ibid., 82.
[459] Ibid., 56.

rite nullifies and voids not only those vows made to men, but also vows made to the Jewish God. One verse reads:

> If any man swear a rash oath, and afterwards repent of it, because he sees that if he keeps this oath it will cause him grief, and therefore changes his mind . . . behold, a person, in such circumstances, is to ask one [rabbi], or three common men in any place where there is not a wise man, and they absolve him from his oath; and then it will be lawful to do a thing which he had sworn not to do, or to leave undone a thing which he had sworn to do: and this is what is called absolution from oaths.[460]

Jews are only allowed to break the Sabbath if they are absolutely certain that a Jew is in danger. Shahak personally witnessed "an ultra-religious Jew refuse to allow his phone to be used on the Sabbath in order to call an ambulance for a non-Jew who happened to have collapsed in his Jerusalem neighborhood."[461] When he brought his complaint before the Rabbinical Court of Jerusalem, the court ruled that "a Jew should not violate the Sabbath in order to save the life of a Gentile . . . [but] if the consequences of such an act puts Jews in danger, the violation of the Sabbath is permitted, for their sake."[462]

Israel is an apartheid state, an explicit Jewish ethnostate in which Gentiles are legally inferior. As Shahak observed, "I suspect that the Jews of the United States . . . would regard it as anti-Semitic if Christians would propose that America . . . should become a 'Christian state,' belonging only to citizens officially defined as 'Christians.'" In 1985, the Israeli Knesset passed a Constitutional Law that "no party whose program openly opposes the principle of 'a Jewish state,' or proposes to change it by democratic means, is allowed to participate in the elections to the Knesset." Rabbi Zalman Melamed said, quite accurately, that "no rabbinical authority disputes that it would be ideal if the land of Israel were inhabited by only Jews."[463] Mordechai Nisan, an Israeli professor and

---

[460] McCaul, *Talmud Tested*, 435.
[461] Shahak, *Jewish Fundamentalism*, 33.
[462] Ibid., 34.
[463] Ibid., 73.

member of the World Zionist Organization, stated that Gentiles permitted to live in Israel "must accept paying a tax and suffering the humiliation of servitude."[464] If Gentiles "refuse to live a life of inferiority, then this signals their rebellion and the unavoidable necessity of Jewish warfare against their very presence in the land of Israel."

The Talmud holds that "Jews must not . . . allow a Gentile to be appointed to any position of authority, however small, over Jews." Gentiles are disqualified from testifying in rabbinical courts, because they are presumed to be "congenital liars." The exception? Shahak remarks:

> The rabbinical court will accept the hearsay evidence of a Jew who testifies to having heard the fact in question mentioned by a Gentile eyewitness, provided the court is satisfied that the latter was speaking casually, rather than in reply to a direct question, for a Gentile's direct answer . . . is presumed to be a lie.[465]

For executing a Gentile, Talmudic law requires only one person's testimony; it should be noted that, of course, Jews are permitted, even encouraged, to perjure themselves in court if a Gentile can thereby be harmed.

Gentiles are prohibited from purchasing land or homes in Israel; a house may be *leased* to a Gentile if not for the purpose of habitation *and* if no more than two adjoining houses are also leased to a Gentile. Upon seeing a large Gentile population, Jews must "utter a curse." The Talmud teaches that "a Jew who passes near an inhabited non-Jewish dwelling must ask [the Jewish] God to destroy it, whereas if the building is in ruins, he must thank the Lord of Vengeance." As we have seen, it became common custom to spit on churches and crucifixes. Shahak explained that it is also forbidden to make:

> [A]ny expressions of praise for Gentiles or for their deeds, except where such praise implies an even greater praise of Jews and things Jewish. . . . For example, the writer Agnon, when

---

[464] Ibid. 73.

[465] Shahak, *Jewish History*, 88.

> interviewed on Israeli radio [after receiving the Nobel Prize for Literature] . . . praised the Swedish Academy, but hastened to add: 'I am not forgetting that it is forbidden to praise Gentiles, but here there is a special reason for my praise'—that is, that they awarded the prize to a Jew.[466]

Jews are not even permitted to "join any manifestation of popular Gentile rejoicing, except where failing to join in might cause 'hostility' towards Jews, in which case a 'minimal' show of joy is allowed."[467] As Rabbi Shneur Zalman puts it, Gentiles "are of a completely different and inferior order. They are totally evil, with no redeeming qualities whatsoever. . . . Their material abundance derives from supernal refuse. Indeed, they themselves derive from refuse, which is why they are more numerous than the Jews."

From earliest youth, Orthodox Jews are thus steeped in a tradition which compares Gentiles to animals (ironic, given the standard Jewish battle cry of "dehumanization") and considers them to be lower than slaves. Indeed, *Jewish* slaves were to be freed after seven years, while *Gentile* slaves must be enslaved forever. As one popular rabbinical commentary explained:

> The Jewish people are the best of the human species, created to know their Creator and worship Him, and worthy of having slaves to serve them. And if they will not have slaves of other peoples, they would have to enslave their brothers. . . . Therefore, we are commanded to possess those for our service.[468]

Jews must "remove themselves" from Gentiles and "speak ill of all their behavior, even of their dress." The Talmud teaches Jews that "when we withhold mercy from others, [it] is equal to . . . doing [merciful deeds] to members of our own people."

As aforementioned, the Talmud states that it is mandatory to "exact as much usury as possible on a loan to a Gentile." The Jewish God has "exposed [Gentiles'] money to Israel." It is

---

[466] Shahak, *Jewish Fundamentalism*, 66.
[467] Ibid., 39.
[468] Shahak, *Jewish History*, 95.

forbidden to give gifts to a Gentile, unless it is an investment, for which some return is expected. Fraud is not applicable to Gentiles; as such, indirect deception is encouraged in business. Jews are not even supposed to pay Gentiles the wages that they have earned for work. After all, they are slaves, and "a Gentile who observes a day of rest deserves death." As one verse reads, "Why should it be unlawful to deal thus with his money, when it is lawful to deal violently with his body, for it is lawful to rend him as a fish."[469] Talmudic teachings preach the virtue of deceptive equivocation. The Talmud forbids the return of lost property to Gentiles, stating furthermore that the Gentile is not to be assisted in his quest to recover the property. One verse reads that the "property of Gentiles is like the desert; whoever among the Jews gets there first, owns it."[470] Jewish robbery of Gentiles is only forbidden "when the Gentiles are not under our rule," but permitted "when they are under our rule."

Shahak explains that adultery between a married Jewess and another man is a heinous offense, but:

> The status of Gentile women is very different. . . . [Gentiles are presumed] to be utterly promiscuous and the verse "whose flesh is as the flesh of asses, and whose issue [of semen] is like the issue of horses" is applied to them. Whether a Gentile woman is married or not makes no difference, since as far as Jews are concerned the very concept of matrimony does not apply to Gentiles. Therefore, the concept of adultery . . . does not apply to intercourse between a Jewish man and a Gentile woman; rather, the Talmud equates such intercourse to the sin of bestiality.[471]

From the Talmud itself, "Let him not marry the daughter of the unlearned, for they are an abomination, and their wives are vermin; and of their daughters it is said, 'Cursed is he that lieth with any beast.'"[472] The punishment for adultery is meted out on the Gentile woman; she must be executed, even if she

---

[469] Quoted in McCaul, *Talmud Tested*, 465.
[470] Quoted in Ibid., 460.
[471] Shahak, *Jewish History*, 87.
[472] Quoted in McCaul, *Talmud Tested*, 6.

was raped by the Jew. In Christian Spain, Jewish women found to be cohabiting or sexually involved with Gentile men had their noses severed by rabbinical decree, because "in this way she will lose her beauty and her non-Jewish lover will come to hate her."

Gentile women are presumed to be whores, treated even worse than the extreme misogyny with which the Talmud beholds Jewish women. One Talmudic verse declares that "there is no matrimony for a heathen"; an alternate version reads, "There is no matrimony to the Gentiles." Indeed, Gentile women are considered prized sexual conquests; the Talmud, for a religious text, has a bizarre sexual fixation and scatological obsession. The *bris* circumcision ritual entails homosexual fellatio of infants. Prohibitions against sodomy are vitiated by, as with all other prohibitions, extremely deferential loopholes, such as claiming "accidental" or "unwitting" penetration. Tel Aviv is home to one of the world's largest homosexual populations. Indeed, pedophilia is explicitly condoned in several verses, among which are: "Intercourse with a boy under nine years old is not considered a significant sexual act"; "A child less than nine years old cannot be the object of sodomy"; "If a girl is less than three years old, it is permitted to be secluded with her. Likewise, if a boy is less than nine years old, a woman is permitted to be alone with him"; and, "If a grown-up man has intercourse with a little girl, it is nothing, for having intercourse with a girl less than three years old is like putting a finger in the eye."

One of the more invidious manifestations of the Talmudic emphasis on Jewish supremacy and Gentile inferiority is organ harvesting. At first glance, the use of a Gentile organ in a Jewish body would appear to contradict the Talmud. Rabbis Ovadia Yosef and Mordechai Eliyahu, both former Chief Rabbis of Israel, ordered "pious Jews not to accept blood donations from non-Jews unless their lives were at risk . . . based upon a Talmudic prohibition that does not allow a non-Jewish nurse to breastfeed a Jewish child." Shahak explains that rabbinical authorities fear that "receiving 'tainted,' secular blood, or non-Jewish blood might cause a pious Jew to behave badly and even, heaven forbid, harm his observance of the Jewish religious laws."[473] Yosef declares that "a pious Jew, who does not urgently need a transfusion and who faces no danger in waiting to receive blood from a strictly religious Jew, should wait."

The same formulation extends to organ transplants, including the exception that a Jew *may* receive blood or organs from a Gentile if necessary. A Gentile, however, may never receive Jewish organs or Jewish blood. Going along with the belief that Gentiles exist for the singular purpose of serving their Jewish overlords, the exception that allows Jews to receive Gentile organs takes on a sinister hue. As Rabbi Yitzchak Ginsburgh muses, "The Torah would probably permit" a Jew to receive the organs of a Gentile. As he explains, "Jewish life has an infinite value. There is something more holy and unique about Jewish life than about non-Jewish life."

As the work of Alison Weir attests, "Israeli organ harvesting—sometimes with Israeli governmental funding and the participation of high Israeli officials, prominent Israeli physicians, and Israeli government ministries—has been documented for many years."[474] Indeed, Israel has been described as *the* global capital of illegal organ trafficking. Nancy Scheper-Hughes, an American medical anthropologist, stated that Israel is "at the top" of the traffic in illegally harvested organs, with "tentacles reaching out worldwide." She described a "pyramid system," with "brokers everywhere, bank accounts everywhere; they've got recruiters, they've got translators, they've got travel agents who set up the visas."[475] Israeli organ traffickers target destitute populations across the world, including Eastern European nations like Moldova, offering one to ten thousand dollars for vital organs. Israelis are large-scale participants in "transplant tourism," traveling to foreign countries expressly to purchase organs. Brazilian authorities have found that Israeli traffickers are not merely after kidneys, but hearts, lungs, livers, corneas, and more. For decades, the Israeli Ministry of Health subsidized these

---

[473] Shahak, *Jewish Fundamentalism*, 43.
[474] Weir, "Israeli Organ Harvesting."
[475] Ibid.

"transplant holidays"; the Ministry of Defense has also been implicated, as, according to Weir, "members of the ministry or those closely related to them accompany transplant junkets."

This is partially motivated by the fact that Israel has the lowest organ donation rate on the planet, stemming from rabbinical injunctions that consider organ removal to be a "desecration of the body." In the United States, for example, nearly sixty percent of adults are organ donors; by the estimate of Israeli outlet *Ynet*, just four percent of Israeli adults are organ donors. In disturbing accord with what we have learned about the Jewish view on Gentiles, Scheper-Hughes states:

> The sale of human organs and tissues requires that certain disadvantaged individuals, populations, and even nations have been reduced to the role of suppliers. It is a scenario in which only certain bodies are broken, dismembered, fragmented, transported, processed, and sold in the interests of a more socially advantaged population . . . of receivers.[476]

Scheper-Hughes has reported that several Israeli organ brokers and transplant surgeons, some of whom work under the auspices of large Israeli hospitals, have named "revenge, restitution, [and] reparation for the Holocaust" as their motivation. One told her that "it's kind of an 'eye for an eye and a tooth for a tooth.' We're going to get every single kidney and liver and heart that we can. The world owes it to us."

In many cases, Gentile organ "suppliers" are unwilling participants in the trade; in 2012, Levy Rosenbaum, an Israeli citizen who lived in Brooklyn, New York, became the first man to be federally convicted in America for profiting from organ trafficking. He was arrested as part of a 2009 sting that indicted dozens of other men, including American rabbis, politicians, and other government officials. Rosenbaum carried a gun, and, according to Weir, "when a potential organ seller wanted to back out . . . would use his finger to simulate firing at the person's head." A horde of Jewish supporters attended his trial and sentencing, which only amounted to two and a half years and possible deportation. Despite this, however,

[476] Ibid.

evidence suggests that the majority of cases of organ theft go even beyond that level of coercion.

Palestinian families have reported for decades that the State of Israel harvests organs from the bodies of those wounded or killed by the IDF. In some cases, families report the IDF returning the bodies of loved ones "late at night, days later, with crudely stitched navel-to-chin incisions," missing eyes, teeth, and other body parts. IDF atrocities against unarmed women and children are well-documented elsewhere, even outside the context of warfare; some American trafficking experts have speculated that people might be killed specifically for the purpose of organ harvesting, although documentary evidence of this has not yet come to light. In 2005, one Israeli soldier described an IDF doctor who gave "medic lessons" using a Palestinian body. The soldier said:

> The Palestinian's body had been riddled with bullets and . . . some of his internal organs had spilled out. The doctor pronounced the man dead and then took out a knife and began to cut off parts of the body. He explained the various parts to us—the membrane that covers the lungs, the layers of the skin, the liver. . . . It was all done very brutally. It was simply contempt for the body.[477]

If all of this seems outlandish, continue reading.

In 2002, Nissim Dahan, then-Minister of Health, was asked whether organs were harvested from the bodies of Palestinians or whether corpses were otherwise experimented on. Dahan replied, "I couldn't say for sure that something like that didn't happen." Israel's very first successful heart transplant used a stolen heart. Weir reports that in 1968, Avraham Sadegat died two days after being hospitalized for a stroke. Though the hospital inexplicably delayed releasing the body to his family, the family eventually obtained it and found that his chest was covered with bandages. Rightfully sensing that this was unusual for the victim of a stroke, they removed the bandages to discover that his heart was missing. During this series of events, the State of Israel announced its first

[477] Quoted in Ibid.

successful heart transplant. The Sadegat family waged a campaign that included petitioning three Cabinet Ministers and signing an agreement not to sue the hospital, after which the hospital admitted that they had, indeed, used Avraham Sadegat's heart. Sadegat's wife was quoted as saying, "From the moment he entered the hospital, they apparently saw him only as a potential source of organs and not as a man in need of treatment. They only thought about how to do the deed without us knowing." Weir notes that "Sadegat's medical condition pre-organ removal is unclear." Weir also notes that it is likely that had Sadegat not been Israeli, the hospital would never have confessed. If this is the contempt with which average Israelis are treated, we need not tax our imagination too much to think of how *Gentiles* are treated.

Yehuda Hiss served as the Chief Pathologist at the Israeli state morgue from 1988 to 2005, later regaining the position before his ultimate dismissal in 2012. Hiss was implicated in several controversies, including the falsification of documents related to the Jewish fundamentalist assassination of Prime Minister Yitzhak Rabin, as well as tampering with DNA evidence related to the Israeli abduction and sale of thousands of Yemeni children from 1948 to 1954. One of the first cases of Hiss' misdeeds involved a Scottish tourist, Alisdair Sinclair. Sinclair was arrested at Ben Gurion Airport for carrying a large amount of cash; in custody, Sinclair died under mysterious circumstances, though Hiss ruled that the man had hung himself. Upon the repatriation of his corpse to Scotland, the Sinclair family commissioned an autopsy at the University of Glasgow; this autopsy revealed that Sinclair's heart and hyoid bone were missing. The British Embassy filed a complaint with Israel, which responded by sending a heart to Scotland. DNA results proved to be inconclusive. Multiple Israeli news reports confirm that Hiss was "involved for years in taking body parts, such as legs, thighs, ovaries, breasts, and testicles, without family permission during autopsies, and selling them to medical schools for use in research and training," and that Hiss "seemed to view every body that ended up in his morgue, whether Israeli or Palestinian, as fair game for organ harvesting."[478] The corpses that were returned to families or buried were stuffed with broomsticks and cotton wool. Hiss has also reportedly done this to the bodies of dead Israeli soldiers, again raising the question that, if this is how Israel treats its own soldiers, how must it treat Gentiles?

Yet another example of Jewish contempt for *Goyim* is the case of Baruch Goldstein. Goldstein was born in Brooklyn, and, after emigrating to Israel, served as an IDF physician. While on active duty, Goldstein refused to treat Gentiles, even those who served in the IDF. He later became an emergency doctor at an Israeli settlement near Hebron, where he became active in extreme ultra-Zionist politics, often seen sporting a yellow star with the word "Jude" on it. In 1994, during the Purim festival, Goldstein entered the Cave of the Patriarchs, considered by Jews to be the second holiest site on earth, and massacred twenty-nine Palestinian Muslims, including children as young as twelve; a further 125 people were wounded. After the massacre, Goldstein, who had been disarmed and beaten to death by the crowd, became something of a Jewish folk hero. Politicians, the press, and leading rabbis all celebrated or minimized the attack; instead of "murder," "massacre," or "killing," media reports spoke of it in terms like "deed," "event," or "occurrence." Why? Simply because the murder of a Gentile by a Jew is, as we have seen, not regarded as a murder at all, and can be perpetrated with impunity.

If killing Gentiles is at all prohibited, it is only because these actions might engender reactions against Jews. The injunction against Jewish murder of other Jews is even excepted, where it might benefit the Jewish nation at large. Thus, there is a long and well-documented history of rabbinical assassination of heterodox Jews, part of a larger trend which largely describes the survival strategy of Judaism—the rigid maintenance of a closed society. Rabbinical courts have the unmitigated power to sentence anyone to death "if it is believed that the world will thereby be improved." This extends to Gentile children, as we have seen. No punishments may be inflicted upon Jewish boys under thirteen, or Jewish girls under twelve;

---

[478] Ibid.

the Talmudic rule is that "any non-Jews, no matter what age, will have to pay for any crime committed." Additionally, "any Jew is capable of judging whether a non-Jewish child should in this sense be considered and punished as an adult."

Goldstein's grand funeral was organized through the office of Israeli President Ezer Weizman. Within just two days of the massacre, Shahak observed:

> The walls of religious neighborhoods of west Jerusalem . . . were covered by posters extolling Goldstein's virtues and complaining that he did not manage to kill more Arabs. Children of religious settlers who came to Jerusalem to demonstrate sported buttons for months after the massacre that were inscribed: 'Dr. Goldstein cured Israel's ills.' Numerous concerts of Jewish religious music . . . often developed into demonstrations of tribute to Goldstein. . . . No major politician protested against such celebrations . . . a massively attended funeral cortege [took] place in Jerusalem [and] the police [closed] some of the busiest streets to traffic in Goldstein's honor.[479]

The teeming throngs of mourners could be heard repeating things like: "What a hero!"; "A righteous person!"; and, "He did it on behalf of all of us."

Rabbi Dov Lior, then-Chief Rabbi of Hebron, declared that "since Goldstein did what he did in [the Jewish] God's own name, he is to be regarded as a righteous man." After the elaborate funeral, the IDF provided an honor guard at Goldstein's tomb, which almost immediately became a popular Jewish pilgrimage site, receiving thousands of pious Jews per year. Rabbi Yisrael Ariel, former Chief Rabbi of Yamit, intoned that "the holy martyr, Baruch Goldstein, is from now on our intercessor in heaven. . . . The Jews will inherit the land . . . only by shedding blood."[480] Lior added that "Goldstein was full of love for fellow human beings. He dedicated himself to helping others," and that "Goldstein could not continue to bear the humiliations and shame nowadays inflicted upon us . . . he took

---

479 Shahak, *Jewish Fundamentalism*, 100.
480 Ibid., 102.

action for no other reason than to sanctify the holy name of God." Needless to say, "human beings" and "others" are categories tainted by Jewish chauvinism, commonly understood to refer only to Jews. Lior is on the record supporting live medical experimentation on Arabs.

Let us conclude with yet more Talmudic teachings regarding the Gentiles. Gentile women are "menstrual filth, slaves, heathen, and whores." Christian women who work for Jews on the Sabbath are called "Sabbath dirt." Sexual slavery is permissible so long as it is a Jew that abducted the Gentile. Gentiles are sexual deviants, inclined to bestiality; indeed, the *Goyim* prefer bovine intercourse to their own wives. One verse reads:

> Animals must not be allowed to go near the *Goyim*, because they are suspected of having intercourse with them . . . when Gentile men come to their neighbors' houses to commit adultery with their wives and do not find them at home, they fornicate with the sheep in the barns. . . . They love the sheep of the Israelites more than their own women.

Gentile children are "animals," "sucklings the same as dogs." The life of a Gentile "and all his physical powers belong to the Jew." The property of the *Goyim* "belongs to the first who can get it," and he must be "wiped off the face of the earth." Murdering the Gentile "will please [the Jewish] God the same as one who offers incense to him." "No mercy" may be shown unto the Gentile, and "their sick must not be cared for, Christian women in childbirth must not be helped, nor must they be saved when in danger of death." Where Jews reign, "no idolater must be allowed to remain."

The "deeds of Israel are righteous, but the Gentiles are capable only of sin." If a Jew finds himself tempted toward evil, "he should put on dirty clothes and go to a city where he is not known, and do the evil there." This same verse is translated alternatively to read, "When one finds that evil appetites are taking hold of his senses, let him repair to some place where he is unknown, let him dress himself in black and follow the impulses of his heart." Rabbi Shimon bar Yochai wrote that "even the best of the Gentiles should be killed." Rabbis Yitzhak Shapira and Yossi Elitzur argue that "non-Jews are uncompassionate by nature and attacks on them curb their evil inclination," continuing that "in any situation in which a non-Jew's presence endangers Jewish lives, the non-Jew may be killed even if he is a righteous Gentile and not at all guilty for the situation that has been created." Paul Eidelberg, an American-born Straussian professor, has stated that "if Germany is peaceful today, it's not only because it was conquered in war, but because the desire to conquer others was bombed out of the German people."

Rabbi Saadya Grama writes:

> The Jew . . . in his very essence is entirely good. The *goy* . . . is completely evil. This is not simply a matter of religious distinction, but rather of two completely different species. Jewish success in the world is completely contingent upon the failure of other peoples. Jews experience good fortune only when Gentiles experience catastrophe. . . . The difference between Jews and Gentiles is not historical or cultural, but rather genetic and unalterable.

Rabbi Ovadia Yosef, a former Chief Rabbi of Israel, said:

> *Goyim* were born only to serve us. Without that, they have no place in the world—only to serve the People of Israel. . . . With Gentiles, it will be like any person—they need to die, but [God] will give them longevity. Why? Imagine that one's donkey would die; they'd lose their money. This is his servant. . . . That's why he gets a long life, to work well for this Jew. Why are Gentiles needed? They will work, they will plow, they will reap. We will sit . . . and eat. That is why Gentiles were created.[481]

[481] Alexis, *Christianity and Rabbinic Judaism*, 296.

9

Case Studies in Jewish Hostility

Degeneracy, Filth, and Pornography

Jews have been the primary driving force behind the gradual abolition of American obscenity laws, being vastly overrepresented as defendants in the landmark obscenity cases *Winters v. New York*, *Burstyn v. Wilson*, *Roth v. United States*, *Freedman v. Maryland*, *Mishkin v. New York*, *Ginzburg v. United States*, *Ginsberg v. New York*, *Cohen v. California*, and *Miller v. California*; Jews are also wildly overrepresented as the activists, attorneys, and judges involved in the initiation and achievement of these victories, and, no less importantly, as the producers of pornographic content. There has been a sort of synergistic relationship between these three categories, all of which are heavily Jewish, in the consummation of a century-long program to promote degeneracy and corrode the Christian morality with which Americans once governed themselves. We will briefly trace the history of this corrosion, discuss the Jewish involvement therein and the motivations that animate that involvement, and conclude by investigating the truly devastating effect that this process has had on the United States, and the West at large.

In 1873, the Grant Administration passed the first federal anti-obscenity law, known as the Comstock Act, which sparked several Comstock Laws. This legislation, due entirely to the tireless lobbying of Anthony Comstock, a U.S. Postal Inspector who also founded the noble New York Society for the

Suppression of Vice, prevented the transmission of obscene materials, including pornography, contraceptives, abortifacients, and infanticidal promotional information. In 1879, its constitutionality was affirmed when the Supreme Court adopted the *Hicklin* definitional test for obscenity, from the 1868 English case, *Regina v. Hicklin*. This test determined that an item was obscene if it tended "to deprave or corrupt those whose minds are open to such immoral influences, and into whose hands a publication of this sort may fall."

Over time, the Comstock Laws were gradually eroded by judicial activists on the high court, as obscenity advocates recast the issue in terms of the First Amendment protections for "speech" and "press"—never mind that the First Amendment was written solely to protect the expression of political ideas, *not* to protect scurrilous filth. Especially during the 1920s, with the growth of the Jewish-controlled film industry, elite support for obscenity regulation declined. As Benjamin Garland observes:

> Much like today, where any and all opposition to the Jewish and [leftist] agenda is silenced through charges of "racism," "bigotry," "hate," and "anti-Semitism" . . . supporters of obscenity regulation were ridiculed in the media with epithets such as "prude" and "Puritan," while their opponents were portrayed as heroic crusaders for freedom of expression.[482]

In *United States v. One Book Called Ulysses*, the United States District Court for the Southern District of New York altered the *Hicklin* test from "those whose minds are open to such immoral influences," restated as those who are susceptible, often taken to include children, to "the average person." In 1957, with *Roth v. United States*, the Supreme Court adopted a new formulation, thereby opening the levees to a flood of refuse. Justice William Brennan wrote for the majority that, while "obscenity is not within the area of constitutionally protected speech or press," "sex and obscenity are not synonymous," as "obscene material is material which deals with sex in a manner appealing to prurient interest."

---

[482] Garland, *Merchants of Sin*, 8.

The *Roth* test was to ask "whether to the average person, applying contemporary community standards, the dominant theme of the material, taken as a whole, appeals to prurient interest." A quite ominous dissent, written by Justice William Douglas and joined by Justice Hugo Black, argued that obscenity *is* protected under the First Amendment. Douglas wrote that "the test that suppresses a cheap tract today can suppress a literary gem tomorrow," citing the Jew William Lockhart, who wrote:

> The danger of influencing a change in the current moral standards of the community, or of shocking or offending readers or of stimulating sex thoughts or desires . . . can never justify the losses to society that result from interference with literary freedom.

Lockhart's argument was itself based on the criminally depraved work of Alfred Kinsey.

After *Roth*, E. Michael Jones notes that there was an explosion "of porn films which sought to evade obscenity convictions by including within them portions which bespoke redeeming social value so that the material 'as a whole' would not be deemed obscene"; for example, the pornographic film *I Am Curious (Yellow)* "was given redeeming social value by making repeated references to the life of Martin Luther King, Jr."[483] Years later, speaking privately with President Richard Nixon, Chief Justice Warren Burger mocked the *Roth* "socially redeeming value" rule as "one of the biggest frauds ever," continuing, "That's a phrase that emanated from some of the campuses. . . . You know this means that if they have one of these outrageous orgies, then if they mention Vietnam or the condition of the ghettos, that 'redeems' the whole thing." As Leo Pfeffer, a leader of the American Jewish Congress, remarked, "Under [the *Hicklin* test], any obscenity in a work, no matter how slight, contaminated the whole; under [the *Roth* test], any slight redeeming trait purified it."

---

[483] Jones, *Libido Dominandi*, 381.

In 1964, Justice Potter Stewart wrote in his *Jacobellis v. Ohio* concurrence that the First Amendment protects all obscenity except "hardcore pornography," of which he famously stated, "I shall not today attempt further to define the kinds of material I understand to be embraced within that shorthand description; and perhaps I could never succeed in intelligibly doing so. But I know it when I see it." *Jacobellis* had the practical effect of making it virtually impossible to obtain a conviction for the dissemination of pornography, further worsened by the Court's ruling in *Stanley v. Georgia* only five years later.

In *Stanley*, Justice Thurgood Marshall, writing for the Court, applied the nonexistent "right to privacy," spuriously and kritarchically read into the First and Fourteenth Amendments, to the possession of pornography. This vicious encroachment upon the Tenth Amendment invalidated all state laws prohibiting the private possession of obscene material, giving each and every American the right to purchase and accumulate any quantity of pornography that they desire. The current definitional test for what constitutes obscenity, however, came into being in 1971, with *Miller v. California*. In *Miller*, the *Roth* standard was reformulated and expanded to determine: "Whether the average person, applying contemporary community standards would find that the work, taken as a whole, appeals to the prurient interest"; "Whether the work depicts or describes, in a patently offensive way, sexual conduct specifically defined by the applicable State law"; *and*, "Whether the work, taken as a whole, lacks serious literary, artistic, political, or scientific value." Evidently, Chief Justice Burger believed that the *Miller* test would function as a conservative doctrine, but it had the opposite effect. As Garland notes, "by this time the Jewish-led Cultural Revolution had been largely victorious. . . . This cultural drift made convictions harder to obtain. Juries were tougher to shock, more reluctant to send people to prison. . . . A more liberal culture reigned in the more conservative doctrine."[484]

In 1996, with *Reno v. American Civil Liberties Union*, the Court defanged the Communications Decency Act, an attempt

---

[484] Garland, *Merchants of Sin*, 84.

to protect children from internet pornography, rendering it impotent. Congress made another attempt at regulating online pornography two years later with its Child Online Protection Act, which met the same fate as its predecessor with *Ashcroft v. American Civil Liberties Union*. In 2000, Congress passed the Children's Internet Protection Act, which was ultimately upheld by the Court in *Ashcroft v. American Library Association*. This was merely a symbolic victory, however, as its only practical effect was to require "age verification" on pornographic websites. We are all aware of the less-than-rigorous "verification" that actually takes place. The culmination of *Miller* was reached in 2002, when the Supreme Court held in *Ashcroft v. Free Speech Coalition* that pornography which involves consenting adults is protected by the First Amendment, even if the models "appear to be" minors but are, in fact of lawful age, and thus virtually enshrines all pornography in the Constitution. Needless to say, Jews are overrepresented in the leadership of the Free Speech Coalition, as well as the ACLU. One such Free Speech Coalition member, John Stagliano, happens to be a major financial contributor to Koch-associated libertarian outfits like the Cato Institute and *Reason*, both of which lionize him as some sort of civil rights hero for the disgusting content he creates. *Reason* referred to pornography as "America's liberty" in an article defending Ira Isaacs, a "filmmaker" whose work involves bestiality.

We begin our brief discussion of Jewish involvement in the entrapment of America into a deluge of degradation by looking at the American film industry. Quite remarkably, Jews had largely captured Hollywood by 1915. From this time through the late 1950s, and continuing until the late 1960s, a war was waged for the cultural soul of America, invisible to all but industry insiders. In 1915, the Supreme Court unanimously ruled in *Mutual Film Corporation v. Industrial Commission of Ohio* that motion pictures were not protected under the First Amendment, and were thus subject to "prior restraint" censorship. Justice Joseph McKenna wrote that "the exhibition of moving pictures is a business, pure and simple." Despite this ruling, which was directly overruled in 1952 by *Burstyn v. Wilson*, Hollywood essentially had free rein. In his *The*

International Jew: The World's Foremost Problem, Henry Ford notes that "as soon as the Jew gained control of the movies, we had a movie problem, the consequences of which are not yet visible. It is the genius of that race to create problems of a moral character in whatever business they achieve a majority." He continues:

> There is little wisdom in discoursing against evil in the movies and deliberately closing our eyes to the forces behind the evil . . . behind the movies there is another group of definite moral and racial complexion . . . the movies are Jewish. It is not a question of morals—that question has been settled; it is a question of management.[485]

In 1922, United States Postmaster General Will Hays was appointed to be the first chairman of the association which later became known as the Motion Picture Association of America, now globalized as the Motion Picture Association. Under Hays, the Motion Picture Production Code was adopted in 1930, but did not begin to be enforced until 1934, with the hiring of Joseph Breen. It is well-established that Hays and Breen were hyper-aware of Jewish power in Hollywood. Breen wrote privately:

> [Jews are] a rotten bunch of people with no respect for anything beyond the making of money. . . . We have Paganism rampant. . . . Drunkenness and debauchery are commonplace. Sexual perversion is rampant . . . any number of our directors and stars are perverts. . . . These Jews seem to think of nothing but making money and sexual indulgence. . . . Ninety-five percent of these folks are Jews of an Eastern European lineage. They are, probably, the scum of the earth.[486]

Through the 1950s and 1960s, the Production Code began to be ignored and unenforced, and was replaced in 1968 by the MPAA ratings system that we are familiar with today, though of course in a different form. The MPAA was at that time led by Jack Valenti, an aide to President Lyndon Johnson who was

---

[485] Ford, *International Jew*, 119.
[486] Garland, *Merchants of Sin*, 72.

installed at the MPAA by Lew Wasserman, the Jewish head of Universal Studios. As an aside, it is perhaps worth noting that when the Hays Office was dismantled in 1966, American Humane lost the ability to monitor film sets for animal cruelty for fourteen years. We need not dwell on Hollywood for long, as its corrosion of American cultural life is manifest.

It is well-documented that members of the first wave of Jewish immigration into the United States from Germany and Eastern Europe, which occurred in the late nineteenth century, were commonly involved in the production and distribution of pornographic smut. This involvement appears to have begun almost immediately after immigration skyrocketed in 1880. One contemporary observer wrote:

> The historian of the future who shall attempt to describe the catalogue of the filthy publications issued by the Jews during the last ten years will scarcely believe the evidence of his own eyes. Scenes of gross debauchery, representing drunken monks in the society of girls, priests lashing nude women . . . and other outrageous pictures, are displayed on all sides, with Jewish effrontery, in the windows and stores.[487]

Anthony Comstock publicly pointed to the fact that the majority of his opponents, including abortionists, pimps, and pornographers, were Jewish, as were their advocates in the legal system.

This involvement continues today; indeed, Nathan Abrams writes in *Jewish Quarterly*:

> Jews have played (and still continue to play) a disproportionate role throughout the adult film industry in America. Jewish involvement in pornography has a long history in the United States, as Jews have helped to transform a fringe subculture into what has become a primary constituent of Americana."[488]

---

[487] Garland, *Merchants of Sin*, 3.

[488] Abrams, "Triple-Exthnics."

Abrams notes that the vast majority of the foundational figures in modern American pornography were and are Jewish, such as Reuben Sturman, known as "the Walt Disney of porn," and Steven Hirsch, founder of Vivid Entertainment Group. Fabian Thylmann is also Jewish; Thylmann founded Manwin, now known as MindGeek, the parent company of several pornographic sites, such as Pornhub, the *ninth* most popular website *on earth*, as well as YouPorn, RedTube, and Brazzers. A quick search will reveal that this pattern persists throughout the "adult film" industry. Abrams also points out that Jews account for most of the leading male performers in pornographic films, such as Ron Jeremy, who "presents an image of a modern-day King David, a Jewish super-stud who supersedes the traditional heroes of Jewish lore."

As aforementioned, Jews and Jewish organizations were at the vanguard of the legal and judicial activism that initiated the current proliferation of filth. Garland notes the supreme irony:

> Since the 1960s, Jews and Jewish organizations have been at the forefront of "free speech" campaigns against the censorship of pornography and obscenity. However, in a remarkable *volte-face*, we now find Jews and Jewish organizations leading the calls to ban First Amendment-protected speech when they disagree with its content. . . . If Jews are against freedom of speech and at the same time committed to the promotion of degeneracy, why should we accept their claim of holding moral authority?

Perhaps more importantly, however, Jews dominated among the foundational figures for the Sexual Revolution itself, which inculcated the culture of degeneracy that made America susceptible to Jewish pornography in the first place. Kevin MacDonald has done yeoman's work in documenting this, so we will not dwell on this point too long, except to simply mention that Freudian psychoanalysis, Frankfurt School Critical Theory, and second-wave feminism were all Jewish-led movements.[489] Jewish figures like Sigmund Freud, Magnus

[489] See MacDonald, *Culture of Critique*.

Hirschfield, Herbert Marcuse, Wilhelm Reich, and Paul Goodman, and Alfred Kinsey (though not Jewish), who were all deeply disturbed and depraved individuals, fundamentally transformed Western civilization by sexualizing, and consequently atomizing, society.

The ethically compromised and fabricated data collected by Kinsey, much of which involved pedophiliac abuse, was cited by Herbert Wechsler, future director of the American Law Institute and the primary developer of the 1955 Model Penal Code, which has largely been adopted by each of the United States. Wechsler used that Code to bring about the abolition of many of the sexual prohibitions that had historically preserved social decency; he basically believed that sex offenders should not be incarcerated, or at least that the standards for what constitutes a sexual offense should be raised much higher. In the wake of *Stanley v. Georgia*, in which, it will be recalled, the Supreme Court held that adults could view whatever material they wish in the privacy of their own homes, the Johnson administration created the President's Commission on Obscenity and Pornography.

The Commission was staffed almost entirely by Jewish ACLU members, including its chairman, William Lockhart, as well as its chief counsel, Paul Bender. Bender went on to become a vociferous advocate for child pornography, testifying in 1977 before the Senate Judiciary Committee that child pornography prohibition is not justifiable because "the conclusion that child pornography causes child abuse involves too much speculation" and "most kids who act on these films probably are doing these acts aside from the films anyway." Not coincidentally, Jews heavily featured in the leadership of the North American Man/Boy Love Association, or NAMBLA, a pedophilia advocacy group—the largest of its kind on earth.

The Commission, to the surprise of nobody, found that there was "no evidence to date that exposure to explicit sexual materials plays a significant role in the causation of delinquent or criminal behavior among youths or adults"; that "a majority of American adults believe that adults should be allowed to read or see any sexual materials they wish"; that "there is no reason to suppose that elimination of governmental prohibitions upon the sexual materials which may be made available to adults would adversely affect the availability to the public of other books, magazines, or films"; that there was no "evidence that exposure to explicit sexual materials adversely affects character or moral attitudes regarding sex and sexual conduct"; and finally, that "Federal, State, and Local legislation prohibiting the sale, exhibition, or distribution of sexual materials to consenting adults should be repealed."[490]

President Nixon, who had succeeded Johnson by the time this report was issued, responded with outrage:

> The Commission contends that the proliferation of filthy books and plays has no lasting harmful effect on a man's character. If that were true, it must also be true that great books, great paintings, and great plays have no ennobling effect on a man's conduct. Centuries of civilization and ten minutes of common sense tell us otherwise. . . . If the level of filth rises in the adult community, the young people in our society cannot help but also be inundated by the flood. Pornography can corrupt a society and a civilization. The people's elected representatives have the right and obligation to prevent that corruption. The warped and brutal portrayal of sex . . . if not halted and reversed, could poison the wellsprings of American and Western culture and civilization. The pollution of our culture, the pollution of our civilization with smut and filth is as serious a situation for the American people as the pollution of our once-pure air and water.[491]

President Nixon, it so happens, was aware of the Jewish menace. In a private conversation with Billy Graham, Graham is heard to say that the Jewish "stranglehold" on the media "has got to be broken or the country's going down the drain." Nixon replied, "You believe that? Oh, boy. So do I. I can't ever say that, but I believe it." Graham made sure to add that "they're the ones putting out the pornographic stuff."[492] In another conversation between the two men, one year later, Graham

---

[490] Garland, *Merchants of Sin*, 81.
[491] Ibid., 82
[492] Ibid., 84.

referred to "the synagogue of Satan" and noted again the Jewish connection to the production and promotion of pornography. This is not all. Gregory Pincus, another Jew, was the primary developer of the combined oral contraceptive pill, colloquially known as "birth control," or "The Pill." Betty Friedan, née Goldstein, whose *The Feminine Mystique* helped spark second-wave feminism, was a Jewess. Friedan went on to found the National Organization for Women. Jews also founded the National Association for the Repeal of Abortion Laws, now known as NARAL Pro-Choice America, the oldest infanticide lobbying group in America.

One of these founders, Bernard Nathanson, admitted decades later:

> [They] persuaded the media that the cause of permissive abortion was a liberal, enlightened, sophisticated one. Knowing that if a true poll were taken, we would be soundly defeated, we simply fabricated the results of fictional polls. We announced to the media that we had taken polls and that sixty percent of Americans were in favor of permissive abortion. This is the tactic of the self-fulfilling lie. Few people care to be in the minority. We aroused enough sympathy to sell our program . . . by fabricating the number of illegal abortions done annually in the United States. The actual figure was approaching one hundred thousand, but the figure we gave to the media repeatedly was one million. Repeating the Big Lie often enough convinces the public. The number of women dying from illegal abortions was around 200 to 250. . . . The figure we constantly fed to the media was ten thousand. These false figures took root . . . convincing many that we needed to crack the abortion law. Another myth we fed to the public . . . was that legalizing abortion would only mean that the abortions taking place illegally would then be done legally. In fact . . . abortion is now being used as a primary method of birth control . . . and the annual number of abortions has increased by fifteen hundred percent since legalization.[493]

It still remains for us to examine *why* Jews have been and are so deeply involved in the culture of degeneracy, *why* it is the case that, as Abrams put it:

---

[493] Ibid., 65.

> Jews in America have been sexual revolutionaries. A large amount of the material on sexual liberation was written by Jews. Those at the forefront of the movement which forced America to adopt a more liberal view of sex were Jewish. Jews were also at the vanguard of the sexual revolution of the 1960s.

Abrams, who celebrates the ascendancy of his brethren in the pornographic film industry, points to two motives.

The first is financial, which is an inadequate explanation for why *Jews* specifically would have been so drawn to this particular business; as to this economic purpose, Abraham Foxman, longtime National Director of the Anti-Defamation League, commented that those Jews who enter the pornography industry have done so as individuals pursuing the American dream." Abrams notes:

> just as their counterparts in Hollywood provided a dream factory for Americans, a blank screen upon which the Jewish moguls' visions of America could be created and projected, so the porn-moguls displayed a talent for understanding public tastes. What better way to provide the stuff of dreams and fantasies than through the adult-entertainment industry?

This proposition presupposes that the Gentile demand for the Jewish product preceded the supply. As we shall see, this is quite a dubious conclusion; indeed, this appears to be exactly the opposite of the truth.

There is, of course, another reason why Jews are so disproportionately involved in filth, deeply rooted and barely concealed: hostility toward Christianity and White, Western civilization. Even Abrams concedes:

> There is surely an element of rebellion in Jewish X-rated involvement. Its very taboo and forbidden nature serves to make it attractive.... [Pornography] signifies the whole world of forbidden sexuality, the sexuality of the *Goyim*, and there all the delights are imagined to lie.

The ubiquitous dichotomy in pornographic productions, that of a Jewish male dominating a White female, is no accident; the formula is "a result a Jewish fantasy of *schtupping* the Catholic *shiksa*." Harvey Cohen affirmed that "it's Jewish fantasy to screw Gentile women."[494] Luke Ford, a pornography columnist and convert to Judaism, wrote that "porn is just one expression of [the] rebellion against standards."[495] Michael Kulich, founder of Monarch Distribution, remarked that Jewish pornographers get to "fulfill every fantasy that every Jewish boy has ever had."[496] Extending this theme of subversion, Abrams explains, "Jewish involvement in the X-rated industry can be seen as a proverbial two fingers to the entire WASP establishment in America. Some porn stars viewed themselves as frontline fighters in the spiritual battle between Christian America and secular humanism." Abrams continues, "Jewish involvement in porn . . . is the result of an atavistic hatred of Christian authority: they are trying to weaken the dominant culture in America by moral subversion."

Ford recalled Jewish porn "performers" gleefully discussing their "joy in being anarchic, sexual gadflies to the puritanical beast." As the Jewish publisher Maurice Girodias sneered, "It was great fun. The Anglo-Saxon world was being attacked, invaded, outflanked, and conquered by this erotic armada." The Jewish pornographer Alvin Goldstein, one of the main forces behind the normalization of hardcore pornography in America, boasted that he was "probably the epitome of everything the Nazis hated: the Jew pornographer who besmirches the pure morals of the white Aryan world." Goldstein spoke even more forthrightly when he said that "the only reason that Jews are in pornography is that we think that Christ sucks. Catholicism sucks. We don't believe in authoritarianism."

Another Jewish "performer," Bobby Astyr, stated that he had "to run or fight for it in grammar school because I was a Jew. It could very well be that part of my porn career is an 'up yours' to these people." Through a character, the Jewish

---

494 Ibid., 84.

495 Ibid., 85.

496 Ibid.

author Philip Roth seethed, "With me money is not the paramount issue. The defiance is. The hatred is. The outrage is." Abrams concludes, then:

> Pornography thus becomes a way of defiling Christian culture and, as it penetrates to the very heart of the American mainstream (and is no doubt consumed by those very same WASPs), its subversive character becomes more charged. Porn is no longer of the "what the Butler saw" voyeuristic type; instead, it is driven to new extremes of portrayal that stretch the boundaries of the porn aesthetic. As new sexual positions are portrayed, the desire to shock . . . seems clear.

The subversive animus toward White Christian America shared by the foregoing Jewish "sexual revolutionaries" becomes even more clear when we examine the social carnage wrought by their sexual revolution. As the Western institutions of romantic love and monogamous marriage were undermined, so too was the very foundation of our society. As Kevin MacDonald explains, one of the most significant effects of Western marriage was the facilitation of high-investment parenting. The Freudian conflation of love and sex was paired with the argument that "sexual liberation," set against "sexual repression," would create a better society. Lasha Darkmoon illustrates the Freudian argument as such:

> The underlying assumption here is that sex is the great liberator and that all political and economic frustrations can be alleviated by sexual activity—particularly by obsessive and addictive sex. People who spend all their waking hours in search of sexual stimulation are obviously unfit to organize pogroms, mount bloody revolutions, or become a threat to the rich and powerful. Sex, according to the philosophers of the Sexual Revolution inspired by Reich, is to be the panacea for all society's problems: the new opium of the people. If people cannot have bread, let them eat cake. If they cannot have jobs, security, fulfillment, and a valid purpose in life, let them have sex as a substitute. If nothing else, recreational sex will provide a useful distraction and give people something to do.[497]

---

[497] Darkmoon, "Masters of Porn."

MacDonald continues this argument, noting that Western social controls "were embedded in Christianity of all stripes and thus seen as part of the alien, anti-Semitic culture to be overcome by intellectually and morally superior Jews."[498] Clearly, then, we cannot help but conclude that "the sexualization of Western culture should be included as a very major component of the Jewish assault on Western peoples."

As MacDonald elaborates:

> The psychoanalytic emphasis on legitimizing sexuality and premarital sex is therefore fundamentally a program that promotes low-investment parenting styles. Low-investment parenting is associated with precocious sexuality, early reproduction, lack of impulse control, and unstable pair bonds.

As is manifest, White America has indeed become "increasingly characterized by low-investment parenting." In other words, MacDonald argues:

> Western religious and secular institutions have resulted in a highly egalitarian mating system that is associated with high-investment parenting. These institutions provided a central role for pair bonding, conjugality, and companionship as the basis of marriage. However, when these institutions were subjected to the radical critique presented by psychoanalysis, they came to be seen as engendering neurosis, and Western society itself was viewed as pathogenic.... Although other factors are undoubtedly involved, it is remarkable that the increasing trend toward low-investment parenting in the United States largely coincides with the triumph of the psychoanalytic and radical critiques of American culture represented by the political and cultural success of the counter-cultural movement of the 1960s. Since 1970 the rate of single-parenting has increased from one in ten families to one in three families, and there have been dramatic increases in teenage sexual activity and teenage childbearing without marriage.[499]

---

498 MacDonald, "Research on Pornography."
499 MacDonald, "Research on Pornography."

MacDonald continues that "there is excellent evidence for an association among teenage single-parenting, poverty, lack of education, and poor developmental outcomes for children." Additionally, rates of divorce and illegitimacy *began* to skyrocket during this period; it is no longer up for debate that the 1960s constituted a watershed moment in our cultural history, a "shift . . . in the direction of 'expressive individualism' among cultural elites and the decline of external controls on behavior that had been the cornerstone of the formerly dominant Protestant culture." The New Left that served in the vanguard of this process was, of course, heavily Jewish. To further illustrate this shift, we point to the alarming data collected by Charles Murray in his *Coming Apart*, which brilliantly traces the evisceration of the White family in a situation where affirmative action, globalization, and the unending ethnic invasion of America have collaborated to create "an ever-increasing gap between the White working class and well-educated Whites in terms of marriage, out-of-wedlock births, single-parenting and divorce." As just one of many indicators, MacDonald notes:

> In 1965, 69 percent of American women and 65 percent of men under the age of thirty said that premarital sex was always or almost always wrong; by 1972, these figures had plummeted to 24 percent and 21 percent. . . . In 1990, only 6 percent of British men and women under the age of thirty-four believed that it was always or almost always wrong.

Furthermore, after the sexual revolution, "the heritability of age of first sexual intercourse increased dramatically."

From an evolutionary perspective, then, MacDonald suggests that Judaism, whether intentionally or not, has reaped inestimably great benefits from this revolution "by increasing Jewish–Gentile differences in resource competition ability . . . Jews suffer to a lesser extent than Gentiles from the erosion of cultural supports for high-investment parenting, and Jews benefit by the decline in religious belief among Gentiles." Indeed, the Jew Norman Podhoretz admitted:

> It is the simple truth that most American Jews . . . have lined up behind policies that are repugnant to the conservative Christian community. Indeed, from the veritably religious passion many Jews have lately invested in the currently most fashionable of these causes, one might think that the only commandments Moses brought down from Sinai were "Thou shalt not oppose abortion," and, "Thou shalt not oppose gay rights." Furthermore, groups like the American Civil Liberties Union, which are not, strictly speaking, Jewish but whose most visible spokesmen are often of Jewish origin, have also taken the lead in the fight against efforts to control the unrestricted spread of pornography, while organizations like the American Jewish Congress, explicitly claiming to speak in the name of the community, have been in the forefront of the campaign to enforce an interpretation of the First Amendment that would bar any and all religious expression from the public square. . . . Far from concealing or making light of all this, liberal Jews are proud of it, often congratulating themselves on their great contribution to the liberal movement. They even link their commitment to that movement directly with the prophetic tradition and the moral imperatives of Judaism, to which they are convinced they are being loyal in being liberal.[500]

MacDonald concludes that the sexual revolution was "a central component of this war on Gentile cultural supports for high-investment parenting," as:

> Freud's war on Gentile culture through facilitation of the pursuit of sexual gratification, low-investment parenting, and elimination of social controls on sexual behavior may therefore be expected to affect Jews and Gentiles differently, with the result that the competitive difference between Jews and Gentiles . . . would be exacerbated.

This is evinced by the fact that "Jews have been relatively insulated from the trends toward low-investment parenting characteristic of American society generally since the countercultural revolution of the 1960s," such that Gentiles have been *far* more affected by "the erosion of traditional Western controls on sexuality."

---

[500] Podhoretz, "In the Matter of Pat Robertson."

This nurturing of our present culture of degeneracy, the moral decay which has rotted the foundational supports that once seemed immovable, has "resulted in an increased competitive advantage for Jews," as well as "a society increasingly split between a disproportionately Jewish "cognitive elite" and a growing mass of individuals who are intellectually incompetent, irresponsible as parents, prone to requiring public assistance, and prone to criminal behavior, psychiatric disorders, and substance abuse." This systematic weaponization of cultural debasement is nothing new. Andrew Joyce, quoting Dirk Moses, writes:

> [These] moral techniques are policies "to weaken the spiritual resistance of the national group." This technique of moral debasement entails diverting the "mental energy of the group" from "moral and national thinking" to "base instincts." The aim is that "the desire for cheap individual pleasure be substituted for the desire for collective feelings and ideals based upon a higher morality."[501]

Joyce notes the example of the Jewish promotion of pornography and alcoholism in Poland prior to the 1939 German invasion, where "Jews were widely understood by both Poles and Germans as having been intimately involved in the alcohol industry." Joyce cites a *Tablet* article affirming that, indeed, Jews "ruled Poland's liquor trade for centuries"; Polish peasants were actually *compelled* to purchase Jewish alcohol. In the nineteenth century, Jews also owned and operated taverns, "in which they established gambling facilities to further squeeze the Poles." Jews have long been associated with the gambling industry, with many sources pointing to the State of Israel as the global capital of online gambling. As we have seen, obscene scatological and sexual language suffuses Talmudic religious literature, so it comes as no surprise that the Jews have long been known as an "obscene people." Sources across England, Estonia, France, Poland, and elsewhere in Europe all confirm the Jewish role in the production and dissemination of obscenity. As Polish Bishop Józef Pelczar wrote, it is

[501] Joyce, "Thoughts on Jews, Obscenity, and the Legal System."

imperative to warn Christian people about "those Jews who intoxicate our people in the tavern and destroy them with usury; against those who maintain houses of debauchery in the towns; who trade in live goods, who poison our young people with pornographic prints and periodicals."

The primacy of Jews in the American legal system is, as Joyce describes it, an example of "Jewish ethnic networking"; in the case of their instrumental role in the repeal of American obscenity laws, Joyce notes that the phenomenon "may be regarded as acting as tactical 'fulcrums' upon which relatively small numbers of influential individuals can 'tilt' the social mores of a host population in directions perceived to benefit Jewish interests." Aside from the foisting of filth upon America, Jews also formed the vanguard of the legal war on Christianity. The modern formulation of "separation of Church and State," which, we must emphasize, is *nowhere* to be found in the text of the Constitution, "is an area where Jews saw a clear Jewish interest in eradicating public displays of Christianity."

This brings us to another facet of the anti-White, anti-Christian animus that undergirds the engendering of sexual profligacy—control. The Marquis de Sade, who was a partisan of the French Revolution, wrote that "the state of the moral man is one of tranquility and peace, the state of an immoral man is one of perpetual unrest." Saint Augustine writes that "a man has as many masters as he has vices." E. Michael Jones notes that Aldous Huxley's *Brave New World:*

> [R]ecognized that sexual passion was an especially effective form of social control because it was so effectively internalized. In defending his passions, the victim thinks he is defending his very self when in fact he is defending the interests of those who give him the permission to gratify them.[502]

As Huxley wrote, the most effective form of totalitarianism would be one in which the subjects need not be coerced, because they were already in love with their own unfreedom. "To make them love it is the task assigned . . . to ministries of

---

[502] Jones, *Libido Dominandi*, 303.

propaganda, newspaper editors, and schoolteachers." Jones pinpoints the true meaning of the Jewish cry for "sexual liberation" and "freedom" when he comments that "liberation from oppression turns out to be a transitional period from the former to the latter condition."[503] Pornography, Jones writes:

> Pornography has nothing to do with freedom. Pornography is a weapon because, as Saint Thomas Aquinas pointed out, lust "darkens the mind." Lust makes you blind. A blind opponent is easily defeated. Pornography is the weaponization of Lust.[504]

Indeed, Jones elaborates:

> If morality is a form of repression, then reason is repressive, and if reason is repressive, then man can become free only by becoming irrational, but once he becomes irrational, the only thing that drives him to act is his appetite, his impulse, his passion. But once man is driven by his passions, he loses all control of his actions. Thus, freedom of this sort . . . becomes a form of slavery. Those who advocate freedom of this sort are promoting . . . a form of social control, because the motive for action which previously lay in reason has now been replaced by the stimulation of passion. Those who control the stimuli now control the stimulated. The purpose of transgressive imagery is social control. Those who relinquish reason are controlled by their passions, which are exploited financially and politically by those who control the flow of transgressive imagery. [Sexuality is] intrinsically other-directed. If it is not directed toward a spouse and put at the service of life, it will be directed toward people who have been turned into objects, and then it will head toward death. [Masturbation] destroys your prayer life, or prayer destroys your ability to enjoy masturbation. The two . . . are psychically mutually exclusive. Anyone interested in changing the default settings of the culture would notice that the settings are binary . . . either/or. There are only two cultural options. Either the State fosters prayer, belief in God, the authority of the father as God's representative, and the social order based on morals, or it fosters masturbation, which is to say, illicit sexual activity, which brings

---

503 Ibid., 267.
504 Jones, "Pornography and Political Control."

> about an inability to pray, the "death" of God, the loss of authority by the father, revolution, and . . . social chaos.[505]

It is the indispensable Richard Weaver, though, who said it best:

> Our most serious obstacle is that people traveling this downward path develop an insensibility which increases with their degradation. Loss is perceived most clearly at the beginning; after habit becomes implanted, one beholds the anomalous situation of apathy mounting as the moral crisis deepens. It is when the first faint warnings come that one has the best chance to save himself; and this, I suspect, explains why medieval thinkers were extremely agitated over questions which seem to us today without point or relevance. If one goes on, the monitory voices fade out, and it is not impossible for him to reach a state in which his entire moral orientation is lost. Thus, in the face of the enormous brutality of our age we seem unable to make an appropriate response to perversions of truth and acts of bestiality. . . . We approach a condition in which we shall be amoral without the capacity to perceive it and degraded without means to measure our descent.[506]

Though we have touched upon the smoking, ruined husk of a nation that the Jewish promotion of the culture of degeneracy has left in its wake, we will here explore some of the more concrete effects by investigating the impact of pornography on American life. Darkmoon cites numerous studies that show that pornography addiction, and its attendant compulsive masturbation, actually alters brain chemistry and reorganizes the *structure* of the brain, which can produce brain *damage*.[507] Sex addiction almost always fueled by internet pornography, has been proven to act on the brain just as cocaine or heroin

---

[505] Jones, *Libido Dominandi*, 265.
[506] Weaver, *Ideas Have Consequences*, 101.
[507] Darkmoon, "Pornography's Effect on the Brain."

addiction does, and its effects are perhaps worse, striking at the very foundation of society.[508]

Research supports the fact that pornographic images lodge themselves in the brain, releasing endorphins that intoxicate people in a way not unlike intoxication to drugs and alcohol. As one neuroscientist has described, "What we are saying here is that an event which lasts half a second [image imprint], within five to ten minutes has produced a structural change . . . as profound as the structural changes one sees in [brain] damage." Judith Reisman refers to this as "brain sabotage," thereby "implying that pornographers are in fact engaged in a species of 'sex terrorism.'"[509]

Because pornography is the provision of sexual stimulus without sex, as we consume ever-increasing quantities of pornography, the brain is "rewired so that what triggers the reward system that is supposed to be linked to sex is no longer linked to sex—to a human in the flesh, to touching, to kissing, to caressing—but to porn." Thus, we are living in the midst of a historically unprecedented epidemic of chronic erectile dysfunction, especially among men under forty. Higher levels of pornographic consumption are correlated with decreased grey matter in the reward system, along with "less reward circuit activation while viewing sexual photos—in other words, porn users were desensitized." Researchers at the Max Planck Institute concluded from this apparent habituation that, just as with drug tolerance, "subjects with high pornography consumption require ever stronger stimuli to reach the same reward level."[510]

This pornographic tolerance, the addictive need for greater amounts of pornography for the same quasi-sexual stimulation, has synergistically led to the increasing popularization of sadomasochism, of violent degradation, rape, and other

---

[508] I point the reader to *Shame*, Steve McQueen's 2011 masterpiece of modern alienation and despair, the finest portrait of sex addiction that will ever be undertaken, starring the devastating Michael Fassbender. The reader should also compare *Don Jon*, Joseph Gordon-Levitt's excellent portrait of porn addiction.

[509] Darkmoon, "Pornography's Effect on the Brain."

[510] Ibid.

manifestations of "extreme" or "hardcore" pornography. For example, two of the pornographic categories that have exploded in the past decade are incestuous and interracial pornography. We could not imagine two categories more representative of the assault on the White social order. Because "Tube" sites nominally ban incest, their popular videos are replete with "stepdads," "stepmoms," and "stepsisters." One of the nastier subgenres of interracial pornography is so-called "cuckoldry," where White actors watch hordes of Black men sexually dominate their White "wives."

Child pornography, the consumption of which has increased astronomically in the last five years, is another manifestation of this trend. Child pornography, i.e., the rape of children, has already been found on popular "Tube" sites, such as those owned by MindGeek, including Pornhub. 2019 marked the first year in recent memory that the "teen" pornographic category did not make the top ten most-searched terms on Pornhub, most likely because "content that fetishizes underage girls and teens is so popular in the porn world that 'teen' porn has been absorbed by many of the other categories." [511] The sexualization of children has by no means become less popular; rather, it has become so dominant that it is taken for granted that pornographic actresses in any given category will automatically be just above the age of majority.

Legalized pedophilia is surely the final frontier of the sexual revolution, looming imminently on the horizon. Already, cries grow apace for the normalization of "minor-attracted persons" as just another "sexual orientation"; as we have already shown, Jews made up the vanguard of this movement as well, with the founding of NAMBLA. We are presumably one Supreme Court ruling away from the Koch-funded cocktail conservative crowd celebrating pederasty as the next great achievement of individual liberty. Child sex trafficking is the fastest-growing business in organized crime, and is an extremely lucrative operation, falling only behind drugs and guns in terms of potential profitability; every year, it is

---

[511] FTND, "Pornhub's Annual Report."

estimated that at least one hundred thousand children in our country are sold into sexual slavery and bought for sex almost three million times.

As pornography "tolerance" increases, the consumer is no longer satiated by what he had been watching; he needs evermore *shocking* content, much like the gateway theory of illicit drug usage. Research suggests that pornography addiction, especially when coupled with stimulant usage, might affect our sexual orientation; if not "turning" heterosexuals into homosexuals outright, pornography can weaken our resistance and lead heterosexual users to experiment with homosexuality. The recent dramatic increase in the consumption of transgender pornography might be evidence of this phenomenon. Anecdotal evidence suggests that serial killers like Gary Bishop, Ted Bundy, and Thomas Schiro were driven insane by their extreme sex addiction. We must also note the prevalence of miscegenation in pornography, and the obvious consequences thereof. Regardless, it is uncontestable that porn fundamentally restructures our minds, altering the very nature and content of our desires.

Victor Cline, an expert on sex addiction, writes that, in his experience:

> Any individual who regularly masturbates to pornography is at risk of becoming, in time, a sexual addict, as well as conditioning himself into having a sexual deviancy. A frequent side effect is that it also dramatically reduces their capacity to love. Their sexual side becomes in a sense dehumanized. Many of them develop an "alien ego state" (or dark side), whose core is antisocial lust devoid of most values.[512]

To those who paint masturbation as some sort of "stress release valve," Darkmoon replies:

> Porn addiction and its invariable accompaniment, compulsive masturbation, are in fact stress *increasers*. They are often found as major symptoms in obsessive-compulsive disorders. Far from relieving depression, they intensify it. Indeed, they

[512] Darkmoon, "Pornography's Effect on the Brain."

> are all too often the underlying cause of the depression in that they generate a huge loss of self-esteem. These are truisms, patently obvious to all except the merchants of lies.

Kevin MacDonald notes that pornography "plugs into male fantasies that are quite incompatible with monogamous relationships based on love and affection toward wives and children."[513] MacDonald cites copious research that supports the conclusion that the consumption of pornography is incompatible with the attitudes and behaviors required for strong family relationships. Frequent consumption of pornography is strongly linked to social anxiety, romantic attachment anxiety, depression, heightened stress, decreased working memory performance, decreased decision-making ability, higher impulsivity, sexually aggressive behavior toward women, the incitement of sexual predators to act on their fantasies, general criminal delinquency, heightened rates of neurosis, decreased altruism, callousness, and, most importantly, attitudes among young adults that sex is a recreational sport, which leads to less involvement with marriage and children, and thus lower fertility. These attitudes foster casual sex, wherein "partners" attempt to mimic the sexual behavior they have seen in pornography, including anal intercourse. Pornographic consumption is also associated with promiscuity, illicit drug use during sex, and the dissolution of relationships, both marital and pre-marital. These issues are exacerbated by the fact that the age of first exposure to pornography continues to decrease; though precise numbers are difficult to obtain, some studies have shown that children begin to encounter pornography at eight years old or earlier. Perhaps even more frightening, a slew of reporting over the past decade has showed a marked decline in sex among young people, both within and without wedlock, as pornography has increasingly turned all sexual behavior inward, producing a world of chronic masturbaters who find no reason to pursue anything beyond narcissistic self-indulgence.

---

[513] MacDonald, "Research on Pornography."

Gobry cites one study that shows that over sixty percent of boys and thirty percent of girls were exposed to pornography in early adolescence, including "bondage, rape, and child pornography," and another which concludes that children *under ten years old* now account for over twenty percent of online pornographic consumption.[514] This is no doubt related to the "embedded sexual content" in popular film, music, and television; as MacDonald defines the term, "this content is not pornographic, but it has positive depictions of teenage sex as normal and 'cool.'" We need only flip television channels once or twice to land on some production, the director, producers, and writers of which are usually Jewish, wherein the camera disgustingly lingers on the body of a teenage girl who has barely reached puberty. This is by no means confined to the media, though the media has certainly normalized and promoted the phenomenon; merely witness what juvenile cheerleading and dance uniforms look like.

Data, both anecdotal and scientific, has long demonstrated that "teenagers are very prone to conforming to media images of what is socially acceptable, especially among their peers, so it is not surprising that the data show that teenagers feel pressure to be sexually active." Nor is this phenomenon confined to adolescence; after all, adolescents become adults. Gobry points to one study, utilizing the General Social Survey, which found that "beginning pornography use between survey waves nearly doubled one's likelihood of being divorced by the next survey period." The study also found that "the group whose probability of divorce increased the most was couples who initially reported being 'very happy' in their marriage and began using porn afterward." Indeed, it has been shown that a majority—in one study nearly sixty percent—of divorces now involve the pornographic or sexual addiction of one spouse.

Pornography advocates argue that the enormous, pervasive (over sixty percent of self-described Christians admit to watching pornography at least once per month), and ever-metastasizing quantity of pornographic consumption is evidence that we have a "natural need to gratify ourselves

---

[514] Gobry, "A Science-Based Case."

through porn." That is so farcical that we need not exert much force against it; it is the same thing as flooding a community with opioid prescriptions and making addicts of the population, and then turning around and stating, without irony, that this is proof that the people had a natural need to drug themselves into oblivion. Lasha Darkmoon notes that pornography is a highly efficient means of social control:

> Most people are only too pleased to live under governments that offer them the seductive pleasures of porn: that is to say, cheap and easy orgasms as substitutes for happiness. . . . Pornography is no longer the relatively mild aphrodisiac it used to be in the Summer of Love, 1967, when the Sexual Revolution first began to take off. With the advent of the internet and the advance in audiovisual communications, its lethality has increased exponentially. Future advances in the area of holographic images and reality drugs threaten to make porn so irresistible to future generations that ordinary sex as we know it will pale into insignificance and fail to exercise its customary charms. Autoeroticism will then reign supreme; and the zombie sex addict, dead-eyed and drooling with unquenchable lust, will inherit the earth and turn it into a vast masturbatorium. This is one vision of the sex dystopia to come: a science fiction nightmare that has every chance of being realized. This is a world in which only the sexually fit will survive as the masters, those schooled to self-discipline and impulse control. The weak-willed and degenerate will not necessarily die out. They will simply sink into the amorphous lumpenproletariat as permanent slaves.

We have established that pornography "damages the character, weakens the will, and produces sexual deviance in those it infects." Can it get worse? Of course. Reginald Thompson takes our aforementioned discussion and follows it to its logical consequence: White genocide. Thompson finds that the corrosion of romantic love, along with its concomitant destruction of stable pair bond-based reproduction, strongly correlates to both the incidence of pornography and the Total Fertility Rate. The American Total Fertility Rate "suffered a *profound* decline" in response to *Jacobellis* and *Stanley*, two of the most important Supreme Court cases for the unrestricted dissemination of pornography.[515] Thompson also shows that there is "a stunningly large gap in fertility between countries where pornography is banned and countries where it is wholly or partially legal."

This discrepancy cannot be explained by the fact that virtually all White countries, or at least those European and American countries which remain White for the time being, have legalized pornography while experiencing lowered fertility rates for other reasons, as the discrepancy remained almost exactly the same when Thompson eliminated the White countries from the equation. This discrepancy also cannot be explained by the possibility that Muslim countries, for example, have widespread illegal pornography while having high fertility for other reasons, as the correlation remained essentially unchanged after tossing the Muslim countries out as well. The conclusion? Pornography seems to be at least one driving factor behind the White fertility crisis. Perhaps this is why there is a pitched campaign against those White men that abstain from pornography. As Grayson Quay reports, *The American Conservative*, *Rolling Stone* and Trevor Noah's *Daily Show*, among others, have trotted out "psychologists" to assert that pornography and masturbation make "a lot of really good things happen in your body and your brain" and that "people who watch more pornography . . . are more feminist" and have "more egalitarian values." Those who dare to refrain from abusing themselves have embraced "the ideology . . . of the far right," including "anti-Semitism," "homophobia," "misogyny," and, you guessed it, "racism."[516] Their argument goes something like, "You know who else hated porn? Hitler!"

We have conclusively established that Jewish leadership and participation was instrumental in, and a necessary condition of, the pornographic war that has struck at the most sacred foundation of the West: the family. A preponderance of the preceding evidence leads us to the inescapable conclusion that this *was* indeed conscious, that the psychosexual carnage of the past sixty years was premeditated. For those of us who

---

515 Thompson, "Legalized Pornography and Demographic Genocide."

516 Quay, "Rolling Stone: Men Who Abstain."

might still have doubts, we will conclude with the remark that Sigmund Freud is supposed to have made to Carl Jung in 1909, as their ship docked in New York Harbor: "They don't realize that we are bringing them the plague."

Jewish Ritual Murder of Christian Children

Finally, we arrive at one of the most sickening manifestations of the Talmudic hatred of Gentiles that permeates Jewish life: the so-called "blood libel," the commonly held historical Christian belief that Jews periodically abducted, crucified, grotesquely tortured, eviscerated, exsanguinated, and ritually murdered Christian children, particularly occurring in conjunction with the Jewish Passover and Purim holidays. This accusation has been dismissed throughout the twentieth century and into the present, used to lampoon Christian "conspiracy theories" regarding Judaism. As with certain other "conspiracy theories," though, considerable evidence suggests that the blood libel is no libel at all; *these bizarre ritual murders actually happened.* Jews, in a seemingly well-organized fashion, *did* abduct, torture, and sacrifice Christian infants and children for the purposes of desecrating and mocking Christ. Jews *did* exsanguinate Christian children for the use of their blood in religious rituals. This claim should not shock us. We have established that the Gentile is not considered to be human, but rather a beast of burden whose worth is wholly derived from the potential benefit that the Jew may extract from him. Orthodox Judaism, especially in the Talmud and the Kabbalah, emphasized (and emphasizes) black magic and other outlandish rites, among which ritual human sacrifice would hardly be surprising.

Harold Covington gives us a good introduction to this sordid topic:

> There is an immense amount of anecdotal and circumstantial evidence that these sacrificial homicides took place in the

past, back in times when concealment was harder and Aryans far more aware and wary of the Jew than they are today. It is significant that ever since the days of Babylon, a period of almost four thousand years, this accusation (like many others) has been leveled against the Jews everywhere they have ever resided in the world. Time and again down through the ages the Jews have been caught literally red-handed, in some cases toting the dead body of the child whose blood they have drained away to dispose of it in sacks or wagons, sometimes with the corpse being found in the synagogue cellars. . . . The Jewish response . . . [maintains] that down through forty centuries of history, there has been a mammoth conspiracy to frame them for ritual murder. According to this theory, in places as far apart as Cochin China, medieval Germany, 1913 Kiev and 1970 Montreal, and among peoples as diverse as knightly Crusaders, Turkish sultans, twelfth-century Yorkshire Saxons, Argentinians, Cossacks, British historians, Renaissance Italian popes, assorted saints and sinners, the burgomasters of Prague, and modern-day Arabs, there exists one big, long, continuous plot periodically to murder small children, drain them of blood, and plant the bodies on Jewish premises or in Jewish vehicles. . . . That's one hell of a conspiracy! Our medieval ancestors were not fools. They lived with the Jews side by side in close-packed urban communities, very small by modern standards, and knew the Jews far more intimately than we do today. Just like people today, they cared about their children and when a child was slain the entire community interested itself not only for purposes of revenge, but to ensure the safety of everyone's kids. We are asked to believe that time and again, insular communities who discovered they had a child-killer in their midst stubbornly refused to apprehend the alleged Gentile 'real killers' and blamed the Jews out of religious bigotry. What possible interest could any community, medieval or otherwise, have in lynching an innocent scapegoat and allowing a real killer of children to go free? Why would everyone in Trier or Lincoln or Spoleto or Kiev go along with such a miscarriage of justice when doing so put other children at risk? Why (so far as we know) did the child-killings cease once the Jews had been punished and (usually) driven from the community? [517]

[517] Covington, "Why I Believe in Jewish Ritual Murder."

We have Ariel Toaff to thank for his singularly instrumental role in documenting the reality of Jewish ritual murder of Christian children. Toaff, professor of Jewish Medieval and Renaissance history at Bar-Ilan University near Tel Aviv, is no anti-Semite; indeed, he is the son of the late Elio Toaff, the former Chief Rabbi of Rome. In 2007, Toaff published *Pasque di sangue*, translated in English as *Blood Passover*, the product of years of deep research into Medieval Jewry, of which he was already a master. Unz remarks that Toaff "certainly seems an extremely erudite scholar, drawing heavily upon the secondary literature in English, French, German, and Italian, as well as the original documentary sources in Latin, Medieval Italian, Hebrew, and Yiddish."[518]

The English translators note that the text, far from being a secret product of niche interest, is the culmination of years of rigorous academic research conducted in public. "The author is extremely careful about what he says, and his conclusions must be taken seriously."[519] We must also recognize that, had *Blood Passover* been published in Hebrew, in Israel, "no one would have cared. There are large bodies of literature in Hebrew that Jews do not wish Gentiles to know about. But Dr. Toaff's announcement of its publication in Italy, in Italian, raised a worldwide firestorm of fury."[520] Almost immediately upon its Italian publication, Toaff came under attack by a legion of Jewish berserkers led by the Anti-Defamation League. As chronicled by Israel Shamir, Toaff initially stood his ground, completely assured in the veracity of his truly brilliant scholarship, declaring that "I will not give up my devotion to the truth and academic freedom even if the world crucifies me."[521]

Soon, though, Toaff "broke down in a mental cellar of Jewish inquisition." Andrew Hamilton notes that "a single positive review of *Blood Passover* appeared before the roof fell in"; Italian Jewish historian Sergio Luzatto praised Toaff's work in the prestigious *Corriere della Sera*, which can be considered Italy's

[518] Unz, "American Pravda."
[519] Toaff, *Blood Passover*, 4.
[520] Ibid., 5.
[521] Shamir, "Bloody Passovers of Dr Toaff."

"paper of record," as a "magnificent book of history."[522] Toaff's elderly father, with whom Pope John Paul II prayed at the Synagogue of Rome, the first-ever visit by a pope to a synagogue, excoriated his son, writing:

> The criticism that everyone has expressed about his book was justified. His arguments were an insult to the intelligence, to the tradition, to history in general and to the meaning of the Jewish religion. It saddens me that such nonsense was put forward by my son of all people.[523]

Toaff's employer, under violent pressure, condemned the book. Though all sources today claim that Toaff still teaches there, this seems highly suspect, as Toaff appears to have dropped off the face of the earth. In the face of such sustained assault, Toaff published an apology, ceased distributing *Blood Passover*, promised to submit to Jewish censors, and vowed to donate all of the proceeds to the ADL. Shamir remarks:

> His last words were as touching as those of Galileo recanting his heresy: "I will never allow any Jew-hater to use me or my research as an instrument for fanning the flames, once again, of the hatred that led to the murder of millions of Jews. I extend my sincerest apologies to all those who were offended by the articles and twisted facts that were attributed to me and to my book."

Shamir also compares Toaff to Uriel da Costa, the Portuguese philosopher who was ostracized for his criticisms of rabbinical Judaism; the poor fellow committed suicide after years as a pariah.

Before we dive further into the sordid details of Toaff's vindication of the reality of Jewish ritual murder, we will outline his findings. In brief, Unz summarizes:

> It appears that a considerable number of Ashkenazi Jews traditionally regarded Christian blood as having powerful magical properties and considered it a very valuable component of

[522] Hamilton, "Diabolical Passion."
[523] Quoted in Ibid.

> certain important ritual observances at particular religious holidays. Obviously, obtaining such blood in large amounts was fraught with considerable risk, which greatly enhanced its monetary value, and the trade in the vials of this commodity seems to have been widely practiced. Toaff notes that since the detailed descriptions of the Jewish ritualistic murder practices are very similarly described in locations widely separated by geography, language, culture, and time period, they are almost certainly independent observations of the same rite. Furthermore, he notes that when accused Jews were caught and questioned, they often correctly described obscure religious rituals which could not possibly have been known to their Gentile interrogators, who often garbled minor details. Thus, these confessions were very unlikely to have been concocted by the authorities.

Though Toaff repeatedly argues that the Ashkenazi Jews involved in ritual murder were isolated members of a tiny fringe sect, Hamilton notes:

> Since the people (both rabbinic and secular) implicated in . . . ritual murder cases were high status, wealthy, powerful members of their communities, Toaff's at times exculpatory comments (especially following the almost-immediate suppression of the first edition of his book) to the effect that only a few marginal, extremist Ashkenazi sects or individuals were involved is constantly belied by his own evidence.

In some of these cases, hundreds of defendants were allegedly involved, with scores of Jews per case convicted and executed. So, rather than say that only some Jews were involved in this practice, "it would be more truthful to say, as the author does at one point, that some Ashkenazim strongly opposed ritual murder and Passover blood ceremonies."[524]

No less than twenty-three innocent children ritually murdered by Jews were canonized or venerated by the Catholic Church, with miracles, healings, and answered prayers documented at their tombs, most of which became pilgrimage sites, including Saint William of Norwich, Blessed Michael of

[524] Ibid.

Sappenfeld, Little Saint Hugh of Lincoln, the Holy Child of La Guardia, Saint Harold of Gloucester, Saint Simon of Trent (whose murder is depicted on the cover of the English translation of *Blood Passover*), and Saint Sigbert of Cologne. Saint Gavril Belostotsky was canonized by the Eastern Orthodox Church. We must again note the sheer volume of cases and accusations, over many centuries, with an essentially identical *modus operandi*; while *some* of these cases may certainly have been falsely attributed to the Jews, by no means could *all* of them be fabrications.

As Philip de Vier explains:

> Each case usually involved the murder of a child or a young woman, on or around the Jewish high holidays of Purim and Passover. Often the bodies of the kidnapped and tortured victims were curiously wounded and drained of blood, though no blood evidence was found nearby, which led observers to suspect ritual abuse. These were comparatively primitive times in the area of forensics. . . . Modern autopsies were virtually unknown and were regarded as ghoulish, forbidden acts. There was little or no refrigeration, and bodies began quick decomposition, making prompt and complete disposal a priority. Any examination of the corpses had to happen soon after the victim's death. Learned people of the day most usually comprised the official court of inquiry. These . . . included physicians, lawyers, judges, civil officials, university faculty, and others . . . the jurists of old were not fools, and they often wrote long, detailed reports of the proceedings, many of which are extant today.[525]

It is also important to note that, especially in the cases of those martyred children who were beatified or canonized, the victims' clothing and the weapons used to slaughter them, when recovered, were stored in cathedral reliquaries.

For vengeance, the vicarious desecration of Christ, and the procurement of young Christian blood for Kabbalistic and other secret Jewish rites, "at Purim and at Passover, a Christian was kidnapped, tortured, often crucified, killed, and

---

[525] de Vier, *Blood Ritual*, 49.

drained of blood destined for use in diabolistic rites. The victim was usually an adult at Purim, but was often a young child at Passover."[526] De Vier notes:

> Whereas Passover required the purity of a child, Purim required an adult to be killed and tortured as a living effigy of the dreaded Haman of the Esther saga. There are . . . cases recorded where bands of drunken Jews attacked Christians at this time of year, and many ritual murder case dates coincide with this Jewish Revenge Feast of Purim.[527]

Purim, one of the most important Jewish holidays, commemorates the deliverance of the Jews from extermination at the hands of the Persian courtier Haman, recounted in the Book of Esther. Early Jewish accounts of Purim describe "a carnival-like atmosphere of celebrations and convivial opulence in which restraint and inhibition were dangerously weakened."[528] For example, one states:

> In memory of everything we read in the Book of Esther, which saved the people of Israel from being exterminated through the machinations of Haman . . . after the ordinary orations, with remembrance only of the escape which occurred at the hour of death, we read the entire History or Book of Esther, written in bulk, on parchment. . . . And some hearing Haman's name mentioned, pound on the tables as a sign to curse him. . . . They make much rejoicing festivities and banquets . . . an effort is made to serve the most sumptuous meal possible and eat and drink more than usual, after which friends go out to visit each other, with receptions, festivities and revelry.[529]

Toaff explains that, "for a number of reasons, not least that of its not infrequent proximity to Holy Week, Purim . . . came, in time, to acquire openly anti-Christian connotations."[530] Over time, Haman became equated with Christ, the new enemy of

---

[526] de Vier, *Blood Ritual*, 22.
[527] Ibid., 23.
[528] Horowitz, *Reckless Rites*, 133.
[529] Ibid., 180.
[530] Toaff, *Blood Passover*, 190.

the Jews whose existence entailed their own destruction. This equation of the two was aided by the fact that Haman was killed by hanging, which the Talmud records as being the method of Christ's death.

Often, Toaff notes, "the ritual of Purim did not always conclude with the bloodless hanging of a mere effigy of Haman. Sometimes, the 'effigy' was a flesh-and-blood Christian, crucified for real, during the wild revelry of the Jewish carnival."[531] A fifth-century source:

> Refers to a case occurring in 415 at Inmestar, near Antioch, in Syria . . . [in which the Jews] took to deriding the Christians and Christ Himself in their boasting; they ridiculed the cross and anyone trusting in the crucifix, putting the following joke in practice. . . . They took a Christian child, tied it to a cross and hanged him. Initially they made him the object of jokes and drollery; then, after a while, they lost control of themselves and mistreated him to such a degree that they killed him.[532]

It is important to note that the Talmud seemingly sanctions and even enjoins such extreme violence by explicitly *commanding* pious Jews to drink themselves into a stupor. Toaff remarks that in the early modern period, "the carnival-like festivities of Purim finally lost those qualities of aggressiveness and violence which had been characteristic since the early Middle Ages, but never renounced the clearly anti-Christian meaning it possessed according to tradition."[533] The narrative of Passover should be familiar to all of us, but the key point here is the tenth plague, God's killing of "all the firstborn in the land of Egypt," sparing, or *passing over*, the Jews who had obeyed his instructions to sacrifice a lamb and smear its blood upon their doors.

Virtually all alleged cases of Jewish ritual murder involved abductions, disappearances, and corpses recovered under remarkably similar circumstances with common causes of death. The Passover and Purim timings were uncannily

[531] Ibid., 192.
[532] Ibid., 193.
[533] Ibid., 195.

consistent. Some cases are obviously more credible and well-supported than others, especially in the case of martyred children who were beatified and canonized, which required multi-adjudication, with evidentiary and trial records pored through thoroughly and laboriously by numerous different courts of inquiry; it is only these cases with the most evidence that we focus on here. There were many trials, many confessions, and many convictions and executions, with just as many acquittals and unsolved incidents; some acquittals were obtained through Jewish bribery of the Church.

Many of the ritual trials featured testimony from Jewish converts to Christianity, who were well-versed in the Talmud; one former Chief Rabbi testified:

> The blood of the victims is to be tapped by force. On Passover it is used in wine and *matzos*. Thus, a small part of the blood is to be poured into the dough of *matzos* and into the wine.... The family head empties a few drops of the fresh or powdered blood into a glass, wets the fingers of the left hand with it, and sprays with it everything on the table. The head of the family then says, "Thus, we ask God to send the ten plagues to all enemies of the Jewish faith." Then they eat, and at the end the head of the family exclaims, "May all Gentiles perish, as the child whose blood is contained in the bread and wine." The fresh (or dried or powdered) blood of the slaughtered is further used by young married Jewish couples, by pregnant Jewesses, for circumcision, and so on. Ritual murder is recognized by all Talmud Jews. The Jew believes he absolves himself thus of his sins. [534]

With remarkable consistency, Jewish converts to Christianity, including former rabbis, swore that "Christian blood, ritually obtained, was an essential part of secret Kabbalistic Jewish rites, of a secret oral tradition."[535] De Vier considered, and Toaff would later confirm, that "transmission by oral lore and initiation rites is ... likely. Writing it down would have been risky." [536]

---

[534] de Vier, *Blood Ritual*, 22.
[535] Toaff, *Blood Passover*, 103.
[536] Ibid., 272.

Though many Jewish confessions to ritual murder were extracted through judicially-administered torture, a fact which is today used to dismiss the confessions altogether, we must remember that torture was a standard method of interrogation in Medieval Europe. Torture does not preclude fact-finding, and indeed, as Toaff notes and as we will explore further, many confessions extracted under torture contained extremely detailed Talmudic language and lore that the Christian authorities had no way of knowing. Additionally, Christian authorities were careful to corroborate any confessions by subjecting defendants to multiple rounds of interrogation over long periods of time; truth was their aim. Jews and philo-Semites today also love to dismiss the ritual murder as an anti-Semitic Christian fantasy; obviously, Christians were uniformly anti-Semitic. That is not the question; most people never pause to ask *why* this was the case, what lay *behind* the anti-Semitism, instead chalking it up to unthinking prejudice.

Accusations of ritual murder have followed Jewry wherever it has set foot; our focus is specifically on Medieval Europe, where the overwhelming majority of cases were reported, though in Europe cases of ritual murder have been cited from Eusebius up through the nineteenth century; for just one example, there is considerable evidence which suggests that Jack the Ripper was Aaron Kosminski or John Pizer, both Polish Jews. Though accusations fell precipitously in the twentieth century—unless, of course, we consider the World Wars, as well as the gratuitous rapine of Jewish-dominated Soviet Russia—this by no means constitutes evidence that Jewish ritual sacrifice has ever stopped.

On the contrary, a probable case occurred from 1955 to 1956, in Chicago. Three young boys and two teenage girls, all White, of course, were abducted and murdered in a manner which is strongly suggestive of Jewish ritual murder. The children were exsanguinated and bore wounds mirroring those of Christ during his crucifixion by Jews, and their skin bore imprinted Kabbalistic symbols, as if they had been tied to a table adorned with them; furthermore, their wounds contained traces of *matzos* grain. When the *Chicago Daily News* reported on the ritualistic aspect to the murders, that edition of the newspaper was almost instantly suppressed; within ten minutes of hitting the street, newspaper trucks collected each one from driveways and newsstands across Chicago. When one woman inquired as to this bizarre behavior, the paper told her that it had been recalled because of potential "racial unrest." The criminal behavior of the investigating police officers ensured that the case was never solved, and the father of two of the murdered boys was, in a common Jewish tactic, involuntarily committed to a Jewish-run asylum, whereupon he was immediately administered electroshock therapy and died that very afternoon. The corpses of another two similarly mutilated children were found in 1957 and 1958, also, of course, unsolved.[537]

To explain the decline in these allegations, we must note that it was during the twentieth century that the Jew conquered the earth and imposed a panoptic social credit regime which is now reaching its zenith, a fact which, aside from limiting the incidence of any members of the general population daring to point the finger at a Jew, would explain why any evidence would be ruthlessly suppressed by the Jewish press. Again, we must recall that ritual murders "are a fact, and not merely the product of an overactive imagination. They are a part of recorded history in many . . . cultures during all ages, including our present one."[538] Why should Jews be exempt? De Vier continues, noting:

> As the twentieth century dawned, almost all the old accusations against the Jews ceased. Yet . . . ritual human sacrifice kept popping up. . . . We know that if the situation were different, and this much evidence pointed toward almost any other ethnic group (especially whites), we would have cries for a wider investigation. If a "white supremacist" . . . group were accused of serial murders over the centuries, mostly of children, we would spend tax dollars investigating, and the victim groups would cry out for justice—and reparations. What if it

537 de Vier, *Blood Ritual*, 156.
538 Ibid., 233.

> were alleged that a cult among white slave owners practiced ritual torture and murder?[539]

One of the earliest cases of Jewish ritual murder in Europe is that of Saint William of Norwich, who disappeared on March 20th, 1144, the eve of Passover. William, only twelve years old, was the son of a peasant, and a tanner's apprentice. His mutilated corpse was found in Thorpe Wood "with countless cuts and stab wounds"; though evidence suggested that he was lured away from home by area Jews, and was apparently last seen entering the home of a Jew, no charges were filed, as the Jews were under the protection of the King of England.

Thomas of Monmouth wrote a contemporary hagiography of the murder:

> Then the boy, like an innocent lamb, was led to slaughter. He was treated kindly by the Jews at first, and, ignorant of what was being prepared for him, he was kept till the morrow. But on the next day, which . . . was the Passover . . . after the singing of the hymns appointed for the day in the synagogue, the chiefs of the Jews . . . suddenly seized hold of the boy William as he was having his dinner . . . and ill-treated him in various horrible ways. For while some of them held him behind, others opened his mouth and introduced an instrument of torture . . . called a teazle (wooden gag), and, fixing it by straps through both jaws to the back of his neck, they fastened it with a knot as tightly as could be drawn. More knots were made, severely constricting his neck and head. . . . Having shaved his head, they stabbed it with countless thorn points, and made the blood come horribly from the wounds they made [as in Christ's crown of thorns] . . . some of those present adjudged him to be fixed to a cross in mockery of the Lord's Passion, as though they would say: Even as we condemned the Christ to a shameful death, so let us also condemn the Christian . . . having lifted him from the ground and fastened him upon the cross, they vied with one another in their efforts to make an end of him . . . we, after enquiring into the matter very diligently, did both find the house, and discovered some most certain marks in it of what had been done there . . . the right hand and foot had been tightly bound and fastened with cords, but the left

[539] Ibid., 243

> hand and foot were pierced with two nails. Now the deed was done in this way . . . lest it look like a crucifixion . . . after all these many and great tortures, they inflicted a frightful wound in his left side, reaching even to his inmost heart . . . [just as] Jesus was similarly pierced by a lance while nailed to the cross . . . to stop the blood and to wash and close the wounds, they poured boiling water over him. . . . Theobald, who was once a Jew . . . verily told us that in the ancient writings of his fathers it was written that the Jews, without the shedding of human blood, could neither obtain their freedom, nor could they ever return to their fatherland. Hence it was laid down . . . that every year they must sacrifice a Christian in some part of the world . . . in scorn and contempt of Christ.[540]

Ariel Toaff fills in more of the details surrounding the sadistic murder of Saint William. Among the clients of the tanner to whom William was apprenticed,

> [W]ere a few local Jews, who are thought to have chosen him as the victim of a ritual sacrifice to be performed during the days of the Christian Easter. On the Monday following Palm Sunday, 1144, during the reign of King Stephen, a man claiming to be the cook for the arch deacon of Norwich presented himself in the village of William, asking his mother Elviva for permission to take William with him to work as an apprentice. The woman's suspicions and hesitation were soon won over thanks to a considerable sum of money. The following day, little William was already traveling the streets of Norwich in the company of the self- proclaimed cook, directly to the dwelling of his aunt Leviva, Godwin Sturt's wife, who became informed of the apprenticeship undertaken by the child and his new patron. But the latter individual awakened numerous suspicions in the aunt, Leviva, who asked a young girl to follow them and determine their destination. The shadowing, as discreet as it was effective, took the child to the threshold of the dwelling of Eleazar, one of the heads of the community of Norwich, where the cook had little William enter the house with the necessary prudence and circumspection. . . . Eleazar's Christian servant . . . the following morning . . . by chance, witnessed, with horror—through the crack of a door left inadvertently open—the cruel ceremony of the child's crucifixion and atrocious

[540] Quoted in Ibid., 82–3.

> martyrdom, with the participation, carried out with religious zeal, of local Jews, "in contempt of the passion of our Lord. . . ." To throw off suspicion, the Jews decided to transport the body from the opposite side of the city to Thorpe Wood, which extended to within a short distance from the last house. During the trip on horseback with the cumbersome sack, however, despite their efforts at caution, they crossed the path of a respected and wealthy merchant of the locality on his way to church, accompanied by a servant; the merchant had no difficulty realizing the significance of what was taking place before his eyes. . . . Young William's body was finally hidden by the Jews among the bushes of Thorpe.[541]

Theobald, a Jewish convert to Christianity who would later become a monk, revealed:

> The Jews believed that, to bring redemption closer, and with it, their return to the Promised Land, they sacrificed a Christian child every year "in contempt of Christ." To carry out this providential plan, the representatives of the Jewish communities, headed by their local rabbis, were said to meet every year in council . . . to draw lots as to the name of the locality where the ritual crucifixion was to occur from time to time. In 1144, the choice fell by lot to the city of Norwich, and the entire Jewish community was said to have adhered to that choice.[542]

Toaff argues that, contrary to the servant's interpretation, the boiling water must have been used not to *staunch* the flow of blood, but rather to *accelerate* it.

The murder of Little Saint Hugh of Lincoln is immortalized in Geoffrey Chaucer's "The Prioress's Tale," in *The Canterbury Tales*: "O you young Hugh of Lincoln, also slain, / by cursed Jews."[543] In 1255, the nine-year-old Hugh "was horribly tortured and slain." De Vier cites a contemporary account stating that "a Jew named Copin enticed the child into his house. A large number of Jews were gathered there and they tortured the nine-year-old Christian boy, scourged and crowned him

---

[541] Toaff, *Blood Passover*, 166.

[542] Ibid., 168.

[543] Chaucer, "Prioress's Tale," II, 232–233.

with thorns, and crucified him in mockery of Christ's death."[544] Copin eventually confessed to the murder, saying that the annual crucifixion of boys was a customary practice among Jews. After his corpse was found in Copin's well, eighteen Jews confessed, and were executed with the approval of King Henry III.

Saint Gabriel of Białystok was murdered on Good Friday in 1690; he was "crucified, his side was pricked, and then he was pierced with different tools until all his blood was spilled." In 1286, Blessed Werner was murdered in Oberwesel-on-the-Rhine, Germany. Only fourteen years old, Werner was tortured for three days at Passover, hung from his feet, and exsanguinated, every artery sliced open and drained. According to de Vier, "Sculpted portrayals of the repulsive crime stayed for centuries in the Oberwesel parish church. . . . [T]he relief was removed from the Werner Chapel in 1968 [under Pope Paul VI]."[545] Saint Andreas of Rinn was murdered on June 12th, 1462, near Innsbruck, Austria. The young Andreas Oxner was kidnapped, sold to Jews, and "ceremonially slain on a large boulder deep in the forested Austrian Alps," "put to death by Jews out of hatred for Christ."[546] No charges were brought, but the investigation concluded that the corpse bore all of the hallmarks of ritual murder, and Saint Andreas was beatified and canonized in the eighteenth century. In 1985, during the pontificate of the philo-Semite John Paul II, the Catholic Church decanonized Saint Andreas and suppressed his shrine; the Bishop of Innsbruck sought to "erase all traces. . . . The boy's remains were exhumed and removed from their place of honor. In 1994 the memorials . . . were officially suppressed by Bishop Reinhold Stecher. Relics and testimonies pertaining to his death were ordered destroyed." [547]

Toaff also gives us a more detailed account of the martyrdom of Saint Andreas of Rinn:

> At Rinn . . . on the road to Innsbruck [Austria], a company of Jewish merchants, returning from the fair at Merano, were

[544] de Vier, *Blood Ritual*, 131.
[545] Ibid., 104.
[546] Ibid., 103.
[547] Hoffman, *Judaism Discovered*, 557–8.

> traversing a small village in the Tyrol and bumped into a three-year old child, Andrea Oxner. Having informed themselves as to his family, the Jews knew that the mother was far from home, in the fields at Ambras reaping wheat, and that little Andrea had been entrusted to the care of his godfather . . . Hannes Mayr. Employing every possible stratagem and pretext, the Jews induced this dishonest peasant to hand the child over to them, promising that they would take him away with them to live a life of ease and comfort. But they had no intention of traveling very far with him. Stopping in a birch tree thicket, a little way above Rinn, "the innocent victim's veins were barbarously and cruelly severed by those inhuman creatures, who then hung the bloodless cadaver from a tree." Having obtained the Christian blood which they needed, the Jewish merchants hurried to leave the scene. . . . The martyred child's body was discovered by the desperate mother. The godfather, under intense interrogation, admitted entrusting Andrea to the Jews on the promise that they would educate the child in luxury and riches. He then confessed that he had been persuaded by innumerable glasses of wine, drunk in the company of those foreigners, and a hatful of gold coins which had been placed in his hand. The impious Mayr's fate was signed, more by God than by men. "The perfidious peasant who sold the child was condemned to perpetual imprisonment in his own house."[548]

From this point forward, we will follow Toaff's inquiry, which focuses mostly on the case of Saint Simon of Trent, the ritual slaughter of whom is depicted on the cover of this book; Toaff devotes most of his time to Saint Simon largely due to the fact that most of the records from the trial are still extant; indeed, Toaff finds:

> A careful reading of the trial records, in both form and substance, recalls too many features of the conceptual realities, rituals, liturgical practices and mental attitudes typical of, and exclusive to, one distinct, particular Jewish world—features which can in no way be attributed to suggestion on the part of judges or prelates—to be ignored.[549]

---

[548] Toaff, *Blood Passover*, 103.

[549] Ibid., 11.

Toaff considers these trial documents to be "priceless":

> The trial records—especially, the cracks and rifts in the overall structure permitting the researcher to distinguish and differentiate, in substance, not just in form, between the information provided by the accused and the stereotypes imposed by the inquisitors—are dazzlingly clear. . . . In many cases, everything the defendants said was incomprehensible to the judges—often, because their speech was full of Hebraic ritual and liturgical formulae pronounced with a heavy German accent, unique to the German Jewish community, which not even Italian Jews could understand; in other cases, because their speech referred to mental concepts of an ideological nature totally alien to everything Christian. It is obvious that neither the formulae nor the language can be dismissed as merely the astute fabrications and artificial suggestions of the judges in these trials. Dismissing them as worthless, as invented out of whole cloth, as the spontaneous fantasies of defendants terrorized by torture and projected to satisfy the demands of their inquisitors, cannot be imposed as the compulsory starting point, the prerequisite, for valid research.[550]

In other words, Shamir explains, these confessions "contained material totally unknown to the Italian churchmen or police. The killers belonged to the small and withdrawn Ashkenazi community, [and] they practiced their own rites, quite different from those used by the native Italian Jews."[551] The Hebraic liturgical incantations and formulas *could not* have been fabricated by inquisitors who had *no way* of knowing of or comprehending them.

On March 21st, 1475, Maundy Thursday of Holy Week, Simon, only two years old, was abducted from his home, ritually tortured, and murdered, his mutilated corpse found two days later, on the eve of Passover. Shamir summarizes that a group of Ashkenazim "murdered the child; drew his blood, pierced his flesh with needles, crucified him head down calling, 'So may all Christians by land and sea.'" As de Vier urges, we cannot lose sight of the fact that these boys were innocent people,

---

[550] Ibid., 15.

[551] Shamir, "Bloody Passovers of Dr Toaff."

real victims, and not mere names found in yellowed trial records, "children, entirely helpless to defend themselves against a gang of savage . . . killers."[552]

De Vier recounts the standard narrative of Simon's martyrdom:

> It seems that Simon played outside after the family dinner, last seen sitting on the front steps of his home. Later testimony revealed that he was approached by one Tobias, a Jewish . . . doctor, a surgeon . . . skilled in the use of knives. . . . Tobias became friendly with the boy, eventually . . . bearing him away to the house of . . . one Samuel. Simon was not seen alive again. . . . Eventually the focus of public attention fell on the Jews. . . . The body was "discovered" by some of the Jews in the . . . Adige River [to create the impression of drowning] that flowed not far from the house of . . . Samuel. . . . The boy's naked body had . . . extraordinary wounds and incisions. The child also showed signs of recent circumcision . . . the body was almost completely bloodless. It was clear that he had not drowned.[553]

Sir Richard Burton wrote a similar version:

> The Jews of Trent . . . decoyed to his house while the Christians were at church, it being Maundy Thursday . . . the principal Jews collected in a room near their synagogue. The child, gagged with a kerchief, was extended in the form of a cross, and held down by his murderers. The blood, pouring from heavy gashes, was collected in a basin, and when death drew near the victim was placed upon his legs by the two men, and the others pierced his body with sharp instruments, all vying in brutality and enjoying the torture . . . the murderers were put to death, the synagogue was razed to the ground, and a church was built over the place where the horrid deed was done.[554]

Simon's body was found in a ravine of the Adige River, in close proximity downstream from the prominent Jew Samuel's

---

[552] de Vier, *Blood Ritual*, 106.
[553] Ibid., 108.
[554] Ibid., 79.

cellar. The killers were arrested, charged, and soon confessed under interrogation in the castle of Buonconsiglio; the conspirators were all burned at the stake or decapitated. The investigation and trial were presided over by the Bishop of Trent; according to the confessions, which will be examined in detail, "all the tortures, including the slow exsanguination, happened while the child was alive and aware."[555] The case was adjudicated at least two more times, including at the Vatican by a commission of six cardinals directly appointed by Pope Sixtus IV. Before the ecclesial high court ultimately affirmed the defendants' convictions, however, the Jews of Italy went to great lengths to free them. Andrew Hamilton explains:

> They bribed powerful Christian officials to interfere in the proceedings, pressured Archduke Sigismund of Austria to free the defendants (he did temporarily suspend the judicial proceedings), won the release of the female defendants by applying pressure to Pope Sixtus IV, criminally schemed to break the prisoners out of jail, and attempted to hire the most prominent and successful Christian lawyer of the day. The Jews also instituted legal proceedings against the prime mover behind the trials, the Prince-Bishop of the independent Bishopric of Trent . . . accusing him of attempting to misappropriate the defendants' property. When all of these subterfuges failed, the Jewish community arranged for a Jewish convert . . . to kill the Prince-Bishop by poisoning his food, in spite of [his] precaution of employing three food tasters. The would-be assassin was caught and executed.[556]

To add even more credence to the proceedings, de Vier noted that Trent was a cosmopolitan city with no record of anti-Semitism; as such, "this was essentially a proven case, and . . . cannot be blamed on ignorance or native anti-Jewish prejudice."[557]

In 1965, the Archbishop of Trent unilaterally, and with no new evidence, declared that the Jews were innocent, and at the behest of the philo-Semitic Pope Paul VI, Saint Simon was

---

[555] Ibid., 118.

[556] Hamilton, "Diabolical Passion."

[557] de Vier, *Blood Ritual*, 109.

decanonized, his veneration forbidden, expunged by the Church. Already, Shamir notes:

> The Church leaders had found the Jews free from guilt for Crucifixion of Christ while admitting the Church's guilt for persecution of Jews; the crucifixion of an Italian baby was a small matter compared with this reversal. In a hasty decision, the bishops ruled that the confessions of the killers were unacceptable because obtained under torture, and thus the accused were innocent, while the young martyr was anything but. His cult was discontinued and forbidden, and the remains of the martyred child were removed and dumped in a secret place to avoid resumption of pilgrimage.[558]

Hamilton remarks that it thus "appears that saints can be 'de-sainted,' just as 'Holocaust deniers' can retroactively lose their academic degrees. As a consequence, Simon no longer appears in the *Roman Martyrology*, or on any modern Catholic calendar."[559]

Toaff discovered that there was indeed a thriving underground trade in blood libations, specifically the blood of Christian children, "for use, not only in the preparation of costly and miraculous medications, but in obscure magical and religious rites as well."[560] Jewish vendors sold Christian blood accompanied by rabbinic certifications of authenticity for "ritual suitability . . . as was customarily done for food products prepared according to" Jewish food regulations.[561] Sometimes, these certificates stated the victim's name, origin, and physical appearance. Clotted, coagulated blood was dried, pulverized, and reduced to powder, which was then used in a variety of rituals. As Toaff notes:

> Reading the depositions of defendants accused of ritual child murder with relation to the utilization of blood, one is left with the clear impression that, rather than explain the need for the blood of a Christian child, the defendants were attempting to

---

[558] Shamir, "Bloody Passovers of Dr Toaff."
[559] Hamilton, "Diabolical Passion."
[560] Toaff, *Blood Passover*, 66.
[561] Ibid., 67.

> provide a description of the wonderful therapeutic and magical properties of blood generally, and of blood extracted from children and young persons in particular.[562]

Scorched and powdered blood was regularly used as a hemostatic agent, or coagulant, in the circumcision ritual, in order to heal the wound in the foreskin; though this claim has long been dismissed by philo-Semitic liars, Toaff counters:

> The texts of the practical Kabbalah, the handbooks of stupendous medications, compendia of portentous electuaries, recipe books of secret cures, mostly composed in the German-speaking territories, even very recently, stress the hemostatic and astringent powers of young blood, above all, on the circumcision wound. These are ancient prescriptions, handed down for generations, put together, with variants of little importance, by Kabbalistic herb alchemists of various origins, and repeatedly reprinted right down to the present day, in testimony to the extraordinary empirical effectiveness of these remedies. . . . It does not, therefore, appear that there can be any doubt as to the fact that, through an antique tradition, never interrupted, empirical healers, Kabbalists and herb alchemists prescribed powdered blood as a healant of proven effectiveness during circumcision or hemorrhage. The fact that this practice was probably anything but generalized should not lead us to suppose that it was not actually in use, particularly in the Ashkenazi Jewish communities, where stupendous "secrets," first transmitted orally, then printed in suitable compendiums, are said to have enjoyed extraordinary success over time.[563]

Yet another form of magical cannibalism is expressed in another grotesque traditional Ashkenazi custom; as Toaff explains:

> The women present at the circumcision ceremony but not yet blessed with progeny of the male sex, anxiously awaited the cutting of the foreskin of the child. At this point, throwing inhibition to the winds, as if at a pre-established signal, the women hurled themselves upon that piece of bloody flesh. The

[562] Ibid., 142.

[563] Ibid., 146–7.

> luckiest woman is alleged to have snatched it up and gulped it down immediately, before she could be mobbed by the competing females, who must have been no less hardened and highly motivated. The triumphant winner was in no doubt whatever that the proud titbit would be infallibly useful in causing the much-coveted virile member to germinate inside the impregnated abdomen through sympathetic medicine. The struggle for the foreskin among women without male progeny appears in some ways similar to today's competition among spinsters and nubile young girls for the conquest of the bride's bouquet after the wedding ceremony.[564]

In the compendia of Kabbalistic incantations and potions, Toaff finds "a broad range of recipes providing for the oral ingestion of blood, both human and animal. These recipes are stupendous electuaries, sometimes complex in preparation, intended to alleviate ailments, act as a remedy, and protect and cure."[565]

Toaff articulates that, as we have already established, rabbinical texts:

> [P]resupposed two different moral codes, one applying to the Jewish world, and the other applicable to the surrounding Christian world. . . . Therefore, that which was prohibited between Jews was not necessarily prohibited in relations between Jews and Christians [including usury and the use of human blood, which was strictly forbidden] . . . when it involved blood extracted from the veins of Jews, but was permitted and even recommended when originating from the body of Christians, or Christian children in particular.[566]

Within the remarkably insular Jewish communities of Medieval Europe:

> Specialty shops offered alchemists and [herbalists] oils and balsams extracted from fetid mummies, miraculous electuaries containing the powder of craniums, often from persons condemned to death, fat from human flesh, distilled from the

---

[564] Ibid., 148.
[565] Ibid., 150.
[566] Ibid., 156.

> bodies of murdered persons and suicides. . . . The sole recommendation in these cases remains the explanation that oils, fats and bones in powder, mummies and human flesh in poultices . . . were not to be extracted from the corpses of Jews. The rabbinical responses were rather clear in this regard, when they hastened to stress that "there is no prohibition against usefully benefiting from the dead bodies of Gentiles."[567]

There was thus an extremely well-established Jewish custom:

> [O]f consuming potions and medications based on . . . human blood . . . not only for therapeutic purposes, but in conjurations and exorcisms of all kinds. . . . The records of the Trent trial were also to reveal, not only the generalized use of blood by German Jews for curative and magic purposes, but the necessity which the accused, according to their inquisitors, are alleged to have felt to supply themselves with Christian blood (and that of a baptized child, in particular), above all, in the celebration of the rites of Pesach, the Jewish Passover. In this case, all they had to do was turn to specialized, acknowledged retailers of blood, or itinerant alchemists and herb alchemists, to obtain the required goods; but it was necessary to ascertain that the object of purchase was actually that precious and much sought-after commodity, young Christian blood, despite the facility of falsification and adulteration. And this was not an easy thing to do, or something to be taken for granted.[568]

Numerous confessions attested to a process whereby the blood of a victim was "poured into the kneaded dough of a pastry consisting of honey, pears, nuts, hazelnuts and other fresh and dried fruits, which all persons present at the ceremony were alleged to have gulped down hastily."[569] Toaff, of course, does not simply take these confessions for granted. The entire point of his inquiry is to determine the veracity of the reports. In order to do so, he finds it necessary to place the alleged blood in brackets, instead examining the other details of the reports, noting to what extent they show a deep familiarity with other Jewish rituals and practices.

---

[567] Ibid., 153.
[568] Ibid., 155.
[569] Ibid., 214.

We should note again that Tobias was the Jew who took Simon, and that the ritual murder occurred in the house of one Samuel, identified by Toaff as Samuele da Nuremberg. Because of the severe risks inherent in the abduction and murder of a Christian child, or any child, for that matter, it was incumbent upon the patriarchs of wealthy households to procure the precious Christian blood. These houses would store reserves of the blood, to be doled out to less fortunate Jews in the community, though, of course, it must be stated that the Ashkenazim were of almost uniformly high status, with all of the social, financial, and political advantages thereof. Tobias, as the head of his family, directly guided the Passover Seder for which Simon had been sacrificed, and "recalled the details, which were furthermore repeated every year at Passover without variation."[570]

Tobias testified that, after he had recited the account in Exodus of the ten plagues, "he then added this phrase: 'Thus we implore God, that you shall similarly send these ten plagues against the Gentiles, who are the enemies of the religion of the Jews,' intending to refer, in particular, to the Christians.'"[571] Samuele, sprinkling the blood of Simon onto the table, mixed with wine, continued to curse Christianity, praying, "We invoke God that he may turn all these anathemas against the enemies of Israel."[572] In unison, the Seder participants chanted, in Hebrew:

> Vomit your anger onto the nations which refuse to recognize you, and their kingdoms, which do not invoke your name, which have devoured Jacob and destroyed his seat. Turn your anger upon them, reach them with your scorn; persecute them with fury, cause them to perish from beneath the divine heaven.[573]

Toaff remarks:

---

[570] Ibid., 251.
[571] Ibid.
[572] Ibid.
[573] Ibid.

> This was one of the most potent, explicit and incisive curses against the Gentiles contained in the Passover liturgy of the Seder. . . . The meaning was obvious. Messianic redemption could only be built upon the ruins of the hated Gentile world.[574]

The intense specificity with which the defendants described the minutiae of Jewish rituals simply could not have been fabricated, nor even understood, by the Christian inquisitors who ordered and executed judicial torture. Toaff explains that the Trent depositions demonstrate that:

> The use of the blood of Christian children in the celebration of the Jewish Passover was apparently the object of minute regulation. . . . These depositions describe exactly what was prohibited, what was permitted, and what was tolerated, all in meticulous detail. Every eventuality was foreseen and dealt with; the use of blood was governed by broad and exhaustive case law, almost as if it formed an integral part of the most firmly established regulations relating to the ritual.[575]

The dried and either powdered or desiccated blood of Christian youths was "mixed into the dough of the unleavened, or 'solemn,' bread."[576] Samuele testified:

> The evening before [Passover], when they stir the dough with which the unleavened bread . . . is later prepared, the head of the family takes the blood of a Christian child and mixes it into the dough while it is being kneaded, using the entire quantity available, keeping in mind that the measure of a lentil is sufficient. The head of the family sometimes performs this operation in the presence of those kneading the unleavened bread, and sometimes without their knowledge, based on whether or not they can be trusted.[577]

All of the defendants separately attested to the same process. Another, Angelo da Verona, elaborated that the ritual kneading of blood into the unleavened dough was carried out:

---

[574] Ibid., 253.
[575] Ibid., 260.
[576] Ibid.
[577] Ibid., 261.

> [A]s a sign of outrage against Jesus Christ, whom the Christians claim is their God. Eating unleavened bread with Christian blood in it means that, just as the body and powers of Jesus Christ, the God of the Christians, went down to perdition with His death, thus, the Christian blood contained in the unleavened bread shall be ingested and completely consumed.[578]

Though Toaff notes that this anti-Christian motivation behind Jewish hematophagy may or may not be completely accurate, it does comport with everything that we have learned of Jewish hatred for Christianity.

Indeed, da Verona "supplied a very colorful and credible representation of the ritual, utilizing the correct formulae from the classical Jewish liturgy."[579] Da Verona described the process thus:

> They place the blood in their unleavened loaves in this manner: after placing the blood in the dough, they knead it and stir it around to prepare the unleavened bread. . . . Then they poke holes in it, pronouncing [in Hebrew] . . . "Thus may our enemies be consumed." At this point, the unleavened loaves are ready to be eaten.[580]

Toaff confirms that this anti-Christian invective is no fantasy; as we have discussed, it is rooted in the blessings and curses recited on Rosh Hashanah; all of the accused at Trent affirmed:

> The head of the family . . . did not shake the blood into the wine before starting the Seder or during the initial phases of the celebration, but only when they were about to recite the ten curses of Egypt.[581]

The head of the family, in this case Tobias, came to the table with a glass vial:

---

578 Ibid., 262.
579 Ibid., 276.
580 Quoted in Ibid.
581 Ibid., 249

> [C]ontaining a small quantity of dried blood, the size of a nut, and shook a pinch of it into the wine, pronouncing the usual formula . . . "This is the blood of a Christian child." He then began the recitation of the plagues, pouring the wine onto the table and cursing the Gentiles hostile to Israel.[582]

What does Toaff make all of this? He concludes:

> Only someone with a very good knowledge of the Seder ritual, an insider, could describe the order of gestures and operations as well as the Hebrew formulae used during the various phases of the celebration, and be capable of supplying such detailed and precise descriptions and explanations. The judges at Trent could barely follow these descriptions, forming a vague idea of the ritual, which was so foreign to their experience and knowledge that they could only reconstitute it in nebulous and imperfect images. The Italian notaries, then, had their work cut out for them in [attempting] to cut their way through this jungle of incomprehensible Hebrew terms, pronounced with a heavy German accent. But on the other hand, what interested them, beyond the particulars of difficult comprehensibility, was establishing where these Jews used Christian blood in their Passover rites, adding it to the unleavened bread and the wine of the libation. Imagining that the judges dictated these descriptions of the Seder ritual, with the related liturgical formulae in Hebrew, does not seem very plausible.[583]

Goy katan, or "little Christian," was the term used to describe the nameless ritual murder victim, and was uttered while his blood was poured into the unleavened dough. Toaff remarks:

> This expression, although not at all neutral in view of the negative and pejorative connotations attributed to Christians in general, was certainly less contemptuous than the term normally used by German Jews with reference to a Christian child. [For example], the word *shekez* possesses the sense of "something abominable," while the feminine, *shiksa* or *shikse*, is a neologism used, in particular, in reference to Christian girls

[582] Ibid., 251

[583] Ibid., 265.

> engaged in romantic relations with young men of the race of Israel.[584]

The preceding rituals held deeply layered meanings. The rite of the blood, or "wine," in conjunction with the anti-Christian invective curses, was most obviously a positive memorial recalling the blood of the lamb spread above the doors of Israelite homes during the Egyptian captivity. The ritual was also conceived of as a *negative* memorial, "intended to bring closer final redemption, prepared by means of God's vengeance on the Gentiles who had failed to recognize Him and had persecuted the Jewish people."[585] Indeed:

> The memorial of the Passion of Christ, relived and celebrated in the form of an anti-ritual, miraculously exemplified the fate destined for Israel's enemies. The blood of the Christian child . . . and the eating of his blood, were premonitory signs of the proximate ruin of Israel's indomitable and implacable persecutors, the followers of a false and mendacious faith.[586]

The Trent defendants emphasized this description of the ritual as an inversion of the Passion of Christ; as one put it, "We use the blood as a sad memorial of Jesus . . . in outrage and contempt of Jesus, God of the Christians, and every year we do the memorial of that passion."[587]

It is crucial to note that Samuele da Nuremberg was a learned man, with "a high degree of Hebrew culture, the fruit of many years of arduous study in the most famous Talmudic academies . . . in Germany."[588] Samuele's family was considered by all observers to have been "the most religious, and the most highly cultivated in terms of Hebrew culture."[589] Another of the Trent defendants was highly educated in rabbinical literature, but neither of the two could (or would) shed any light on the origins of ritual murder or ritual hematophagy, or of

---

[584] Ibid.
[585] Ibid., 302.
[586] Ibid., 268.
[587] Ibid., 281.
[588] Ibid., 269.
[589] Ibid., 270.

the names of the rabbinical authorities who instructed them in the practice. All that they would admit is:

> The ritual was based on ancient traditions which were only transmitted orally, for obvious reasons of prudence, and that no written traces of it remain in the texts of ritual law. Just when these traditions were formed, and why, was, for them, an unresolved mystery, enveloped in the mists of the past. Samuele vaguely attributed these traditions to the rabbis of the Talmud . . . who were said to have introduced the ritual in a very remote epoch, "before Christianity attained its present power." Those scholars, united at a learned congress, were said to have concluded that the blood of a Christian child was highly beneficial to the salvation of souls, if it was extracted during the course of a memorial ritual of the passion of Jesus, as a sign of contempt and scorn for the Christian religion. Over the course of this counter-ritual, the innocent boy, who had to be less than seven years old and had to be a boy, like Jesus, was crucified among torments and expressions of execration, as had happened to Christ.[590]

The other learned defendant, Mosè, "the Old Man" of Würzburg, affirmed that "that the blood ritual was not recorded in any of the ritualistic scripts of Judaism, but was transmitted orally, and in secret, by rabbis and scholars in Jewish law," and that indeed, "the Christian boy who was to be crucified during the rite in commemoration of the Christ's shameful Passion had to be less than seven years old and of the male sex."[591]

Despite the lack of direct evidence proving the existence of secret, oral rabbinical traditions intentionally left unwritten, Toaff finds these allegations to be "quite plausible," noting that "medieval Ashkenazi Judaism made up a hermetically sealed orthodoxy."[592] Other oral rabbinical polemics are known to have existed.

Toaff points to a passage in the Talmud that "might be interpreted as an indirect confirmation of the phenomenon of ritual murder during an ancient epoch, although we don't

---

590 Ibid., 269.
591 Ibid., 269.
592 Ibid., 273.

know how widespread or how widely approved it may have been."[593] This passage:

> [C]oncerns a so-called "outside" *baraita*, or *mishnah*, i.e., one not incorporated into the codified and canonical text of the *mishnah* (dating back approximately to the third century A.D.)—which seems to be one of the oldest—and may therefore be traced back to Palestine at the time of the second Temple.[594]

Toaff also points out that there were definitely recorded allegations of ritual human sacrifice occurring in the Temple, dating back to the second century before Christ; in any case, the passage reads:

> A man is killed, leaving a son of a tender age in the care of his mother. When the father's heirs approach and say, "Let him grow up with us," and the mother says "Let him grow up with me," he (the boy) should be left with the mother, and should not be entrusted to the care of anyone entitled to inherit from him. A case of this kind happened in the past and (the heirs) killed him on Passover Eve.[595]

Noting that the Hebrew verb used in the foregoing passage, *shachet*, means "butcher," "kill," and, in the sacrificial sense, "immolate," Toaff argues, quite convincingly:

> If the case in question were merely a matter of a simple murder committed by heirs for profit, the statement that the murder was committed 'on Passover Eve' would be quite superfluous. In fact, in support of the law providing that the child should be entrusted to the mother instead of persons entitled to inherit his property, it would have been sufficient merely to state that, in the past, a child had been killed by his heirs. When and how the murder occurred is in fact superfluous, except to remind the reader of a case, which was presumably well known, in which such a child murder, which deserved to be condemned, actually occurred, but only for material and egotistical motives.... It is advisable to stress that the reading,

---

[593] Ibid., 186.
[594] Ibid.
[595] Quoted in Ibid.

> "They killed (or immolated) him on Passover eve" . . . appears in all the manuscript and ancient versions of the . . . treatise in question, as well as in the first edition of the Talmud. . . . Later, no doubt for the purpose of defending themselves against the ritual murder accusation brought by those who had, in the meantime, discovered the potential value of the embarrassing passage, the Jewish editors of the Talmud replaced the passage with a more anemic, less embarrassing reading: "They killed him on New Year's Eve," or, "They killed him the first evening. . . ." The latter version might suggest that the child's heirs got rid of him in a violent way as early as the evening of the day upon which he was entrusted to them, with the obvious intention of getting their hands on the estate as soon as possible.[596]

The established fact that Christian Europe feared Jews must be traced to its origin. *Why* did rumors of the ritual murder of Christian children by Jews first begin to circulate, aside from the actual existence of the phenomenon? Toaff speculates that these fears might have initially arisen during the ninth and tenth centuries, when Jews dominated the slave trade in Islamic Spain, abducting Christians on a vast scale and selling them into slavery. The first primary testimony relating to the Jewish abduction of Christian children for Muslim slavers comes from the Archbishop of Lyon in the late ninth century, and has been incontrovertibly established for quite some time. As we have set forth, our Christian forefathers were wise to the vitriolic contempt that Jews directed at them. Toaff cites cases in which Jews placed chamber pots below crucifixes, and the Jews of Medieval Europe commonly made images of Christ and the Virgin Mary, only to smear excrement upon, trample, and burn them. In 1451, during Passover week in present-day Crete:

> [The local Jews] were accused of crucifying suckling lambs . . . in contempt of the Christian religion, with a grotesque and sacrilegious anti-ritual. Symbolism of the suckling lamb placed on the cross seemed obviously linked, in an intolerable and obscenely blasphemous manner, to the passion of Christ, the

---

[596] Ibid., 187.

> *Agnus Dei* [Lamb of God]. The accusation does not appear to have been completely groundless, in view of the ancient Hebraic custom of roasting the Passover lamb skewered on the spit in a vertical position, with the head upwards, to ridicule and deride the crucified Christ.[597]

During the crucifixion of the victim, numerous trials revealed that the Jews present chanted a wide range of anti-Christian anathemas, such as, "Thou shalt be martyred as Jesus, the hanged God of the Christians, was martyred: and thus may it happen to all our enemies," and, "You have been crucified and pierced like 'Jesus the Hanged,' in ignominy and shame, like Jesus."[598] These anathemas were:

> Generally reinforced by appropriate gestures of mockery and contempt, often taking the form of obscene and scurrilous jests . . . [including] the rhythmic stamping of the feet to create an ear-splitting din intended to drown out any mention of the memory or even the very voice of the adversary; the act of sticking out the tongue and/or making faces, the act of spitting in the face, the act of uncovering the buttocks and the gesture of "doing the fig." The latter, considered a particularly insulting gesture of contempt, was performed by displaying the hands with the thumb tightly inserted between the index and middle fingers, a symbolic allusion to the female genital organ during the act of copulation.[599]

For the participants, the victim symbolically *becomes* Jesus Christ; the Christian child loses his identity, if the Jews had ever even granted him one, and is transformed into Christ, "the crucified and hanged." The child is transformed symbolically into the Christian community broadly construed, allowing the Jews to enact vengeance upon their enemies.

His murderers confessed that, before Saint Simon's life was finally ended, Samuele delivered a Talmudic sermon on the life of Christ, which, now that we have explored that Talmudic account, mercifully need not be repeated. A crescendo of

[597] Ibid., 70.
[598] Ibid., 291.
[599] Ibid., 303.

obscenity was then hurled at poor young Simon, directed not at *him*, but rather at Christ, whom Simon was taken to personify. As summarized by Andrew Hamilton, on the Sabbath immediately following Simon's martyrdom, his corpse was displayed on the *almemor*, the "pulpit" of the synagogue, and the Jews of Trent "abandoned themselves to excessive gestures absolutely without inhibition or restraint":

> [The rabbi] after concluding his fiery anti-Christian sermon against Jesus and his Mother, rushed up to the *almemor*, and, after "doing the fig" [an obscene hand gesture signifying sexual intercourse performed before the eyes of the dead child], slapped the corpse of the 2-year-old in the face and spat upon it. Other members of the congregation (women were also present) followed suit, slapping, biting, and spitting upon the mutilated body, making faces and obscene gestures. One man, "coarsely raising his caftan, displayed his buttocks [and genitals] shamelessly."[600]

Is this inhuman wickedness some aberration from what we already know of Jewry? Of course not. The *Midrash*, a rabbinical form of biblical exegesis, teaches that Abraham actually slaughtered his son, Isaac, upon the very spot of the future Temple of Jerusalem; after burning Isaac's body in crematory sacrifice, God is supposed to have brought the boy back to life. This rabbinical text also contends that the blood smeared upon the Israelites' doors for the tenth plague was "the spilt blood of the sacrifice of Isaac."[601] Tellingly, Talmudic Judaism deliberately chose to ignore the biblical emphasis of God's aversion to human sacrifice, preferring instead to refer to a heretical account whereby Abraham literally murdered his son in the name of God. Perhaps this explains why Jews throughout Medieval Europe unhesitatingly slit their own children's throats rather than allow them to convert to Christianity.

There are hundreds of accusations and cases of Jewish ritual murder, each just as sadistically depraved as the last,

---

600 Ibid., 304.
601 Ibid., 205.

involving barrels of nails, crucifixion, decapitation, spit-roasting, stoning, and a litany of other barbaric evils; we could fill entire volumes with the accounts of each of these innocent lives so cruelly taken from this world. The fact that the case of Saint Simon of Trent has more concrete support and copious documentation than most ritual murders does *not* imply in any way that those cases which lack this level of specificity are not credible. After all, these events occurred, in most cases, hundreds of years ago. Christian authorities had no reason to obfuscate the truth and allow child murderers to go free, especially if we are to believe the laughably absurd Jewish position that every Christian for two thousand years has been totally consumed with and deranged by anti-Semitic prejudice.

PART III

Toward a Doctrine of Christian Racialism

As with so many issues that we have thus far discussed, there is a bold line of partition between traditional Christianity and the deviant aberration that is egalitarian Christianity, the heresy that afflicts contemporary organized Christianity. Catholic and Protestant clergy of all denominations thunderously decry the contemporary Satan, "racism," from their pulpits each Sunday. They fall over themselves in the promotion of every faith *but* Christianity, seeing it as their duty to use the Christian faith as a vehicle for egalitarian dispossession.

As H. A. Scott Trask has pointed out, the only difference between "conservative" churches and "liberal" churches is:

> More liberal churches openly support the multicultural and anti-white agenda, while the conservative churches ignore it. Of course, ignoring an agenda that pervades everything from politics to advertising is a form of tacit acceptance. The question is not whether Western churches are betraying their predominantly White congregations; they are. The question is whether they have doctrinal justification to do so.[602]

Of course, they do not. As John Vinson writes, "the Bible does not require American Christians to sacrifice their country and their children's future on an altar of false generosity."[603] Christianity is fundamentally *anti*-egalitarian. Trask correctly

---

[602] Trask, "Christian Doctrine of Nations."
[603] Vinson, *Immigration and Nation.*

notes that "Biblical illiteracy, illogic, and historical ignorance have created an environment in which the Scriptures have been perverted into a religious justification for racial liberalism."

Our forefathers, whose Christianity was on far firmer ground than our own, did not share the suicide drive that has yoked our culture under the bondage of ethnomasochism. Were they "wrong"? Is our theology simply "better," more "advanced" than theirs? Of course not. We will thus begin to articulate a theory of Christian racialism, demonstrating biblically that ethnonationalism is most certainly *not* "un-Christian," that White pride is not "un-biblical." Furthermore, while we do not—indeed, cannot—deny that Christianity is indeed *open* to all races, we must vehemently oppose the idea that equality before *God* is anything remotely approximating equality among men. For an illustration of this vitally important fact, we will discuss pro-slavery theology to conclusively demonstrate that, contrary to the self-flagellation of the Southern Baptist Convention, slavery was not and is not a biblical sin. We will also demonstrate that the non-White "Christianity" of the Global South that the Church celebrates as successful world evangelism is *not* Christian, but rather a bastardized and amalgamated paganism masquerading as Christianity. Non-White "Christianity" in the United States is also not necessarily Christian, as we understand the term.

Unless we resurrect the historical Christian recognition of race and nation, and then *act* upon this recovered knowledge, we will have no recourse than to lament, "Our inheritance is turned to strangers, our houses to aliens." (Lamentations 5:2) If we do nothing, God promises:

> Thy sons and thy daughters shall be given unto another people, and thine eyes shall look, and fail with longing for them all the day long: and there shall be no might in thine hand. The fruit of thy land, and all thy labours, shall a nation which thou knowest not eat up; and thou shalt be only oppressed and crushed always: So that thou shalt be mad for the sight of thine eyes which thou shalt see. . . . The Lord shall bring thee . . . unto a nation which neither thou nor thy fathers have known. (Deut. 28:32–36)

10

Christian Ethnonationalism

The most commonly cited verse that Christian ethnomasochists use to justify their subversion of the West is that in which Paul wrote that "there is no difference between the Jew and the Greek; for the same Lord over all is rich unto all that call upon him." (Rom. 10:12) While this verse obviously and quite simply means that God's grace is available to all who come to him through Jesus Christ, it is instead cited as some sort of call to eradicate racial and ethnic distinctions, to condemn even thinking in racial terms. A parallel verse is Paul's statement that "there is neither Jew nor Greek, there is neither bond nor free, there is neither male nor female: for ye are all one in Christ Jesus." (Gal. 3:28) Contrary to what liberal theologians might have us believe, this does *not* mean that there are no social distinctions, that there should be no social or sexual distinctions, that sexuality is fluid, that we are all "equal."

Indeed, this verse conveys the *opposite* meaning by acknowledging those very rigid distinctions. This is merely another statement on the universal *offer* of salvation through faith in Christ, which itself is tempered by the fact of predestination, which is to say that we are not all meant to be saved; with that in mind, this verse emphasizes that *before Christ*, there are no distinctions, that one class will not be exalted over another *in Heaven*. Trask explains that these verses do *not* mean "that such distinctions should be ignored, that they are unimportant, that acting upon them is sinful, or that they should be overthrown."[604] If we followed the liberal theological interpretation to its logical conclusion, Christ would become a communist and a sexual revolutionary, a hero of the contemporary American left. Trask asks, "If the Bible supports racial liberalism, why has this fact come to light only in the past century, a century known for its secularism and declining moral and cultural standards?"

Trask elaborates that "the Bible supports racial preservation and even separation," teaching that "mankind is composed not of an amorphous mass of individuals but of nations," and:

> The basis of all genuine nations is a common ethnic stock, which is more important even than a common language, culture, political allegiance, or locale. The Bible praises homogeneity as a blessing, and posits it as the basis of love, friendship, social peace, and national harmony. The Bible also sanctions love of nation and fatherland, a virtue antagonistic to indiscriminate and large-scale immigration.

After the Flood, God divided humanity into discrete and separate nations, descending from Noah's sons, Shem, Japheth, and Ham; these nations shared a common ancestry and thus race, a common language, and a specifically delineated land. (Gen. 10) Nations were not, then, the arbitrary creation of men, or "imagined communities," but were rather instituted by and ordained by God, and thus created according to his inerrant plan. All nations are, of course, *not* equal. The antithesis of God's plan, the design of fallen and degraded man, was the Tower of Babel.

Immediately after God's division of humanity into separate and discrete nations, man rebelled against God by hubristically building the Tower of Babel. Even if, as some have argued, this event occurred before God's partition of man, the point remains the same.

> [When] the whole earth was of one language, and of one speech . . . [men] said one to another, Go to, let us . . . build us

---

[604] Trask, "Christian Doctrine of Nations."

> a city and a tower, whose top may reach unto heaven; and let us make us a name, lest we be scattered abroad upon the face of the whole earth. And the Lord came down to see the city and the tower, which the children of men builded. And the Lord said, Behold, the people is one, and they have all one language; and this they begin to do: and now nothing will be restrained from them, which they have imagined to do. Go to, let us go down, and there confound their language, that they may not understand one another's speech. So the Lord scattered them abroad from thence upon the face of all the earth: and they left off to build the city. Therefore is the name of it called Babel; because the Lord did there confound the language of all the earth: and from thence did the Lord scatter them abroad upon the face of all the earth. (Gen. 11:1–9)

Does this sound familiar? It should. Since the end of the Second World War, humanity has been engaged in rebuilding the Tower of Babel; with the dawn of the twenty-first century, these efforts have reached a feverish pitch.

Liberal theologians would have us believe that Babel was God's plan, a complete inversion of the account given in Genesis. Humanity was never intended to be united; division is our earthly state, union the state of eternity. As national borders bleed and blur into the abyss of mass immigration and multiculturalism, or rather *a*culturalism, the *absence* of culture, as racial distinctions are assailed through miscegenation, as the satanic, secular humanist New World Order is erected, God's plan is violently overthrown. This is further evinced by the Hebraic juxtaposition between the word "brick," the material created by men to build their symbol of rebellion against God, and the confusion that God then created among men in response; the Hebrew "brick" contains the sound sequence *l-b-n*, while his "confounding" contains the sound sequence *n-b-l*, signifying that, indeed, Babel was a direct inversion of God's will. How dare we attempt to annihilate that which God wrought?

We must remember that God "divided to the nations their inheritance" and "separated the sons of Adam," setting "the bounds of the people." (Deut. 32:8) Trask makes the insightful argument that the ascendant globalism of today:

> [S]ullies the beauty and diversity of God's human creation, in that it suggests that the existence of different races, which vary markedly in physical appearance, is a mistake that man is to remedy by racial intermarriage. In this warped version of creation, God is the bungler and man the redeemer.

If we acknowledge that God created man, we must also acknowledge that he created our differences; it thus follows that these differences are to be *preserved*, not muddied into oblivion. God knows that the Ethiopian can no more change his skin than the leopard can change his spots; why can we not grasp this eternal truth? (Jer. 13:23)

Biblical references to the separate and discrete nature of the nations of men abound; some of these references, however, have been used to argue *for* amalgamation, for the browning of the West. For example, the Psalmist writes, "All nations whom thou hast made shall come and worship before thee, O Lord; and shall glorify thy name." (Ps. 86:9) Does this mean that national divisions must be abolished, that all of humanity is to commingle into a shapeless and faceless throng? Of course not. This simply means that the sovereignty of God will come to be universally recognized, that God exercises dominion over all the earth, that, as Trask writes, "although the nations join in praising God, they by no means lose their national identities." Likewise, when Christ gives his disciples the Great Commission, commanding, "Go ye, therefore, and teach all nations, baptizing them in the name of the Father, and of the Son, and of the Holy Ghost," he is not declaring that henceforth all borders and distinctions are to be dissolved. (Matt. 28:19) He is instead confirming that Christianity must be transmitted to Gentiles, that the disciples are to go forth and evangelize each nation, acknowledging that there are such differentiations among men. World evangelism, despite what liberal theologians may assert, categorically does *not* mean that God's partition of man must be undone, that divisions must be leveled and extinguished. Indeed, numerous prophetic verses attest to the eternal permanence and indestructibility of the nations of men; in other words, national identity is ineradicable, even upon our election to salvation in Heaven. (Ps. 22:27, Rev. 21:24, 21:26, and 22:2)

A more creative ethnomasochistic argument is that Christ's commandment to "love your enemies, bless them that curse you, do good to them that hate you, and pray for them which despitefully use you, and persecute you" is, as Trask describes:

> A radical, all-embracing injunction that would do away with ethnic or national differences. Greek, however, distinguishes between personal enemies and foreign enemies. It has three words for enemy: *polemios* (a foreign enemy), *agonistes* (a competitor or rival), and *echthros* (a private enemy; literally, one whom you hate). When Christ commands Christians to "love their enemies," he uses the word for one's private enemy, that is to say someone with whom a Christian has quarreled. Never is this injunction applied to foreign enemies, the enemies of one's people. (Matt. 5:44, Luke 6:27 and 6:35, Rom. 12:14 and 12:20)

This area of Scripture is expounded upon more fully in our discussion of Christian violence.

Throughout the Bible, miscegenation is explicitly forbidden, ethnic homogeneity explicitly commanded by and ordained by God. (Gen. 24:1–4, Ex. 34:11–16, Deut. 7:3, Ezra 9:1–2) Indeed, homogeneity is a virtue, a wholly positive good that, as Trask notes, "contributes to peace, harmony, and happiness, whether it be in marriage, friendship, or society." The Bible is very much concerned with purity. We have God's commandment that "thou shalt not let thy cattle gender with a diverse kind: thou shalt not sow thy field with mingled seed: neither shall a garment mingled of linen and woolen come upon thee." (Lev. 19:19) Continuing in this line, God commands that "thou shalt not sow thy vineyard with divers seeds: lest the fruit of thy seed which thou hast sown, and the fruit of thy vineyard, be defiled." (Deut. 22:9) Christ admonishes us to "give not that which is holy unto the dogs, neither cast ye your pearls before swine, lest they trample them under their feet, and turn again and rend you." (Matt. 7:6) We might consider in parallel the words of Paul, who wrote, "What communion hath light with darkness . . . ? Wherefore come out from among them, and be ye separate, saith the Lord, and touch not the unclean thing; and I will receive you." (2 Cor. 6:14–17)

Although liberal theologians argue that these prohibitions are based on religion, rather than race, they fail either to recognize or to acknowledge that they are both religious *and* racial. Egalitarian Christians conclude that while White Christians cannot marry White non-Christians, they can marry non-White Christians. As Trask explains, "God does not condemn interethnic or interracial marriage *per se*, but he does lay down a principle that would forbid it as a common or widespread practice," citing the late Reformed theologian R. J. Rushdoony, who noted that "the burden of the law is thus against inter-religious, interracial, and inter-cultural marriages, in that they normally go against the very community which marriage is designed to establish." Foreign, interracial marriages and ethnically mixed households are almost exclusively depicted ruinously in the Bible; think Abraham and Hagar (Gen. 16–18 and 21), Esau and his Canaanite wives (Gen. 26:34–35), or, most devastatingly of all, Samson and Delilah (Judg. 16).

Though God did indeed bless certain interethnic marriages, Trask notes that these were "always between Israelites and members of other Semitic peoples who were their ethnic kin, [the] descendants of Shem." As an example, Trask recalls that Joseph married a member of the Egyptian ruling class, and that two of their sons, Manasseh and Ephraim, went on to become the patriarchs of two of the twelve tribes of Israel. (Gen. 41:50–52) This Egyptian woman, Asenath, along with the rest of the Egyptian ruling class, were Hyksos, another Semitic group and thus racial kin to the Hebrews. Yet another example is the marriage of Boaz to Ruth, a Moabite, which also did not violate "the principle of ethnic consanguinity, for the Moabites too were Semites." John Vinson makes an even more important point with respect to Ruth by noting that she, a naturalized Israelite, "identified completely with her new nation, and made no boast about 'enriching' it with her previous background."[605] (Ruth 1:16)

[605] Vinson, *Immigration and Nation*.

John Calvin affirmed the necessity and the benevolence of God's national partition, writing:

> Just as there are in a military camp separate lines for each platoon and section, men are placed on the earth so that each nation may be content with its own boundaries. . . . God, by his providence, reduces to order that which is confused.[606]

The Russian Orthodox Church, one of the few Churches that still propounds true Christianity, released a statement which urges Christians to develop "national Christian cultures." The bishops emphasize:

> The universal nature of the Church, however, does not mean that Christians should have no right to national identity and national self-expressions. . . . Christian patriotism may be expressed at the same time with regard to a nation as an ethnic community and as a community of its citizens. The Orthodox Christian is called to love his fatherland, which has a territorial dimension, and his brothers by blood who live everywhere in the world. . . . The patriotism of the Orthodox Christian should be active. It is manifested when he defends his fatherland against an enemy, works for the good of the motherland, cares for the good order of [a] people's life through, among other things, participation in the affairs of government. The Christian is called to preserve and develop national culture and people's self-awareness.[607]

No wonder that the Jewish press routinely attacks Russian Orthodoxy as "anti-Semitic" and "White supremacist."

---

[606] Bouwsma, *John Calvin*, 35.
[607] Sacred Bishops' Council, "Social Concept of the Orthodox Church."

11

Evangelism at What Cost? Non-White "Christianity"

It is often said that Blacks are "more religious" than Whites, and Republicans celebrate Latin American mass immigration into our country by virtue of the "fact" that they are generally "very religious" groups. Similarly, Catholics and Protestants rejoice over their achievements in global evangelism, as Christianity appears to be soaring in the Global South, or Third World. Liberal theologians in the West seize upon these factors and furiously urge their congregations to flagellate themselves in penitence for the "sin" of racism, contending that we "privileged" Christians must dispossess ourselves for the benefit of our non-White "brothers and sisters in Christ."

These arguments are, however, predicated upon the dubious assumption that the Black, Brown, and global Christianity that our "Christian brothers and sisters" practice is actually the same faith that we know as Christianity—that is, the Christianity that built Western civilization, the Christianity that served as the foundation of both Europe and the United States of America. If *their* Christianity is not *our* Christianity, or even similar enough to constitute doctrinally *true* Christianity, then we must acknowledge that we are *not* kindred spirits, that they are not our "brothers and sisters," that, as Thomas Jackson writes, "Nothing—not a neighborhood, not a school, not a city, not a country, not even God almighty—remains the same once it falls into the hands of non-Whites."[608]

[608] Jackson, "Christianity Turns Brown."

Hilaire Belloc noted in 1920 that "Europe is the Faith and the Faith is Europe." Christendom *was* Europe. Christianity *was* White. As we shall see, while Europe is no longer equivalent with Christendom, Christianity is still, for all practical purposes, White. In short, non-White Christianity is not Christian, just as egalitarian "Christians" are not Christian.

Let us first take a brief look at non-White Christianity in America. With respect to Hispanic Christianity, merely witness the behavior of Hispanics; clearly, whatever Christianity they espouse does not further their assimilation into American life. Theologically, Vinson notes that their "Christianity quite often is a blend of Christian sentiments and symbols, pre-Colombian Indian or African religions, and various folk superstitions."[609] The bizarre cartel cult of folk Catholicism, centered upon the veneration of Santa Muerte, "Our Lady of Holy Death," is an instructive example. Calling some system of ritual worship "Christian" does not make it so. Liberation theology, which is perhaps best described as Christianity interpreted through a thoroughly Marxist hermeneutic, reigns ascendant in Global South Catholicism, especially in Africa and Latin America. The White-led churches that cater to Hispanics, as mentioned in the introductory essay, often facilitate legal and illegal mass immigration *and* provide social services, calling into question whether or not faith is even the purpose for Hispanic association with these churches. A large part of our inquiry, and a recurring question, is to ask at what point the syncretic infusion of folk tradition and ritualism into Christianity subsumes and devours the Christianity, to leave behind merely a disguised paganism.

Black Christianity is an even more instructive phenomenon; the stereotypical image of the jolly, obese Black woman in the gospel choir is deeply-rooted. An overwhelming majority of Blacks self-identify as Christian, yet despite this, the Christianity that Blacks practice very clearly has no transformative effect on their lives. For Blacks, the church is a social space, one in which they may hoot and holler in an unrestrained, hyper-expressive atmosphere; after church, as those

---

[609] Vinson, *Immigration and Nation.*

of us in the American South know very well, Blacks go out to lunch, decked in their Sunday finery, the men walking slowly and solemnly, arm folded over with one hand over their breast, the women topped with obscenely gaudy hats. After lunch, they return to their homes and resume their squalid, violent lives. To illustrate our point more fully, let us examine the birth of Black Christianity. In America, Blacks were evangelized by their masters, who saw it as their duty to convert them and rescue them from the savage jungles of paganism. In the antebellum South, Black slaves sat in the galleries of White churches, their masters below. After the War for Southern Independence, however, everything changed. We will quote at length E. Merton Coulter on the birth of this new, *Black* Christianity:

> When freedom came, the Negroes found in their religious organizations a jewel of great value. Being by nature highly emotional and excitable, and now unrestrained by the hand of former masters, they carried their religious exercises to extreme lengths, both in time and content. Their evening services began at nightfall or later and continued frequently far into the next morning. Meetings might degenerate into blabberings, yellings, and groanings, and even into indecent orgies. Signs of voodooism were detected from the swamps of Louisiana to as far north as North Carolina. Chants and dismal howls the Negroes called "mourning for their sins, as the angels mourn." Their services recalled to one Northerner the performances of the heathen in Africa or the rites of the savages of the Fiji Islands, leaving out the feast in human flesh. The most widespread was the shout, which consisted of a combination of singing and a sort of holy dance or shuffle in which the feet were dragged along the floor. This is a stanza from one of their chants: "*We's be nearer to de Lord / Den de White folks; and dey knows it; / See de glory-gate unbarred—walk in, darkeys, past de guard, / Bet your dollar He won't close it!*"
>
> For the mass of Negroes, religion had no relation to morality. It was an emotional orgy which they enjoyed no less than did their preachers who promoted it. Dressed in their florid and ornate colors and styles Negroes passed from their day services to a night "dance break-down"; and from their night services they might likely adjourn to a watermelon patch not their own. A half-hour after a Negro had left a shout he might

> be "begging the overseer for a drink of whiskey." Sympathetic Southerners firmly declared that good Negro workmen were ruined by their churchgoing: "Instead of assembling there together and holding services for a reasonable length of time, they frequently prolong them all night, disturbing everybody in the neighborhood, and hatching up enough devilment to run a small-size hot country." Sometimes the churchgoers would "get tired of listening, even to their own florid preachers, and frequently fall asleep in the midst of the most glowing descriptions of the torments of the damned." Some Negro preachers were of a degenerate and vicious character, who after their services might engage with the worst part of their congregations in carousals. A Northerner declared they were "infinitely worse than no preachers." They had great influence over their congregations and were uniformly Republican political leaders. A Floridian said in 1868: "The colored preachers are *the great power* in controlling and uniting the colored vote, and they are looked to, as political leaders, with more confidence and sincerity than any other source of instruction and control."
>
> Before the War, all Negro church members had belonged to the churches of their masters; but with the coming of freedom they wanted to run their own organizations. . . . The Negroes wanted their own churches wherein they could do as they pleased, unchaperoned and uninstructed by Northerners or Southerners. Methodist Negroes found already in existence . . . churches of that persuasion . . . [including] the African Methodist Episcopal Zion Church . . . which had been organized in the North many years before the War. These churches came South to reap a rich harvest. . . . Having a freer hand, [the Negro] erected a greater independency in the field of religion than in any other endeavor, but the character of his progress recommended him no more than in other activities where the restraining hand of the Whites was still felt.[610]

Though a minority of Blacks, typically of a relatively more militant worldview, saw Christianity as "the tool of the slavemasters" and opted for Islam, Blacks overwhelmingly adopted a form of Christianity as their own. Throughout the mid-twentieth century and into the present, Black churches and

[610] Coulter, *South During Reconstruction*, 338.

Black Christian organizations were instrumental in the civil rights revolution; it became a common activist tactic to clothe agitators in their "Sunday best" and equip them with a Bible. Today, Black churches still serve at the vanguard of the racial extortion industry, as is evinced by the notorious hustler, Al Sharpton, and foster anti-White vitriol from such proponents of Black theology as President Obama's favorite preacher, Jeremiah Wright.

Most concerning of all, though, is the rise of Global Christianity, the final consequence of centuries of global evangelism missions whose guiding maxim appears to have been: "Proclaim Christian conversion at any cost, doctrine be damned." Philip Jenkins notes that in 1900, Europe was home to two-thirds of the world's Christian population, and that 83 percent of the world's Christians lived in Europe and North America.[611] By 2050, Whites will constitute a tiny and precipitously declining subset of Christians, with 72 percent of the world's Christians projected to live in Africa, Asia, and Latin America; a great number *above* that 72 percent may *live* in Europe and North America, but will hail from the Global South. By 2030 at the latest, Africa will be home to more Catholics than Europe.[612] By 2025, less than 20 percent of the world's Christians will live in Europe, once inextricable from and synonymous with "the faith." Jenkins states that "the era of Western Christianity has passed within our lifetimes, and the day of the [Global] Southern Christianity is dawning."[613] Jenkins, rather disquietingly, remarks that "if we want to visualize a 'typical' contemporary Christian, we should think of a woman living in a village in Nigeria, or in a Brazilian *favela*."[614] The "center of gravity" of Christianity has "shifted inexorably away from Europe, southward, to Africa and Latin America, and eastward, toward Asia."[615]

---

[611] Jenkins, *Next Christendom*, 21.
[612] Ibid.
[613] Ibid., 3.
[614] Ibid., 2.
[615] Ibid.

In this new bastard Christianity, theological doctrine and religious practice is rife with extreme heresy. As Jenkin explains:

> If demographic change just meant that Christianity would continue to be practiced in more or less its present form, but by people of a different ethnic background, that would of itself be a fact of some historical moment. But the changes of the coming decades promise to be much more sweeping than that.[616]

The new Christianity of the Global South, which missionaries have allowed to thrive either through convenience, neglect, or active subversion, is:

> [F]ar more enthusiastic, much more centrally concerned with the workings of the supernatural, through prophecy, visions, ecstatic utterances, and healing. In fact, they have differed so widely from the cooler Northern norms as to arouse suspicion that [they] are essentially reviving the pagan practices of traditional society.[617]

The Christianity of the Global South is highly emotive, expressive, and physical, replete with synchronous swaying and dancing, as well as the trappings of the animistic ritualism, voodoo, and witchcraft that were supposedly vanquished by faith in Jesus Christ.

In the pulsing megalopolises of Africa, witchcraft accusations still flourish; Jenkins explains:

> Even today, a single outbreak of witch-panic can lead to hundreds of murders in a period of weeks or months. Moreover, one of the main centers of modern witch-hunting activity has been South Africa, the most developed state on the whole continent.[618]

---

[616] Ibid., 107.
[617] Ibid.
[618] Ibid., 123.

With that in mind, Jenkins asks, "Just how are Western Christians meant to respond to modern-day churches that hold firm opinions about the reality of witchcraft—beliefs, of course, that are by no means confined to Africa?"[619] The answer of the Christian missionaries seems universally to have been pyrrhic "compromise," or rather, no answer at all.

Rather than deal with the intractable challenge posed, they capitulated, essentially allowing the core features of the extant paganism to continue under the guise of Jesus Christ; in other words, what we are left with is pagan practice cloaked in superficially Christian language. The Christian churches "eventually acknowledged that the older beliefs were too deeply embedded to be removed, and either made their peace with tradition or else made it an integral part of their own system."[620] When assimilation crosses the line into accommodation, "what is being transformed is not merely the trappings, but the core of the faith. What is being practiced, it appears, is not inculturation but syncretism, the blatant adulteration of Christianity by elements of other religions."[621]

To continue with the example of African Christianity, Christ has been incorporated into ancestral worship, with Jesus Christ becoming the great common ancestor, among other animistic spirits. The Holy Spirit is transformed into "the Earthkeeping Spirit," and vernacular prayers and liturgies come to be associated with new or existing holy places based entirely on local folkways. In sub-Saharan Africa, so-called "Christian" churches "have retained a wide range of traditional practices, including polygamy, divination, animal sacrifices, initiation rites, circumcision, and the veneration of ancestors." Highly-placed Catholic officials in South Africa even go so far as to *promote* animal sacrifice.[622] The new Christian religious leaders often style themselves as "apostles," performing elaborate healing rituals; as Jenkins describes them, they, "like the pagan diviners before them, are healer figures who possess supernatural gifts and act as channels to the

[619] Ibid.
[620] Ibid., 124.
[621] Ibid.
[622] Ibid., 132.

ancestors. In some cases, they seem to be superhuman and become messiah figures."[623] In Asia, aside from the continuation of ancestral veneration, themes of karmic reincarnation have been fused into Christian doctrine.

The act of translation is fundamentally antagonistic to the original language; inherently, even the slightest linguistic alteration is capable of wreaking major doctrinal changes, with ramifications of great consequence. Nowhere could this process be more vitally important than in the sphere of faith. In each new outpost of Global Christianity, Jesus Christ is depicted in the same garb and with the same skin color and facial features of whatever ethnicity is dominant; translation "transforms Jesus and his followers into Africans for African hearers, makes them Chinese for a Chinese audience."[624] Through translation, including the use of highly specific local terms and even place-names, the Scripture becomes amenable, or "relevant," to each particular culture. Obviously, "as worship patterns change, so do the underlying beliefs, and changes in practice in the Global South will inevitably have their consequences in terms of belief and theology."[625] Moreover, though, as Christianity is simultaneously globalized and particularized, "it cannot fail to absorb the habits and thought-worlds of the regions in which it is strongest."[626] Indeed, these new churches, paired with the process of cultural amalgamation, use entirely new hermeneutical strategies that render the Bible a sort of meaningless chimera. In other words, in order to make Christianity recognizable to non-Whites, White Christianity is eviscerated and made unrecognizable.

Because much of the Global South remains mired in direst poverty, the prosperity gospel heresy is common. Preachers teach the doctrine of consumerism, promising material blessings in this present life; this bastard Christianity is generally focused more on present reward than eternal salvation, its eyes fixed in immediacy. The "health-and-wealth" heresy lends itself quite easily to clerical corruption, as their

---

[623] Ibid., 121.

[624] Ibid., 113.

[625] Ibid., 115.

[626] Ibid.

exorbitant material wealth is interpreted as the physical representation of spiritual purity and wholesomeness. A different consequence of the impoverished state of the Global South actually partially explains the success of this nominal Christianity, especially among Hispanics. The new churches "do best among young and displaced migrants in mushrooming cities. The most successful new denominations target their message very directly at the have-nots, or rather, the have-nothings."[627]

Hispanic theology is heavily inflected with covert and overt anti-White sentiment, the theme of:

> [L]iberation, suffering, and social justice, while matters of race are also paramount. . . . This approach profoundly affects readings of the Bible . . . [and] presents Jesus as a *mestizo* son of Galilee's mixed and marginalized society, who enters the city of Jerusalem in order to challenge its wealth, to confront the racial arrogance of the pure-blooded elite.[628]

Liberation theology emphasizes social issues and political repression. The Virgin Mary has come to represent the "feminine face of God," and is often depicted *only* in her apparition as the Virgin of Guadalupe, who for Mexicans has become "the mother of all border-crossers." The provision of social services has become an instrumental church function, over and above the proclamation of the gospel; further, the new churches provide immigrants with a sense of:

> [C]ohesion and community, and offer them hope, so that exile and return acquire powerfully religious symbolism. [These themes] also exercise a powerful appeal for . . . the tens of millions of migrant workers who have sought better lives in the richer lands.[629]

Much like the United States of America, a Christianity divorced from its people is no longer Christianity at all, but

---

[627] Ibid., 92.
[628] Ibid., 117.
[629] Ibid., 209.

some other hostile, foreign faith. Christianity is, like America, not in practice a mere "universal creed," but is rooted in cultural specificity. While Christianity has been fundamentally transformed before, the current phenomenon has no real historical precedent. Must Christianity be historically and culturally specific? Yes, because in our fallen state, no universal cultural vacuum is possible, nor even desirable. The Christianity that built the West is *necessarily* the only true Christianity. Certainly, all can come to God through Jesus Christ, our Lord and Savior; yet merely because one claims to be a Christian does not make it so. A Christianity that has allowed itself to be inverted and even devoured by the idols that came before is not Christianity at all, nor even a remote approximation thereof; Christianity demands assimilation into itself, and *never* vice versa.

12

Proslavery Theology: Slavery is Not a Biblical Sin

At the outset, I must state that, of course, I do not support slavery. My "abolitionism," however, is not motivated by the same spirit that the average American would cite for his position. I do not believe Blacks and Whites are "equal"; they are not. Nor do I believe that Blacks are equipped with the requisite faculties to live among Whites. My opposition to slavery stems from the fact that our slave-owning ancestors saddled us with a burden, a curse with no end in sight; without slavery, there simply would not be such a large population of Blacks that menace and financially and spiritually tax our nation today. Tens and perhaps hundreds of thousands of Americans would still be alive today, had they not been sacrificed at the altar of diversity as the propitiation of our "sin" of "White privilege."

Had I lived in the antebellum South, I would have made every effort to return the Black population, to expel them back to the dark continent from whence they were so fatefully brought. The purpose of this section is not, then, to argue in favor of Black slavery, or of any slavery, but rather to demonstrate that, contrary to modern "Christian" authorities, slavery is indeed biblically justifiable. One may wish to make any argument he wishes against slavery, but any abolitionist argument cannot be grounded in the Scripture; simply put, one cannot craft a biblical argument against slavery. Does the Bible *command* slavery? Of course not. But the Bible *does* permit slavery, as we shall see.

Slavery was not, is not, and will never be a sin, let alone, as so many cocktail conservative commentators assert, "America's Original Sin"; understanding this might very well help White Christians to see that the reparations demanded of them under this artificial pall of moral opprobrium are nothing but an extortive transfer of wealth. There is, at this late hour, no doubt that Blacks fared far better under slavery than they do now, basking in the "freedom" of crack addiction, crime, and Mammon-worship. In a review for *Antebellum Slavery: An Orthodox Christian View* by Gary Lee Roper, Dr. Clyde N. Wilson writes:

> Servitude has been an almost universal institution and is by no means incompatible with Scripture. . . . On the long list of the crimes, follies, and misfortunes of mankind through history, slavery in the antebellum United States does not rank very high. It is past time Americans understood this and disdained talk of reparations.[630]

A former Chaplain-in-Chief of the Sons of Confederate Veterans affirms that "we need not apologize for the Southern slave owner who observed the Scriptural instructions to masters in the treatment of their servants."[631] Gary Roper suggests, quite rightly, that there is a thinly-veiled ideological purpose for recasting slavery as a "sin"; by doing so, our enemies are able to paint the South, in one broad stroke, as irredeemably evil, thus kneecapping the Confederate States of America, the model White Christian ethnostate. As Roper puts it:

> You cannot hate slavery without hating the slave owner. . . . "There is no abstract sin that can be hated apart from the persons in whom that sin is represented and embodied. . . ." There would be no murder without the murderer. There would be no robbery without the robber.[632]

---

[630] Quoted in Roper, *Antebellum Slavery*, 7.
[631] Quoted in Roper, *Antebellum Slavery*, 10.
[632] Roper, *Antebellum Slavery*, 27–8. Interior quote from Christian Theology by E. H. Bancroft. See Ps. 5:5 and 9:17.

Roper assails the army of so-called "unreconstructed" Southerners who nevertheless make sure that they go out of their way to decry slavery and "racism"; these ostensibly patriotic Southerners praise "the South" and "the Confederacy," while in the same breath vilifying their slave-owning forefathers. These men make tortured arguments that are destined to fail, for once the "sinful" status of slavery is conceded, the entire argument has been ceded. If we are truly proud of our forefathers, if we truly honor our ancestors, we cannot also contend that slavery was "evil" or "sinful." He goes on to say:

> Southerners of today are continually bombarded with messages that they should feel self-reproach, self-condemnation, contrition . . . humiliation, embarrassment, shame, remorse, regret, and guilt, guilt, guilt for the imaginary sin of the antebellum slavery of their forefathers. Therefore, they make haste to bow the knee, make penitence, and submit their mea culpa. The barking of the hounds, the cracking of the whip against quivering flesh, and the glorification of the underground railroad are the images that most people immediately see when the word slavery is mentioned.[633]

Think *Django Unchained*. From 1936 to 1938, the Federal Writers' Project, a program of the New Deal's Works Progress Administration, produced the *American Slave Narratives*, an ambitious undertaking in which more than 2,300 former slaves were interviewed. Roper, analyzing these primary accounts, finds that they are "overwhelmingly favorable in the judgment of masters as good men."[634] Nearly ninety percent of the interviews attested to the benevolent nature of antebellum slavery.

Yet another ideological interest is served by singularly linking slavery to one specific context, that of the antebellum South. The brutal White slavery practiced throughout the United Kingdom and the British colonies,[635] the horrific conditions of White Christian slavery in Muslim North Africa,[636]

---

633 Ibid., 163–4.

634 Ibid., 166.

635 Hoffman, *They Were White and They Were Slaves.*

636 Davis, *Christian Slaves, Muslim Masters.*

and the twenty-first-century White slave trade, generally of a sexual nature, all of which were and are far crueler than the greatly exaggerated Atlantic slave trade, are utterly ignored. Slavery is the norm, the *default*, of human civilization; freedom is the aberration. Why, we wonder, do Blacks not thank us for the freedom which we generously granted them, for the invitation, long since rejected, to join our society?

There are a variety of extremely compelling justifications and apologetics for Black slavery, but they are mostly beyond the purposes of our current discussion. As such, our examination of antebellum slavery focuses solely on the theological justification for slavery, the biblical grounding of the master-slave relation. As we begin, however, it will certainly be beneficial to briefly examine the true conditions of the slavery which we seek to justify. Black slaves, by and large, enjoyed lives that were comparable to, and in many respects *better than*, the lives of White factory workers in the North.[637] There are several factors that created the generally benevolent nature of Southern slavery, including economic, social, and religious considerations.

First, it is of the utmost importance to understand that slavery *was* profitable, and that as such, slaves were highly valuable commodities. Why would a master harm his own economic productivity? Second, the nature of Southern society was such that any master who abused his slaves suffered quite severe social, if not always legal, consequences, essentially becoming a pariah cast into outer darkness. Third, as we shall elaborate upon, the masters were Christians before they were anything else, and tried to the best of their abilities to treat their slaves in the manner regulated and prescribed by the Bible. The late Eugene Genovese noted that on all of these fronts:

> Slaveholders lived on a high wire. They had to balance a public stake in the decent treatment of slaves; a compelling need to support their authority at almost any cost; and a psychological

---

[637] Fogel & Engerman, *Time on the Cross*.

> as well as ideological need for reassurance that they were kind as well as stern.[638]

The masters' collective struggle for self-justification betrays a deep concern with justice, with ensuring that they were living up to the ideal of the chivalrous Southern gentleman and the kind Christian master. Slavery was virtually universally conceived as a perfected form of organic social relations, the archetypal model of Christian hierarchy, of the subjection and dominion that typifies the patriarchal family, which itself typifies the Church's relationship with Christ. As Roper ably describes this relationship, "Being a bondslave of Jesus Christ is freedom from a cruel master, and the gift of God is eternal life."[639] Indeed, Paul often refers to himself as a "slave," or "servant," to express his relationship with Christ. (Rom. 1:1, 1 Cor. 6:19–20, Gal. 1:1, Phil. 1:1, Titus 1:1)

Blacks were viewed as part of the master's extended family, as his symbolic children. Roper confirms that the average member of the Southern aristocracy viewed himself "not only as the master of the slaves, but also as the undershepherd of Christ. He saw himself responsible for taking good care of his family, and that family included the slaves whom he considered blessings from God."[640] Slaves were thus not merely considered to be property, or abstract economic units, but were rather seen as human beings, for whose welfare the master was wholly responsible. Indeed, "the Christian South refused to view slaves as mere chattel." As Genovese explains:

> Slaveholders, including the most pious, stoutly defended slavery as a system of organic social relations that, unlike the market relations of the free-labor system, created a bond of interest that encouraged Christian behavior. When interest and humanity clashed, piety and honor demanded a decision for humanity, but slaveholders considered a social system good if it kept clashes to a minimum. . . . Sensible slaveholders understood that brutality, neglect, and inconstancy provoked covert

---

[638] Fox-Genovese & Genovese, *Mind of the Master Class*, 370.
[639] Roper, *Antebellum Slavery*, 270.
[640] Ibid., 95.

> or overt slave resistance that, in turn, threatened social order.[641]

The preservation of the social and economic cohesion of the community was of paramount importance. Genovese noted that "sternness and severity were one thing, neglect and cruelty another. The one sustained good order; the other subverted it." As the prominent South Carolinian William Harper wrote:

> It is wise, too, in relation to the civilized world around us, to avoid giving occasion to the odium which is so industriously excited against ourselves and our institutions. For this reason, public opinion should, if possible, bear down even more strongly on masters who practice any wanton cruelty on their slave. The miscreant who is guilty of this not only violates the law of God and of humanity, but as far as in him lies, by bringing odium upon, endangers the institutions of his country, and the safety of his countrymen.[642]

If this sounds self-serving, think again. By all accounts, the masters truly did go to great lengths to fulfill their duties, wonderfully set forth by Genovese:

> Every Southern slaveholder . . . was supposed to treat his slaves as part of his "family, white and black," and yet keep his head above water in a competitive market. While managing the work of his slaves, supervising their lives, paying bills, and getting the crop out, he was simultaneously to be gentle, forbearing, and kind—but stern, even severe, when duty, dignity, and preservation of authority required. His character and reputation depended upon his ability to resolve the attendant contradictions.[643]

It was a ubiquitous honorific to describe the benevolence of a master; as Genovese astutely observed:

> Masters thought they knew what God and their consciences expected—and what their neighbors expected. . . . Many

[641] Fox-Genovese & Genovese, *Mind of the Master Class*, 368.
[642] Ibid., 365.
[643] Ibid., 369.

> tombstones in old Southern graveyards identify "kind" and "'affectionate" masters.... Tombstones speak especially to families, to grandchildren and generations to come. We find engraved on them what the closest survivors wanted to convey.[644]

Genovese confirmed that, "as [the slaveholders'] diaries and letters attest, they could hardly believe it when, during the War, thousands of presumably loyal and contented slaves deserted to the Yankees and told horror stories."[645] Those farcically embellished "atrocity stories" are eerily similar to the ridiculous exaggerations of the Holocaust.

The character of a gentleman hinged upon the manner in which he treated his slaves, as Southerners were raised under a code of honor that emphasized the duty of the stronger to defend the weaker, including especially the slaves in their charge. Future Confederate General Albert Sidney Johnston wrote to his son that "a man has no right to inflict upon any creature of God unnecessary pain."[646] The key word in this formulation is "unnecessary"; as Genovese elaborates:

> Southerners maintained that no gentleman would dream of oppressing slaves or anyone else deemed in his charge, but requiring obedience and subordination was not oppression. A master who abused his slaves . . . would strike his wife or beat his horse.[647]

To impose stern, even severe, corrective discipline was not considered to be abuse; future congressman William Elliott affirmed that "against *insubordination alone*, we are severe."[648] Roper urges us to remember that "the master, not the State, was responsible for maintaining law and order among the slaves."[649]

Genovese noted:

---

[644] Ibid., 367.
[645] Ibid., 368.
[646] Ibid., 366.
[647] Ibid.
[648] Ibid., 368.
[649] Roper, *Antebellum Slavery*, 62.

> John Taylor of Caroline offered what became a [S]outhern motif in which the master's concern for his own reputation, as well as his material interest, weakened any inclination to overdriving. In the free-labor system, to the contrary, the market disguised the relation of master and man and imposed "a slavery, in which the sufferer is ignorant of his tyrant, and the tyrant is remorseless, because he is unconscious of his crime."[650]

This critique of Northern industrial capitalism is similar to that offered by George Fitzhugh, whose argument for a system of universal slavery was an early and iconoclastic formulation of anti-egalitarian and non-Marxist socialism, which can still be seen as the most courageous conception of the logical consequence of socialism that we have yet encountered. In contrast to the truly brutal and soulless nature of Northern capitalism, wherein White workers who fell ill or were gruesomely mangled or killed on the job were simply tossed out into the bitter cold, Black slaves could count on being cared for, in sickness and in health, from cradle to grave.

Genovese explains that "proslavery theologians believed that slavery encouraged moral evil to a lesser extent than did the North's free-labor system."[651] He goes on to note that "respectable Southerners scorned neighbors who failed to provide for their old slaves."[652] Many masters did what they could to prevent slave families from being separated as well. Bearing in mind the sheer devotion of the Southern masters to their Christian faith, Roper asks:

> Does it seem reasonable that Southern men of honor who were so aware of their responsibility before God would abuse their families? If they were not God-fearing men, they certainly cared about the defense of their sacred honor. A man who beat his slaves was looked down upon in the antebellum South as much as a man who beat his wife or children.[653]

---

[650] Fox-Genovese & Genovese, *Mind of the Master Class*, 371.
[651] Ibid., 521.
[652] Ibid.
[653] Roper, *Antebellum Slavery*, 98.

When, in infrequent cases, masters did commit acts of cruelty or "go too far" in their administration of discipline, the perpetrator was either legally punished or socially ostracized. Genovese remarks, contrary to popular opinion:

> Although juries seldom convicted a malicious and negligent master, they did so on occasion and sometimes on circumstantial evidence—which suggests that the master's neighbors considered him a savage. Public opinion expressed circumspect approval for a slave who killed a barbaric overseer or even a barbaric master.[654]

Public opinion obviously carried the greatest weight in rural communities, those which constituted and still largely do constitute the American South. Genovese emphasizes that "the prevalence of small towns and villages in the South offered considerable scope for social, political, and religious leaders to encourage humane treatment of slaves by all those, high and low, who valued respectability."[655] From Virginia to Texas, spanning the entire South, "notorious slaveholders—most notably those who killed slaves—found it advisable to relocate in some far-off place. Although juries might be loath to acquit even when faced with damning evidence, the wretch could face the wrath of irate citizens."[656]

Evangelism was one of the primary reasons cited by Southern theologians in their defenses of Black slavery; in other words, slavery was conceived of as a positive good, by virtue of its "bringing heathens to be Christianized." Episcopal Bishop John Henry Hopkins wrote:

> The South has done more than any people on earth for the Christianization of the African race. The condition of slaves here is not as wretched as Northern factions would have men believe, but prosperous and happy, and would have been more so, but for the mistaken zeal of abolitionists. . . . Thus has God blessed us in gathering into His Church from the children of Africa more than twice as many as are reported from all the

---

[654] Fox-Genovese & Genovese, *Mind of the Master Class*, 374.
[655] Ibid., 375.
[656] Ibid., 374.

> converts in the Protestant missions throughout the heathen world. . . . I see no reason to deny the statement of our Southern friends, that their slaves are the happiest laborers in the world. Their master provides for all their wants. Their families are sure of a home and maintenance for life. In sickness, they are kindly nursed. In old age, they are affectionately supported. They are relieved from all anxiety for the future. Their religious privileges are generously accorded to them. Their work is light. Their holidays are numerous.[657]

Most of the formative Christian leaders in the early republic were slaveowners, as were, of course, the overwhelming majority of the Founding generation, along with its progeny, the generations that shepherded the United States into the mid-nineteenth century. Ministers wrote about half of all pro-slavery tracts. Historically, Christian churches *always* regulated and even *promoted* slavery, yet *never* condemned the system. Jesus Christ, who most certainly did not mince words, never once criticized slavery, and indeed, the Bible provides strict regulations for masters and slaves in their dealings with one another. (Gen. 17:12, Ex. 20:10, 20:17, 21:20–21, 21:26, 22:3, 1 Cor. 7:20–24, Eph. 6:5–9, 1 Tim. 6:2, Titus 2:9–10, 1 Pet. 2:18) Roper notes, "Only mortal men, who profess themselves wiser than God, have declared slavery a sin."[658] Despite living at a time when slavery was rampant, and far crueler than antebellum slavery, Christ deigned not to open his mouth against human bondage. Would God have regulated slavery if it were a sin? As Roper asks, "Can you imagine the thrice-Holy God giving rules on the proper way to commit adultery or murder?"[659] Charles Hodge writes:

> The fact that the Mosaic institutions recognized the lawfulness of slavery is a point too plain to need proof, and is almost universally admitted. Our argument from this acknowledged fact is that if God allowed slavery to exist, if he directed how slaves might be lawfully acquired, and how they were to be

---

[657] Quoted in Roper, *Antebellum Slavery*, 222, 163.
[658] Roper, *Antebellum Slavery*, 28.
[659] Ibid., 24.

> treated, it is vain to contend that slaveholding is a sin, and yet profess reverence for the Scriptures.[660]

Again, we must recall that the South has always been fervently Christian; Southerners uniformly swore that they would abhor slavery if it were truly sinful, if it were truly in violation of biblical Christianity. This was not mere rhetoric; Southerners thought long and hard about whether or not a contemplated action could be reconciled with Scripture before undertaking to do *anything*. For example, upon learning of the fall of the Confederate States of America, the arch-Fire Eater, Edmund Ruffin, consulted his Bible, poring over it to ensure that what he was about to do was not a sin. After concluding that suicide is never once condemned in the Bible, even in the few places where it does occur, Ruffin committed suicide by shooting himself in the head. As an aside, we must applaud his final diary entry:

> And now with my latest writing and utterance, and with what will [be] near to my latest breath, I here repeat, & would willingly proclaim, my unmitigated hatred to Yankee rule—to all political, social and business connections with Yankees, & to the perfidious, malignant, & vile Yankee race.

In any case, the Baptist Reverend Thornton Stringfellow confirmed that "if slavery be thus sinful, it behooves all Christians who are involved in the sin, to repent in dust and ashes, and wash their hands of it, without consulting with flesh and blood."[661] James Henley Thornwell, the greatest of the Southern divines, wrote:

> If I know the character of our people, I think I can safely say, that if they were persuaded of the essential immorality of Slavery, they would not be backward in adopting measures for the ultimate abatement of the evil.[662]

---

[660] Quoted in Roper, *Antebellum Slavery*, 234.
[661] Fox-Genovese & Genovese, *Mind of the Master Class*, 505.
[662] Ibid., 506.

Roper asks the key question to our inquiry: "Is morality decided by the prevailing opinion of the majority or by the Almighty?"[663]

The weakest Scriptural pro-slavery argument, and thus the sole strawman cited by leftists today, is Noah's curse of his son, Ham; we need not dwell on this point, aside from noting that this theory held slavery to be a corrective punishment instituted by God. (Gen. 9:18–27) With many holding that Ham was the common ancestor of the African race, the curse of Ham provided a justification specifically for *Black* slavery. Of course, this argument was weak merely because it simply is not textual, requiring quite a bit more exegesis than we are comfortable with; R. L. Dabney described the curse of Ham as "not essential to our argument."[664] Indeed, there is little biblical evidence to support the *necessity* of racially-based slavery, for the Bible sanctions *all* slavery; nor does this mean that racial slavery is condemned, for it is not—racial slavery is simply one form of slavery, which is biblically justified.

The Israelites held slaves, both in bondage and in freedom. (Ex. 12:44, Ezra 2:64–65) Abraham owned a great many slaves, and indeed the Bible explicitly states that God himself *blessed* Abraham with his many slaves. (Gen. 12:16, 14:14, 20:14, 24:35) Isaac, Jacob, and Job were also slaveowners. (Gen. 26:14 and 30:43, Job 31:13–14) As Roper writes, "One cannot say that the institution of slavery is sinful without accusing Almighty God of immorality." Genovese reinforced this, noting that "Man cannot reject or call sinful that which God has commanded."[665] As Christians, we must understand that "the thing proceedeth from the Lord: we cannot speak unto thee bad or good." (Gen. 24:50)

As one antebellum pastor declared, "In its moral aspect, slavery was not countenanced, permitted, and regulated by the Bible, but it was positively instituted by God himself—he had, in so many words, enjoined it."[666] God commanded the

[663] Roper, *Antebellum Slavery*, 207.
[664] Fox-Genovese & Genovese, *Mind of the Master Class*, 523.
[665] Fox-Genovese & Genovese, *Mind of the Master Class*, 510.
[666] Ibid.

Israelites to enslave the Canaanites in perpetuity; Genovese explains that some abolitionists interpreted this:

> [A]s historically specific, not a general license. Jesus, [they] argued, taught meekness and submission to slaves, but their very enslavement encouraged the vices he everywhere combated . . . [but they] had surrendered the argument . . . even if God's command to the Israelites to slaughter and enslave the Canaanites was historically specific. Since he surely could not have commanded them to sin, slavery could not be sinful.[667]

Many liberal theologians make the facile argument today, as did the abolitionists before them, that the Golden Rule, Christ's commandment that "therefore all things whatsoever ye would that men should do to you, do ye even so to them," forbids slavery. (Matt. 7:12, Luke 6:31) Roper provides an excellent rejoinder:

> We are to apply the Golden Rule provided it is just and reasonable to do so. A child would never be restrained or punished by a parent if he put himself in the place of the child. A judge would never condemn a criminal if he put himself in the mind of a criminal who desires to be released. The Golden Rule does *not* require a master to free his slave, but *does* require him to treat his slave the way he would want to be treated *if he were the slave*. The Golden Rule cannot conflict with the biblical arrangement of dominion and subjection.[668]

R. L. Dabney wrote:

> [S]urely, the principle of the Golden Rule binds the slave just as much as the master. If the desire which one would feel must govern each man's conduct, then the slave may be very sure that were he the master, he would naturally desire to retain the services of the slaves who were his lawful property.[669]

Richard Furman explained that the Golden Rule is:

---

[667] Ibid., 509.
[668] Roper, *Antebellum Slavery*, 262.
[669] Quoted in Roper, *Antebellum Slavery*, 262.

> [N]ever to be urged against the order of things, which the Divine government has established; nor do our desires become a standard to us, under this rule, unless they have a due regard to justice, propriety, and the general good. A father may very naturally desire that his son should be obedient to his orders. Is he, therefore, to obey the orders of his son? A man might be pleased to be exonerated from his debts by the generosity of his creditors; or that his rich neighbor should equally divide his property with him; and in certain circumstances might desire these to be done. Would the mere existence of this desire oblige him to exonerate his debtors, and to make such a division of his property?[670]

Abolitionists seized upon the biblical injunction that "thou shalt not deliver unto his master the servant which is escaped from his master unto thee" to attack the Fugitive Slave Laws; as with all of the other necessarily feeble abolitionist attempts to muster the Scripture, this argument is *prima facie* nonsensical. (Deut. 23:15) Indeed, the abolitionists violently tore this verse from its context, which is a passage dealing with the paramount importance of maintaining the *purity* of Israel, as against its heathen enemies, the enemies of God. This verse means only that if one of the slaves of the heathen is able to escape and come into Israel *in order to convert and know God*, he is not to be returned to the heathens. As Charles Hodge elaborates:

> The thing there forbidden is the restoration of a slave who had fled from a heathen master and taken refuge among the worshippers of the true God. Such a man was not to be forced back into heathenism. This is the obvious meaning and spirit of the command. That it has no reference to slaves who had escaped from Hebrew masters, and fled from one tribe or city to another, is plain from the simple fact that Hebrew laws recognized slavery. It would be a perfect contradiction if the law authorized the purchase and holding of slaves, and yet forbid enforcing that right of possession.[671]

---

[670] Richard Furman, "Exposition of the Views."

[671] Quoted in Roper, *Antebellum Slavery*, 237.

The illicit "liberation" of slaves outside of express manumission was a violation of the Eighth Commandment, functioning as simple theft. Remember that in the abstract, a slave is an economic unit of property; though, as we have established, Christians are enjoined to treat their slaves as more than mere chattel, this is what they were. Abolitionists would have done well to remember that "if thou meet thine enemy's ox or his ass going astray, thou shalt surely bring it back to him again." (Ex. 23:4)

The greatest illustrations of the biblical doctrine of slavery are the only two accounts of runaway slaves, Hagar and Onesimus; in both narratives, the slaves are returned to subjection under their masters. Hagar was the slave of Sarah, Abraham's wife, and:

> When Sarai dealt hardly with her, she fled from her face. And the angel of the Lord found her. . . . And he said, Hagar, Sarai's maid, whence camest thou? and whither wilt thou go? And she said, I flee from the face of my mistress Sarai. And the angel of the Lord said unto her, Return to thy mistress, and submit thyself under her hands. (Gen. 16:6–9)

The angel of the Lord thus reminded Hagar that in the sight of God, she is still Sarah's slave, regardless of her physical location; slavery is her station in life. As John Calvin elaborates:

> The angel declares that she still remained a servant, though she had escaped the hands of her mistress; because liberty is not to be obtained by stealth, nor by flight, but by manumission. But Hagar was now out of her place, and out of the way of her duty, and going further astray, when the angel found her. It is a great mercy to be stopped in a sinful way either by conscience or by Providence. Sarai's maid ought to be in Sarai's tent, and not wandering in the wilderness.[672]

Hagar sinned in "abandoning the station in which his Providence had placed her"; as such, she was compelled by God to return and submit to her duty.

---

[672] Quoted in Roper, *Antebellum Slavery*. From Calvin's Commenteries.

The second runaway narrative, that of Onesimus, is recounted in the Epistle of Paul to Philemon, Paul's only private letter contained in the Bible. Onesimus robbed his master, Philemon, and escaped from Colossae to Rome, whereupon he met the apostle Paul. Paul wrote his letter to Philemon, sending it to Colossae along with Onesimus. Baptist theologian John Gill summarizes the narrative thus:

> Philemon's servant, Onesimus, having either embezzled his master's goods or robbed him, ran away from him and fled to Rome. While in Rome, Onesimus, the fugitive slave, was converted under the preaching of the apostle Paul. In this epistle it is the purpose of Paul to reconcile Philemon to his slave, and to beseech him to receive Onesimus back not only as a slave, but also as a brother in Christ. In this epistle, we see the wonderful providence of God in overruling that which was sinful in itself, running away from his master, to the greatest good, even the conversion of him. [Paul] would do nothing with another man's servant without his consent; he would not seem to alienate, or engross another man's right and property, whatever power he might have as an apostle, to have returned Onesimus as a minister to him.[673]

Dabney explained:

> Paul judged it proper to send him back to his master, to whom he wrote this epistle, that he might procure Onesimus a more favorable reception than he would otherwise have expected. . . . Onesimus was Philemon's legal property, and Saint Paul had required, and prevailed with him, to return to him. . . . The transaction clearly implies a moral property or ownership in Onesimus' labor, as pertaining to Philemon; of which the latter could not be rightfully deprived without his consent.[674]

Presbyterian theologian Joseph Wilson, father of Woodrow Wilson, writes:

> Being converted, what was [Onesimus'] duty to his defrauded master? The spirit of Christianity, which now resided in his

[673] Fox-Genovese & Genovese, *Mind of the Master Class*, 543.
[674] Quoted in Roper, *Antebellum Slavery*, 259.

> heart, informed his conscience of the fact that he was the property of Philemon, and that while he remained away from his owner's home and authority, he was committing the sin of robbery. He consulted the apostle. What was his advice? [Paul] did not hesitate to urge Onesimus to go at once to his master, confess at his feet the grievous fault he had committed, and beg to be received once more among the number of his slaves.[675]

We must remember that Jesus Christ *never* condemned, nor criticized in the slightest, the institution of slavery, which Moses had introduced to the Israelites under God's command. In fact, as Genovese notes:

> Ancient slaves were treated more harshly than modern and yet Jesus had not condemned slavery. . . . Jesus witnessed a Roman slave system "more absolute and objectionable" and more "abject and degrading" than anything seen in America.[676]

All of the early Christian churches named in the New Testament, along with virtually all Christian churches through the mid-nineteenth century, were open to both slaveholders and their slaves. Christ never once excluded masters from the Church, unlike the moneychangers whom he unceremoniously evicted from the premises.

Had Jesus considered slavery sinful, Genovese correctly asserts, "he would certainly have preached against it as he did against other socially entrenched sins."[677] Christ went to great pains to decry all of the corruption and evil that permeated society, suffering and paying the ultimate price for these condemnations. He emphatically did *not* exclude any evil from his judgment. Legions of Christian martyrs proclaimed the gospel and suffered excruciating and gruesome torture and murder for their actions; this is to say that clearly, Christians, as well as Christ himself, were not afraid to speak the truth, no matter the social cost for doing so. Slavery passed unscathed because it was not and is not a sin. Taking again the example of Paul's

---

[675] Ibid.

[676] Fox-Genovese & Genovese, *Mind of the Master Class*, 516.

[677] Ibid.

letter to Philemon, nowhere is emancipation suggested, and, as Genovese noted, "not a word . . . condemns slavery as *malum in se* or criticizes slavery at all."[678] Genovese continues:

> As Southerners knew, when Paul wrote 1 Corinthians at least a fifth and perhaps a third of the population of Corinth was enslaved; another third were freedmen, some descended from former slaves whom Julius Caesar had sent out as colonists. Paul observed that many slaves fared much better than did free laborers. His Epistle manifested his "theology of the calling," which demanded fidelity to Christ in every earthly occupation and status. It contained no criticism of slavery.[679]

Yet another illustration of Christ's attitude toward slavery is his interaction with the Roman centurion. (Matt. 8:5–13, Luke 7:1–10) The centurion approached Christ in Capernaum, asking him to heal his grievously ill slave; when Christ responds that he will go and heal the man, the centurion cries:

> Lord, I am not worthy that thou shouldest come under my roof: but speak the word only, and my servant shall be healed. For I am a man under authority . . . and I say . . . to my servant, Do this, and he doeth it.

Christ marvels at the centurion's faith in his power to heal the slave remotely, stating, "Verily I say unto you, I have not found so great faith, no, not in Israel." Roper remarks:

> Jesus highly praised the Roman centurion without one word of condemnation regarding the institution of slavery. When we consider how our Lord never missed an opportunity to correct ancient errors and expose sin, we must come to certain conclusions: Had the institution of slavery been morally wrong and sinful, this would have been . . . too great an opportunity to be lost in not setting a good precedent against it.[680]

As we have stressed, Christ never fails to denounce sin in the most explicit terms.

---

678 Ibid., 518.

679 Ibid.

680 Roper, *Antebellum Slavery*, 244.

Further expounding upon pro-slavery theology, colonial theologian and slaveholder Jonathan Edwards, best known for his masterfully written sermon *Sinners in the Hands of an Angry God* wrote that "I am God's servant as they are mine, and much more inferior to God than my servant is to me." James Henley Thornwell elaborates that

> The Apostles did not regard the personality of the slave as lost or swallowed up in the propriety of the master. They treat him as a man, possessed of certain rights, which it was injustice to disregard; and, make it the office of Christianity to protect these rights by the solemn sanctions of religion—to enforce upon masters the necessity, the moral obligation, of rendering to their bondsmen that which is just and equal.[681]

John Calvin explained that slaves are enjoined to their masters "not only to the good. . . . When a superior abuses his power, he must hereafter render an account to God, but he does not for the present lose his right."[682] Men are inherently *unequal* in this fallen world. Roper remarks, "Unto whom much is given shall much be required. We live in a world of dominion and subjection. Without dominion and subjection, our whole society would crumble."[683] Charles Hodge explains:

> Slaves were to regard their obedience to their masters as part of their obedience to Christ. This, as the Scriptures teach, is not peculiar to the obedience of the slave to his master, but applies to all other cases in which obedience is required from one man to another. It applies to children in relation to their parents, wives to husbands, and people to magistrates. Those invested with lawful authority are the representatives of God.[684]

To conclude our exposition of pro-slavery theology, Baptist theologian John Dagg writes, "If the relation of master were unlawful, to instruct them how to exercise the authority of

---

[681] Quoted in Roper, *Antebellum Slavery*, 241.
[682] Quoted in Roper, *Antebellum Slavery*. From Calvin's Commenteries.
[683] Roper, *Antebellum Slavery*, 246.
[684] Quoted in Ibid., 250.

master would be to instruct them how to sin. The Scriptures nowhere instruct us in what manner we ought to commit [sins]."[685] Roper puts it more succinctly: "Either you believe the whole Bible or you believe none of it." If slavery be recognized, regulated, and sometimes even commanded in both the Old and New Testaments, how could Christians in good conscience refer to the institution as a sin?

Because there is no Scriptural argument against slavery to be made, Genovese noted:

> The abolitionists did not make their case for slavery as sin—that is, as condemned in Scripture. The proslavery protagonists proved so strong in their appeal to Scripture as to make comprehensible the readiness with which Southern whites satisfied themselves that God sanctioned slavery.[686]

To this very day, Christian churches harp on and on about the sinfulness of racism and slavery, but every time, their theologians fail to marshal Scripture against slavery, an institution affirmed throughout the Bible. The solid defense of slavery articulated by the Southern divines has yet to be answered by the partisans of egalitarianism.

---

[685] Quoted in Ibid., 249.
[686] Fox-Genovese & Genovese, *Mind of the Master Class*, 526.

PART IV

Theories of Christian Violence

Christianity is not the sing-song *kumbaya* religion of pusillanimous cuckoldry and "the brotherhood of man" that it has so often been portrayed as by the cultured despisers of the White race; as we have seen, the fallen state of our faith today is a gross aberration from the true Word of God. One of the greatest misconceptions of Christianity, promulgated by nearly all of our contemporary clergymen, is that it teaches absolute pacifism, that violence is *never* the answer, that we are supposed to bend the knee and submit to every oppression that we face, that we must "hate the sin, and love the sinner." This is all poppycock, for we shall see that there is an ironclad Scriptural justification of and for Christian violence; we will show that Christianity emphatically does *not* support absolute pacifism, and recognizes that violence is necessary under the proper circumstances.

Consider the tale of Tommie Lindh, a hero whose name shall grace our martyrology for all time, as a proper example of Christian violence. Lindh, only nineteen years old, was at a party in Härnösand, Sweden, where he saw a Sudanese invader raping a Swedish girl. Lindh immediately intervened to save his kinswoman from dishonor, and was summarily stabbed to death for his courage. Many nominally Christian preachers would have us believe that Lindh should not have acted, that those who live by the sword die by the sword, that he should instead have called the impotent police and let the girl be raped and potentially murdered. We do not know whether Lindh was a Christian or not, but his actions are a perfect illustration of reactive Christian violence in the defense of others. We will begin by investigating a general theory of Christian violence, and then proceed to explore Christian violence as it was specifically theorized and manifested during the First Crusade. Along the way, we will briefly discuss Islamic hostility to Christianity, focusing on the rampant Islamic sexual exploitation of White girls as a searing reproach to the milquetoast "Christianity" practiced by the Church today. We will conclude by examining the theological chassis of another particularized manifestation of Christian violence, the anti-infanticide or pro-natalist Army of God.

13

Against Absolute Pacifism

God is not merely love, but rather love and wrath. Though no man may serve two masters, love and hatred go hand in hand. While hatred is certainly not dependent upon love, love is utterly dependent upon hatred; how can a man truly love something without also hating that which has as its animating spirit the annihilation of that object of his affections? Christians *must* hate Satan and all of the anti-Christian forces he has arrayed against us. That tired adage, "love the sinner, hate the sin," appears nowhere in the Bible; it is purely the creation of liberal theologians. Throughout the Bible, God does indeed hate sinners, along with and because of their sins. (Lev. 20:23, Ps. 5:4–6 and 11:5, Prov. 6:16–19, Hos. 9:15, Mal. 1:3, Rom. 9:13) God engages in holy warfare against his enemies and those who revolt against him. He eradicates whole cities (not only Sodom and Gomorrah) and even whole peoples. He even employed the Flood to destroy all life on earth aside from Noah and his ark. Biblical heroes such as David, Moses, and Esther fought to destroy evil; they were not known to be meek pacifists. Biblical sins carry a death sentence.

Jesus Christ *is* God, and has always existed. (John 1:1) There is no difference between the Old and the New Testament, save for the transformation of the covenant; the old *covenant* was fulfilled in and superseded by Christ, the new covenant. The Old *Testament* was not overwritten. Though God's covenant was formerly with the Jews, his chosen people, they rebelled against him and broke the covenant; God then sent Jesus

Christ, the fulfillment of Old Testament prophecy, to establish the new covenant. God's chosen people are now no longer the Jews, but *Christians*; all Christians now continue his lineage. The God of the Old Testament is the same God of the New; the two form a unified whole. Jesus Christ is not some hippie peacenik preaching a different gospel than that of the Father; he *is* his Father, the commonly-believed distinction between the Old and New Testaments merely a heresy spun out of whole cloth by a second-century man named Marcion of Sinope. Marcion believed that the Old Testament should simply be jettisoned.

Christ refers to his disciples James and John as "sons of thunder." (Mark 3:17) In Gethsemane, when Jesus is arrested, Peter cuts off the ear of Malchus, the servant of the high Jewish priest; thus, we have definitive evidence that at least some of the disciples were armed (Matt. 26:47–54). Indeed, as the servants approached, the disciples asked Christ, "Lord, shall we smite with the sword?" (Luke 22:49) When Jesus violently cleansed the Temple by driving out the merchants and moneychangers, "he had made a scourge of small cords"; in other words, he was so incensed by the Jewish corruption of the Temple that he took the time to braid a whip from strips of leather or rushes. (John 2:13–16)

The most commonly promulgated verses in perpetuating the myth of absolute pacifism are Matthew 5:38–39:

> Ye have heard that it hath been said, An eye for an eye, and a tooth for a tooth: But I say unto you, That ye resist not evil: but whosoever shall smite thee on thy right cheek, turn to him the other also.

There is a Bible page, supposedly found fused to a piece of the World Trade Center's rubble, on display at the 9/11 Memorial in Manhattan (as of last spring). Quite conveniently, this page is the very page containing these verses that to the layman, whose mind has been warped by liberal theology, are an injunction against any and all retaliation for any wrongs committed against us.

This concept of turning the other cheek is recapitulated throughout the Bible, including Lamentations 3:30: "He giveth *his* cheek to him that smiteth him: he is filled full with reproach." Ancient Hebrew law considered a slap on the cheek as the infliction of shame, and as such provided for recompense; an openhanded slap resulted in a fine of two hundred *zuzim*, while a backhanded slap resulted in a fine of four hundred *zuzim*. This discrepancy was because a backhanded slap was considered to be twice as offensive as an openhanded slap. Importantly, in Middle Eastern culture, as in most cultures, it is customary to use the right hand; to use the right hand to slap someone on their right cheek, then, would require a backhanded slap.

Thus, when Christ tells us to turn our *left* cheek to the person who has already stricken us on our *right* cheek, he is not only *not* speaking of physical violence, but only mild insults, but he is additionally telling us that because we have already been dealt a highly offensive backhanded slap, we might as well present our left cheek and accept lesser insults. Again, Christ is *not* telling us to respond to physical violence by suicidally exposing ourselves to further injury. Christ is *not* establishing an absolute injunction against retaliation. Christ *is* establishing a tiered response of degree; we should not respond to petty insults by lowering ourselves to our opponent's level and escalating the frivolous situation into something worse. To reiterate once more, Matthew 5:39 does not command us not to resist *the* Enemy, whom we *must* resist, but rather to respond to petty humiliations from personal enemies by letting them go and waiting for future vindication, whether in this life or the next.

As Jack Kerwick has argued, Matthew 5:39 *only* applies to an insult, as perfectly represented by a slap on the face; one cannot insert more serious offenses into the verse, or it would be antithetical: "But I tell you, whoever rapes you in one bodily orifice, offer him another"; "I say to you, whoever bludgeons you with a pipe on one side of the skull, turn to him the other side"; or "But I tell you, if someone abducts one of your children, give him another."[687] Furthermore, as Kerwick refutes the aforementioned "love the sinner, hate the sin" fallacy, sin is inseparable from he who sins. Moreover:

> The idea that acts can be divorced from and morally evaluated independently of the moral agents who performed them is an essentially modern one. In the ancient and medieval eras, it did not exist. Indeed, it was the agent, as opposed to the act, that assumed moral primacy. . . . Virtuous and vicious actions were recognized as those actions in which virtuous and vicious people, respectively, would engage. Thus, in the Bible, evil or sinful activity is that activity conducted by evil or sinful people.

Additionally, Kerwick notes that God does not punish abstract sin, but rather sinners; so, "while God can and does forgive sin, his hatred of it can be, will be, and must be asserted by way of his judgment upon the sinner." Our hatred and retaliation should not be directed at our personal enemies if solely based on petty personal conflict, but rather at enemies who we hate because they are evil; from Kerwick:

> Whether that person is, subjectively speaking, [our] enemy or not. If, though, the person is [our] enemy, [we are] to hate him, but not hate him as [our] enemy, or *because* he is [our] enemy; [we are] to hate him *because he is a wicked being*. To put it another way, an objective evildoer and [our] enemy *can* be one and the same person. But they do not *have* to be one and the same person.

If we are truly called to *love* sinners, it logically follows that we must love Satan, whom we categorically *cannot* love and in fact *must* abhor, for, as Kerwick elucidates:

> To hate Satan for God's sake is to love for God's sake. To be filled with the love of God is to burn with hatred of the wicked. God may love Satan insofar as he loves every being that he has created, just inasmuch as being itself is good. From a moral, as opposed to an ontological perspective, though, God, it seems painfully, shockingly clear, hates the Devil. So too should

---

[687] Kerwick, "Christianity's Divine Hatred."

> Christians pray for, not Satan's salvation, but his destruction. And this is nothing if not hatred.

Paul reinforces the meaning of Matthew 5:39 when he writes,

> Recompense to no man evil for evil. Provide things honest in the sight of all men. If it be possible, as much as lieth in you, live peaceably with all men. Dearly beloved, avenge not yourselves, but rather give place unto wrath: for it is written, Vengeance is mine; I will repay, saith the Lord. (Rom. 12:17–19)

We are not to avenge *ourselves* of personal slights or to retaliate against *our* personal enemies, but rather await our vindication by the Lord. God *will* vindicate us in the end. With respect to objective *evildoers*, however, we *must* respond. Peace is to be our primary response *when peace is possible*; this is a clear acknowledgement that sometimes peace is *not* possible, that sometimes violence is the answer. That we are prohibited from avenging *ourselves* does not necessarily mean that we are precluded from avenging *others*, or even the Lord himself.

This true meaning of "turning the other cheek" is quite aptly illuminated in the excellent Kenny Rogers song, "Coward of the County." A young man named Tommy is the titular coward; his father died in prison, and his last words to Tommy were:

> Son, my life is over, but yours has just begun.
> Promise me, son, not to do the things I've done.
> Walk away from trouble if you can.
> Now it don't mean you're weak if you turn the other cheek.
> I hope you're old enough to understand.
> Son, you don't have to fight to be a man.

Tommy lives his life according to his father's dying wish, and "never stood one single time to prove the county wrong." Becky, the woman that Tommy loves, is brutally gang-raped by the Gatlin boys while Tommy is away at work; when he comes home, he:

> [O]pened up the door and saw his Becky crying.
> The torn dress, the shattered look was more than he could stand.
> He reached above the fireplace [and] took down his daddy's picture.
> As a tear fell on his daddy's face, he heard these words again.

As his father's words reverberate in his mind, Tommy goes to the bar to find the Gatlin boys. They laugh at him and call him yellow, but fall silent when Tommy locks the door behind him. He unleashes his "twenty years of crawling" upon them and "let 'em have it all." When "Tommy left the bar room, not a Gatlin boy was standing. He says, 'This one's for Becky' as he watched the last one fall." As he leaves the bar, Tommy says,

> I promised you, Dad, not to do the things you've done.
> I walk away from trouble when I can.
> Now please don't think I'm weak, I didn't turn the other cheek.
> And Papa, I sure hope you understand.
> Sometimes you gotta fight when you're a man.

Though this vigilantism is perhaps problematic, the song accurately shatters the misconception of what "turning the other cheek" truly means. While one does not have to fight in order to be a man, sometimes a man has to fight. There comes a time in every man's life when he must stand. Obviously, in a perfect world there would be no violence; but of course, men are fallen, evil, incapable of perfection. In the 1981 film adaptation of the song, Kenny Rogers plays a pastor, the narrator of the song; he tells his nephew Tommy, "You know, a man's only got two cheeks. He don't say what to do after that. You might want to think about that."

God understands that violence is sometimes a necessary part of our lives as imperfect, inherently sinful beings; after all, "to every thing there is a season, and a time to every purpose under the heaven: . . . A time to kill, and a time to heal." (Eccles. 3:1–4)

Another series of verses that trouble Christians who attempt to reconcile the liberal theological doctrine of pacifism with what they feel is the correct meaning of "turning the other cheek" occur in the First Epistle of Peter. Peter discusses Christian persecution at great length; importantly, Peter was writing during the reign of Nero, whose government brutally murdered and otherwise oppressed Christians. Peter's purpose was to encourage Christians in the midst of their agonies by urging fellow believers to recognize that the suffering of this world, in which they were powerless, would be wiped away by the coming of the next. Peter writes that "it is thankworthy, if a man for conscience toward God endure grief, suffering wrongfully. For what glory is it, if . . . when ye do well, and suffer for it, ye take it patiently, this is acceptable with God." (1 Pet. 2:19–20) God's grace is extended to unwarranted suffering dealt us by the world, and *not* merited punishment for our sins. It is crucial to note that the immediately preceding verse is an exhortation for slaves to be subject to their masters; the immediately following lines thus apply to slaves, and not necessarily to free men. (1 Pet. 2:18)

Perhaps more important, though, is the rhetorical purpose of this call to suffer patiently. Just as Christ promised us that "ye shall be hated of all men for my name's sake: but he that endureth to the end shall be saved," and that "if the world hate you, ye know that it hated me before it hated you," this is spiritual ammunition for our persistence in our faith in God in the face of adversity, even against overwhelming odds. (Matt. 10:22, John 15:18) Our suffering *as believers*, and not merely as imperfect mortals, is often paralleled with that of Jesus Christ, who "also suffered for us, leaving us an example. . . . Who did no sin. . . . Who, when he was reviled, reviled not again; when he suffered, he threatened not; but committed himself to him that judgeth righteously." (1 Pet. 21–23) We *will* suffer and be suppressed for our faith; to endure this patiently is to persevere in our faith, to not waver and turn away from God in embrace of the world, or Satan. This does *not*, however, mean that we are to sit idly by as our loved ones are exterminated or as our government is turned against us. This is merely a powerful call to maintain our faith and understand that Christ suffered worse than we, that if we are not facing persecution, we are doing something wrong; for "the friendship of the world is enmity with God." (James 4:4)

As followers of Christ, we must understand that we travel an arduous path, and as such are called to lead strenuous lives. Christ said, "The foxes have holes, and the birds of the air have nests; but the Son of man hath not where to lay his head." (Matt. 8:20) The life of a believer is not easy; it is full of pain. Faith and worldly comfort, Christ has definitively stated, are mutually exclusive; this worldly comfort does not mean material wealth, which is not mutually exclusive with faith, but rather means the praise and accolades of the world, Satan's domain, which necessarily hates God. To endure suffering patiently is to not shrink from performing our Christian duty as his warriors, to "gird up now thy loins like a man." (Job 38:3) Once more, the patient endurance of pain, the patient wait for our future inheritance and vindication, is a call to steadfast *faith*, not to absolute pacifism. Christianity is not a suicidal faith, but rather the opposite. We are to be "fruitful, and multiply; bring forth abundantly in the earth, and multiply therein." (Gen. 9:7)

Christian holy war occurs throughout the Bible. Some of God's victories were recorded in a now-lost ancient text referred to as *The Book of the Wars of the Lord*; obviously, then, some wars were waged on his behalf. (Num. 21:14) As such, they were his wars, the victories belonging to God, not the men who waged them vicariously. When God's people warred with the Hagarites, "they cried to God in the battle" and were rewarded, "for there fell down many slain, because the war was of God." (1 Chron. 5:19–22). Chronicles is suffused with wars in which God's people failed on their own strength, but were blessed with miraculous victories when God fought the war. War, then, *can* be just when waged for God, and thus become *his*. God's enemies "shall fall before [his people] by the sword." (Lev. 26:7–8)

Holy warfare was generally initiated by God to fulfill the inheritance of his chosen people and to purify the community, scourging it of toxins. In an exemplary instance, God commanded Moses to send his people to war against the Midianites. The priest Phinehas accompanied the army into battle, along with "the holy instruments," further evincing the holy nature of the war. God's people "slew all the males," taking the women and children captive, and put the cities to the torch. (Num. 31:1–11) When the children of Reuben and Gad prevaricated on crossing over the Jordan and completing the conquest of Canaan, Moses expressed God's anger at their disobedience; Moses told them that if they refused to go to war, they "have sinned against the Lord: and be sure your sin will find you out." (Num. 32:20–23) In the case of holy war, then, pacifism is a sin. If we are not *with* God, we are *against* him.

When engaged in holy war, God's people were told:

> When thou goest out to battle against thine enemies, and seest horses, and chariots, and a people more than thou, be not afraid of them . . . let not your hearts faint, fear not, and do not tremble, neither be ye terrified because of them; For the LORD your God is he that goeth with you, to fight for you against your enemies, to save you. (Deut. 20)

Cities that were outside the realm that God promised his people as their inheritance could be approached with an offer of peace. If the city responded positively and surrendered, "all the people that is found therein shall be tributaries unto thee, and they shall serve thee." (Deut. 20) If the city refused, it was to be besieged, and once God delivered the city unto His people they were to "smite every male thereof with the edge of the sword" and capture the women, children, and spoils. (Deut. 20) Distant cities, then, were still to be subdued, though at least given the chance to surrender. (Josh. 9:26–27, 2 Sam. 10)

As for the cities that were within the realm promised by God as the inheritance of his people, God commanded that they "save alive nothing that breatheth," that they "utterly destroy them." (Deut. 20) This total annihilation was important for the sake of purity, so that none of the "abominations" of the conquered people could contaminate the community of God's people. (Deut. 20) When "the Lord thy God shall deliver" the enemies of his people unto dispossession, his people are commanded to "smite them, and utterly destroy them

. . . make no covenant with them, nor shew mercy unto them." His people are not to have any relations whatsoever with the conquered enemy. (Deut. 7:1–6) The cultural and physical genocide inherent in the divine command to "utterly destroy" is the ultimate act of self-preservation for his community.

Jesus Christ declares, "Think not that I am come to send peace on earth: I came not to send peace, but a sword." (Matt. 10:34) The angel of the Lord slaughtered a "hundred fourscore and five thousand" Assyrians. (2 Kings 19:35) God is described as a warrior-king; of Edom, representing all of the enemy nations, God says:

> I have trodden the winepress alone; and of the people there was none with me: for I will tread them in mine anger, and trample them in my fury; and their blood shall be sprinkled upon my garments, and I will stain all my raiment. For the day of vengeance is in mine heart, and the year of my redeemed is come. And I looked, and there was none to help; and I wondered that there was none to uphold: therefore mine own arm brought salvation unto me; and my fury, it upheld me. And I will tread down the people in mine anger, and make them drunk in my fury, and I will bring down their strength to the earth. (Isa. 63:1–6)

The image of God trampling his enemies as grapes crushed in a winepress is repeated in Revelation. Jesus Christ is there referred to as the "Word of God," hearkening back to the first verse of the Gospel of John, and is described as being:

> Clothed with a vesture dripped in blood. . . . And out of his mouth goeth a sharp sword, that with it he should smite the nations: and he shall rule them with a rod of iron: and he treadeth the winepress of the fierceness and wrath of Almighty God. (Rev. 19:11–18)

This bloodstained robe looks backward to his crucifixion and forward to the wrath of his final judgment. Furthermore, the Word, referring to Christ himself as well as the gospel, is described as a sharp sword, hearkening back to Matthew 10:34.

God imbues his people with the traits for warfare to ensure that they are always the pursuers, never the pursued; King David celebrates:

> It is God that girdeth me with strength. . . . He maketh my feet like hinds' feet. . . . He teacheth my hands to war. . . . I have pursued mine enemies, and overtaken them: neither did I turn again till they were consumed. I have wounded them that they were not able to rise: they are fallen under my feet. (Ps. 18:32–38)

He praises God:

> Thou hast subdued under me those that rose up against me. Thou hast also given me the necks of mine enemies; that I might destroy them that hate me. They cried, but there was none to save them: even unto the Lord, but he answered them not. Then did I beat them small as the dust before the wind: I did cast them out as the dirt in the streets. (Ps. 18:39–44)

We are called:

> [T]o put on the whole armour of God, that ye may be able to stand against the wiles of the devil. For we wrestle not against flesh and blood, but against principalities, against powers, against the rulers of the darkness of this world, against spiritual wickedness in high places. Wherefore take unto you the whole armour of God, that ye may be able to withstand in the evil day, and having done all, to stand. Stand therefore, having your loins girt about with truth, and having on the breastplate of righteousness; And your feet shod with the preparation of the gospel of peace; Above all, taking the shield of faith, wherewith ye shall be able to quench all the fiery darts of the wicked. And take the helmet of salvation, and the sword of the Spirit, which is the word of God: Praying always with all prayer and supplication in the Spirit, and watching thereunto with all perseverance and supplication for all saints; And for me, that utterance may be given unto me, that I may open my mouth boldly, to make known the mystery of the gospel, For which I am an ambassador in bonds: that therein I may speak boldly, as I ought to speak. (Eph. 6:11–20)

It is worth noting that in this description of the "whole armour of God," no armor is mentioned for our backs; it seems then that we are meant to press forward unrelentingly.

As we have said, when the authorities came to arrest Christ in the Garden of Gethsemane, Peter severed the ear of Malchus, servant of the high priest, with his sword; Jesus, in a verse erroneously yet ubiquitously believed to be an absolute injunction against violence, admonishes Peter to "put up again thy sword into his place: for all they that take the sword shall perish with the sword." (Matt. 26:47–52) Those who cite this for their liberal theology never fail to elide over the next two verses; after telling Peter to put away his sword, Jesus continues by asking him, "Thinkest thou that I cannot now pray to my Father, and he shall presently give me more than twelve legions of angels? But how then shall the scriptures be fulfilled, that thus it must be?" (Matt. 26:53–54) Christ, therefore, is not admonishing Peter for the act of violence in cutting Malchus' ear (which Christ restores), but rather for his intervention in the fulfillment of God's plans for him. By attempting to save Jesus, Peter is directly acting against what *must* happen: Christ's sacrifice. Moreover, not only was it Christ himself who told the disciples to obtain the swords in the first place, but, as John of Mantua noted, when Christ directed Peter to put away his sword, he told him to *sheathe* it in its scabbard, rather than discard it.

Another common misconception comes in the context of revolution, with liberal theologians promoting the notion that Christians cannot resist or revolt against their government; this logic was first articulated in the early modern period by divine right theorists, and held little sway during antiquity and the Middle Ages, when, to name but one instance, Thomas Aquinas defended the right of subjects to rise up against tyrants. If our Christian forefathers had believed in this particular formulation, they would not have rebelled against Great Britain, nor would they have seceded from the Union. While, indeed, everything that occurs does so as a part of God's predetermined plan, it is also made manifest throughout the Bible that this world is the realm of Satan, that "the rulers of the darkness of this world" embody "spiritual wickedness in high places." (Eph. 6:12)

Paul writes:

> Let every soul be subject unto the higher powers. For there is no power but of God: the powers that be are ordained of God. Whosoever therefore resisteth the power, resisteth the ordinance of God: and they that resist shall receive to themselves damnation. For rulers are not a terror to good works, but to the evil. Wilt thou then not be afraid of the power? do that which is good, and thou shalt have praise of the same: For he is the minister of God to thee for good. But if thou do that which is evil, be afraid; for he beareth not the sword in vain: for he is the minister of God, a revenger to execute wrath upon him that doeth evil. Wherefore ye must needs be subject, not only for wrath, but also for conscience sake. For this cause pay ye tribute also: for they are God's ministers, attending continually upon this very thing. Render therefore to all their dues: tribute to whom tribute is due; custom to whom custom; fear to whom fear; honour to whom honour. (Rom. 13:1–7)

Similarly, we are told to "render therefore unto Caesar the things which are Caesar's; and unto God the things that are God's." (Matt. 22:21) Peter writes:

> Submit yourselves to every ordinance of man for the Lord's sake: whether it be to the king, as supreme; Or unto governors, as unto them that are sent by him for the punishment of evildoers, and for the praise of them that do well. For so is the will of God, that with well doing ye may put to silence the ignorance of foolish men: As free, and not using your liberty for a cloke of maliciousness, but as the servants of God. (1 Pet. 2:13–16)

The key to unlocking this problem is provided by Peter and the other apostles; they said, "We ought to obey God rather than men." (Acts 5:29) Thus, we are presented with our answer: God's law is supreme. In the case of conflict between the laws of governments and the laws of God, God must always prevail. We are called, then, to submit to *legitimate* authorities; this injunction against *unwarranted* rebellion does not apply to *illegitimate*, satanic rulers that oppress God's people. When Paul urged us to submit, he presumed that rulers were "not a terror to good works, but to the evil," that governments would act as God's instruments of justice in this world, that they would not bear "the sword in vain"; the very fact that Paul included this detail of the benevolent nature of legitimate government suggests that we *must* take into account the nature of the regime that we are to obey. The command, then, is not absolute. *All* governments are not to be obeyed; indeed, illegitimate and oppressive governments are rather to be resisted, just as Satan is to be resisted. When we consider the fact that Paul's government executed him, we may also examine what exactly is meant by being an obedient subject.

When Christ tells us to render "unto Caesar the things which are Caesar's," when Peter urges us to submit "to every ordinance of man for the Lord's sake," we must ask what that means. It seems clear that the things which are Caesar's are the general components of civil order, including paying taxes or obtaining proper licensure for businesses, and *not* such things as allowing our dispossession or allowing violence committed against us to go unpunished. Again, we are presented with a tiered system of degree. As Peter himself said, one cannot submit to "every ordinance of man" if that ordinance contradicts God's ordinances. Examples of violative ordinances are manifest in our presently fallen and degraded society, from infanticide to homosexuality, from transgenderism and the mutilation of children to saturated obscenity and promiscuity. We must understand that we would be sinning if we literally obeyed "every ordinance of man," if we actually completely submitted ourselves; as elaborated upon at length already, we *must* resist Satan. We certainly are not commanded to stand by as we are attacked, exploited, and replaced. We also cannot forget that the Mark of the Beast will be instituted by law. (Rev. 13:17)

14

Christian Holy War: Crusade Theology

Saint Augustine laid the foundations of Christian just war theory. He writes in Chapter 7 of Book XIX of his *City of God*, entitled "The misery of war, even when just":

> The wise man . . . will wage just wars. Surely, if he remembers that he is a human being, he will rather lament the fact that he is faced with the necessity of waging just wars; for if they were not just, he would not have to engage in them, and consequently there would be no wars for a wise man. For it is the injustice of the opposing side that lays on the wise man the duty of waging wars; and this injustice is assuredly to be deplored by a human being, since it is the injustice of human beings, even though no necessity for war should arise from it.

He continues in Chapter 12, entitled "Peace is . . . the ultimate purpose of war":

> There is no man who does not wish for peace. Indeed, even when men choose war, their only wish is for victory; which shows that their desire in fighting is for peace with glory. For what is victory but the conquest of the opposing side? And when this is achieved, there will be peace. Even wars, then, are waged with peace as their object, even when they are waged by those who are concerned to exercise their warlike prowess . . . it is an established fact that peace is the desired end of war. For every man is in quest of peace, even in waging war, whereas no one is in quest of war when making peace. In fact, even when men wish a present state of peace to be disturbed,

> they do so not because they hate peace, but because they desire the present peace to be exchanged for one that suits their wishes. Thus, their desire is not that there should not be peace but that it should be the kind of peace they wish for. Even in the extreme case when they separated themselves from others by sedition, they cannot achieve their aim unless they maintain some sort of semblance of peace with their confederates in conspiracy.

In the same chapter, Augustine explains:

> All men desire to be at peace with their own people, while wishing to impose their will upon those people's lives. For even when they wage war on others, their wish is to make those opponents their own people, if they can—to subject them, and to impose on them their own conditions of peace.

He notes that "even the most savage beasts . . . safeguard their own species by a kind of peace, by coition, by begetting and bearing young, by cherishing them and rearing them." Though Christian just war theory went on to be developed further by later theorists, most notably Thomas Aquinas, the key components of Christian just war are based in Augustinian theory, including just cause, legitimate authority, right intention, last resort, and proportionality. In other words, violence committed in the name of the Lord must be reactive rather than preemptive, formally authorized, and waged justly. Just wars are a form of retributive justice, initiated only in direct and proportional retaliation against grievous, intolerable injuries, when all other solutions have been exhausted, and only in order to restore the *status quo antebellum.*

Since unjust aggressions or oppressions tend to disturb earthly order, which reflects the divine order, resistance to them was an absolute necessity for good men. In Augustine's *Contra Faustum Manichaeum*, the illustrious doctor elaborated that "right intention," as the great Crusade scholar Jonathan Riley-Smith explains, requires that Christian violence be motivated by love, proportional to the injury received, and circumscribed to ensure that the innocent suffer as little as possible. To understand Augustinian theory, it is crucial to understand the ethical neutrality of violence. As Riley-Smith paraphrases, Augustine basically asked,

> What was evil in war of itself . . . ? The real evils were not the deaths of those who would have died anyway, but the love of violence, cruelty, and enmity; it was generally to punish such that good men undertook wars in obedience to God or to some lawful authority [as the earthly representative of God]. It was the intention of the perpetrators . . . that provided force with a moral dimension.[688]

From the earliest days, Christians killed in wars against infidels and other enemies of the Church were referred to as martyrs; indeed, Pope Gregory VII spoke of "the soldiers of Christ" who fought for God, literally rather than metaphorically. Pope Alexander II had argued that force could be applied to remedy present, apparent, and material injury, such as military aggression, the occupation of Christian property, or insurrection; past acts were only relevant insofar as they may have continual injurious impact. It was Pope Urban II, however, who elucidated the most interesting and most impactful theory of Christian violence, in his preaching of the First Crusade, the purest and most spectacularly triumphant of the Crusades, and thus that which we will focus our efforts on.

Before we delve into Crusade theology, we must contextualize the First Crusade within the greater narrative of the threat, since the time of Muhammad, of global Islamic conquest. As Thomas Madden summarizes, the Crusades were wholly defensive wars, the European answer to a dire mayday from the Byzantine emperor, to "more than four centuries of conquests in which Muslim armies had already captured two-thirds of the old Christian world."[689] Christianity faced a choice: Christendom as faith and polity must either defend itself or be devoured by Islam. The Crusades were that defense, precipitated by centuries of the foulest Islamic provocations. The Byzantine emperor wrote to Urban, detailing unfathomably brutal Muslim atrocities against native Christians and

---

688 Riley-Smith, *Crusades, Christianity, and Islam*, 13.
689 Madden, *Crusades Controversy*, 45.

European pilgrims, as well as sounding the alarm of the Islamic advance, warning that, were Constantinople to fall (as seemed likely), thousands more Christians would be enslaved, tortured, raped, and butchered. The emperor called for the aid of his Christian brethren, writing, "In the name of God . . . we implore you to bring . . . all the faithful soldiers of Christ . . . you will find your reward in Heaven, and if you do not come, God will condemn you."

In stark juxtaposition with Pope Francis, an Islamic apologist who declared in 2013 that Islam and the Qur'an "are opposed to every form of violence," Urban answered the emperor in this dark hour, and called the First Crusade. The pope proclaimed of the Muslim savages:

> They ruin the altars with filth and defilement. They circumcise Christians and smear the blood from the circumcision over the altars or throw it into the baptismal fonts. They are pleased to kill others by cutting open their bellies, extracting the end of their intestines, and tying it to a stake. Then, with flogging, they drive their victims around the stake until, when the viscera have spilled out, they fall dead on the ground. . . . And what shall I say about the shocking rape of women?[690]

As Madden notes:

> For knights steeped in a culture of militant Christianity, these were stories to make the blood boil. The shouts of Europe's fighting men, filled with righteous anger, rang out across the land: "God wills it! God wills it!"[691]

This was the battle-cry of the Crusaders. Riley-Smith emphasizes that, although Pope Urban II technically initiated this First Crusade, "no Crusade could ever have left Europe merely because a pope had authorized it."[692] The Crusaders were volunteers, meaning that the laity *and* the nobility had to respond positively to an appeal from the Church; although the number of Crusaders, those men who "took the cross," was always a

---

690 Quoted in Madden, *Concise History of the Crusades*, 8.
691 Ibid.
692 Riley-Smith, *Crusades, Christianity, and Islam*, 5.

numerical minority of the Western Europeans who were qualified to do so, they enjoyed the near universal enthusiasm of the general population.

The success of the call throughout Christendom is explained largely by Urban's brilliant theological innovation; Riley-Smith elaborates that, "for Augustine, violence was justified in response to *injury*," whereas, "for Urban, this response took the form of a war of liberation."[693] Urban thus infused love into the Augustinian theory of Christian violence, casting Christian holy war, the Crusade, as an act of charitable love for our aggrieved Christian brethren. Urban also expounded a theory of penitential warfare, of war as penance for our sins. This penance was enhanced through the inherent dangers and privations of the Crusade itself, which the pope understood to be a pilgrimage both internal and external, and was compounded by a parallel monasticization of war. As Rodney Stark explains, Urban directed the European knighthood toward a sacred cause, preaching a Crusade doctrine wherein "participation in the Crusade was the moral equivalent of serving in a monastic order."[694] In other words, Urban promised salvation through penitential warfare against the enemies of the Lord. To employ the terminology of Riley-Smith:

> [These were] penitential war-pilgrimages . . . proclaimed not only against Muslims, but also against pagan Wends, Balts and Lithuanians, shamanist Mongols, Orthodox Russians and Greeks, Cathar and Hussite heretics, and those Catholics whom the Church deemed to be its enemies. . . . [To crusade was] to engage in a war that was both holy, because it was believed to be waged on God's behalf, and penitential, because those taking part considered themselves to be performing an act of penance. The war was authorized by the pope as a vicar of Christ.[695]

Urban employed Scripture impressively, often repeating Christ's exhortation, "If any man will come after me, let him

---

[693] Riley-Smith, *First Crusade*, 17.
[694] Stark, *God's Battalions*, 16.
[695] Riley-Smith, *Crusades, Christianity, and Islam*, 18

deny himself, and take up his cross, and follow me," "And whosoever doth not bear his cross, and come after me, cannot be my disciple." (Matt. 16:24, Luke 14:27) Urban recalled those words of the Psalmist, "O God, the heathen are come into thine inheritance; thy holy temple have they defiled; they have laid Jerusalem on heaps." (Ps. 79:1) Pope Innocent III would later ask:

> How does a man love according to divine precept his neighbor as himself when, knowing that his Christian brothers in faith and in name are held by the perfidious Muslims in strict confinement and weighed down by the yoke of heaviest servitude, he does not devote himself to the task of freeing them . . . ? Is it, by chance, that you do not know that many thousands of Christians are bound in slavery and imprisoned by the Muslims, tortured with innumerable torments?

To the Knights Templar, Innocent cited another brilliant verse, declaring to the knights, "You carry out in deeds the words of the gospel, 'Greater love hath no man than this, that a man lay down his life for his friends.'" (John 15:13)

Urban wrote that the Crusaders were engaged directly "in the service of God," acting out of love for Him, as "knights of Christ," "the army of God," and "the army of the Lord." The First Crusade was known throughout France as "the way of God," and throughout Christendom as "the way of the cross." God was understood to be waging war himself, through his servants, in "God's own war." In fact, Madden notes, the word "crusade" is derived from *cruce signati*, "those signed by the cross," a descriptor used after the twelfth century to refer to the Crusaders. Muslims were "enemies of the cross," barbaric enemies of God and of Christianity, the servants of Satan, while Crusaders were the very knights of Christ. Martyrdom, Riley-Smith explained, "the voluntary acceptance of death for the sake of the Faith and reflecting the death of Christ, is the supreme act of love of which a Christian is capable and is the perfect example of a Christian death."[696] Martyrdom, dying for Christ who died for us, was thus the highest expression of love

[696] Riley-Smith, *First Crusade*, 115.

for Christ and for Christians, a voluntary exchange of ephemeral mortality for incorruptible permanence.

There is no reason to doubt (and mountains of incontrovertible evidence affirm) the fact that the Crusaders, already raised within chivalric culture, truly were the agents of altruistic violence, that in taking the cross and making vows symbolized by the wearing of the cross, they really were "motivated by Christian charity . . . the preachers who recruited them tended to stress love of God and of brothers and sisters in the Faith."[697] Riley-Smith notes:

> To crusade was to engage in a serious business, dangerous, debilitating, and impoverishing, and one that was . . . primarily a penitential exercise. It was also to enter for a Divine examination. The idea of the summons to take the cross as God's own test of an individual put it on a different plane from those feats of knightly endurance in fiction that appealed so much to contemporaries.[698]

The Crusaders took the cross, "moved by love of God and their neighbor, renouncing wives, children, and earthly possessions, and adopting temporary poverty and chastity" to enter a self-imposed exile and embark on a rigorously liturgical expedition to wage war for the Lord on his enemies.[699] The Crusades, especially this First, were thus the epitome of devotional sacrifice, of pious idealism, of the belief in that which is greater than oneself. The Crusaders attributed, to a man, their stunning victory to God, their strength a miraculous gift for their military service rendered unto him, often cast in terms of feudal lordship. Their swords were collectively his sword, the sword of Christ; as Eudes of Châteauroux wrote:

> The cross is the sword with which the Lord fought the earthly powers and their followers, and up to now he has not ceased fighting them. . . . And today, who but the knights more aptly

---

[697] Riley-Smith, *Crusades, Christianity, and Islam*, 23.
[698] Ibid.
[699] Ibid., 32.

> and more evidently trust that Christ is their Lord. They follow his call and form his army.[700]

Much later, in 1212, Pope Innocent III wrote to King Alfonso VIII of Castile after the great victory over the Almohads at Las Navas de Tolosa, cautioning:

> It was not your highness's hands but the Lord who has done all these things. . . . For that victory took place without doubt not by human but by divine agency; and the sword of God, not of man . . . destroyed the enemies of the cross. . . . So do not walk proudly because those who work wickedness have fallen there, but give glory and honor to the Lord, saying humbly . . . *the zeal of the Lord of Hosts* has done *this*.[701]

The letters of the First Crusaders reflect this sentiment precisely, almost all of them containing phrases like the following: "Truly, God fights for us"; "How one against a thousand . . . ? We do not trust in any multitude nor in power nor in any presumption, but in the shield of Christ"; and, "We had the most victorious hand of the Father with us."[702]

Riley-Smith emphasizes:

> [The Crusaders] were not fools. They knew how weak they were and what risks they took. It is not surprising that they attributed their triumph to divine assistance or that their achievement enthralled their contemporaries and was venerated as a model of heroism and endurance for many centuries to come.[703]

They recognized full well how ill-equipped and under-prepared they were, and experienced extreme privation. Horrendous conditions on their journey left at least one third of the knights dead, the peasantry obviously faring even worse:

---

[700] Ibid., 41.
[701] Ibid., 24.
[702] Riley-Smith, *First Crusade*, 100.
[703] Ibid., 3.

> [There was] no system of provisioning and for long periods the Crusaders were far from potential supply-points. Most of their time was taken up in foraging. They had to fight most of their battles on foot, because they lost nearly all their horses and, even more seriously, their pack animals, so that they had to carry their baggage themselves.[704]

The only plausible explanation for their victory, then, "was the fact that they really were fulfilling the intentions of God. They had set out, of course, convinced that they were involved in God's work."[705]

Crusaders, Madden notes, were men who, "at great expense and personal peril, sought to rescue the downtrodden, defend the defenseless, and restore to Christendom what had been violently taken away."[706] The cost of crusading was enormous, often involving the impoverishment of one's own family and the abandonment of that family for years at a time; only about half of these men ever returned home, and when they did so they carried not material wealth, but the faith with which they had departed. How can we understand why thousands of knights from the greatest families of Europe made such profound sacrifices? Stated simply, we must remember that they were medieval, not modern, people.

Madden explains:

> The culture of nobility in the eleventh century was one of public displays of piety. Lords were known as much for their love of God as for their skill on the battlefield. Indeed, the two were seen as different sides of the same coin, neither possible without the other. With open hands, these families had showered lands and wealth upon Europe's churches and monasteries for centuries. It was the duty of the nobility, who were blessed by God, to return the fruits of that blessing to God's people and His Church. The Crusade was simply another means of doing that. Knights were willing to make profound sacrifices for the Crusade because it was in the nature of their class to do so. By expending great wealth, they were storing up treasure where

---

[704] Ibid., 2.

[705] Ibid., 99.

[706] Madden, *Concise History of the Crusades*, 12.

> rust and moth could not corrupt. By defending the Church, they defended all that was good and true in their world. In short, most noblemen who joined the Crusade did so from a simple and sincere love of God.[707]

The Knights Templar were established for the protection of European pilgrims. These knights lived lives of monastic asceticism. One pilgrim to Jerusalem, writing some years prior to 1187, described the Templars thus:

> The Templars are most excellent soldiers. They wear white mantles with a red cross, and when they go to the wars . . . [t]hey go in silence. Their first attack is the most terrible. In going they are the first, in returning the last. . . . When they think fit to make war and the trumpet has sounded, they sing in chorus the Psalm of David, "Not unto us, O Lord," kneeling on the blood and necks of the enemy, unless they have forced the troops of the enemy to retire altogether, or utterly broken them to pieces. Should any of them for any reason turn his back to the enemy, or come forth alive [from defeat], or bear arms against the Christians, he is severely punished; the white mantle with the red cross, which is the sign of his knighthood, is taken away with ignominy, he is cast from the society of brethren, and eats his food on the floor without a napkin for the space of one year. If the dogs molest him, he does not dare to drive them away. But at the end of the year, if the . . . brethren think his penance to have been sufficient, they restore him the belt of his former knighthood. These Templars live under a strict religious rule.[708]

This lifestyle was influenced primarily by Bernardine theology, set forth by Saint Bernard of Clairvaux in his *De laude novae militiae*. This new knighthood, Malcolm Barber elaborates, pursued "a double conflict against both flesh and blood and the invisible forces of evil."[709] This hybridized warrior-monk *ethos* was inculcated to produce "men who need have no fear. Since they fought with a clear and pure conscience, these men had no dread of death, confident in the knowledge that in the

---

[707] Ibid., 13.
[708] Barber, *New Knighthood*, 179.
[709] Ibid., 45.

sight of the Lord, they would be his martyrs."[710] Bernard saw the Crusade as "a form of pilgrimage in which the Christians became participants in the Passion of Christ and therefore his heirs. Conversely, Muslims were unjustified invaders of Christ's patrimony."[711] Bernard wrote that, when the Templars joined battle, they at last cast aside restraint, as if to say, "Have I not hated those, Lord, who hated you and languish upon your enemies?"[712]

Pope Celestine II would later write of the First Crusade that "God liberates the Eastern Church from the filth of the pagans."[713] Two brothers en route to Jerusalem explained that they took the cross for the precise reasons Urban had called them:

> On the one hand for the grace of the pilgrimage and, on the other, under the protection of God, to wipe out the defilement of the pagans and the immoderate madness through which innumerable Christians have already been oppressed, made captive, and killed with barbaric fury.[714]

Urban had preached, "May the stories of your ancestors move you and excite your souls to strength; the worth and greatness of King Charlemagne . . . who destroyed the kingdoms of the pagans and extended into them the boundaries of Holy Church," and later wrote that the Church was "stimulating the minds of knights to go on this expedition, since they might be able to restrain the savagery of the Muslims by their arms and restore the Christians to their former freedom."[715]

Baldric of Bourgueil recounts a sermon preached beneath the walls of Jerusalem on this First Crusade:

> Rouse yourselves, members of Christ's household! Rouse yourselves, knights and footsoldiers, and seize firmly that city, our commonwealth! Give heed to Christ, who today is banished

---

[710] Ibid.
[711] Ibid.
[712] Ibid., 181.
[713] Ibid., 58.
[714] Ibid.
[715] Ibid., 59.

> from that city and is crucified . . . and forcefully take Christ away from these impious crucifiers. For every time those bad judges, confederates of Herod . . . make sport of and enslave your brothers they crucify Christ. Every time they torment them and kill them, they lance Christ's side with Longinus. Indeed, they do all these things and, what is worse, they deride and cast reproaches on Christ and our law and they provoke us with rash speech. What are you doing about these things? Is it right for you to listen to these things, to see these things done and not to lament them? I address fathers and sons and brothers and nephews. If an outsider were to strike any of your kin down, would you not avenge your blood-relative? How much more ought you to avenge your God, your father, your brother, whom you see reproached, banished from his estates, crucified; whom you hear calling, desolate, and begging for aid.[716]

The Crusade was, as Robert the Monk wrote, "not human work, but divine," fought against "a race absolutely alien to God," the agents of Satan himself.[717] Guibert of Nogent wrote of the Crusaders' commonly stated devotion to:

> [O]ur brothers, members of Christ's body. . . . Your blood-brothers, your comrades-in-arms, those born from the same womb as you, for you are sons of the same Christ and the same Church . . . Christian blood, which has been redeemed by Christ's blood, is spilled and Christian flesh, flesh of Christ's flesh, is delivered up to execrable abuses and appalling servitude.[718]

Violence was considered to be justified if meted out for the recovery of property unrightfully stolen, a category to which the recent Muslim conquests definitely belonged; as Riley-Smith notes, "the region rightfully belonged to Christendom because before it had been seized by Muslims, it had been part of the Christian Roman Empire."[719] One contemporary affirmed this, writing:

---

[716] Riley-Smith, *First Crusade*, 48.
[717] Ibid., 139.
[718] Ibid., 145.
[719] Ibid.

> [The land] is not theirs, although they have possessed it for a long time, for from the earliest times it was ours and your people attacked it and took it . . . and so it ought not to be yours just because you have held it . . . for by heavenly judgment it is now decreed that that which was unjustly taken from the fathers should be mercifully returned to the sons.[720]

While Muslims were the primary enemy, that which Pope Urban II had initially raised the First Crusade for, many, if not most, of the Crusaders rightfully held Jews to be equally detestable, if not more so. At Rouen, men who had come to take the cross began to say, "We wish to attack the enemies of God in the East, once we have crossed great tracts of territory, when before our eyes are the Jews, more hostile to God than any other race. The enterprise is absurd."[721] Indeed, many French Crusaders argued likewise, noting that they were "going to a distant country to make war against mighty kings and are endangering our lives to conquer kingdoms which do not believe in the crucified one, when it is actually the Jews who murdered and crucified him."[722] Some later Crusaders were influenced by a scene in the *Chanson d'Antioche*, the great vernacular epic of the First Crusade, in which Christ was pictured crucified between the two thieves; the good thief comments, "It would be most just, moreover, if you should be avenged on those treacherous Jews by whom you are so tormented."[723] Our Lord turns to him and says:

> Friend, the people are not yet born who will come to avenge me with their steel lances. So they will come to kill the faithless pagans who have always refused my commandments. Holy Christianity will be honored by them, and my land conquered and my country freed. . . . Know certainly that from over the seas will come a new race which will take revenge on the death of its father.[724]

---

720 Ibid., 146.
721 Ibid., 54.
722 Ibid., 55.
723 Ibid.
724 Ibid., 56.

The long, blood-drenched history of Islamic hostility to Christianity is well-documented and set forth in innumerable books that still grace the shelves of mainstream White conservatives, so we will not undertake a full exposition here. Instead, we focus our efforts on one particular aspect of that hostility, indeed its most gut-wrenching facet: the systematic sexual enslavement of White women. The Qur'an explicitly legitimates not only the Islamic enslavement of Christians, but more particularly the *sexual* enslavement of Christians, including boys and girls of *all* ages—look no further than Muhammad himself, who, aside from being a vicious warlord, was a pedophiliac rapist.[725] This deep tradition of Muslim pederasty continues today, in the barracks of our "allies" in the "War on Terror." In an early *hadith*, Muhammad offered a new convert "the girls of the yellow-haired pale people." He often demanded, "Give me that girl." Raymond Ibrahim explains that Islam traditionally conflates Christian piety with sexual promiscuity.[726] A celebrated Persian court scholar gave us a characteristic example in his description of the arrival of a ship full of Frankish women who had just been enslaved:

> They glowed with ardor for carnal intercourse. They were all licentious harlots . . . who took and gave, foul-fleshed and sinful . . . with nasal voices and fleshy thighs, blue-eyed. . . . They dedicated as a holy offering what they kept between their thighs. . . . They maintained that they could make themselves acceptable to God by no better sacrifice than this. . . . They made themselves targets for men's darts.[727]

The fiend was fixated on one girl in particular, who "walked proudly with the cross on her breast," signifying that she "longed to lose her robe and her honor."[728]

Ibn Hazm, an esteemed Islamic theologian, wrote that White women "have nothing else to fill their minds, except

---

[725] McLoughlin & Robinson, *Mohammed's Koran*. Note: Despite the authors' philo-Semitism, this translation of the Qur'an, organized chronologically, is the best English edition available.

[726] Ibrahim, *Sword and Scimitar*.

[727] Ibid., 49.

[728] Ibid.

[sex] and what brings it about. . . . This is their sole occupation, and they were created for nothing else."[729] Ibrahim notes that Muslim men have long held an obsession for White women; to entice his men to make war, Muhammad, and jihadi leaders ever since, promised them blonde-haired women as spoils.[730] Abd al-Rahman III, the caliph most associated with the Andalusian "golden age" of Islam, had White women and children brutally tortured and murdered for refusing his sexual advances.[731] During the Barbary trade, most young White children, both boys and girls, were retained for sex; by 1541, Muslim Algiers so teemed with White slaves that it became a common saying that "a Christian slave was scarce a fair barter for an onion." As Father Dan, a contemporary observer, wrote, "No Christian could witness what took place without melting into tears, to see so many honest girls and so many well-brought-up women abandoned to the brutality of these barbarians."

When the Hagia Sophia was sacked, as embalmed saints were disinterred and dumped into filthy latrines, Christian men and women alike were gang-raped under the crucifix. Aside from drawing the Janissaries from the Christian population, the Ottomans demanded an annual "blood tribute" from Christian subjects, consisting of boys as young as eight. Ibrahim details:

> [It] was collected variously. Sometimes, Ottoman officials would go door to door, other times fathers were ordered to bring their sons to the public squares. After the boys were examined, the very best—the handsomest and halest—were hauled off, often torn from the grips of their hysterical mothers. Any father who dared offer resistance was executed on the spot.[732]

The slave markets of the Ottomans were so full of White slaves that European children sold for pennies; Ibrahim remarks that

---

[729] Ibid., 54.

[730] Ibrahim, "'A Piece of Meat.'"

[731] Fernández-Morera, *Myth of the Andalusian Paradise.*

[732] Ibrahim, *Sword and Scimitar*, 207.

"a very beautiful slave woman was exchanged for a pair of boots, and four Serbian slaves were traded for a horse."[733] In Crimea, where at least three million Slavs were enslaved by Muslim Tatars, one eyewitness described how Christian men were castrated and brutalized, including having their eyes gouged out, while "the youngest women are kept for wanton pleasures."[734]

Our Christian forefathers did not countenance these atrocities. Of all the symptoms of fallen Christendom, the most awful portent of our psychological emasculation is the inexcusably bleak fact that the Church, and White civilization writ large, behaves with utter passivity today in the face of the rampant rape of White girls in their own homeland. White silence *is* violence indeed. The phenomenon of Islamic "grooming gangs" is a prime illustration. Across Western Europe, as far afield as Finland, in *every* town with even a middling Muslim population, these gangs lure White schoolgirls (and schoolboys, though the targets are primarily girls between the ages of eleven and sixteen, with some younger than ten) into putrid lives of addiction and prostitution, enslaving them into extraordinarily well-organized rape networks.[735] In the UK alone, while Rochdale and Rotherham are the most infamous scapegoats atop an iceberg, these gangs have been discovered operating, in some cases since early Islamization in the late 1980s, in Accrington, Aylesbury, Barking, Barrow-in-Furness, Birmingham, Blackburn, Blackpool, Bradford, Brierley Hill, Bristol, Burton, Chesham, Coventry, Derby, Dudley, Huddersfield, Ipswich, Keighley, Lancaster, Leeds, Leicester, London, Luton, Lye, Manchester, Middlesbrough, Morcombe, Nelson, Newcastle, Oldham, Oxford, Peterborough, Preston, Sandwell, Sheffield, Skipton, Slough, Smethwick, Solihull, Telford, Tipton, Walsall, Willenhall, Wolverhampton, *and more.*

One of the reasons that Rotherham has remained so memorable is that its case is the one that provided us the greatest glimpse into the systematic cover-up that must also be

---

[733] Ibid.

[734] Ibid., 275.

[735] Dutton, *Silent Rape Epidemic.*

happening even now, in countless other Islamized cities across the whilom West. These gangs, comprised primarily of Pakistanis, North Africans, Syrians, Afghans, Turks, and Somalis, were permitted to operate in the open for decades, claiming an industrial-scale number of victims. While in Rotherham, the conservative cumulative total is estimated at fourteen hundred, there have been as many as one million White victims of Islamic "grooming gangs" in Europe. Consider this number alongside the approximate fifteen million Whites historically enslaved by Muslims. Peter McLoughlin explains that, for decades, "thousands of professionals who pride themselves on supposedly protecting our society turned a blind eye to the organized seduction and rape of schoolgirls."[736] These "professionals" include social workers, teachers, school administrators, medical professionals, law enforcement officers, charities, academics, journalists, and Members of Parliament; *they all knew*. As with most other truths too terrible to bear, including several other international pedophile rings with friends in high places, this cover-up was for years derided as a "right-wing conspiracy theory" and consigned to Outer Darkness.

Just as the profaning of American culture was accomplished through Jewish ethnic networking, these systematized rape gangs are examples of Muslim ethnic networking. The debasement, torture, and murder of White schoolgirls was a community affair, involving nearly all of the Muslims in the area; Muslims from all walks of life, including taxi drivers, store owners, security guards, and public officials, all colluded to support, aid, or participate in the evil. Andrew Hamilton notes that, although Pakistani taxi drivers were instrumental in organized rape, the only taxi driver that has ever been barred from transporting girls was White.[737] Indeed, White girls were often lured to their doom by young Muslim peers, utilizing their family networks to traffic the girls across the country and across Europe. Another fifth of the known victims came from children's homes or social services guardianships.

---

[736] McLoughlin, *Easy Meat*, 123.
[737] Hamilton, "Rotherham."

Gangs of adult Muslim men loitered brazenly about schoolyards. Girls would disappear for days at a time, returning to school dirty, disheveled, ill, and covered with sores and injection marks, all with nary a question asked or an action taken. The evidence of daily starvation and rape before their very eyes, the teachers did nothing. Children weren't even warned, the problem wholly ignored. The Rotherham government shuttered its own youth program to silence its reports. Douglas Murray reports that in 2004, a documentary on Bradford's social services was suppressed after "antifascists" and local police chiefs lodged complaints, deeming the sections dealing with the sexual exploitation of White girls by "Asian" gangs to be "potentially inflammatory"; in particular, these authorities insisted that "the screening ahead of local elections could assist the British National Party."[738]

"Grooming gangs" were an open secret. Muslim clerics gave their followers detailed instructions on sexual subjugation. Families spoke of having to cut ties with their own daughters in order to prevent them from luring other relatives into putrescence. Victims contacted local police departments and social services agencies, offering ironclad evidence in many cases, none of which was acted upon. One mother found her thirteen-year-old daughter in their home with a Muslim in his thirties—her daughter had been burned. When this mother contacted the police, they allowed the girl to tell them that she had burned herself, despite her prior classification as at-risk of sexual exploitation. They took no action, not even deigning to follow standard procedure and notify social services, who admittedly would not have acted even then. One mother, aware that her daughter was being trafficked, copied the names of hundreds of Muslims, including a police officer, from her girl's phone. When her daughter went missing for five days, this mother gave the names to the local police, who promptly replied that "using the information would infringe the girl's and the men's human rights."[739] In another case, two girls who had been abducted and raped were able to contact

---

[738] Murray, *Strange Death of Europe*, 47.
[739] McLoughlin, *Easy Meat*, 124.

the police, who rescued them and then proceeded to release them without conducting any semblance of an investigation.

Even now, British police, and the police services of other European nations, rarely take action; if Muslims do happen to be arrested, they are rarely prosecuted, and even when they are, they are treated with extreme leniency, given inexplicably soft sentences that fall far short of guidelines. In cases where the gangs have been exposed, such as in Rotherham, the overwhelming majority of Islamic rapists walk free to this day, no doubt continuing to ply their trade. As just one example, several of the Rochdale rapists continue to reside in the town where they brutalized girls as young as twelve, despite having their citizenship revoked and being ordered deported years ago.

British judges routinely cite *sharia* law to legitimate or minimize Islamic rape and White slavery; McLoughlin notes one typical example, in which the judge spared from prison a Muslim in Nottingham who raped a thirteen-year-old girl. Why the leniency? The judge heard that the "naïve" man was taught in his *madrassa* that White women are worthless, or rather that "women are no more worthy than a lollipop that has been dropped on the ground."[740] Not to be outdone, the Finnish Supreme Court ruled in 2018 that sex between a ten-year-old Finnish girl and a Muslim "refugee" nearly two-and-a-half times her senior did not constitute rape. After more than 120,000 people signed a petition demanding the release of a report on the ethnic makeup of the rape gangs, Boris Johnson's government simply rejected it, stating as explanation that "child sexual abusers come from all walks of life, and from many different age groups, communities, ethnicities and faiths," despite the fact that a hundred thousand signatures requires consideration by Parliament; one month later, the Home Office reversed course and announced that it would publish the report—without specifying a date.

How could this have happened? The most simplistic explanation, given credence by the fact that policemen and bureaucrats were warned by superiors both to not report the rapes

---

[740] Ibid., 229.

at all and to especially avoid reporting the Muslim identity of the rapists, is that Western European Whites were afraid of being tarred and feathered as "racists" and facing the inevitable Two Minutes' Hate that would follow. While it is absolutely the case that these hollow men feared the consequences of being declared heretics from egalitarian-totalitarian orthodoxy, Hamilton makes the point that this "does *not* mean that they are secret dissenters from it." Indeed, Hamilton notes:

> In Rotherham the System performed according to specification, consistent with the beliefs and values of both rulers and functionaries. They are *de facto* revolutionaries whose job is to transform society and commit genocide. They are not "afraid." They are not moral, good, or trying to do what is right. Their mission is to transform society and exterminate "racism."[741]

He continues that "the acquiescence of officialdom was *necessary* for the crimes to occur year after year regardless of evidence and the power of a totalitarian state to easily stop them if it desired to." A perfect illustration of this anarcho-tyrannical policy is the fact that Rotherham social services removed three White children from the home of their White foster parents. The parents' crime? Supporting the United Kingdom Independence Party, a moderate civic nationalist political party. A local official explained that the government was concerned about opposition to "the active promotion of multiculturalism." Yet, where these same bureaucrats knew that children were actively being gang-raped and tortured, they turned a blind eye. Hamilton points out:

> If the cases instead involved peaceful, noncriminal White writers, activists, or Holocaust revisionists, police, prosecutors, and judges would certainly examine and publicize the defendants' computer files, reading matter, and writings—as well as enormously increase the length of criminal sentences meted out for practicing free speech by utilizing the "hate crime" "enhancement' provisions drafted by Jewish organizations.

---

[741] Hamilton, "Rotherham."

Another aspect of any explanation of this phenomenon is Lawrence Auster's "First Law of Majority-Minority Relations in Liberal Society," which holds essentially that the worse the behavior of a protected class, the greater the cover-up must be to preserve and enforce egalitarian *pravda.*[742] Auster identified the logical corollary of this truism, that "the more egregiously any non-Western or non-White group behaves, the eviler Whites are made to appear for noticing and drawing rational conclusions about that group's bad behavior," for "once the equality of all human groups is accepted as a given, any facts that make a minority or foreign group seem worse than the majority native group must be either covered up or blamed on the majority." This victim-blaming certainly carried the day among the pedophiles' facilitators by omission in media and government. As Colin Liddell has explained, this victim-blaming is so insidious because "there is indeed an element of willingness in crimes like this, with the victims—usually children from poor or broken homes—being lured in by initially friendly male attention, presents, drink, drugs, and etcetera."[743] This element of conscious volition is gradually "intermixed with increasing amounts of violence, abuse, intimidation, and outright degradation as the girls fall deeper into the traps created by these gangs."[744]

As one victim explained:

> These are evil yet clever men. They know how to manipulate, convince and threaten girls into staying, and when they can't they use extreme violence. I used to believe that these people loved me, but I realize now that they used me for their own gain and profit. They have beaten me on multiple occasions sometimes for no reason at all. They have given me drugs to the point where I was nearly addicted to heroin. They have stripped me naked, beaten me and dumped me in the middle of nowhere with nothing, I mean nothing, no money, phone, ID, clothes, shoes, nothing. They did this once in winter where I got found with bad hypothermia. They have broken my ribs, many bones in my face, they have split my ear, cut my throat,

[742] Auster, "First Law of Majority-Minority Relations."
[743] Liddell, "Ellie Williams Case."
[744] Ibid.

> attempted to cut my boobs and nipples off, they have carved words into my body, branded me with letters, they have dislocated my elbow, they have stabbed me, they have burnt me and used me as an ashtray to stump cigarettes out, they have beaten me black. I have had a bleed on the brain from a head injury, I have lost some vision in one of my eyes from being smacked so badly. Now I have had my finger cut. They have put lit petrol rags and threatening letters through my letter box, they have followed me home, tried to drown me, strangled me and they have stalked me. They have had guns they have waved around and held to my head. They have abused me in every way possible. They have emotionally abused me calling me every name. It got to the point where I was being abused all the time and being hit and hurt weekly! I am incredibly lucky not to be dead already! I thought the only way I could escape this life was to marry one of them, get pregnant or kill myself.[745]

Innumerable White children, girls as young as *ten*, were abducted, trafficked across the continent, gang-raped, beaten, burned, and tortured. Raymond Ibrahim gives an account of one case that actually made it all the way to trial, a British girl was "passed around like a piece of meat" between Muslims who violated her countless times from the age of twelve to fourteen; she told the court that she eventually "lost count of how many men I was forced to have sex with" during two years of "hell" when she often considered suicide. Among other sordid memories, the court heard that she "was raped on a dirty mattress above a takeaway and forced to perform oral sex acts in a churchyard," and that afterwards, one of her rapists "urinated on her in an act of humiliation." In another case, a girl "had her tongue nailed to the table when she threatened to tell."[746] Douglas Murray reports that girls were doused in gasoline and threatened with being set on fire, while others were held at gunpoint and forced to watch the violent rape of other girls as a warning.[747]

---

[745] Ibid.
[746] Ibrahim, "'A Piece of Meat.'" For all previous in paragraph.
[747] Murray, *Strange Death of Europe*, 47.

Hamilton describes another case in which a British girl reported that she was gang-raped daily, from age twelve to fifteen, by hundreds of men, sometimes five at a time; as per usual, "although the girl reported the rapes to police when she was 13 and 14, the authorities did nothing . . . police treated White victims with contempt." In Telford, cases commonly involved Muslims "who would ejaculate and then urinate in children's mouths, violating them in every orifice, as well as gang-rape by queues of men while girls were held hostage for hours, sometimes days." Girls were branded and tattooed with their rapists' initials, sexually assaulted with knives and baseball bats, and even forced to undergo female genital mutilation, too horrific to detail. If parents find out and try to intervene, the gang often alienates the schoolgirl from her parents "by accusing the parents of being racists and convincing the girls that all White people are racists."[748] If this fails, the gangs simply threaten the families with death.

The rampant rape of White women by Islamic savages is not confined to the "grooming gang" phenomenon, which is but one particularly invidious facet of the larger descent of Christendom into Eurabia. Within a generation, Europe has ceased to be European, an unprecedented transformation, one of the greatest symbols of which is the fact that, despite British sophistry in listing each variant of "Muhammad" separately, it is the most common boy's name in England and Wales. White women and children live in fear of simply leaving their homes, and even at home their safety is dubious; the epidemic is so severe that blonde-haired Scandinavian women have begun to dye their hair black in the hopes of warding off Muslim predators. Escalating rapes, in the hundreds and then in the thousands, primarily of women but also of men, were all swept under the rug, uninvestigated, unpunished, and suppressed.

One such incident, unreported by legacy media but now infamous, occurred in Germany on New Year's Eve 2015. Murray explains:

---

[748] Hamilton, "Rotherham." For all previous in paragraph.

> On one of the busiest nights of the year, as the city was celebrating, crowds of up to two thousand [all Muslim] men sexually assaulted and robbed something in the region of twelve hundred women in the main square outside the central railway station and cathedral of Cologne and in the adjoining streets.[749]

The rape was not confined to Cologne, as these seemingly coordinated sexual attacks occurred throughout the country, from Hamburg to Stuttgart. Tellingly, only one year prior, the anti-immigration Pegida movement, the members of which have been described by the genocidal Angela Merkel as having hearts that are "cold and often full of prejudice, and even hate," held a peaceful protest in Cologne.[750] The very same cathedral "announced in advance that it would turn off its lights in protest at the gathering," the significance of which is not lost on Murray; he notes that "few people in Cologne would miss the symbolism of the fact that, almost exactly a year later, the cathedral's lights were blazing as hundreds of local women were molested, raped, and robbed by [Muslims] in the same streets."[751] At the 2014 "We Are Stockholm" music festival:

> Dozens of girls as young as fourteen were surrounded by gangs of immigrants, particularly from Afghanistan, molested and raped. Local police covered up the case, making no mention of it in their report on the five-day festival. There were no convictions, and the press avoided any mention of the rapes.[752]

Similar organized rapes by "migrant" gangs occurred at music festivals the next year across Sweden, including heavily-Muslim Malmö. By then, Sweden had the highest level of rapes per capita of any country aside from Lesotho.[753] When the Swedish press did report these events, they willfully misrepresented them; for example, Murray recalls the gang-rape of a young

[749] Murray, *Strange Death of Europe*, 160.
[750] Ibid., 196.
[751] Ibid.
[752] Ibid., 203.
[753] Ibid.

girl on a ferry from Stockholm to Abo, Finland, after which the Somali culprits were reported to be "Swedish men."

We must again emphasize that these cases are merely representative samples of countless others, each as tragic as the last. Perhaps more tragic than any are the White ethnomasochists who sympathize with their own attackers; in one striking, but by no means uncommon case, a twenty-four-year-old woman who serves as a spokesperson for an "antifascist" group was gang-raped by three Muslims in Mannheim in 2016. This victim lied about the identity of her rapists, in order to avoid "helping to fuel aggressive racism." The woman then wrote an open letter to her attackers, *apologizing* to them:

> I wanted an open Europe, a friendly one. . . . I am sorry. For us both, I am so incredibly sorry. You, you aren't safe here, because we live in a racist society. I, I am not safe here, because we live in a sexist society . . . what truly makes me feel sorry, are the circumstances by which the sexist and boundary-crossing acts that were inflicted on me, make it so that you are beset by increasing and more aggressive racism. I promise you; I will scream. I will not . . . stand by idly and watch as racists and concerned citizens call you a problem. You are not the problem. You are not a problem at all. You . . . are a wonderful human being, who deserves to be free and safe like everyone else.[754]

The prior year, a young woman working with "No Borders" activists at the Ventimiglia crossing between Italy and France was gang-raped by a group of Sudanese men. Murray explains that her fellow egalitarians "persuaded her to keep the attack quiet in order not to damage their cause. When the woman did finally admit to the attack, they accused her of reporting her own rape out of 'spite.'" [755]

Hamilton rightly emphasizes the evolutionary aspect of the Islamic enslavement of White girls, especially girls at the aforementioned young ages; these are the very girls who, "in a racially healthy society, would soon constitute the next

[754] Ibid., 161.
[755] Ibid., 162.

generation of wives and mothers." There is essentially no hope that the legion of White girls now being sexually exploited by industrial pornography, prostitution, and casual nihilism will reproduce White children within the nuclear family; Hamilton thus predicts that, of the progeny of this generation, "many, eventually most . . . will be interracial." Though Hamilton correctly points to one of the underlying drivers of this disease as pornography, which indeed depicts and valorizes precisely these things, the primary engine is Islam itself. Indeed, Ibrahim reminds us that when Muslims rape White women while saying things like, "You White women are good at it," or, "German women are there for sex," or, "All Australian women are sluts and deserve to be raped," they are simply being pious, drawing on "a long tradition of seeing pale infidels as the epitome of promiscuity." When White schoolgirls are called "easy meat" and "White trash," they are practicing the precepts of their Qur'an. In fact, many "grooming gang" victims report being given Islamic names and forced to read the Qur'an.

When Islamic State jihadists sexually enslave Christians, they are fully convinced not only that it is their Muslim *right* to rape "infidels," but also that it is their pious *duty*, a kind of perverse sacrament. All non-Muslim women are "fair game for abducting and enslaving"; as one Muslim rapist told a terrified Christian girl before brutally murdering her, "Christian girls are only meant for one thing, the [sexual] pleasure of Muslim men." White women are "meat," their slightest glance or physical proximity taken to be valid provocation for rape. Ibrahim gives an account from 2015:

> In the moments before he raped the twelve-year-old girl, the Islamic State fighter took the time to explain that what he was about to do was not a sin. Because the preteen girl practiced a religion other than Islam, the Quran not only gave him the right to rape her—it condoned and encouraged it, he insisted.[756]

[756] Ibrahim, "Sex Slavery."

As his victim recalled, "He said that by raping me, he is drawing closer to God." From the same article, another victim of Islamic rape, only fifteen, explained:

> Every time that he came to rape me, he would pray. He said that raping me is his prayer to God. I said to him, "What you're doing to me is wrong, and it will not bring you closer to God." And he said, "No, it's allowed. It's halal."

One schoolgirl in Paris reported that the gang of African Muslims who raped her "repeatedly cited Allah, the Qur'an, and Mecca." This is quite common, with many of the countless rape victims reporting that their abusers quoted the Qur'an as they beat them. In numerous cases that have gone to court, Muslims confidently declare that sharing non-Muslim girls for sex was "a religious requirement." Christian girls are considered "goods to be damaged at leisure. Abusing them is a right. According to the community's mentality it is not even a crime. Muslims regard them as spoils of war."[757] As aforementioned, jihad is largely carnally motivated; the Islamic reward for martyrdom is literally a harem of virgins and a permanent erection.

The greatest reason for the Islamization of Western Europe is, of course, European ennui, perhaps best encapsulated in the German term, *Geschichtsmüde*, or "weary of history." As Murray puts it, the problem in Europe is "an existential tiredness and a feeling that perhaps for Europe the story has run out and a new story must be allowed to begin."[758] He notes, chillingly, that "the fact that a society should feel like it has run out of steam at precisely the moment when a new society has begun to move in cannot help but lead to vast, epochal changes." Nietzsche wrote that "we are no longer accumulating. We are squandering the capital of our forebears, even in our way of knowing."[759] Twentieth-century deconstruction and critical theory finished the job begun by nineteenth-century German higher literary criticism as applied to the Bible.

---

[757] Ibid.

[758] Murray, *Strange Death of Europe*, 7.

[759] Ibid., 170.

After the Jewish-initiated World Wars, Christian Europe "lost faith not only in its God, but in its people as well."[760] As Christianity has collapsed, so too has Christendom. Nature abhors a vacuum, as they say, and Islam has stepped in to take its place.

Murray, following the thesis of our introductory essay on Christian leftism, notes that organized Christianity has "lost the confidence to proselytize or even believe in its own message," having become "a form of [leftist] politics, diversity action, and social welfare projects." It was not Islam that changed, but the West; Ibrahim explains that "Muslims still venerate their heritage and religion—which commands jihad against infidels—whereas the West has learned to despise its heritage and religion, causing it to become an unwitting ally of the jihad."[761] Murray refers to the great cathedrals of Europe as "glorious debris" that "still signify something, though we do not know exactly what."[762] When Europe turned away from God, it lost itself, its identity and narrative of mission wholly subverted and turned against it; after the Second World War:

> To be on the side of the incomers was to be on the side of the angels. To speak for the people of Europe was to be on the side of the Devil. And all the time, there existed that strange assumption that Europe was simply letting one more person into the room. . . . Europe could no longer be bothered to turn anyone away. And so, the door just remained open to anyone who wanted to walk through it.[763]

This lifeboat so sags that it now scrapes the sea floor.

Faustian Europe was once animated by conquest in the name of the Lord. From Spain, we conquered the New World. We conquered the North American continent. We conquered the *earth*. We traveled to the stars, and yet we were pulled back from this final frontier, stifled by the anchor of tens of trillions of dollars squandered in our decades-long exercise in

---

[760] Ibid., 179.
[761] Ibid., 215.
[762] Ibid., 173.
[763] Ibid., 238.

glorified babysitting. Our animating spirit was this sense of destiny, of mission. The Promethean fire has foundered, and we fumble in growing darkness, mired in ethnomasochistic doubt. No people can survive without a past. By contrast, Murray notes, the people of the Global South:

> [S]hare none of these fears, distrusts, or doubts. They do not distrust their own instincts or their own actions. They do not fear acting in their own interest or think that . . . the self-interest of their kind should not be furthered. They seek to further their own lives.[764]

Islam is still driven, as it has always been, by its mission of global conquest. Herein lies the rub—as Ibrahim writes, "If Islam is terrorizing the West today, that is not because it can, but because the West allows it to. For no matter how diminished, a still-swinging Scimitar will always overcome a strong but sheathed Sword." It is long past time to unsheathe the Sword of Christ.

Edward Dutton elaborates:

> In the struggle for the future of the world, victory for the West is more likely if Europeans are more religious, less cerebral, and possessed by feelings of camaraderie and destiny—in other words, if they become more like those against whom they are competing. In this regard, Islam is right about many things.[765]

What are these things? For one thing, we must contemplate the virtue of the closed mind; our Semitic Enemy retains power at least partially through its enforcement of rigid dogma, of ideological orthodoxy. Similarly, Muslims simply do not permit their faith to be criticized or even deeply analyzed. We should, to whatever extent practicable while still remaining true to ourselves and to our tradition of open inquiry, emulate that. We must not tolerate subversion. Liberalism must

---

[764] Ibid., 183.

[765] Dutton, *Why Islam Makes You Stupid*, 14.

go; we cannot afford to repeat the mistakes of the Enlightenment. We cannot afford to countenance any further anti-American, anti-family, anti-White speech, and this should be reflected in a *new* Constitution. Just as conservatism was not enough, the United States Constitution was not enough, with gaps that left it gaping wide for judicial "interpretation." For another thing, we must circle the wagons and inculcate the *männerbund*, restraining our individualism at least for the time being. For another, we must return to our Lord and Savior. A nation without faith can have no guiding light, no purpose, no drive, no Mission. Izaak Walton, writing of his friend John Donne's last days, described the body "which was once a temple of the Holy Ghost and is now become a small quantity of Christian dust." His last line: "But I shall see it reanimated."

15

Anti-Infanticide, or Pro-Natalist, Violence

In 1973, the United States Supreme Court unilaterally enshrined infanticide in our Constitution by reading into it a protected "sexual liberty" interest, along with a fundamental "right to privacy" conjured especially for the occasion. Fifty years have passed since *Roe v. Wade*; the continuing holocaust unleashed by that depredation has claimed more than sixty million lives, about half of which have been White. Even with the overturning of *Roe* in 2022, abortion remains the law of the land in most states, with many adopting even more radical abortion regimes that would have been impossible to imagine under *Roe*. Witness, for instance, the proliferation of programs in states like California that aim to ship in women from states that have rightfully outlawed abortion with the aim of destroying their unborn children.

Formed in 1982, the Army of God is an extremely loose, leaderless, and decentralized organization whose associates practice violent resistance against infanticide. This anti-infanticide, pro-natalist violence has included actions by such individuals as Michael Bray, Michael Griffin, Shelley Shannon, Paul Hill, Eric Rudolph, James Kopp, and Scott Roeder. These actions have included the arson and destruction of infanticide "clinics," as well as the murder of abortionists. This program of violent resistance is approached from a comprehensive theological justification of and for Christian violence, as against absolute pacifism; the following exposition is taken from materials promulgated by the Army of God, including a polemic written by Eric Rudolph, most widely known as the Olympic Park bomber, from prison.

Infanticide may be seen as a return to the pagan child sacrifice practiced by the Canaanites and Moabites, who ritually murdered their children in worshipping Moloch. (Deut. 12:31 and 18:10, 2 Kings 3:27, Ps. 106:37–38) God told Moses, "And thou shalt not let any of thy seed pass through *the fire* to Molech, neither shalt thou profane the name of thy God: I *am* the Lord." (Lev. 18:21) God continued:

> Whosoever . . . giveth *any* of his seed unto Molech; he shall surely be put to death. . . . And I will set my face against that man, and will cut him off from among his people; because he hath given of his seed unto Molech, to defile my sanctuary, and to profane my holy name. And if the people of the land do any ways hide their yes from the man . . . and kill him not: Then I will set my face against that man, and against his family, and will cut him off, and all that go a whoring after him, to commit whoredom with Molech, from among their people. (Lev. 20:2–5)

Jephthah sacrificed his own daughter as the result of a rash vow. (Judg. 11) Evil rulers practiced sacrificial infanticide in Israel at sites such as Tophet, in the valley of the son of Hinnom, or Gehenna. (1 Kings 11:7, 2 Kings 16:3, 17:17, 17:41, 21:2–6, 23:10, Isa. 57:1–5, Jer. 7:31, 19:5, 32:35, Ezek. 16:20–21, 20:26, 20:31, 23:37) When Josiah, the sixteenth king of Judah, instituted a purgative restoration to recommit his nation to God, one of his actions was to desecrate the site at Tophet, where "he brake in pieces the images, and cut down the groves, and filled their places with the bones of men"; then, he slaughtered the pagan priests, scattering and burning their bones upon their own altars. (2 Kings 23:10–20)

Michael Bray notes in A *Time to Kill* that Mosaic law established that blood must be repaid by blood for the sake of the community. Moses conveys from God that "so ye shall not pollute the land wherein ye are: for blood it defileth the land: and the land cannot be cleansed of the blood that is shed therein, but by the blood of him that shed it." (Num. 35:33) God tells Noah that "whoso sheddeth man's blood, by man shall his blood be shed: for in the image of God made he man." (Gen. 9:6) Implicit in this injunction is that *unauthorized* and *unjust* bloodshed, thus murder, the killing of an innocent, is prohibited. Therefore, because man will justly punish unjust bloodshed by the execution of murderers, this must mean that some bloodshed is divinely sanctioned. As Cathy Ramey discovered in her research on the Sixth Commandment, "Thou shalt not kill," the Hebrew word used for "kill" was *ratsach*, one of seven Hebrew words in the Old Testament for the taking of a life.[766] *Ratsach* means "murder," such that the Commandment should read, "Thou shalt do no murder," as in Matthew 19:18. This word is never used in the context of holy war, self-defense, accidental killing, or just execution; it was also not used when Moses slew the Egyptian taskmaster. (Ex. 2:12 and 22:2, Deut. 19:5) As in the case of that taskmaster, God commanded the killing of individuals *outside* the context of war in several cases. (Ex. 21:12–17 and 21:29, Lev. 20:1–5, Deut. 17:2–7, 2 Kings 9:6–10) Although *ratsach* is used to refer to killings of revenge, there is an exemption for the "revenger of blood," a victim's next of kin. (Num. 35:27)

Governments are entrusted with the punishment of the wicked; what, then, when the government rewards and sanctions evil? The government necessarily loses its legitimacy. (Prov. 16:12) Ramey, after noting that nothing could be more innocent than an unborn infant, clearly sees abortionists as the condemned sinners who lie in wait for blood and "lurk privily for the innocent without cause," those men whose hands "shed innocent blood" and whom the Lord hates. (Prov. 1:10–11 and 6:17) Ramey thus argues that the killing of abortionists is not a usurpation of authority to *punish* the wicked for past evils, but rather a proactive effort to *prevent* the future *ratsach* killings of the unborn that are forbidden by the Sixth Commandment. The abortionists (and, we must note, doctors who perform "gender affirming" mutilation on children) themselves "have sown the wind, and they shall reap the whirlwind." (Hos. 8:7)

---

[766] Ramey, *In Defense of Others.*

Ramey explains that Scripture contains numerous instances of taking life as a defensive action, whether in self-defense or in defense of others; in each of these instances, the actor is praised, unblemished by any expression of moral disapprobation. (Gen. 14:14–16, Ex. 2:11–12, Heb. 11:24–27, Acts 7:23–25, Judg. 4:17–21 and 5:24–31) To defend his nation, in accord with God's command in Exodus 22:20, slew four hundred and fifty prophets of the false god Baal. (1 Kings 18) Ramey also points out that, although property crimes are not capital offenses in the Old Testament, breaking into a home at night does expose the burglar to death, for the homeowner is free to kill the intruder (whose motives are unknown) *in defense of his family*. (Ex. 22:2) This comports with a well-established pattern throughout the Bible expressing God's hierarchical preference for the innocent over the guilty. In fact, the first occurrence of the "eye for eye, tooth for tooth" formulation of *lex talionis* punishment is in the context of a pregnant woman who is assaulted and whose baby is injured as a consequence; in other words, this most basic stricture of retributive justice is clearly prescribed for the case of the injury of an unborn child, whose life is given the same weight as an adult. (Ex. 21:22–25) Whatever injury the child was dealt, including murder, the inflictor is to receive in kind.

There is further evidence that the lives of the unborn are clearly given the same value as born children and adults, their undifferentiated personhood affirmed throughout the Bible. (Amos 1:13) As the Psalmist sings, "For thou hast possessed my reins: thou hast covered me in my mother's womb." (Ps. 139:13) Children are "an heritage of the Lord: and the fruit of the womb is his reward." (Ps. 127:3) God tells Jeremiah, "Before I formed thee in the belly I knew thee; and before thou camest forth out of the womb I sanctified thee, and I ordained thee a prophet unto the nations." (Jer. 1:5)

With his crucifixion imminent, Jesus tells his disciples that they must prepare for the storms to come, that they must take care of their physical needs and protection, saying, "But now, he that hath a purse, let him take it, and likewise his scrip: and he that hath no sword, let him sell his garment, and buy one." (Luke 22:36) His disciples respond by presenting two swords, to which Christ said, "It is enough." (Luke 22:38) Two swords for twelve men, Ramey emphasizes, is more indicative of defensive action than offensive. It follows that if we may defend *our* lives, and are to love our neighbors as ourselves, we may also defend our defenseless neighbors; and who is more defenseless than an infant? (Mark 12:31, Luke 10:25–37) Liberal theologians teach today that the sword Christ commanded his disciples to obtain is figurative or spiritual; the purse, scrip, and garment are all certainly physical, so it is quite a stretch to contend that the sword alone is not really a sword. As Ramey provocatively asks, "Can a spiritual sword be purchased for the price of a cloak?"

Eric Rudolph elaborates even further on the theological foundation of legitimate defensive violence. To love one's neighbor as oneself inherently includes coming to his defense. (Matt. 22:39) Rudolph additionally argues that absolute pacifism is sinful pride:

> Since normal, mentally healthy people will defend themselves against an unjust aggressor, if able, rather than submit to being killed, it is the height of narcissism for the pacifist to presume otherwise about his neighbor. It may be permissible for the Christian to refuse to defend his own life, but it is not permissible to refuse to defend his neighbor's. [767]

Rudolph refers to Christian pacifism as an anti-Christian heresy which he terms "milquetoastism," an individualized postmodern religion that serves only as:

> A declaration of disarmament, an acknowledgement of liberalism's hegemony over public policy. The milquetoast Christian holds dual citizenship: on the one hand, he claims to be a child of God, and on the other, a loyal citizen of liberal society. But the two are incompatible. The values of liberal society—abortion on demand, no-fault divorce, normalized homosexuality—are antithetical to Christianity. Hence the need for dual citizenship.[768]

---

[767] Rudolph, *A Time of War*, 2.
[768] Ibid., 3.

Rudolph takes the Amish as an example, calling such Anabaptist societies "parasitic" for their dependence "upon the larger society in which they live to do the things they refuse to do themselves."[769]

Rudolph cites the litany of genocidal violence that God directed his people to implement in order to receive their inheritance, and emphasizes the fact that in at least five places, the New Testament refers to Jesus as the son of the warrior-king David; Christ himself proclaimed, "I am the root and offspring of David, and the bright and morning star." (Rev. 22:16) As all Christians trace their new lineage to Christ, we may logically extend this back to David as well. Rudolph underlines the distinction between justified killing and prohibited murder, noting that liberal theologians recast the Sixth Commandment as meaning:

> [T]he intentional killing of another human being, regardless of the circumstances or the motives of the killer, is always morally wrong. There's no difference between an act of unprovoked aggression and self-defense. . . . Such reasoning takes no cognizance of free will, without which discussion about moral responsibility is meaningless. The moral quality of any act depends mostly on the motives of the actor. The fact that a blade is being used to damage human flesh tells us nothing about the moral quality of the act, until we learn the motives of the man who wields it. All killing ends the life of a human being, but not all killing is murder.[770]

After all, if all killing is proscribed, how is the death penalty to be carried out for the dozens of capital sins listed throughout the Bible?

God often delegates his wrath to his people to carry out, such as Ehud, who assassinated the Moabite despot Eglon with a hidden dagger. Ehud sought an audience with Eglon, claiming he bore him a present; when Ehud approached the tyrant, he whispered:

---

[769] Ibid., 5.
[770] Ibid., 9.

> I have a message from God unto thee. And he arose out of his seat. And Ehud put forth his left hand, and took the dagger from his right thigh, and thrust it into his belly: And the haft also went in after the blade; and the fat closed upon the blade, so that he could not draw the dagger out of his belly; and the dirt came out. (Judg. 3:20–22)

Ehud then returned to his countrymen, God's chosen people, and declared, "Follow after me: for the Lord hath delivered your enemies the Moabites into your hand." Ehud then led his people to slaughter ten thousand Moabites, of whom "there escaped not a man." (Judg. 3)

Moses slew the Egyptian taskmaster, a government official, for his murder of a Hebrew slave; as Rudolph points out:

> He committed an act of insurrection for the sake of justice. He took the law into his own hands. Which law? By Pharaoh's law, Moses was a "murderer" and a "fugitive from justice." But by God's law Moses was justified.[771]

Indeed, the New Testament martyr Stephen justified and praised Moses when he said, "And seeing one *of them* suffer wrong, he defended *him*, and avenged him that was oppressed, and smote the Egyptian." (Acts 7:24) Jesus was the fulfillment of the Law; as Rudolph argues, "turning the other cheek" is not a repudiation of *lex talionis*, but rather a guideline enjoining believers from being quick-tempered and retaliating for relatively minor insults.

Christ's command to "love your enemies, bless them that curse you, do good to them that hate you, and pray for them which despitefully use you, and persecute you" does not preclude one from killing the enemy. (Matt. 5:44) Rudolph explains:

> A man might kill an aggressor not out of hatred or malice, but simply because he can find no other way to prevent him from harming innocent people. Any student of military history

[771] Ibid., 12.

> knows that what motivates soldiers in combat is not hatred of the enemy but concern for their comrades; i.e., love.[772]

Criminals are punished for the benefit of society.

Another perniciously misconstrued set of verses is cited by liberal theologians as a "get out of jail free card," the validation of postmodern deracinated individualism. In these verses, Christ says:

> Judge not, that ye be not judged. For with what judgment ye judge, ye shall be judged: and with what measure ye mete, it shall be measured to you again. And why beholdest thou the mote that is in thy brother's eye, but considerest not the beam that is in thine own eye? Or how wilt thou say to thy brother, Let me pull out the mote out of thine eye; and, behold, a beam is in thine own eye? Thou hypocrite, first cast out the beam out of thine own eye; and then shalt thou see clearly to cast out the mote out of thy brother's eye. (Matt. 7:1–5)

Rather than being a *kumbaya* statement of egalitarianism, or a paean to a dissipated culture where "every man does that which was right in his own eyes," this is merely an admonition against hypocrisy.

Rudolph explains just war theory, adding:

> Christian just war doctrine holds to the ancient wisdom: it identifies human nature as the ultimate cause of war. It's not land, nor resources, nor justice, nor the lack thereof that causes wars. Sinful man carries war around with him like syphilis, its symptoms flaring up or in remission like the changing of the seasons. Just war doctrine says that evil must be opposed, fought off, and reversed, or worse evil will surely follow. Indifference is not an option. Not to respond to evil is to say that it does not matter, and therefore its victims do not matter. Retribution ultimately derives from the Christian ethic of love of our neighbor, for the just warrior does not fight for glory, or revenge, or booty. He fights to protect the innocent and to punish the aggressor "with a sort of kind harshness," to impel him to "repent and embrace peace."[773]

---

[772] Ibid., 13.

[773] Ibid., 20.

One of the aforementioned keys to just war doctrine is that it is may only be justified "once all peaceful efforts have failed."

Aquinas teaches that it is not inherently evil to kill an evildoer, because such a man "falls away from the dignity of his manhood . . . and falls into the slavish state of the beast."[774] The many corpses of God's enemies littered through the Bible are nowhere mourned; Rudolph notes that "in each case the Bible suggests the world was made a better place without them."[775] The Psalmist sings:

> Let the saints be joyful in glory: let them sing aloud upon their beds. Let the high praises of God be in their mouth, and a twoedged sword in their hand; To execute vengeance upon the heathen, and punishments upon the people; To bind their kings with chains, and their nobles with fetters of iron; To execute upon them the judgment written: this honour have all his saints. Praise ye the Lord. (Ps. 149:5–9)

Rudolph asserts that Christian pacifism is essentially conditional, that "in extremis, the Christian must be prepared to use lethal force in defense of the innocent."[776] He traces the long history of holy warfare waged by Christianity against Islam for its very survival, illuminating the storied tradition of the archetypal Christian soldier in comparison to the weak and subservient milquetoast Christianity of our own day. Rudolph states:

> Milquetoasts preach indifference to or surrender to the dominant liberal culture. Either strategy will lead to the extinction of Christianity. Conservative Christians are still fighting a rearguard action. The fight for traditional marriage, for the family, and for the unborn is Christianity's last battle. . . . The abortion controversy is not a religious debate, as liberals prefer to frame it. Child baptism versus adult baptism is a religious debate. Abortion, on the other hand, is about a fundamental question of justice: Is it permissible for one class of persons (adults) to kill another class of persons (unborn children) for

---

[774] Ibid., 22.
[775] Ibid.
[776] Ibid., 25.

> reasons of social engineering and simply as a matter of convenience?[777]

Rudolph concludes his polemic by arguing:

> Any government, democracy or dictatorship, that enshrines child murder into law has abrogated the natural law and declared war on its people; and it is the right of the people to defend themselves. Whether the people, collectively or individually, decide to take up arms in defense of its right in this circumstance is a matter of expediency, not morality. There may be solid practical reasons for not resorting to lethal violence against abortion, but there are no moral ones . . . absolute pacifism is incompatible with Christianity. The Scripture, both Old and New Testaments, consistently uphold just war and just retribution in response to evil. Indifference is not an option for the Christian, as it is for the Buddhist. In a sinful world, Christians must sometimes use lethal force to uphold the law and defend society. To be or not to be, that is the question at stake. . . . Christians face an existential crisis every bit as vital as Charles Martel faced at Tours. Consider that militant Islam failed to destroy Christian Europe in a thousand years of war, but liberalism has secularized Western Europe in less than a generation. Why? Because the Church declared itself neutral in the ideological battles of the 19th and 20th centuries. And when the dust had settled after the World Wars, the people silently shifted their loyalty and worship to the victor, the social-democratic welfare state. Travel across Western Europe today and you'll find empty churches. These are the monuments of milquetoastism. Europe today is America tomorrow. The Church militant is the only thing that can save the faith, and Western civilization.[778]

---

[777] Ibid., 32.
[778] Ibid., 43.

Revival

By now, we have learned that Christianity—more specifically, *real*, fundamental, traditional, orthodox, *biblical* Christianity—is wholly of the right, standing in diametric opposition to the Leviathan which has seized the Church in its bloody talons. Now, we understand that:

1. Organized Christianity *is* corrupt, an engine of White dispossession and White racial suicide. This bastard, egalitarian "Christianity" is, however, an aberration from the rich, robust Christianity which guided our forefathers as they built Christendom, Western civilization itself.

2. Jews are the avowed Enemy of Christianity, and, for all intents and purposes, Jewish hatred for Christianity is the origin of Jewish hatred for Whites, who are still practically understood as inseparable. Christian Zionism is the greatest heresy to have ever afflicted our faith, and serves primarily to facilitate the Jewish coup which has consumed our nation over the past century.

3. The Jewish promotion of sexual degeneracy, including but not limited to pornography, is a psychological warfare operation, an artificial weapon of White humiliation, control, and genocide. The Jewish inculcation of sexual nihilism has fundamentally torn asunder the very foundation of White civilization: the family.

4. The “blood libel” is real. Jews did, and likely still do, ritually murder White Christian children.

5. Though Christianity is not *necessarily* racialist, most non-Whites simply are not Christians, unless we consider animistic voodoo syncretism to be an acceptable form of our faith. In any case, Christianity fully supports a doctrine of racialism, for the Christian doctrine of ethnonationalism courses throughout the Bible. There is nothing “un-Christian” about loving and fighting for your race and your homeland.

6. Black slavery was not, is not, and will never be a biblical sin. Christianity is necessarily anti-egalitarian and hierarchical, our world being ordered according to relationships of dominion and subjection.

7. Christianity does not support a doctrine of absolute pacifism or suicidal passivity. God and His Son, Jesus Christ, our Lord and Savior, command, sanction, and even perpetrate violence throughout the Bible. The Crusades, and Christian holy warfare in general, are theologically justified as wars of reactive defense against the enemies of the Faith and of our White Christian brethren. One of those enemies, Islam, is currently ascendant in the ruins of Christendom now known as the European Union.

8. Affirmative Christian violence, such as that practiced by the anti-infanticide or pro-natalist Army of God, is justified and even commanded based upon the same theological doctrine which frames Christian holy warfare in terms of reactive defense. The argument for pro-natalist violence is broad, applying not only to abortionists, but also physicians who practice sexual reassignment on children.

Christianity is not irredeemable. Indeed, Christianity is not even in need of redemption, for its foundation, the Word of God, is incorruptible. The organizational edifice is that which has sunken into debauched disrepair, marked by empty cathedrals whose failed glory echoes today as a challenge to be taken up, dying embers which cry for fire. The fallen Church can be healed and erected again with the effort of only a handful of young preachers, trained in true biblical orthodoxy, ready to unsheathe the sword of Christ and carry His fire into the stinking, filthy brothel once known as the United States. This handful of young preachers will most likely come not from the seminaries, but rather from the laity. They must be prepared to enact a new Great Awakening, hopefully our last, and initiate a Christian ethnonationalist revival, an American renaissance. I do not propose this national revival out of any castle-in-the-sky naïveté, for the path ahead will be difficult. But it will not be as difficult as we might imagine, provided that we locate its leaders. The larger purpose for my proposal, though, is to state unequivocally that only something as massive as this national revival is capable of serving as a mission around which we can organize and save ourselves. Without faith, we have no reason to live, let alone to fight.

Go forth, and conquer

Deus Vult

Bibliography

Books Cited and for Further Reading

Augustine. *The City of God*. London: Penguin, 2003.

Barber, Malcolm. *The New Knighthood: A History of the Order of the Temple*. Cambridge: Cambridge University Press, 2018.

Bass, Clarence B. *Backgrounds to Dispensationalism: Its Historical Genesis and Ecclesiastical Implications*. Eugene, Oregon: Wipf and Stock Publishers, 1960.

Bouwsma, William. *John Calvin: A Sixteenth-Century Portrait*. New York: Oxford University Press, 1988.

Bray, Michael. *A Time to Kill*. Portland, OR: Advocates for Life Publications, 1994.

Canfield, Joseph M. *The Incredible Scofield and His Book*. Vallecito, CA: Ross House Books, 2004.

Chaucer, Geoffrey. "The Prioress's Tale." In *The Riverside Chaucer*, 2nd ed., 441–48. Oxford: Oxford University Press, 1988.

Chrysostom, John. *Against the Jews*. CreateSpace Independent Publishing Platform, 2013.

Coey, John Alan. *A Martyr Speaks: Journal of the Late John Alan Coey*. Boring, OR: CPA Book Publishers, 1994.

Coulter, E. Merton. *The South During Reconstruction: 1865–1877*. Baton Rouge, LA: Louisiana State University Press, 1947.

Davis, Robert. *Christian Slaves, Muslim Masters: White Slavery in the Mediterranean, the Barbary Coast, and Italy, 1500-1800*. Basingstoke: Palgrave Macmillan, 2003.

Dutton, Edward. *The Silent Rape Epidemic: How the Finns Were Groomed to Love Their Abusers*. Independently Published, 2019.

Dutton, Edward. *Why Islam Makes You Stupid . . . But Also Means You'll Conquer the World*. Whitefish, MT: Washington Summit Publishers, 2020.

Fernández-Morera Darío. *The Myth of the Andalusian Paradise: Muslims, Christians, and Jews Under Islamic Rule in Medieval Spain*. Wilmington, DE: ISI Books, 2018.

Fogel, Robert William, and Stanley L. Engerman. *Time on the Cross: The Economics of American Negro Slavery*. New York, NY: W. W. Norton & Co., 1995.

Ford, Henry. *The International Jew*. Detroit, MI: Don Lohbeck, 1947.

Fox-Genovese, Elizabeth, and Eugene D. Genovese. *The Mind of the Master Class: History and Faith in the Southern Slaveholder's Worldview*. Cambridge: Cambridge University Press, 2005.
Francis, Samuel T. "All Those Things to Apologize For." In *Essential Writings on Race*. Oakton, VA: New Century Foundation, 2007.
Francis, Samuel T. "The Christian Question." In *Essential Writings on Race*. Oakton, VA: New Century Foundation, 2007.
Freedman, Benjamin H. *The Hidden Tyranny: The Issue That Dwarfs All Other Issues*. Reedy, WV: Liberty Bell Publications, 2000.
Garland, Benjamin. *Merchants of Sin*. Independently Published, 2017.
Gottfried, Paul. *Multiculturalism and the Politics of Guilt: Toward a Secular Theocracy*. Columbia, MO: University of Missouri Press, 2004.
Hoffman, Michael A. *Judaism Discovered: A Desideratum*. Coeur d'Alene, ID: Independent History and Research, 2008.
Hoffman, Michael A. *Judaism's Strange Gods*. Coeur d'Alene, ID: Independent History and Research, 2011.
Hoffman, Michael A. *They Were White and They Were Slaves: The Untold History of the Enslavement of Whites in Early America*. Coeur d'Alene, ID: Independent History and Research, 1993.
Horowitz, Elliott S. *Reckless Rites: Purim and the Legacy of Jewish Violence*. Princeton, NJ: Princeton University Press, 2006.
Ibrahim, Raymond. *Sword and Scimitar: Fourteen Centuries of War between Islam and the West*. New York, NY: Da Capo Press, 2018.
Jenkins, Philip. *The Next Christendom: The Coming of Global Christianity*. Oxford: Oxford University Press, 2011.
Jones, E. Michael. *Libido Dominandi: Sexual Liberation and Political Control*. South Bend, IN: St. Augustine's Press, 2005.
Jordan, Don, and Michael Walsh. *White Cargo: The Forgotten History of Britain's White Slaves in America*. New York, NY: New York University Press, 2008.
Luther, Martin. *On the Jews and Their Lies*. Austin, TX: RiverCrest, 2014.
Lutz, David W. "Unjust War Theory: Christian Zionism and the Road to Jerusalem." In *Neo-Conned! Again: Hypocrisy, Lawlessness, and the Rape of Iraq*, edited by J. Forrest Sharpe and D. Liam O'Huallachain, 127–70. Vienna: Light in the Darkness Publications, 2005.
MacDonald, Kevin. *The Culture of Critique: An Evolutionary Analysis of Jewish Involvement in Twentieth-Century Intellectual and Political Movements*. Westport, CT: Praeger, 1998.
MacDonald, Kevin. *Separation and Its Discontents: Toward an Evolutionary Theory of Anti-Semitism*. Bloomington, IN: 1stBooks, 2004.
Madden, Thomas F. *The Concise History of the Crusades*. Lanham: Rowman & Littlefield, 2014.
Madden, Thomas F. *The Crusades Controversy: Setting the Record Straight*. North Palm Beach, FL: Beacon Publishing, 2017.
Malkin, Michelle. *Open Borders, Inc.: Who's Funding America's Destruction?* Washington, D.C.: Regnery, 2019.
McCaul, Alexander. *The Talmud Tested: A Comparison of the Principles and Doctrines of Modern Judaism with the Religion of Moses and the Prophets*. Coeur d'Alene, ID: Independent History and Research, 2013.

McLoughlin, Peter, and Tommy Robinson. *Mohammed's Koran: Why Muslims Kill for Islam*. Independently Published, 2019.
McLoughlin, Peter. *Easy Meat: Inside Britain's Grooming Gang Scandal*. Nashville, TN: New England Review Press, 2016.
Mearsheimer, John J., and Stephen M. Walt. *The Israel Lobby and U.S. Foreign Policy*. New York, NY: Farrar, Straus and Giroux, 2007.
Murray, Douglas. *He Strange Death of Europe: Immigration, Identity, Islam* . London: Bloomsbury, 2018.
Oliver, Revilo P. *Christianity and the Survival of the West*. Sterling, VA: Sterling Enterprises, 1973.
Origen. *Contra Celsum*. Freiburg: Herder, 2011.
Pranaitis, I. B. *The Talmud Unmasked: The Secret Rabbinical Teachings Concerning Christians*. Ostara, 2018.
Ramey, Cathy. *In Defense of Others*. Portland, OR: Advocates for Life Publications, 1995.
Riley-Smith, Jonathan. *The Crusades, Christianity, and Islam*. New York, NY: Columbia University Press, 2011.
Riley-Smith, Jonathan. *The First Crusade and the Idea of Crusading*. Philadelphia: University of Pennsylvania Press, 2009.
Roper, Gary Lee. *Antebellum Slavery: An Orthodox Christian View*. Xlibris Corp, 2009.
Rudolph, Eric. *A Time of War: Is Armed Resistance to Abortion Morally Justified?* Army of God, 2018.
Russell, James C. *The Germanization of Early Medieval Christianity: A Sociohistorical Approach to Religious Transformation*. Oxford: Oxford University Press, 1994.
Schäfer, Peter. *Jesus in the Talmud*. Princeton, NJ: Princeton University Press, 2009.
Shahak, Israel. *Jewish Fundamentalism in Israel*. London: Pluto Press, 2004.
Shahak, Israel. *Jewish History, Jewish Religion: The Weight of Three Thousand Years*. London: Pluto Press, 2008.
Sizer, Stephen. *Christian Zionism: Roadmap to Armageddon?* Westmont, IL: IVP Academic, 2004.
Sizer, Stephe. *Zion's Christian Soldiers?* Westmont, IL: IVP Academic, 2008.
Sniegoski, Stephen J. *Transparent Cabal: The Neoconservative Agenda, War in the Middle East, and the National Interest of Israel*. Norfolk, VA: IHS Publishing Group, 2008.
Spengler, Oswald, and Charles Francis Atkinson. *The Hour of Decision*. New York: Knopf, 1963.
Stark, Rodney. *God's Battalions: The Case for the Crusades*. New York, NY: HarperCollins, 2009.
Tacitus. *The Histories*. New York: Penguin, 1975.
Toaff, Ariel. *Blood Passover: The Jews of Europe and Ritual Murder*. Translated by Gian Marco Lucchese and Pietro Gianetti. Lucchese-Gianetti Editori LLC, 2016.
de Vier, Philip. *Blood Ritual: An Investigative Report Examining a Certain Series of Cultic Murder Cases*. Hillsboro, WV: National Vanguard Books, 2001.

Vinson, John. *Immigration and Nation: A Biblical View*. Monterey, VA: American Immigration Control Foundation, 1997.
Weaver, Richard M. *Ideas Have Consequences*. Chicago, IL: University of Chicago Press, 2013.
Weir, Alison. *Against Our Better Judgment: The Hidden History of How the U.S. Was Used to Create Israel*. CreateSpace, 2014.

Articles and other Resources Cited

Abrams, Nathan. "Triple-Exthnics." *Jewish Quarterly* 51, no. 4 (2004): 27–31. https://doi.org/10.1080/0449010x.2004.10706874.
Alexis, Jonas E. *Christianity and Rabbinic Judaism: A History of Conflict*. Bloomington, IN: WestBow Press, 2013.
Apple, Raymond. "There Is No 'Judeo-Christian' Tradition." *The Jerusalem Post*, January 8, 2018. https://www.jpost.com/Opinion/There-is-no-Judeo-Christian-tradition-533166.
AR News. "O Tempora, O Mores!" *American Renaissance*, February 1, 1992. https://www.amren.com/news/1992/02/o-tempora-o-mores-february-1992/.
Auster, Lawrence. "The First Law of Majority-Minority Relations." *Views from the Right*, November 1, 2002. http://www.amnation.com/vfr/archives/000933.html.
Banks, Adelle. "Southern Baptist President: 'As a Gospel Issue, Black Lives Matter.'" *Charisma News*, June 10, 2020. https://www.charismanews.com/us/81524-southern-baptist-president-as-a-gospel-issue-black-lives-matter.
BP Staff. "Southern Baptist Leaders Issue Joint Statement on the Death of George Floyd." *Baptist Press*, May 30, 2020. https://www.baptistpress.com/resource-library/news/southern-baptist-leaders-issue-joint-statement-on-the-death-of-george-floyd/.
Brahmin, Mark. "'1917': A Fateful Reference to the Scofield Reference Bible." *The Occidental Observer*, January 22, 2020. https://www.theoccidentalobserver.net/2020/01/22/1917-a-fateful-reference-to-the-scofield-reference-bible/.
Breitman, Kendall. "Coulter Hits 'Moral Show-off' Dolan." *Politico*, July 23, 2014. https://www.politico.com/story/2014/07/ann-coulter-timothy-dolan-109295.
Carlson, C. E. "The Source of the Problem in the Mid East – Part II: Why Judeo-Christians Support War." *Serendipity*, 2002. http://www.serendipity.li/zionism/carlson01.htm.
Ó Cathail, Maidhc. "The Scofield Bible: The Book That Made Zionists of America's Evangelical Christians." *Washington Report on Middle East Affairs* XXXIV, no. 7 (October 2015): 45–46.
Chaput, Charles. "Statement of Archbishop Charles J. Chaput, O.F.M. Cap. Regarding Racial Violence in Charlottesville, Virginia." Archdiocese of

Philadelphia, August 13, 2017. https://archphila.org/statement-of-archbishop-charles-j-chaput-o-f-m-cap-regarding-racial-violence-in-charlottesville-virginia/.

Cohen, Arthur A. "The Myth of the Judeo-Christian Tradition." *Commentary*, November 1969. https://www.commentary.org/articles/arthur-cohen/the-myth-of-the-judeo-christian-tradition/.

Comtaose, F. C. "Subversion in Red America Part I: Religion." *Counter-Currents*, February 5, 2020. https://counter-currents.com/2020/02/subversion-in-red-america-part-i-religion/.

Covington, Harold. "Why I Believe in Jewish Ritual Murder." *Heretical*, September 29, 1997. http://www.heretical.com/miscella/jrm.html.

Craig, Victor. "A Defense of Faith." *American Renaissance* 8, no. 9 (September 1997). https://www.amren.com/archives/back-issues/september-1997.

Darkmoon, Lasha. "Masters of Porn: The Systematic Promotion of Sexual Deviance." *The Occidental Observer*, June 6, 2012. https://www.theoccidentalobserver.net/2012/06/06/portraits-of-masters-of-porn-the-systematic-promotion-of-recreational-sex-sexual-callousness-and-sexual-deviancy/.

Darkmoon, Lasha. "Pornography's Effect on the Brain, Part 1 of 2." *The Occidental Observer*, September 28, 2012. https://www.theoccidentalobserver.net/2012/09/28/pornographys-effect-on-the-brain-part-1/.

Darkmoon, Lasha. "Pornography's Effect on the Brain, Part 2 of 2." *The Occidental Observer*, September 30, 2012. https://www.theoccidentalobserver.net/2012/09/30/pornographys-effect-on-the-brain-part-2/

Duffy, JP. "Chick-Fil-A Once Inspired Me to Live out My Faith in the Workplace. Those Days Are Gone." USA *Today*, December 4, 2019. https://www.usatoday.com/story/opinion/voices/2019/12/04/chick-fil-a-southern-poverty-law-center-donation-column/2588820001/.

Fernández-Morera Darío. *The Myth of the Andalusian Paradise: Muslims, Christians, and Jews Under Islamic Rule in Medieval Spain* . Wilmington, DE: ISI Books, 2018.

framingtheworld. "New World Order Bible Versions (Full Movie)." March 24, 2014. YouTube, 1:46:45. https://www.youtube.com/watch?v=kFtI_mVOXbQ.

Francis. "Message of His Holiness Pope Francis for the 106th World Day of Migrants and Refugees 2020." The Vatican, September 27, 2020. https://www.vatican.va/content/francesco/en/messages/migration/documents/papa-francesco_20200513_world-migrants-day-2020.html.

FTND. "Pornhub's Annual Report: Can You Guess the Most Popular Porn Categories in 2019?" *Fight the New Drug*, December 17, 2019. https://fightthenewdrug.org/2019-pornhub-annual-report/.

Furman, Richard. "Exposition of the Views of the Baptists Relative to the Coloured Population of the United States in Communication to the Governor of South Carolina." Charleston, 1823. Reprinted in Rogers, James A. Richard Furman: Life and Legacy. Macon, GA: Mercer University Press, 1985. 274–286. December 24, 1822

Gobry, Pascal-Emmanuel. "A Science-Based Case for Ending the Porn Epidemic." *American Greatness*, December 15, 2019. https://amgreatness.com/2019/12/15/a-science-based-case-for-ending-the-porn-epidemic/.

Hamilton, Andrew. "Diabolical Passion: Ariel Toaff's Blood Passovers." *Counter-Currents*, April 6, 2012. https://counter-currents.com/2012/04/diabolical-passion-ariel-toaffs-blood-passovers/.

Hamilton, Andrew. "Rotherham: The Product of a Diseased Ruling Class." *Counter-Currents*, September 5, 2014. https://www.counter-currents.com/2014/09/rotherham/.

Ibrahim, Raymond. "Sex-Slavery: An Islamic Sacrament?" *American Renaissance*, February 22, 2020. https://www.amren.com/news/2020/02/sex-slavery-an-islamic-sacrament/.

Ibrahim, Raymond. "'A Piece of Meat'—How Muslim Men See White Women." *American Renaissance*, December 20, 2019. https://www.amren.com/news/2019/12/a-piece-of-meat-how-muslim-men-see-white-women/.

Jackson, Thomas. "Christianity Turns Brown." *American Renaissance*, December 23, 2018. https://www.amren.com/news/2018/12/christianity-next-christendom-philip-jenkins/.

Jones, E. Michael. "Pornography and Political Control." *The Unz Review*, December 15, 2019. https://www.unz.com/ejones/pornography-and-political-control-the-hexenhammer-debate/.

Joyce, Andrew. "Thoughts on Jews, Obscenity, and the Legal System." *The Occidental Observer*, November 27, 2017. https://www.theoccidentalobserver.net/2017/11/27/thoughts-on-jews-obscenity-and-the-legal-system/.

Kerwick, Jack. "Christianity's Divine Hatred." *The Agonist*, February 10, 2019. https://the-agonist.github.io/essays/2019/02/10/essays-kerwick-christianitys-divine-hatred.html.

Kimble, Lindsay. "Pastor Speaks out after Arrests in Murder of His Pregnant Wife: 'I Choose the Route of Forgiveness, Grace and Hope.'" *People*, November 23, 2015. https://people.com/crime/davey-blackburn-i-chose-the-route-of-forgiveness-grace-and-hope/.

Leggate, James. "Chick-Fil-A CEO Dan Cathy on Racism in America: 'We're Shameful.'" *Fox Business*, June 19, 2020. https://www.foxbusiness.com/lifestyle/chick-fil-a-ceo-comments-racism-america-were-shameful.

Liddell, Colin. "Ellie Williams Case Reveals How Britain Tries to Cover Up Grooming Gang Rape." *The Occidental Observer*, May 27, 2020. https://www.theoccidentalobserver.net/2020/05/27/ellie-williams-case-reveals-how-britain-tries-to-cover-up-grooming-gang-rape/.

MacDonald, Kevin. "Research on Pornography and the Sexualization of Culture." *The Occidental Observer*, June 9, 2012. https://www.theoccidentalobserver.net/2012/06/09/research-on-pornography-and-the-sexualization-of-culture/.

Masters, Michael W. "How Christianity Harms the Race." *American Renaissance* 8, no. 9 (September 1997). https://www.amren.com/archives/back-issues/september-1997.

Miller, Emily. "ELCA Declares Self a 'Sanctuary Church Body,' Marches to Ice Building in Milwaukee." *Religion News Service*, August 8, 2019. https://religionnews.com/2019/08/07/elca-declares-self-a-sanctuary-church-body-marches-to-ice-building-in-milwaukee/.

Moore, Russell. "A White Church No More." *The New York Times*, May 6, 2016. https://www.nytimes.com/2016/05/06/opinion/a-white-church-no-more.html.

Moore, Russell. "Have Evangelicals Who Support Trump Lost Their Values?" *The New York Times*, September 17, 2015. https://www.nytimes.com/2015/09/17/opinion/have-evangelicals-who-support-trump-lost-their-values.html.

Moore, Russell. "Perspective | Russell Moore: White Supremacy Angers Jesus, but Does It Anger His Church?" *The Washington Post*, August 14, 2017. https://www.washingtonpost.com/news/acts-of-faith/wp/2017/08/14/russell-moore-white-supremacy-angers-jesus-but-does-it-anger-his-church/.

Moore, Russell. "The Cross and the Confederate Flag." *Russell Moore*, December 4, 2017. https://www.russellmoore.com/2015/06/19/the-cross-and-the-confederate-flag/.

Moore, Russell. "The Weight of Glory in a Time of Blood and Fear." *Russell Moore*, June 23, 2020. https://www.russellmoore.com/2020/06/05/the-weight-of-glory-in-a-time-of-blood-and-fear/.

Parke, Caleb. "Mark Levin, John Hagee fight anti-Semitism, raise more than $1M for Israeli and Jewish charities." *Fox News*, October 29, 2019. https://www.foxnews.com/faith-values/mark-levin-hagee-israel-anti-semitism-christian.

Podhoretz, Norman. "In the Matter of Pat Robertson." *Commentary*, August 1995. https://www.commentary.org/articles/norman-podhoretz/in-the-matter-of-pat-robertson/.

Preston, Keith. "Zionism and the Power Elite." *The Agonist*, December 31, 2019. https://the-agonist.github.io/essays/2019/12/31/essays-preston.html.

Quay, Grayson. "Rolling Stone: Men Who Abstain From Porn Are Dangerous Alt-Righters." *Intellectual Takeout*, November 18, 2019. https://intellectualtakeout.org/2019/11/rolling-stone-men-who-abstain-from-porn-are-dangerous-alt-righters/.

Roberts, Chris. "When One Crime Becomes Two." *American Renaissance*, April 22, 2019. https://www.amren.com/commentary/2019/04/when-one-crime-becomes-two/.

Rosenberg, Eli. "Mollie Tibbetts's Father Decries Vitriol against Hispanics, Saying They're 'Iowans with Better Food.'" *The Washington Post*, October 29, 2019. https://www.washingtonpost.com/nation/2018/08/28/mollie-tibbettss-father-rebukes-anti-hispanic-sentiment-saying-theyre-iowans-with-better-food/.

Sacred Bishops' Council. "Social Concept of the Orthodox Church." Russian Orthodox Church of Three Saints. Accessed November 9, 2022. http://3saints.com/social-concept.html.

Shamir, Israel. "The Bloody Passovers of Dr Toaff." *The Unz Review*, February 19, 2007. https://www.unz.com/ishamir/the-bloody-passovers-of-dr-toaff/.

Shellnutt, Kate. "Evangelical Advisers Condemn Charlottesville Rally More Than Trump." *Christianity Today*, August 13, 2017. https://www.christianitytoday.com/news/2017/august/trump-evangelical-advisers-charlottesville-white-supremacis.html.

Smietana, Bob. "Millennial Evangelicals on Israel: 'Meh.'" *Christianity Today*, December 4, 2017. https://www.christianitytoday.com/news/2017/december/us-evangelicals-support-israel-peace-survey-millennial-meh.html.

Southern Baptist Convention. "Resolution on Racial Reconciliation on the 150th Anniversary of the Southern Baptist Convention." SBC.net, June 1, 1995. https://www.sbc.net/resource-library/resolutions/resolution-on-racial-reconciliation-on-the-150th-anniversary-of-the-southern-baptist-convention/.

Strode, Tom. "SBC Denounces 'Alt-Right White Supremacy.'" *Baptist Press*, June 14, 2017. https://www.baptistpress.com/resource-library/news/sbc-denounces-alt-right-white-supremacy/.

Taylor, Jared. "The White Man's Disease." *American Renaissance* 14, no. 1, January 2003. https://www.amren.com/ar/pdfs/2003/200301ar.pdf.

Taylor, LaTonya. "Church, Community Stand by Refugee Charged with Rape." *Christianity Today*, October 1, 2001. https://www.christianitytoday.com/ct/2001/octoberweb-only/10-8-35.0.html.

Thompson, Reginald. "Legalized Pornography and Demographic Genocide." *The Occidental Observer*, January 23, 2010. https://www.theoccidentalobserver.net/2010/01/23/reginald-thompson-legalized-pornography-and-demographic-genocide/.

Thorpe, Vernon. "Ben Shapiro and the Myth of the Judeo-Christian West." *The Unz Review*, July 19, 2019. https://www.unz.com/article/ben-shapiro-and-the-myth-of-the-judeo-christian-west/.

Tisby, Jemar. "Black Ministers Release Charlottesville Declaration." *Mississippi Clarion Ledger*, August 25, 2017. https://www.clarionledger.com/story/magnolia/faith/2017/08/25/black-ministers-release-charlottesville-declaration/601309001/.

Trask, H. A. Scott. "The Christian Doctrine of Nations." *American Renaissance* 12, no. 7, July 2001.

Unz, Ron. "American Pravda: Oddities of the Jewish Religion." *The Unz Review*, July 16, 2018. https://www.unz.com/runz/american-pravda-oddities-of-the-jewish-religion/.

USCCB. "A Call for Prayer and Unity in Response to Deadly Charlottesville Attack." USCCB, August 13, 2017. https://www.usccb.org/news/2017/usccb-president-and-domestic-justice-chairman-call-prayer-and-unity-response-deadly.

VD. "'Judeo-Christian' Is Anti-Christian." *Vox Popoli*, August 26, 2016. https://voxday.net/2016/08/26/judeo-christian-is-anti-christian/.

Vezner, Tad. "St. Paul Rabbi's Comments on Arabs Spark Outrage." *Twin Cities Pioneer Press*, November 13, 2015. https://www.twincities.com/2009/06/02/st-paul-rabbis-comments-on-arabs-spark-outrage/.

Walters, Joanna. "Oxycontin Maker Expected 'a Blizzard of Prescriptions' Following Drug's Launch." *The Guardian*, January 16, 2019. https://www.theguardian.com/us-news/2019/jan/15/oxycontin-purdue-pharma-massachusetts-opioid-crisis.

Weir, Alison. "Israeli Organ Harvesting." *CounterPunch*, August 28, 2009. https://www.counterpunch.org/2009/08/28/israeli-organ-harvesting/.

Weir, Alison. "Israeli Organ Harvesting: From Moldova to Palestine." *Washington Report on Middle East Affairs*, November 26, 2009. https://www.wrmea.org/009-november/israeli-organ-harvesting-from-moldova-to-palestine.html.

Williams, Thomas D. "Jesuit Chief: No Country Has the Right to 'Reject Migrants.'" *Breitbart*, August 24, 2019. https://www.breitbart.com/europe/2019/08/24/jesuit-chief-no-country-has-the-right-to-turn-away-migrants/.

ANTELOPE HILL
PUBLISHING

www.ingramcontent.com/pod-product-compliance
Lightning Source LLC
Chambersburg PA
CBHW030326130626
46554CB00011B/23
9798892520256